ALSO BY JOHN MCCAIN AND MARK SALTER

Faith of My Fathers: A Family Memoir

Why Courage Matters: The Way to a Braver Life

Thirteen Soldiers: A Personal History of Americans at War

THE
RESTLESS
WAVE

Good Times, Just Causes, Great Fights,
and Other Appreciations

JOHN McCAIN

and Mark Salter

Simon & Schuster

NEW YORK · LONDON · TORONTO
SYDNEY · NEW DELHI

Simon & Schuster
1230 Avenue of the Americas
New York, NY 10020

First Simon & Schuster hardcover edition May 2018

SIMON & SCHUSTER and colophon are registered trademarks
of Simon & Schuster, Inc.

For information about special discounts for bulk purchases,
please contact Simon & Schuster Special Sales at 1-866-506-1949
or business@simonandschuster.com.

The Simon & Schuster Speakers Bureau can bring authors to your
live event. For more information or to book an event, contact the
Simon & Schuster Speakers Bureau at 1-866-248-3049
or visit our website at www.simonspeakers.com.

Interior design by Paul Dippolito

Manufactured in the United States of America

1   3   5   7   9   10   8   6   4   2

Library of Congress Cataloging-in-Publication Data has been applied for.

ISBN 978-1-5011-7800-9
ISBN 978-1-5011-7801-6 (ebook)

To the people of Arizona, in gratitude
for the privilege of representing them
in the United States Senate

Eternal Father, strong to save,
Whose arm hath bound the restless wave,
Who bidd'st the mighty ocean deep
Its own appointed limits keep;
Oh, hear us when we cry to Thee,
For those in peril on the sea!

—Navy Hymn

CONTENTS

THE
RESTLESS
WAVE

ACCUMULATED MEMORIES

TEARS WELLED IN MY EYES AS I WATCHED THE OLD MEN march. It was a poignant sight, but not an unfamiliar one, and I was surprised at my reaction. I have attended Memorial Day and Veterans Day parades in dozens of American cities, watched aging combat veterans—heads high, shoulders back—summon memories of their service and pay homage to friends they had lost. I had always kept my composure.

It was the fiftieth anniversary of Japan's surprise attack on Pearl Harbor and I had been invited to the official commemoration. The President of the United States, George H. W. Bush, was there and would give an emotional, memorable address at the USS *Arizona* memorial. I assumed that I, a first-term senator, had been included with more important dignitaries because that famous ship was named for the state I represent. Or perhaps I had been invited because I'm a Navy veteran, the son and grandson of admirals, and this was a Navy show.

My best friend from the Naval Academy, Chuck Larson, acted as host and master of ceremonies for the proceedings at the *Arizona*. Chuck had a far more distinguished naval career than I had, continuing a divergence that had begun in our first year at the Academy, where he had graduated at the top of our class and I very near the bottom. We had gone through flight training together, and remained the closest of friends. Chuck had been an aviator, then a submariner and a military aide to President Richard Nixon. He had been a rear admiral at forty-three, one of the youngest officers in Navy history to make that rank. He was the only person to serve as superintendent of the U.S. Naval Academy twice. On the fiftieth anniversary of Pearl Harbor, he had four stars and was commander in chief of all U.S. forces in the Pacific, CINCPAC, the largest operational command in the U.S. military, my father's old command, headquartered in Hawaii.

The *Arizona* ceremony was the main event of the weekend. The President would also pay a visit to the battleship USS *Missouri*, as would I. She had come from operations in the Persian Gulf to join in the Remembrance Day tribute. It was her last mission before she would be decommissioned. The war that had begun for America in Pearl Harbor had ended on her deck. My grandfather had been there, standing in the first line of senior officers observing the surrender ceremony.

My father, a submarine skipper, was waiting in Tokyo Harbor to meet him for—as it turned out—the last time. They lunched together that afternoon in the wardroom of a submarine tender. When they parted that day my grandfather began his journey home to Coronado, California. He died of a heart attack the day after he arrived, during a welcome home party my grandmother had arranged for him. He was only sixty-one years old, but looked decades older, aged beyond his years from "riotous living," as he called it, and the strain of the war. My father, who admired his father above all other men, was inconsolable. Many years later he recalled in detail their final reunion and the last words his father spoke to him, "Son, there is no greater thing than to die . . . for the country and principles that you believe in."

The day before the ceremony on the *Arizona* I had joined a small group of more senior senators and combat veterans, among them Senate Republican leader Bob Dole and the senior senator from Hawaii, Dan Inouye. Bob had served in the Army's 10th Mountain Division. A few weeks before the end of the war in Europe, in Italy's Apennine

Mountains, he was grievously wounded by a German machine gun while trying to rescue his fallen radio operator. His wounds cost him the use of his right arm, and much of the feeling in his left. Around the same time, Dan had led an assault on a German bunker in Tuscany. He was shot in the stomach and a grenade severed his right arm. He kept fighting, and would receive the Medal of Honor for his valor. Bob and Dan had been friends longer than either had been a senator. They had met while recuperating from their wounds in Percy Jones Army Hospital in Battle Creek, Michigan, along with another future senator, Phil Hart, who had been wounded on D-Day.

That day, we watched two thousand Pearl Harbor survivors march to honor their fallen. Most appeared to be in their seventies. Neither the informality of their attire nor the falling rain nor the cheers of the crowd along the parade route detracted from their dignified comportment. A few were unable to walk and rode in Army trucks. All of a sudden I felt overwhelmed. Maybe it was the effect of their straight faces and erect bearing evoking such a hard-won dignity; maybe it was the men riding in trucks managing to match the poise of the marchers; maybe it was the way they turned their heads toward us as they passed and the way Bob and Dan returned their attention. A little embarrassed by my reaction, I confessed to Dan, "I don't know what comes over me these days. I guess I'm getting sentimental with age." Without turning his gaze from the marchers, he answered me quietly, "Accumulated memories."

That was it. Accumulated memories. I had reached an age when I had begun to feel the weight of them. Memories evoked by a connection to someone or to an occasion, by a familiar story or turn of phrase or song. Memories of intense experiences, of family and friends from younger days, of causes fought, some worth it, others not so much, some won, some lost, of adventures bigger than those imagined as a child, memories of a life that even then had seemed to me so lucky and unlikely, and of the abbreviated lives of friends who had been braver but not as fortunate, memories brought to mind by veterans of a war I had not fought in, but I knew something of what it had cost them, and what it had given them.

I had been a boy of five, playing in the front yard of my family's home in New London, Connecticut, when a black sedan pulled up and a Navy officer rolled down the window and shouted to my father, "Jack, the Japs bombed Pearl Harbor." The news and the sight of my father leaving in that sedan is one of my most powerful memories, the only memory of my father during the war I've managed to retain all these years. I know he didn't go to sea immediately and I know we were briefly reunited with him when he was reassigned from a submarine command in the Atlantic to another in the Pacific theater. But I don't recall seeing my father again after he got into that car until the war was over, and he had lost his father and many of his friends. He returned changed in the way most combat veterans are, more self-possessed and serious. I understood the journey the Pearl Harbor veterans had made. That empathy stirred by my own memories had made me weep.

I feel the weight of memories even more now, of course. I've accumulated so many more of them. I was in my midfifties in 1991. I'm eighty-one now, twenty years older than my grandfather had been when he died, and more than ten years older than my father when we buried him, as it happened, on the day I left the Navy, a year before I was elected to my first term in Congress.

A quarter century's worth of new memories, of new causes, won and lost, more fights, new friendships and a few new enemies, of more mistakes made and new lessons learned, of new experiences that enriched my life so far beyond my wildest dreams that I feel even luckier than I did in 1991.

Of course, the longer we live, the more we lose, too, and many people who figure prominently in my memories have left the scene.

Friends from prison have passed away. Bob Craner, my closest confidant in prison, the man who got me back on my feet after the Vietnamese forced me to make a false confession and propaganda statement, died many years ago. Bill Lawrence, my exemplary senior ranking officer, died in 2005. Ned Shuman, whose good cheer was a tonic in the worst of times, is gone now, too. And Bud Day, the toughest man I ever knew, veteran of three wars, who wouldn't let me die in those hard first months of my captivity, left us four years ago.

Close Senate friends have passed as well, including brave Dan Inouye. My pal Fred Thompson, whose company was a delight, died two years ago. Lion of the Senate Ted Kennedy, with whom I worked and fought and joked in some of the more memorable moments of my time in the Senate, succumbed in 2009 to the cancer that I now have. Ted and I shared the conviction that a fight not joined is a fight not enjoyed. We had some fierce ones in our time, fierce, worthwhile, and fun. I loved every minute of them.

Other friends have left, too. I'm tempted to say, before their time, but that isn't the truth. What God and good luck provide we must accept with gratitude. Our time is our time. It's up to us to make the most of it, make it amount to more than the sum of our days. God knows, my dear friend Chuck Larson, whom I had looked up to since we were boys, made the most of his. Leukemia killed him in 2014. He was laid to rest in the Naval Academy's cemetery on Hospital Point, a beautiful spot overlooking the Severn River, near where our paths first crossed.

I've been given more years than many, and had enough narrow escapes along the way to make me appreciate them, not just in memory, but while I lived them. Many an old geezer like me reaches his last years wishing he had lived more in the moment, had savored his days as they happened. Not me, friends. Not me. I have loved my life. All of it. I've wasted more than a few days on pursuits that might not have proved as important as they seemed to me at the time. Some things didn't work out the way I hoped they would. I had difficult moments and a few disappointments. But, by God, I enjoyed it. Every damn day of it. I have lived with a will. I served a purpose greater than my own pleasure or advantage, but I meant to enjoy the experience, and I did. I meant to be amazed and excited and encouraged and useful, and I was.

All that is attributable to one thing more than any other. I have been restless all my life, even now, as time grows precious. America and the voters of Arizona have let me exercise my restlessness in their service. I had the great good fortune to spend sixty years in the employ of our country, defending our country's security, advancing our country's ideals, supporting our country's indispensable contributions to the progress of humanity. It has not been perfect service, to be sure, and there were times when the country might have benefited from a little less of my help. But I've tried to deserve the privilege, and I have been repaid a thousand times over with adventure and discoveries, with good company, and with the satisfaction of serving something more important than myself, of being a bit player in the story of America, and the history we made. And I am so very grateful.

I share that sentiment with another naval aviator, the good man and patriot we elected our forty-first President, George Herbert Walker Bush. He paid tribute twenty-six years ago to those fellow patriots whose service to America was not repaid with a long life of achievement and adventure.

We had assembled at the *Arizona* memorial around seven o'clock the morning of December 7, 1991. President and Mrs. Bush and their party arrived shortly after. Chuck opened the proceedings and introduced a Navy chaplain to give an invocation. At 7:55, fifty years to the minute since the attack on Pearl Harbor had commenced, the cruiser USS *Chosin* crossed in front of the memorial and sounded its horn as its officers and crew standing along its rails saluted. The minute of silence we observed ended when four F-15 fighters roared overhead, and one pulled up and away in the missing man formation. A bugler sounded attention at eight o'clock, the colors were raised, and the national anthem sung. President and Mrs. Bush dropped flower wreaths into the well of the memorial.

Secretary of Defense Dick Cheney introduced retired USN Captain Donald Ross, who had been a warrant officer on the USS *Nevada*, one of eight battleships stationed at Pearl Harbor when the Japanese attacked. He was the senior engineer on the ship and managed to get her under way in the firestorm, the only one of the battleships to do so. The *Nevada* was struck by six bombs and a torpedo. Ross lost consciousness twice from the smoke and was twice resuscitated. He was blinded by an explosion, but he kept the ship steaming long enough to run her aground where she wouldn't block the entrance to the harbor. He received the Medal of Honor for his valor. He was eighty-one years old in 1991, slight and stooped in his Navy whites, and walked with a cane. He would die the next spring. But he was exuberant that morning and emotional as he introduced his fellow World War II veteran, almost shouting, "Ladies and Gentlemen, I give you the President of the United States."

The President read from a printed text. He would give another, longer speech later that day about America's leadership of the postwar world, and the international order we had superintended for nearly fifty years. But his speech at the memorial was devoted to the Americans who had fought and perished there at the dawn of the American century. "The heroes of the harbor," he called them.

As he closed the speech, his voice grew thick with emotion. I think he must have felt not only the sacrifices made at Pearl Harbor, but the weight of his own memories, the memories of friends he had lost in the war, when he was the youngest aviator in the Navy.

"Look at the water here, clear and quiet," he directed, "bidding us to sum up and remember. One day, in what now seems another life-time, it wrapped its arms around the finest sons any nation could ever have, and it carried them to a better world." He paused and fussed with the pages of his speech, struggling to compose himself before deliver-ing the last line of the speech. "May God bless them, and may God bless America, the most wondrous land on earth."

The most wondrous land on earth, indeed. What a privilege it is to serve this big, boisterous, brawling, intemperate, striving, daring, beautiful, bountiful, brave, magnificent country. With all our flaws, all our mistakes, with all the frailties of human nature as much on display as our virtues, with all the rancor and anger of our politics, we are blessed. We are living in the land of the free, the land where anything is possible, the land of the immigrant's dream, the land with the storied past forgotten in the rush to the imagined future, the land that repairs and reinvents itself, the land where a person can escape the consequences of a self-centered youth and know the satisfaction of sacrificing for an ideal, where you can go from aimless rebellion to a noble cause, and from the bottom of your class to your party's nomi-nation for President.

We are blessed, and in turn, we have been a blessing to humanity. The world order we helped build from the ashes of world war, and that we defend to this day, has liberated more people from tyranny and poverty than ever before in history. This wondrous land shared its treasures and ideals and shed its blood to help make another, better world. And as we did we made our own civilization more just, freer, more accomplished and prosperous than the America that existed when I watched my father go off to war.

We have made mistakes. We haven't always used our power wisely. We have abused it sometimes and we've been arrogant. But, as often as not, we recognized those wrongs, debated them openly, and tried to do better. And the good we have done for humanity surpasses the damage caused by our errors. We have sought to make the world more stable and secure, not just our own society. We have advanced norms and rules of international relations that have benefited all. We have stood up to tyrants for mistreating their people even when they didn't threaten us, not always, but often. We don't steal other people's wealth. We don't take their land. We don't build walls to freedom and opportunity. We tear them down.

To fear the world we have organized and led for three-quarters of a century, to abandon the ideals we have advanced around the globe, to refuse the obligations of international leadership for the sake of some half-baked, spurious nationalism cooked up by people who would rather find scapegoats than solve problems is unpatriotic. American nationalism isn't the same as in other countries. It isn't nativist or imperial or xenophobic, or it shouldn't be. Those attachments belong with other tired dogmas that Americans consigned to the ash heap of history.

We live in a land made from ideals, not blood and soil. We are custodians of those ideals at home, and their champion abroad. We have done great good in the world because we believed our ideals are the natural aspiration of all mankind, and that the principles, rules, and alliances of the international order we superintended would improve the security and prosperity of all who joined with us. That leadership has had its costs, but we have become incomparably powerful and wealthy as well. We have a moral obligation to continue in our just cause, and we would bring more than shame on ourselves if we let other powers assume our leadership role, powers that reject our values and resent our influence. We will not thrive in a world where our leadership and ideals are absent. We wouldn't deserve to.

I have served that cause all my adult life. I haven't always served it well. I haven't even always appreciated that I was serving it. But among the few compensations of old age is the acuity of hindsight. I was part of something bigger than myself that drew me along in its wake even when I was diverted by personal interests. I was, knowingly or not, along for the ride as America made the future better than the past.

Yes, I have enjoyed it, all of it, and I would love for it to continue. A fight not joined is a fight not enjoyed, and I wouldn't mind another scrap or two for a good cause before I'm a memory. Who knows, maybe I'll get another round. And maybe I won't. So be it. I've lived in this wondrous land for most of eight decades, and I've had enough good fights and good company in her service to satisfy even my restless nature, a few of which I relate in the pages that follow.

Who am I to complain? I'm the luckiest man on earth.

John McCain
Cornville, Arizona

CHAPTER ONE

NO SURRENDER

ON AN ORDINARY NOVEMBER MORNING IN PHOENIX, SUNNY and warm, Cindy and I walked the two blocks from our building to the nearest Starbucks. We stood in line with other early risers, and made our purchases. We walked back to our condo, coffees in hand, and got ready to drive to our place in Northern Arizona, where we go to rest and relax in good times and bad. Friends would join us there for a few days, and our conversations would inevitably return now and again to the intense experience we had just shared. But whenever it looked like we were about to dwell at length on that subject, I would steer the conversation in another direction, toward the future. And that morning in Phoenix, we were left entirely to ourselves, just another couple in need of their morning coffee, which made for a welcome change.

The night before, I had conceded the election to the man who had defeated me and would be our forty-fourth President, Barack Obama. After I had left the stage, Mark Hughes, the agent in charge of my Secret Service detail, started to brief me on the schedule and security procedures for the trip north. The Secret Service customarily continues to protect defeated presidential candidates for a little while after the election. I suppose they worry some fool might think the losing candidate deserved a more severe sanction than disappointment. I thought it unlikely, and while I regretted losing the election, I did not expect to regret recovering autonomy over decisions about where I would go and when and with whom. Wherever the hell I wanted, I thought to myself, and the notion brightened a day that might otherwise have been spent contemplating "if only."

If only we had done this. If only we hadn't done that. I intended to leave those questions to reporters and academics. They were unproductive. I still had a job, a job I enjoyed and looked forward to resuming. And, as I said, I looked forward to resuming the routine habits of a man without a security detail: opening doors, driving my car, walking to a coffee shop. Being at liberty. Having spent more than five years of my life in prison, I tend to appreciate even the more mundane exercises of my freedom more than others might.

Mark Hughes had done a fine job supervising my protection, as had Billy Callahan, the agent in charge of my other Secret Service detail, which alternated weeks with Mark's crew. All the agents protecting Cindy and me, and my running mate, Sarah Palin, and her family, had been consummate professionals and had at my repeated requests exercised as much restraint as circumstances and good sense allowed. I was appreciative and grateful. But that didn't stop me from taking a little pleasure in interrupting Mark's briefing.

"Mark, my friend, you guys have been great, and I appreciate all your concern and hard work. I've enjoyed getting to know you. But tomorrow, I want all of you to go home to your families like I'm going home to mine. I'd appreciate a ride home tonight. Then we'll say goodbye, and we probably won't see each other again."

Mark was accustomed to my chafing at restrictions imposed on my independence, and did not argue. He smiled, and said, "Yes, sir." I liked him all the more for it. We said goodbye that night. And the next morning, Cindy and I walked to Starbucks without any more protection than a little sunscreen. An hour or so after that, I was happily driving north on Interstate 17, a free man at last.

It had been an exhilarating and exhausting two years. And though almost every defeated candidate insists the experience was wonderful and satisfying, I imagine I was only slightly less pleased that it was over than was President-elect Obama. Don't get me wrong, I fought as hard as I could to win, and I really don't enjoy losing. We had triumphant moments, and deeply touching experiences in the campaign. We had disappointing experiences as well, and days that were blurred by adrenaline-fueled activity and stress. It was like drinking from a firehose all day, every day, especially in the months between the party conventions and Election Day. But it had been for the most part a wonderful experience.

While some might find it odd, the part I had enjoyed the most were the days when I was again an underdog for the Republican nomination. I'm not sure why, but my enjoyment of a fight of any kind is inversely proportional to the odds of winning it. And in July of 2007 the odds that I would win the Republican nomination for President were starting to look pretty long.

I had formally announced my candidacy in April, but the campaign had been under way for months before then. I had started out as the presumed front-runner for the nomination, and my friend Hillary Clinton, whom I had gotten to know and like while serving with her on the Armed Services Committee, was the front-runner for the Democratic nomination. Her status would last a bit longer than mine. We had built a front-runner's campaign with a large and experienced staff and a big budget. Much too big, it turned out. We were spending a lot more than we were raising. I'm not the most prodigious fund-raiser, to be sure. I don't mind asking people for money, but I don't really enjoy it, either, and I certainly wasn't as good at it as was my principal rival for the nomination, Governor Mitt Romney. I suppose it didn't help matters with many donors that I was the leading Republican proponent of limiting campaign donations or that I was inextricably tied to the deeply unpopular surge in Iraq. My support for comprehensive immigration reform was proving to be a liability as well, although majorities of Americans then and now support its provisions. I had sponsored an immigration bill that year with Ted Kennedy. The bill was as unpopular with some conservatives as Ted was. Some of the other candidates, particularly Mitt, were already making an issue of it, and it was starting to generate grassroots opposition to my candidacy.

Whatever the reasons for my failure to outraise the competition, our spending should have been more in line with our financing. We shouldn't have assembled an operation with as big a payroll and expenses as we had until my front-runner status was earned by winning primaries. In the spring and early summer of 2007 it was based on not much more than the fact that I had been the runner-up for the nomination in 2000, and was at the moment better known nationally than Governor Romney.

I was, to put it mildly, unhappy with my situation and considering what to do about it when I left for an overseas trip in early July. The whole thing just didn't feel right to me. I felt as if I was running someone else's campaign or pretending my campaign was something it wasn't or shouldn't have been. I had enjoyed my experiences as the underdog in the 2000 Republican nomination race partly because hardly anyone expected me to win and I felt as if I had nothing to lose. Then we caught fire in the fall of 1999, won the New Hampshire primary in a landslide, and had a rocket ride for a couple months, losing South Carolina, winning Michigan, before crashing in the Super Tuesday primaries. I left the race having outperformed expectations, possessing a much bigger national reputation, increased influence in the Senate, and an abundance of truly wonderful memories. Not bad for a defeat. Before I made the decision to run again, I had nagging doubts that I mentioned frequently to aides that we weren't likely to bottle lightning twice.

Compounding my concern over spending and the direction of the campaign in 2007 were my concerns about the surge in Iraq, which preoccupied me more than the campaign did. There had not been many advocates in Congress, even among Republicans, for President George W. Bush's decision to surge troops to Iraq to run a counterinsurgency under the command of General David Petraeus. The war had been almost lost in 2006. A Sunni insurgency had grown much stronger as it claimed more territory, and more Iraqis and foreign fighters were joining its ranks. Shia militias were working with Iran to terrorize Sunnis and, when the spirit moved them, to kill Americans. They operated practically unfettered in some neighborhoods. We were obviously losing ground and were at risk of losing the war. That reality wasn't altered by repeated assurances from senior commanders in Baghdad and from Defense Secretary Donald Rumsfeld that the American effort in Iraq was meeting all its targets (principally, the number of Iraqi troops trained, which proved as useless as a measure of success as body counts had in Vietnam). And a majority of the American people, which grew larger by the day, wanted us to get out.

I had been advocating for a counterinsurgency campaign in Iraq since August 2003. I had lost all confidence in Secretary Rumsfeld's willingness to change what clearly wasn't working, and I said so. To my and many others' relief, President Bush asked for his resignation in November 2006. Knowing the President was actively considering the idea, I had urged for months that we surge thousands more troops to Iraq. I knew it was a decision that some officials in his administration opposed, that Democrats and more than a few Republicans would strongly criticize, and that most of the American people would not agree with. They had already punished Republicans for Iraq in the 2006 midterm election. They would likely want to rebuke us again in 2008, and that probability would loom larger as casualties spiked in the first months of the surge.

President Bush knew all this as well or better than I did. Good man that he is, I knew he was deeply pained by the loss of Americans he had sent to Iraq. He knew that if he decided to order the surge the situation would get worse and more Americans would die before it got better. He knew there was no guarantee it would succeed.

We had gone into Iraq based on faulty intelligence about weapons of mass destruction, and destroyed the odious Saddam Hussein regime. Bad tactics, a flawed strategy, and bad leadership in the highest ranks of uniformed and civilian defense leadership had allowed violent forces unleashed by Saddam's destruction to turn Iraq into hell on earth, and threaten the stability of the Middle East. The situation was dire, and the price that we had already paid in blood and treasure was dear. But we had a lot at stake and we had a responsibility to attempt one last, extremely difficult effort to turn it around, to test whether a genuine counterinsurgency could avert defeat. The President chose to do the right thing, and the hardest. I imagine it was a lonely, painful experience for him, and I admired his resolve. I admired also his choice to lead the effort, General David Petraeus.

I believed that we should have responded to the insurgency at its inception, and I was increasingly convinced with every month that followed that only a full-fledged counterinsurgency, with all the force it required, had any chance for winning the war. But I didn't know in late 2006 whether or not the situation was too far gone to salvage. Advisors whose counsel I trusted believed it still could be won. General Petraeus believed it could be. But none of us felt as confident about the outcome as we would have liked, and we knew most Americans believed we were wrong.

Five additional Army brigades were deployed to Iraq, and Marine and Army units already in country had their tours extended, providing just enough force to support a counterinsurgency. The numbers of Americans killed or wounded in the first months of 2007 increased substantially, as additional forces arrived and fought to take back territory from Sunni insurgents and Shia militias. For the first time in the war on a large scale, they held the ground they took and provided security for the affected populations. The spike in casualties was expected, but it was hard not to worry you were needlessly sending young kids to their death in a war that had been a mistake. You couldn't help but wonder if maybe the best thing now was to cut our losses. But I believed our defeat would be catastrophic for the Middle East and our security interests there as terrorists and Tehran gained power and prestige at our expense. And I was worried about the humanitarian implications of our withdrawal, fearing that the raging sectarian war might descend into genocide. Of course, if the surge failed, there would be nothing we could realistically do to prevent that defeat or prevent history and our own consciences from damning us for having made this last, costly effort.

So, as I considered what to do about my campaign, I did so recognizing that I would be spending more time and energy focusing on the issue that was likely to cost me votes. Nowhere was that likelier to be the case than in my favorite state after Arizona, New Hampshire, scene of my 2000 landslide win. In the 2006 election, Democrats had swept almost every state and federal contest in New Hampshire, a Republican wipeout blamed on voters' deep dissatisfaction with the war. There was no credible scenario in which I could win the nomination without winning the New Hampshire primary, as I had in 2000. And even Granite State voters who had supported me seven years before and who still liked me were not pleased with my support for the war. It was increasingly apparent that many of them would express their displeasure by voting for a candidate other than me.

Anxious about the surge, upset with the state of my campaign, increasingly aware of the extent of the challenge before me, I was in a bad frame of mind that summer. My uncertainty about what to do only aggravated my condition. There have been very few times in my life when I have felt I might be in a predicament that I could not eventually escape. But I had serious doubts that I could win an election and maintain my position on Iraq. In fact, I was beginning to ask myself if I should even be trying. And that was my attitude as I departed with my friend Senator Lindsey Graham for a long-scheduled trip to Iraq, leaving decisions about how to repair my campaign or even whether to continue it for my return.

On the flight over I confided to Lindsey my unhappiness with the campaign, and we discussed what I ought to do about it. I told him I was leaning toward getting out of the race. I wasn't sure I could win. I wasn't sure I wanted it badly enough to do what I had to do to win. We were broke. Unlike our merry little band of insurgents in 2000, factions had formed in the campaign, and they were sniping at each other in the press. Old friendships were becoming rivalries. It was an increasingly joyless experience, and I had begun to worry that it would ultimately prove pointless. Lindsey thought it was salvageable, that we could downsize, and fight more like a challenger than a front-runner. If nothing else, that would feel more natural to me. But I was skeptical. I would need to raise a lot more money to run any kind of serious campaign, and that would get harder, not easier, as donors saw us cutting payroll, shedding talented staff, and closing state offices six months before the Iowa caucuses. We were about to become in the eyes of the press and donors the first casualty of the 2008 Republican nomination race.

The worst violence had started to subside by the time of our July visit to Baghdad, which strengthened our faith that the surge could succeed. Casualties had peaked in May. The number of killed and wounded declined every month thereafter. General Petraeus and Ambassador Ryan Crocker and their staffs briefed us on the military and political gains that had been made since our last visit. We could see for ourselves that things were improving. There were visible signs of progress almost everywhere in Baghdad. Dangerous neighborhoods had been quieted, commercial activity was resuming. There wasn't enough progress to convince you that victory was assured. Far from it. But it was enough to think that maybe, to quote Churchill, we were at the end of the beginning. I was more hopeful that the decision I had long advocated would not end up sacrificing the lives ransomed to it in a failed effort to rescue an already lost cause.

The experience that made the biggest impression on me was a ceremonial one. General Petraeus had asked us to participate in an Independence Day event at Saddam's al-Faw Palace at Camp Victory that included the reenlistment of over 600 soldiers and the naturalization of 161 soldiers, mostly Hispanic immigrants, who had risked life and limb for the United States while they waited to become citizens. Some of these soldiers, the reenlisted and the newly naturalized, were on their second and third combat tours. Some of them had just had their current tour extended. Most were kids, of course, and some of them had spent two or three years of their short lives living with fear and fatigue, cruelty and confusion, and all the other dehumanizing effects of war. They had seen friends killed and wounded. Some had been wounded themselves. They had seen firsthand the failed strategy that had allowed the insurgency to gain strength, and had risked their lives to reinforce what they knew was a mistake. They had retaken the same real estate over and over again. They had conducted raids night after night looking for insurgents and caches of arms. They had been shot at by snipers and blasted by IEDs, and buried friends who hadn't survived the encounters, while month after month the situation got worse. And here they were, re-upping again, choosing to stay in harm's way. Most of them, it appeared, were excited to be finally doing something that made sense, taking and holding ground, protecting and earning the trust of the locals. Lindsey and I spoke at the ceremony.

We were awed by them. It was hard to keep our composure while witnessing that kind of courage and selfless devotion to duty. And it was all the harder after·General Petraeus recognized the sacrifice made by two soldiers who had planned to become naturalized citizens at the ceremony, and were now represented by two pairs of boots on two chairs, having been killed in action two days before. "They died serving a country that was not yet theirs," Petraeus observed.

I wasn't the only person there with a lump in his throat and eyes brimming with tears. I wish every American who out of ignorance or worse curses immigrants as criminals or a drain on the country's resources or a threat to our "culture" could have been there. I would like them to know that immigrants, many of them having entered the country illegally, are making sacrifices for Americans that many Americans would not make for them.

The ceremony was one of the most inspirational displays of genuine loyalty to country and comrades I'd ever witnessed, and I'll never forget it. On our return flight, Lindsey and I again discussed my political predicament and what to do about it. But I had decided before we boarded the flight that whatever I was risking by remaining a candidate, which wasn't much more than embarrassment, it was nothing compared to what those kids were risking and the cause they were fighting for. I decided to stay in the race.

We had to downsize substantially. Many staffers left of their own accord and others involuntarily. We closed our operations in a number of states. We borrowed money to keep the thing going. We developed a "living off the land" strategy that relied on debates and other free media opportunities to get out our message. We couldn't afford to pay to advertise. And we had to adjust our expectations accordingly. I wasn't able to run campaign operations with paid staff in as many primaries and caucuses as we had planned. We were going to have to downplay our involvement in the Iowa caucuses, as we had eight years before, and bet it all on New Hampshire again. We would be active in the states that immediately followed New Hampshire—Michigan, which was Governor Romney's native state, and South Carolina. We knew we would have to win at least one of those to have a decent shot at winning the Florida primary. Whoever won Florida would have the most momentum going into Super Tuesday, when twenty-one states would hold primaries or caucuses. But for all practical purposes it was New Hampshire or bust for us again. There wasn't a way to win without it.

I made one other commitment. I wouldn't just stand by my position on the surge, I would make it the centerpiece of our campaign, arguing for its necessity and predicting its success if sustained, a message that many New Hampshire voters did not welcome. I couldn't win the nomination without winning New Hampshire. I probably couldn't win New Hampshire if I continued to support the surge. But I was going to make defending the surge my principal message in New Hampshire. An underdog again.

My very first campaign stop after returning from Iraq was in Concord, New Hampshire, where I was scheduled to deliver a speech on Iraq. Before we left, I planned to speak in the Senate about the progress Lindsey and I had witnessed and the necessity of sustaining the surge beyond its difficult first months. Before the speech, in difficult conversations with senior staff, I ordered the downsizing that necessitated staff departures, provoked bitter feelings between former colleagues and angry recriminations in the press, and spawned hours of political prognostication that our campaign was for all practical purposes "a corpse" as my days as a front-runner came to an abrupt and messy end.

I didn't have an elaborate response to the situation. Rick Davis, my campaign manager, was working on a plan to run a smaller campaign, and find the money for it. I decided the best thing I could do was to put my head down and plod through the next few weeks. I'd like to say I ignored the skepticism and mockery directed my way. But I heard it and read it and felt it. I didn't like it but I didn't let it intimidate me. I intended to go to New Hampshire and make my case to people I had a pretty good rapport with even if they were no longer supporting me. If they didn't buy it, so be it. I wouldn't be President. I don't want this to sound flip because it's not as if I didn't want to win. I did. I'm a very competitive person. But I just decided that if I was likely to lose and was going to run anyway, I shouldn't be afraid of losing. I had something to say. I thought it was important that I say it. And I would see the damn thing through.

On a Friday morning in July, I boarded a flight to New Hampshire at Reagan National Airport with my youngest son, Jimmy, a Marine, who was about to deploy on his first combat tour, and my administrative assistant and co-writer, Mark Salter. No other staff accompanied me. Flights to Manchester, New Hampshire, in primary season are usually crowded with Washington reporters. Press accounts quickly proliferated that I had been spotted in much reduced circumstances carrying my own bag to the gate. I had carried my own bag before then. I almost always carried it, as a matter of fact (although it was another thing I was accustomed to doing for myself that the Secret Service would eventually relieve me of). I didn't care that reporters remarked on it. The image gave them a handy metaphor for our humbled campaign. I kind of liked it.

When we arrived at the venue in Concord, which if I remember correctly was hosted by the local Chamber of Commerce, the room was congested with reporters, including some of the most well-known and respected in the country. I knew most of them, and I liked many of them. A half dozen TV cameras were there to record the moment. Although we had announced I would be making remarks about the situation in Iraq, reporters, seeing what they thought was the chaos and confusion that beset a campaign in its death throes, suspected or hoped that I would withdraw from the race then and there. They were like crows on a wire, watching the unfortunate roadkill breathe its last before they descended to scavenge the remains.

I made my speech. It wasn't a memorable one, I'm afraid. But it did not include an announcement that I was ending my campaign. Professionals that they are, none of the reporters present betrayed their disappointment that they had been denied their deathbed scene. Most of them believed I was a ghost candidate, who would sooner or later realize that he was not part of this world any longer. For my part, I would stick to my scheduled appearances for the time being while we sorted through tough decisions we would have to make about strategy, staffing, and financing. The next morning, I held a town hall meeting at the American Legion post in Claremont. Most of the questions were about Iraq. Many of them were skeptical, and a few hostile.

On a summer night a month later, I was halfway through a town hall meeting in Wolfeboro, and had answered the usual questions about the war, federal spending, immigration, climate change, veterans care, questions I got at every event. Nothing out of the ordinary had yet occurred when a middle-aged woman stood and gestured to the staffer holding the microphone. When he handed it to her she started speaking in a quiet voice. When you've done as many town halls as I have, you can tell in an instant the people who are used to questioning candidates and those who are uncomfortable with public attention. Lynne Savage, a special education assistant in the local school system, and a mother, was the latter. I sensed as I called on her that she had something to say that would affect me. I thought it might be a criticism. She was standing just a few feet from me. Shy but purposeful, she prefaced her question by recalling that during the Vietnam War she had "proudly worn a silver bracelet on her arm in support of a soldier who was fighting." Then she got to her point. "Today, unfortunately I wear a black bracelet in memory of my son who lost his life in Baghdad."

My first thought in the instant she uttered her statement was that she would hold me responsible for her loss, and she would be right to do so. By my vote in support of the war and my support for the surge, I assumed a share of that responsibility, and a Gold Star mother was well within her rights to resent me for it. But she didn't speak of resentment or accountability. She didn't ask any questions about the war. She had only come to ask me if I would wear his bracelet, "so you could remember your mission and their mission in support of them." The room was completely still. My emotions began to swell and I worried I would lose my composure. I managed to get out "I would be honored and grateful" before giving her a hug. "Don't let his sacrifice be in vain," she instructed me. I took the bracelet from her and read the name inscribed on it, Matthew Stanley. I asked how old Matthew had been. "Twenty-two," she replied. "Twenty-two," I repeated. My voice cracked a little as I thanked her for his service. All I could find the wit and will to say after that was, "Yes, ma'am, I will wear this. Thank you."

Specialist Matthew Stanley was two months into his second tour in Iraq in December 2006 when an IED destroyed the Humvee he was in, killing him and four other soldiers. He was ten days shy of his twenty-third birthday and was still a newlywed, having married Amy the previous New Year's Eve. I wore Matthew Stanley's bracelet every day of the campaign, and I've worn it every day since. I'll wear it for the rest of my life.

"Why not make a virtue of necessity?" Steve Schmidt, who was acting as a volunteer strategist for us, had proposed a few days before the Wolfeboro town hall. His pitch went something like this: You're broke. You're down in the polls. You're not drawing crowds. The press has moved on. Why not get some of your POW buddies and other friends to travel with you while you hold small events all over New Hampshire, and make the case for the surge. Go to VFW and American Legion halls, to people's backyards if you have to, and tell them you're not quitting on the men and women we sent to fight for us in Iraq, even if it costs you the election. Voters like seeing politicians stick to their guns, especially if it looks like it's going to cost them the election. Call it the "No Surrender Tour."

It made sense to me. We began that September and traveled in vans and cars at first. Buses were expensive. Some of the earliest events were held in people's homes, which weren't exactly bursting with crowds of cheering people. I traveled with old pals from prison, Bud Day, Orson Swindle, and others, as well as my dearest friends in the Senate, Lindsey Graham and Joe Lieberman. I got to say what I wanted to say, what I believed was important to say and true, ending every speech with what, depending on your point of view, was either a boast or a prediction: "I'd rather lose an election than see my country lose a war."

Being an underdog with low expectations can be liberating and fun. The humor gets a little dark, but that's often the most fortifying kind. I have a quote I jokingly attribute to Chairman Mao that I like to use in tough situations: "It's always darkest before it's completely black." I remember Lindsey and I were excited when we arrived at a VFW hall one Friday night and found the place packed with people. "We must be catching on," we congratulated ourselves, only to learn that it was fried fish night, an event so popular with the locals they were willing to put up with the annoyance of politicians interrupting their supper. We eventually got a bus, wrapped it in our new motto, "No Surrender," and rolled along the highways of the Granite State, stumping for the surge and my struggling candidacy wherever we could find people to listen.

It worked. We slowly started to revive. The crowds grew modestly, my poll numbers improved slightly, and the press started paying a little more attention. I doubt reporters thought I was a serious contender for the nomination again, but they believed I might fight until the New Hampshire primary. I think most of them appreciated that I was a proven campaigner in New Hampshire. I also think most of them expected Governor Romney to win the expensive, labor-intensive Iowa caucuses, and probably have enough momentum coming out of Iowa to beat me in New Hampshire, where he had a vacation home and was well known and liked.

A defeat in New Hampshire would surely force my exit from the race. We had to hit a triple bank shot to stay viable. I had to place respectably in Iowa without being seen to have made a major investment of time and money there. One of the other candidates had to win or come awfully close to winning Iowa so the press would declare Governor Romney had underperformed expectations. Then I had to win New Hampshire on the strength of a good grassroots organization, nostalgia for my 2000 campaign by independents who can vote in New Hampshire party primaries, respect for my open style of campaigning, taking all questions and abuse, and my willingness to tell people what they didn't want to hear and still ask for their vote.

I like and respect Mitt Romney. I think he would have made a very good President. I liked him before we ran against each other and I liked him after we were finished running against each other. In between, I and my more demonstrative staffers worked up a little situational antipathy for the governor and his campaign. That's natural, of course. Presidential campaigns are exhausting, stressful experiences, run on coffee, adrenaline, and fear, and when you need a little extra boost, resentment of your opponent can be a handy motivator. Mitt is an intelligent, accomplished, decent, convivial man, who is really good at raising money and looks like a movie star. Deep into the endless series of primary debates, I and the other candidates were looking a little worse for wear. Mitt always arrived looking as if he had just returned from a two-week vacation at the beach, tanned, smiling, and utterly self-possessed. If you're not constantly reminding yourself to behave like an adult, you might start getting a little pissed off at your opponent's many fine attributes. That kind of childishness usually ends when the contest is over as it did with our campaigns. But when the game is on between very competitive people something akin to trash talking to the press can happen, as was the case with us. Nothing below the belt, really, from either side, just jabs here and there, enough to make you want to, well, beat the other guy.

We had worked hard. We had a strategy we could afford. And we got lucky. Iowa worked out about as well as it could have under the circumstances. A late-surging Governor Mike Huckabee, who had extensive support in Iowa's evangelical community, the most influ-ential and well-represented bloc of Republican caucus voters, caught Mitt and a lot of the press if not by surprise (it was evident in the last rounds of polls) then unprepared for the magnitude of his victory. Huckabee ended up winning the thing by a nine-point margin, which meant Mitt wouldn't only be deprived of momentum coming out of Iowa, he would drop in the polls in reaction to the unexpected size of his defeat there. I had managed to come in a respectable fourth, only a couple hundred votes behind the third-place finisher, my friend Fred Thompson. It's all an expectations game. The press thought I hadn't put in the time in Iowa and didn't have a real organization there, but I had just enough of both to do well enough to avoid hurting myself in New Hampshire.

I wasn't overconfident after learning the Iowa results, but I did think I was now the candidate to beat in the New Hampshire primary five days later. I had a small lead in most of the latest polls. Huckabee didn't have much support there, but his win in Iowa had likely cost Mitt some of his support. So, as I heard the news from Iowa that night after finishing an event in New Hampshire, the guy who had come in fourth in a six-man field was, after the actual winner, the happiest candidate in the race.

I didn't expect to win a blowout as I had in 2000. My lead in the latest polls was in the two- to three-point range, way too tight to get cocky. But I was confident enough to ignore my usual superstition about not discussing my primary-night speech before I knew whether we would celebrate a victory or concede a defeat. The victory I and just about everyone expected would be the biggest that night would likely belong to the candidate riding the most momentum out of Iowa and the biggest wave of enthusiasm. That was Senator Barack Obama, the eloquent newcomer to American politics, who had just defeated the front-runner, Hillary Clinton, in Iowa and given a victory speech that captured the imaginations of Americans who were tired of politics, including many first-time voters. He appeared unstoppable after Iowa. Everyone assumed he would win New Hampshire, too, and drive Hillary out of the race. I discussed with Davis, Salter, and Schmidt the right message for my speech that night, and we agreed I should begin by saluting Senator Obama's historic achievement, and recognize what it meant to his supporters and to the entire country. I would also express my hope that should I be the Republican nominee, our contest would be conducted in a way that would impress Americans in both parties as respectful.

That sentiment wasn't only a sincere wish for more civility in politics. The country wanted change. They wanted the biggest change they could get. Barack Obama was offering them change, and he had advantages I did not. He was not a member of the party in power. I was. He was young and cool and new to national politics. I was seventy-one years old and had been a known commodity for some time, with a long record of votes and statements to criticize. He opposed the unpopular war in Iraq. I supported it. He would be the first African American to earn a major party's presidential nomination. He represented change in his very person. I had to convince people I, too, was a change candidate. But the most effective means I had to convey that message was campaigning in ways that might appear novel and authentic to cynical voters. I intended to use my victory speech to start that effort.

When it became clear that night that I had managed a come-from-behind victory, beating Mitt by about five points, it was looking like Hillary might be doing the same. When the networks declared me the New Hampshire winner, the Democratic race was still too close to call, and we revised my speech accordingly. I began by noting I was too old to be called any kind of kid, "but we sure showed them what a comeback looks like." I thanked the people of New Hampshire for hearing me out even when they disagreed with me. We were down in the polls and written off when we came here, I reminded them, "and we had just one strategy: to tell you what I believe."

Unable to congratulate the winner of the Democrats' primary, I paid my respects to the supporters of all the candidates, Republicans and Democrats, who "worked for a cause they believe is good for the country we all love." We had a long way to go. The Michigan primary was a little more than a week away. Mitt would be hard to beat there. South Carolina would be a close contest between Huckabee, Fred Thompson, and me. I needed to win one of them to continue. Winning both would be preferable, but South Carolina, the place where my rocket ride out of New Hampshire in 2000 crashed, loomed larger. Eight years before, I had stood on the steps of the Bedford, New Hampshire, town hall the night before the primary and looked out on a sea of faces. There were people crowding the streets and intersection, extending several blocks. It was thrilling, and I knew I was on the cusp of my biggest political triumph. It remains to this day my favorite campaign memory.

My 2008 primary win was not as heady as our victory in 2000. But I was deeply touched by it, and have had ever since a special affection for the proud voters in the first-in-the-nation primary. "These people have been so good to us," I told Cindy that night. "I owe them so much."

The next day, somewhere in Iraq's Anbar Province, my son Jimmy helped dig an MRAP, a heavily armored personnel carrier, out of the mud in a wadi that had flooded in a downpour. He was knee-deep in the muck working a shovel, and sweating in the oppressive heat, when his sergeant walked over to him.

"McCain."

"Yes, Sergeant."

"Your dad won New Hampshire."

"Did he?"

"Yeah, keep digging."

"Yes, Sergeant."

I laughed when Jimmy recounted the exchange for me when we were reunited some months later, and I laugh every time I retell it to friends. But as I have remembered it in the years that followed, and remembered, too, my worry then that my ambitions had exposed my youngest son to even greater danger, I'm moved to tears.

CHAPTER TWO

COUNTRY FIRST

I RECEIVED A DECENT BUMP IN THE NATIONAL POLLS FOL-
lowing my New Hampshire win, and our fund-raising picked up,
although we still had to pay off the bank loan we borrowed in the
summer to keep the campaign running. National polling leads can create a false impression that someone is a front-runner. We don't have
national primaries. The next contest was in Michigan on January 15,
and Mitt and I were running neck and neck there. Michigan wasn't
do-or-die for me, but it was for Mitt. Huckabee and I had split the first
two contests. Mitt had to get into the picture now or risk being written off by reporters and donors. South Carolina was four days after
Michigan, and Mitt wasn't competing there. I saw the chance to finish
him off and secure a nearly invincible position by winning Michigan
and beating Huckabee and Fred Thompson in South Carolina. I had
upset George Bush in the 2000 Michigan primary, and believed I had
a good feel for campaigning there. It's obviously a lot more populous
and urban than New Hampshire, and I had spent a lot more time in
New Hampshire than we could spend in Michigan. But I felt Michigan
voters in 2000 had responded as well as New Hampshire voters had
to my candor, which occasionally offered uncomfortable truths to an
audience that might disagree. The Straight Talk Express, our boasting
motto in 2000, mostly avoided being sanctimonious because now and

again I had to pay a real price for it. I would say something in the name of straight talk that got me in trouble.

We both fought hard for Michigan, and threw punches that aggravated our campaigns' already healthy game-day animosity for the other. I took a shot at Mitt's record on taxes as Massachusetts governor. He accused me of being that most odious of characters, the "Washington insider." Most polls had us less than a percentage point apart. Then I offered Michigan voters a little dose of straight talk. It was true, but hard to hear, and I have to watch myself and not appear smug when I'm offering a hard truth. I can seem to enjoy being impolitic.

Michigan was in the throes of a deep recession and had the highest unemployment in the nation. Technology-driven productivity gains in the automobile industry and foreign competition had cost the state tens if not hundreds of thousands of high-wage manufacturing jobs. I campaigned on ideas to help people whose lives were disrupted by the global economy, getting workers into improved retraining programs, and having the government make up some of the difference between the wages they had lost and the lower pay they were now earning in service industry jobs. But I wanted to acknowledge that work was permanently changing in the U.S. in ways that would put a premium on education reform and highly skilled training to achieve the same standard of living that had been common for manufacturing workers in the last century. In a debate, I blurted out that "there are some jobs that aren't coming back to Michigan."

Mitt jumped on it instantly, grabbing the opportunity to portray me as unsympathetic to dislocated workers and underscore his credentials as a successful businessman, who specialized in turning around failing companies. In addition to having been governor of Michigan, Mitt's father, George, had been president of American Motors. "I've got the automobile industry in my veins," Mitt reminded voters, promising to turn Washington inside out to turn Michigan's economy around, and accusing me of undue pessimism. It was the smart play. It emphasized his connections to the state, and offered voters that most potent of political appeals—hope. I had offered grim reality, which made a negative impression on Michigan voters that overshadowed the policies I proposed to improve it.

Mitt won the Michigan primary. It wasn't close, 39 to 30 percent. I had missed the chance to land a knockout blow on my most dangerous opponent. Good thing for me Mitt had effectively abandoned South Carolina. A win there could offset the damage that losing Michigan had done, and give me back the advantage going into Florida. I had to beat Mike Huckabee, who was gaining ground in South Carolina with his strength in the Upstate evangelical communities. But Mitt's absence in South Carolina wasn't my only piece of good luck. Fred Thompson had decided to stay in the race after losing the first three major contests. He was popular with the base, and he and Huckabee divided voters who were unlikely to support me. My strength was in South Carolina's Lowcountry, from Myrtle Beach to Charleston to Hilton Head, where social conservatives aren't as prominent as they are Upstate. But I had found out in 2000 that I couldn't win the primary with Lowcountry voters alone if one opponent won everywhere else.

The Associated Press had called the race earlier in the evening when the exit polls and early returns were indicating a five- or six-point McCain win. But the wire service had to retract the projection a short while later when the count unexpectedly tightened, my stomach with it. The next couple hours were agonizing. I wanted badly to win South Carolina not just for the advantage it would give me in upcoming contests, but because South Carolina had been a bitter defeat in 2000. I had something to prove. To myself, if no one else. As it turned out, Fred won enough votes to dilute Huckabee's strength, and I did better than expected in the Upstate, even winning Greenville, where I'd been clobbered eight years before. Still, it was a narrow victory, only three points, and Huckabee did well enough to be encouraged.

He would win quite a few more primaries and caucuses, mostly in the South, before it was over. But I was the recognized front-runner going into Florida, which was setting up to be the decisive contest. Rudy Giuliani had bet everything on the state. He had mostly avoided Iowa because his positions on abortion and other issues made him unacceptable to social conservatives. He hadn't campaigned much in New Hampshire, either, which I thought was a mistake on his part that redounded to my benefit. He's the kind of candidate who appeals to New Hampshire Republicans and independents, outspoken, authentic, and confrontational. He chose to save his resources for a last-stand fight in Florida, where quite a few retired New Yorkers reside. But by then the press narrative was firmly fixed and voters were only hearing about a three-person race, McCain, Romney, and Huckabee. I don't think a lot of Floridians even knew Rudy was still running. He and I were friends, and in the days between the South Carolina primary and Florida's, as Rudy sensed his gambit had failed, we stayed on good terms, even hinting that he would encourage his organization and endorsements to support me in the primaries that followed.

Mitt had a good organization in Florida, and was managing to keep the debate focused on economic issues rather than national security, where I was stronger. He reminded voters that in another burst of straight talk I had publicly acknowledged I knew less about the economy than national security. He assured them he could do both jobs competently. He hadn't finished taking advantage of my Michigan jobs remark, either.

I was also on the receiving end of daily attacks from talk radio blowhards. They had some effect, but they aren't as influential as they like their listeners to believe. They make quite a living from promoting polarization in the country, and scaring politicians who can only win races in gerrymandered districts. And when they're in high dudgeon they can be amusing in an over-the-top, vaudevillian kind of way. They had been after me episodically for years, pounding my positions on campaign finance reform and immigration and other apostasies. I had learned to laugh it off. They could tie up our front-office phones for an hour or so by exhorting their listeners to give the traitor McCain a piece of their mind. But they had a negligible impact on my national popularity. In Florida, their antipathy toward me was frenzied. Even Mitt, the moderate former governor of Massachusetts, whom they would disparage four years later, was an acceptable alternative as long as I was in the race.

We feared that as long as Mitt stuck with his disciplined message on the economy and emphasized his business skills, the race would stay too close for comfort. Our last debate just five days before the primary had focused on economic policy, and Mitt was far outspending us on television and radio ads. I needed to change the subject. Our research guys dug up a quote by Mitt about Iraq, which interpreted very literally could be portrayed as advocating a schedule for withdrawing our troops based on dates rather than conditions on the ground. I accused him of wanting to cut and run before victory was achieved. It was a stretch, according to the fact-checkers, and I caught flak for it. I don't think we took any more liberties with the quote than Mitt had taken with my jobs remark or my immigration views, but the attack angered him, and he wouldn't let it go for three days, which played to my advantage since it kept the debate focused on Iraq and not the economy.

I knew from personal experience how he felt. I'd gotten angry over attacks in South Carolina eight years before, and strayed from my reform message to air my grievances. Mitt called our tactics in Florida Nixonian, but he kept talking about them, which is probably a reaction that would have pleased Richard Nixon. He had a point, though, and as I said, getting pissed off by an opponent's attack is something I could relate to empathetically. But the comeback phase of my campaign was over. I had made my point about the surge and proved that I was resilient. Now I was running to win the thing.

An endorsement by Charlie Crist, Florida's Republican governor, the night before the primary gave us a last burst of speed across the finish line. According to Rudy, Crist had promised his endorsement to him. Mitt thought he had received encouragement, too. Rudy was angered by the betrayal, but not at me. He knew his candidacy was finished. That night he and I talked on the phone, and our staffs conferred about working together after Florida. I won the Florida primary by a little more than I thought we would, five points, and with it all fifty-seven of its delegates. Mitt wasn't going anywhere yet, but I would be hard to stop now. Super Tuesday with its twenty-one primaries and caucuses, and California the biggest prize, was a week away. Rudy endorsed me the day after the Florida primary, and helped us get his supporter Texas governor Rick Perry's endorsement the same day that California governor Arnold Schwarzenegger endorsed me, giving our campaign the appearance of the train to ride as it was leaving the station. We had a debate that night at the Reagan Library with Nancy Reagan in attendance. All the remaining candidates were tired and aware that the contest would soon be over. It might have been a comparatively sedate event, but Mitt and I mixed it up anyway, too heatedly, irritability being fatigue's main effect on me.

We were in Phoenix for Super Tuesday. Arizona held its primary that day. I won my home state and eight other primaries, including the biggest ones, California and New York, as well as Illinois, New Jersey, Missouri, and others. Mitt won seven primaries and caucuses and Mike Huckabee won five southern contests that night. But my delegate take was three times the size of Mitt's and four times larger than Huckabee's. I was the presumptive nominee. Two days later in a speech in Washington, Mitt ended his campaign. He endorsed me a week after that. Our antagonism quickly cooled as our competitive natures found other outlets, and developed into a genuine friendship, which, I'm privileged to say, continues to this day. He was an indefatigable and effective surrogate in the general election, who never refused to help. I enjoyed reciprocating in 2012, endorsing him before the New Hampshire primary.

Huckabee remained in the race, as did libertarian Ron Paul. Huckabee won a few more southern contests but formally withdrew in March after I had accumulated enough delegates to secure the nomination. Paul stayed in until June, when he suspended his campaign having never won a single primary or caucus, but having made a point of some kind to his passionate followers.

I had the advantage of being able to prepare for the general election while Barack Obama and Hillary Clinton were still in a dogfight. Hillary was proving to be a tough, resilient competitor. But Obama had something special going on. His crowds were enormous. His appeal for a campaign that aspired to more than the usual smash-and-grab tactics tapped into a yearning in people alienated from contemporary politics. Much of the press was infatuated with him. I didn't underestimate him. I was impressed by him, and I knew I would be the underdog in the race were he to be my opponent. I had to present myself as a different kind of politician, too, if I was to have a fighting chance. And I had to start right away.

I received President Bush's endorsement at the White House the day after Mike Huckabee had withdrawn. I appreciated it, and the gracious consideration that he extended me throughout the campaign. The President's approval rating was at its lowest due to widespread unhappiness with the Iraq War and the federal response to Hurricane Katrina. To state the obvious, the image conveyed by his endorsement wasn't likely to reinforce the idea that I was a different kind of Republican. Rather it would be interpreted as a ritual anointing of an heir apparent to a then unpopular President, an interpretation Democrats were quick to publicize. Neither did the trip to Iraq I took later that month with Lindsey Graham and Joe Lieberman have the appearance of change, either. The progress we had made there since our last trip was noticeable and encouraging, and I said so, which might have sounded to many voters as the same old empty assurances they'd been hearing for five years.

I had been a U.S. senator for over twenty years, and a nationally known politician for almost a decade. But while Obama and Clinton were slugging it out, and consuming most of the public's appetite for politics, my advisors thought I should reintroduce myself to voters who might still be paying attention. We decided I would give several speeches in locations that had been important in my life. The subjects of each speech would be mostly biographical, emphasizing my service to the nation. We started at Episcopal High School. The Naval Academy was the second stop. By the third speech, in Pensacola where I had trained as a naval aviator, I started getting bored with the story. I expect voters were, too, and likely returned their attention to the close race for the Democratic nomination, while I regaled a few more audiences with favorite tales from my colorful past.

I was more enthusiastic about the series of campaign stops that followed my biography tour. Most were in hard-pressed communities that wouldn't vote for me, places that hadn't shared in the prosperity of the previous quarter century. We went to a shuttered steel mill in Youngstown, Ohio, a coal-mining hollow in Eastern Kentucky, and to New Orleans's Ninth Ward. We began the tour in Alabama's "Black Belt," named for the richness of its soil. It's a mostly rural, economically distressed section of the state, where the majority of voters are African American and Democrat. It was a politically inhospitable section of a state that would vote overwhelmingly for the Republican nominee for President, whether he campaigned there or not. Campaigning anywhere in Alabama wouldn't gain or cost a single vote. But that was sort of the point. I wanted to stress that ours wasn't like Republican campaigns of the past. I wasn't interested in sharpening old divisions, emphasizing partisan differences, and trying to run up the score with the base without scaring off too many moderates and independents. I wanted to show I cared about every American community, that all Americans are my responsibility, and would be my concern were I to become their President.

We kicked off the tour on an April morning in Selma, Alabama, at the foot of the Edmund Pettis Bridge, where forty-three years earlier Alabama state troopers and local police had savagely beaten peaceful civil rights marchers, men, women, and children, including John Lewis, a man I greatly admired. "There must be no forgotten places in America," I said to the 150 or so Selma residents who gathered to listen, "whether they have been ignored for long years by the sins of indifference and injustice or have been left behind as the world grew smaller and more economically interdependent." I recounted John Lewis's story, how he had bravely stood to take the expected blows from the troopers' batons, and collapsed unconscious in his bloodstained raincoat.

> In America, we have always believed that if the day was a disappointment, we would win tomorrow. That's what John Lewis believed when he marched across this bridge.

The audience was mostly white. Selma is mostly black. After my remarks, reporters were quick to point out the difference as if I hadn't been aware of it myself. "I'm aware the African American vote has been very small in favor of the Republican Party," I responded. "I am aware of the challenges, and I am aware of the fact that there will be many people who will not vote for me. But I'm going to be the president of all the people."

We traveled from Selma to other stops in the Black Belt, Camden and Thomasville, where I held a town hall at a packed junior college auditorium, and to Gee's Bend on the Alabama River, where lived a remote but somewhat famous community of quilters, whose work had been nationally and internationally recognized. There I received what is probably the most effusive reception I have ever received in my political career. The women of Gee's Bend all turned out to welcome us as our bus pulled to a stop. They shouted, sang, and danced—and tried to get me to dance, as ungainly a sight as any they had seen before—as they escorted Cindy and me around their little community, and to see and admire their quilts. They recalled how the local ferry service had been terminated in 1962 to prevent them from crossing the river to register to vote in the county seat. It hadn't stopped them. The ferry wouldn't be restored until 2006. They thanked us for coming, and wished us good luck in the election. And they meant it, even though they were surely going to vote for my opponent. They were the warmest and most genuine people I have ever met.

I loved it, the entire day. It remains one of my fondest memories of the campaign and in all my public life. Noted in many of the news accounts of the day's events was the fact that I was a rare Republican politician in those parts. I loved that. The headline for the *Birmingham News*'s report proclaimed, "In Black Belt, McCain Wins Hearts, Not Votes." I loved reading that, too.

We visited the weathered porch of the Fletcher family's house in Inez, Kentucky, where Lyndon Johnson had announced the War on Poverty in 1964, and where the coal industry's decline had sunk the area deeper into the poverty Johnson had promised they would escape. Inez remained one of the poorest communities in Appalachia. I made a brief speech at the Martin County courthouse before taking questions. I acknowledged that I had been raised in the Navy, and had an easier start in life than the families who worked the mines and farms of Appalachia, and my life continued to be easier than theirs. "But you are . . . my fellow Americans, and that kinship means more to me than almost any other association." Then I answered questions, joked around, and swapped stories with them for a while, refusing a few invitations to attack Obama, who had lost the Pennsylvania primary the night before but was still viewed as the likely Democratic nominee. There would come a time, soon enough, when our campaigns would trade accusations and batter each other. For now, I wanted to do what I was doing, talking with Americans I didn't know and who didn't really know me, and assure them of my concern for their situation. A reporter for *The New Yorker* described my Inez town hall as a "remarkably subdued performance." I didn't mind. I followed the town hall with a fairly lively press conference. The same reporter had also noted that "McCain doesn't try to stir the crowd's darker passions or its higher aspirations. He doesn't present himself as a conservative leader. He is simply a leader. . . . Here I am, a man in full, take me or leave me. This might be the only kind of Republican who could win in 2008." I liked that thought quite a bit whether it was true or not.

We ended the tour walking the streets of New Orleans's Katrina-ravaged Ninth Ward, past abandoned homes and huge heaps of debris. Reporters rode in front of us in a flatbed truck, captives for the moment, and unhappy they couldn't interview the locals as we toured their devastated neighborhood. I promised to expedite the building of a new levee system and restore wetlands that could absorb storm surges. I swore never again would the federal government fail Americans as disgracefully as it had failed the people of New Orleans.

We followed the tour with a series of policy speeches, on health care, national security, economic policy, the environment, and tax reform. I gave a speech in Columbus, Ohio, that envisioned the progress I hoped to achieve by the end of my first term in office, listing a number of bi-partisan accomplishments that included a successful conclusion to the war in Iraq and most of our troops returned home. I wanted to run the kind of substantive campaign the press and public claim to want while they focus their attention on the horse race. They had quite a race running in the other party, and while we received dutiful attention for my campaign stops and policy speeches, it was usually relegated to the inside pages of the newspaper while the Obama-Clinton contest owned the front page.

Then it was over. In the first week of June, on the night of the last Democratic primaries, Obama collected enough delegates to be the presumptive nominee. Hillary conceded and endorsed him a few days later. Turnout in the Democratic contests had set records. Even in some red states, more people had voted for Obama or Clinton than had supported me and the other Republican candidates. Obama looked on top of the world the night he clinched the nomination. He gave a speech that captivated his supporters, and most of the press. I made a speech that night, too. I didn't want to concede to him any news cycle from that day on, if I could help it. It was a mistake in hindsight. I wasn't going to own even a small share of the attention on the night a young African American with an exotic name, who had come from obscurity a few years before, captured the hearts and minds of millions of excited voters and won a major political party's presidential nomination. Not much was noted in the press about my speech other than that I had the temerity to distract attention from my opponent's triumph and that I'd spoken in front of a bright green background that looked odd on television.

There would be other nights throughout the general election campaign when I would find it difficult if not impossible to compete with the publicity and excitement my opponent generated. I had two imperatives before me that were clear from the beginning of my contest with Barack Obama. The first was obvious. I was the more experienced public official, having had a career in the military as well as a career in politics. I had to make the case that experience was still crucially important in choosing a President. My military credential was more of an advantage than my long career in Congress, which wasn't something that thrilled voters in 2008. It hampered my second, more important objective—convincing skeptical voters that I, too, could be counted on to change Washington.

The only way I could persuade voters I would bring change as President was to conduct my campaign for the office in ways that were noticeably different from presidential campaigns of the past. But the idea wasn't just tactical. I truly did want to campaign in a way that was more honest and, I hoped, inspiring. And to do that I needed my opponent to be my partner. I loved the story that Jack Kennedy and Barry Goldwater had agreed to travel together on the same plane in 1964 if Barry were to win the Republican nomination, and hold a series of informal debates or dueling speeches in small and large communities across the country. We proposed something along that line to the Obama campaign. We suggested holding ten joint town hall–style debates, and traveling together to each of them. They countered by offering one town hall event on the Fourth of July, and the three traditional debates the Commission on Presidential Debates had already proposed. They were silent about the plane.

That was disappointing. I'm not naive. I had a lot to gain. Obama had a lot to lose. He was the front-runner. He had lots more money than we had. He was getting a lot more attention than I was. And he owned the change message. All those advantages might have been risked or at least diminished had he agreed to share the spotlight with his opponent in such a novel way. But I believed then that by our willingness to trust voters' intelligence and decency, and to an extent, to trust each other, we would have called out some of the BS in the way politics is routinely practiced, and conducted ourselves in a way that we and the country could be proud of. I loved the idea. I suspect he saw the appeal of it, too. But front-runners are risk averse, challengers are risk-takers, and that's how his advisors likely saw the proposal, as an unnecessary risk. Yet his very decision to run had been a risk. I hoped some of that daring would have influenced his decisions in the general election campaign. But he decided not to squander his advantages. It was the prudent thing to do.

When Nancy Reagan and Lyndon Johnson's daughters invited us to hold joint town halls at the Reagan and Johnson libraries, we agreed. The Obama campaign declined. When we agreed to abide by campaign spending limits in order to receive the millions of dollars in public financing we needed, the Obama campaign, knowing they had an immense financial advantage, announced Obama would be the first nominee to opt out of the public financing system. That was also the prudent thing to do. We expected that the press would support our position on debates and public financing, and punish Obama for rejecting them. That turned out to be a misjudgment on my part. Most reporters liked the idea of joint town halls and spending limits. But they liked the Obama story better, and the fallout he experienced for rejecting them was negligible.

There isn't any way the loser in an election can criticize the press without appearing to be a sore loser. So I won't complain here. Not much, anyway. Most of the coverage I received was fine. I didn't agree with all of it. I disliked the criticism I received, although I earned some of it. I also understand why my opponent's campaign made such good copy and attracted more attention than ours did. He was new news. I wasn't. And most reporters were more aligned with his politics than mine. Above all, his success seemed to transcend political tribalism and represent real progress against the racism that had afflicted our society from its founding, and reporters, like most people, didn't want to see that progress set back.

The press had a finger on the scale for Obama, both in the primaries and the general election. They gave him more favorable attention
than they gave his opponents. They defended him from attacks, unfair
and fair, and criticized his opponents for making them. I don't think
that's disputable or surprising. The favoritism wasn't universal and it
didn't determine the outcome. It was just a challenge we had to factor
into our decision making. I didn't like it. But given the media environment we live in today, where we can restrict information gathering to
sources that tell us only what we want to hear, where crackpot conspiracy websites like InfoWars and Breitbart, and Russian propagan-
dists such as Russia Today and WikiLeaks, are taken more seriously by
their credulous followers than journalism practiced with professional
standards and ethics, the problem of routine liberal bias in the media
seems positively quaint.

I'm familiar with how reporters can favor and protect one candidate over another. I had that advantage in the primaries in 2000, and
I know it when I see it. It's certainly helpful, but you can't win a presidential election on better press alone. The irony here is that Obama
didn't need it. He was running a hell of a campaign. He had bottled
lightning in a political environment that couldn't have been more favorable to the party out of power. He was in accord with the country
and the times. He was the biggest political show on earth.

His first trip overseas as the Democratic nominee in July generated much more excitement than mine had. He stopped in Iraq and
Afghanistan, as well as Jordan, Israel, and the West Bank before visiting
the capitals of our main European allies. He was greeted effusively not
just by the government leaders he met. His public reception at some of
his stops was rapturous. He gave a speech in Berlin that drew a crowd
estimated to be as many as a quarter of a million people. It was a spec-
tacle that led the news broadcasts and dominated the front page. He
had something going on all right, and figuring out how to challenge

it and divert a little more interest in our direction was as difficult as it was imperative.

Win or lose, I didn't want anyone ever to have fair grounds to criticize us for resorting to any kind of racist dog whistling. I wanted to win. I wanted to be President. But I, too, recognized the social progress Obama's candidacy represented, and I didn't want to impede it by inciting, even with a wink and a nod here and there or with language that had double meanings, the prejudices that have marred our history. I cautioned staff repeatedly, and senior staff reiterated it repeatedly, to steer clear of any communication, formal or informal, or an event or any person that could be interpreted as suggesting race as a reason to vote for me and against Obama. That meant our criticism of him and any of his associates had to be carefully screened for a meaning we didn't intend. We were on the receiving end of quite a number of attacks by his campaign and assorted Democratic entities on people working with or associated with us in some way. We had to be more restrained in that line of attack, as we would learn again and again. The press was primed to prosecute any hint of racism. Every now and again I had to chastise someone introducing me or warming up the crowd or asking me a question for what could be construed as at least an implicit racist remark. Emphasizing Obama's middle name. Claiming he was a secret Kenyan or Arab or Muslim, and somehow disloyal to the country. Questioning his patriotism, his parentage, his travels and experiences as a young man. The occasional vulgar or cruel or racist shout from the crowd. I condemned them when I heard them.

I forbade all mention of the Reverend Jeremiah Wright, Obama's controversial pastor, whose sermons had been the reason Obama felt it necessary to give his much-praised speech on race the previous March. Fred Davis, who led our media team, had prepared an ad that attacked Obama's relationship with Wright. I rejected it. In July, Fred, Rick Davis, and Steve Schmidt proposed a kind of jujitsu ad that used my opponent's strength against him. In this case, the ad used Obama's global celebrity to raise doubts about his preparation for the job of President, and by inference contrasted his experience unfavorably to mine. I thought it was fair play, and still do.

It was a thirty-second spot with a female narrator. Over images of his Berlin event, and pop culture celebrities of the time, and above the sound of a crowd chanting Obama's name, the narrator intoned, "He's the biggest celebrity in the world, but is he ready to lead?" That was it. The ad took a couple quick shots at his positions on oil drilling and taxes, but they were sort of beside the point. Its purpose was to suggest that his sudden celebrity was not based on real achievements or better ideas. It didn't mention my record. It didn't need to. We would do that in our earned media. Our message through that summer had two parts: ready on day one and country first. My war record, Navy career, long involvement with national security issues, long-standing relationships with foreign leaders, and record of bipartisan accomplishments demonstrated more experience than could my opponent, who had been a state senator and briefly a U.S. senator before becoming "the biggest celebrity in the world." My support for the surge, and other views that weren't always popular with Republican leaders or the conservative base, as well as my conduct as a POW were presented as proof that I put the country before myself. It was our best case at the time, and it worked. By the end of the month we had put a dent in Obama's lead, and in August a few polls, including Gallup's, had me slightly ahead.

Everything we did was scrutinized by the other side and the media for any trace of below-the-belt insinuations. That included the "celebrity" ad. Questions were raised about whether we used Paris Hilton's and Britney Spears's images in the ad to appeal to prejudiced white voters' fear of miscegenation or if we had darkened Obama's skin in the photograph we used. Silly shit like that was tossed at us regularly.

We didn't intend to play those games. We didn't want to play those games. And we didn't play those games. We didn't want to set the country back or undermine the social significance of Obama's candidacy. We took pains to stay clear of that stuff. We denounced anyone who resorted to it, and we were proud we did.

Nevertheless, we were frequently accused without evidence of racist insinuations or worse. *Newsweek* ran a cover story in May that didn't just imply but openly assumed we would make or secretly support racist attacks on my opponent. The Obama campaign and reporters relying on Democratic opposition research regularly assailed members of my campaign staff, my donors, and supporters for their businesses and associations. But we were restrained from doing the same by our own and the media's insistence that we take extreme care to avoid the appearance of appealing to people's prejudices. Our surrogates were criticized for making fun of Obama's experience as a community organizer, which I sort of regret. There's nothing wrong with and probably much that's admirable about the occupation. But our ridicule wasn't racist, as some alleged. We were accused of racism for calling Bill Ayers, my opponent's early supporter and former member of the Weather Underground, a terrorist despite the fact that he was white and had been involved in bombings at New York City's police headquarters, the Pentagon, and the U.S. Capitol. When the housing market crashed in the fall, and with it much of the global credit system, Democrats fixed the blame on George Bush and his heir apparent, me. That's politics. I would've done the same if I'd been them. When we responded by pointing out that the people who ran Fannie Mae, one of the institutions responsible for the housing market collapse, were all Obama supporters, including its CEO, Franklin Raines, we were accused of invoking race because Raines was black. It was the predicament we had to learn to operate within and not take personally.

I didn't like it, of course, at all. But in only one instance did I take

lasting offense at a false accusation. Citing reports that fall that racist insults were shouted from the crowd at some of my events, John
Lewis, a personal hero of mine, accused our campaign of sowing hatred, compared me to George Wallace, and said that, like Wallace, we
were creating the kind of political atmosphere that got four little girls
killed in a Birmingham church. I couldn't believe it, and I couldn't
forgive it. I still can't.

My biggest predicament was my difficulty convincing voters I was an
agent of change. That was our principal concern as we assembled a list
of potential vice presidents that summer. I wanted to choose someone
I respected, and I wanted the choice to represent change. We had a list
of names with twenty to thirty people. The lawyers vetting candidates
for us, led by the able A. B. Culvahouse, a prominent Washington attorney, did a public records search for all of them, and several were
removed from the list. I admit I didn't give the attention they deserved
to all the prospects who remained on the list. I gave most thought to
people with whom I had an established relationship. I thought a lot
about choosing Mitt Romney. He had been my most formidable opponent in the primaries, and is a smart, capable, and appealing candidate
with expertise in issues where I was a little deficient. Tim Pawlenty
was another successful blue state governor I got along well with. Mike
Bloomberg, a friend, brilliant businessman, and innovative mayor, was
on the list, too.

All the choices had some downside. Had I asked Governor Romney
to join the ticket, the Democrats would have greeted the decision by
reminding voters of the attacks and recriminations we had exchanged
during the primaries. That's standard practice when the nominee asks
a rival to join the ticket. It's annoying, but it's fair, and it's a surmount-
able problem. Tim Pawlenty didn't have much national name iden-

tification, which was fine. He would have been a fresh face. He had widespread appeal in Minnesota, and I liked him and his wife, Mary, a lot. He would be viewed as a safe, conventional choice, solid on the merits, but not an outsider or a credible change agent. Mike Bloomberg would be viewed as a change. He had an impressive record of accomplishment in New York, but one not always admired by conservatives, nor were his views on guns, abortion, and other social issues. Conservatives didn't consider Mike to be a moderate Republican or RINO (Republican in Name Only), an epithet often hurled at me. They viewed him as a liberal, along the lines of John Lindsay, a species of Republican that hasn't existed in any numbers for quite a while. They viewed his affiliation with the Republican Party as weak and opportunistic. Mike is smart, shrewd, and not given to posturing. When we informed him he was on the short list and asked if he would agree to be fully vetted, he responded with, "Are you sure about this?"

I had met with several prospects under consideration and read vetting summaries for others. In May, I had invited a few of them to our place in Northern Arizona for the weekend in the hope that a relaxed social setting among our family and friends would give me a better sense of their personalities. I didn't like the idea of conducting formal interviews, and I left routine issue and background questions to the lawyers and staff. I did want to know, if I didn't already, what issues were their priorities, and I wanted to be confident they would share mine. I admired many of the candidates, and I enjoyed the company of most of them.

By late June, I had mentally culled a shorter list from the short list, consisting of three or four names. Each had appeal, and I liked them all. But I kept coming back to one name, one name that would have certainly represented change, although that wasn't the principal reason I wanted to pick him. Joe Lieberman and I shared the same worldview and concerns, and we were the best of friends. I trusted him completely, and valued his counsel. He was no longer formally a Democrat, having won his last reelection as an Independent. But he caucused with Senate Democrats, and he had been the Democratic vice presidential nominee in 2000. He had endorsed me in December when I wasn't the presumptive nominee or the favorite to win, when there was no advantage for him to risk his relationships with Democrats. Were Joe to join the ticket it would send a clear message of change. It would be an emphatic statement that I intended to govern collaboratively with an emphasis on problem solving not politics, which in 2008 would have been very good politics. The more I thought about asking Joe, the more the idea felt right to me.

By the end of July, I had decided. I would ask Joe to join what I hoped would be seen as a national unity ticket pledged to avoid partisan excesses in the hope of overcoming Washington gridlock. I shared the decision with my closest advisors, including Lindsey Graham, who enthusiastically endorsed the idea. We agreed to keep my decision a closely held secret while Rick Davis and others began gauging how difficult it would be to get convention delegates to vote for a vice presidential nominee whose views on various social issues, including abortion, were to the left of mine, and far to the left of most of the delegates. Of course, as soon as they began raising the idea with state and national party leaders, speculation ensued about who McCain's prochoice pick might be, which in turn aroused the conservative base, and brought private and public recriminations from a broad array of Republicans, some of whose opinions I valued and some I didn't. Their argument was that a pro-choice pick, whoever it was, might survive the convention but would fatally divide the Republican Party. The reality of Republican politics set in. Even were Joe to give assurances that he would be duty bound to uphold my positions on all issues were he to assume the presidency, it wouldn't stop the intraparty brawl that would be the only story coming out of the Republican convention, and would dominate coverage of our campaign in the critical first weeks of the fall campaign.

With the exception of Lindsey, who remained supportive, everyone else I had entrusted with my decision advised me against it. They had liked the idea initially, and thought we could still get Joe through the convention, barely. But they thought we would discourage activists and depress Republican turnout more than we would attract Independents and crossover Democrats. I didn't agree with the advice, or more accurately, I didn't like the advice, and I continued to insist on naming Joe my running mate, while the window for making and preparing for another choice was rapidly closing.

They were giving me their best counsel. It was sound advice that I could reason for myself. But my gut told me to ignore it, and I wish I had. America's security and standing in the world were my principal concerns and the main reason, other than personal ambition, that I ran for President. Joe and I share those priorities, and on most related issues we agree on how best to serve them. I completely trusted, liked, and worked well with Joe. And I still believe, whatever the effect it would have had in some quarters of the party, that a McCain-Lieberman ticket would have been received by most Americans as a genuine effort to pull the country together for a change. I don't like not doing what I know in my gut I should do. I made it known that I reluctantly accepted my advisors' concerns. Then I sulked about it for a little while.

We were nearly out of time. The Republican convention was a week away, and when Steve Schmidt and Rick Davis raised Sarah Palin with me, I was intrigued. Steve had spent time in Alaska on business in recent months and had been impressed by what he had learned about her. Rick had reviewed what research was immediately available and watched recordings of some of her press interviews. He was impressed as well. Sarah had been among the names on the initial, longer list of

VP prospects, most of whom had received a cursory public document vetting before being dropped for other, more serious prospects. I had met her briefly at a recent National Governors Association meeting in Washington, and had been seated at her table at a dinner that night. I had liked her. She had spirit and charisma.

She had been governor less than two years, but her involvement in state politics had begun a decade and a half before, and she had been active in the local politics of the town where she'd been mayor, Wasilla, since the early 1990s. She was a popular, energetic, and accomplished reformer as mayor, governor, and as a campaigner. She had been appointed by her predecessor, Frank Murkowski, to the state's oil and gas commission. Her lack of experience with energy issues hadn't prevented her from recognizing and criticizing ethical breaches committed by a fellow commissioner and other public officials, who had conflicts of interest involving oil and gas companies. She had cooperated with a Democratic legislator to make the case for their removal from office. She ran for governor on an ethics reform platform against the incumbent and most influential Republican in Alaska for the nomination. She beat a former Democratic governor in the general. The underestimated small-town mayor was an underdog and vastly outspent in both races, but she had won. As governor, she passed an ethics reform bill her first year in office and raised taxes on the biggest interest in Alaska, the oil and gas industry, and used the revenues to offset the high fuel prices Alaskans were paying at the time.

Her profile as a reformer and as someone who managed to get important stuff done without years of experience or deferring to established interests was her main appeal. The fact that she was an accomplished woman succeeding in a male-dominated profession didn't hurt, either. We felt, and polling confirmed, that there were moderate and conservative Democrats who had voted for Hillary Clinton and might be persuaded to vote for a Republican presidential candidate with a record of working with both sides, and the female chief executive he had picked as his running mate.

On several issues, Sarah held more conservative positions than mine, from drilling in the Arctic National Wildlife Refuge to public funding for stem cell research. As my running mate she would be expected to defer to my views, and she did. But the expectation she would excite conservatives who hadn't reconciled themselves to my nomination, and who were at present unlikely to work hard to turn out Republican voters, was a consideration, too. Not the main one, but not a negligible one. Her reformer credentials, the surprise her selection would be, her gender, and her naturalness as a political personality were what made her so appealing to us.

I called her and asked if she would agree to a formal vetting, and to come to Arizona to meet with me. Although she had to have been surprised by the call, she answered affirmatively very calmly as if she'd been expecting the call. I told her we would be in touch shortly with the details, and she thanked me for calling. The experience reminded me a little of the time I'd received a call from Bob Dole during the 1996 Republican convention asking me if I would mind putting his name in formal nomination the next night, offering me a prime-time speech a little more than twenty-four hours before it had to be delivered. That's quite an honor and opportunity for a junior senator, and Bob had made the offer with all the ceremony of someone asking me the time. I had just dangled before Sarah Palin an opportunity to become overnight a nationally known figure, with all that means, good and bad. She had responded as if it had been a routine request, and she was open to the idea.

A few days later Sarah and an aide flew to Flagstaff, where she interviewed first with Schmidt and Salter, and then with A. B. Culvahouse and his team. If after their conversations, they and Rick Davis agreed she was the wrong pick, they would thank her for her time and arrange for her flight back to Alaska. But if they felt it was worthwhile for me to meet with her, they would bring her to our place an hour from Flagstaff.

She arrived the next day after spending all night on the phone with the lawyers. We sat next to the creek and talked for an hour. I liked her right away. She spoke with genuine passion about government reform and fighting corruption. She acknowledged our differences, but noted that we shared an independent streak that put the country above party. She is uncannily self-possessed, and has an authentic warmth as a campaigner. I sensed how appealing a performer she would be, and her self-confidence allayed concerns we had that she might not be able to withstand the scrutiny and rigors of a presidential campaign. I walked away from our meeting confident that she could. Whatever stumbles she would have in the blindingly intense experience she was about to enter would be on us, on our judgment, not hers.

Cindy sat with Sarah after we finished our conversation, and showed her around the place while I talked with Salter and Schmidt. I'd spoken to A. B. earlier, who counseled that she would be a "high risk, high reward" pick. He saw her appeal and potential, and the vulnerabilities that could be exposed by the battering of a national campaign that can test the fortitude of more experienced politicians. Salter worried that Sarah's scant exposure to national politics, and her self-admitted knowledge deficiency in national security issues, would undermine the experience advantage we had over Obama. He argued for Tim Pawlenty. Schmidt made the case for her, which essentially boiled down to "she could shake up the race and the other candidates can't." She was a fresh face, an outspoken reformer, a wife and mother who had fought the special interests and won. She could appeal to conservative Democrats and women voters not yet sold on Obama or me. She was tough and could handle pressure. She was smart, hardworking, and willing to learn. We had three opportunities, he argued, to stop the race from trending inevitably to the challenger in an environment where over 70 percent of voters believed the country was going in the wrong direction: my vice president selection, my convention speech, and the debates. If we failed to use any one of those opportunities to convince voters we would bring change to Washington, we would lose. Sarah was the biggest change message on the list of possible choices. I thought Schmidt made the better argument probably because it echoed my own thoughts about Sarah and the challenges ahead. I walked back to the deck of our house where Cindy and Sarah were sitting, and offered her the nomination. We talked a while longer, then she left with Salter and Schmidt to fly to Dayton, Ohio, where we would announce her the day after the Democratic convention had closed with Obama's soaring acceptance speech (except for the parts where he blasted me, which didn't soar as much as they irritated).

We successfully kept Sarah's selection secret until we introduced her. She had flown to a private airfield twenty miles from Dayton, and stayed in a nearby hotel under an assumed name. A small group of staff, sworn to silence, spent the night working with her on her speech. Her family arrived later that night.

The lack of time and our emphasis on secrecy deprived the media of a chance to scrutinize her strengths and weaknesses before the announcement. It also left the rest of the campaign staff unprepared to answer questions about her. Getting up to speed on Sarah Palin for both reporters and staff would happen after her first public appearance. We had left too little time to prepare thoroughly for the announcement, to defend it and get a VP operation staffed and running, especially considering the unconventional choice I had made. Those things would happen in a rush in the days immediately after the announcement, and during our convention. It was chaotic. Again, that was on us, not her.

When she strode out onto the auditorium stage at Wright State

University that morning with her beautiful family, and introduced herself to the fifteen thousand people there and the nation, she was a pitch-perfect performer and the crowd was completely smitten. She conveyed her natural appeal as if she were one of the most practiced political communicators in the country. I was beaming as I watched her. We weren't the only Americans excited by her selection. The campaign raised more than $7 million in twenty-four hours, a sum greater than any total we had raised in a week's time.

Four days later, she delivered her acceptance speech in St. Paul, Minnesota, another bravura performance that had the hall on its feet, fired up the grass roots, captivated a lot of undecided voters, and impressed even reporters who questioned her qualifications for the job.

You have to have extraordinary strength, confidence, and ability to be suddenly plucked from your life, and in less than a week present your best self to an audience of tens of millions, who are watching and wondering who the hell you are, while you, your family, your friends are furiously scrutinized by hundreds of reporters. She handled it with resolve and grace even when her single daughter's pregnancy was disclosed, igniting a brief, intense media storm that included ugly speculation that her youngest son, Trig, then an infant, was her daughter's child. She did what we asked of her and more. She was a concerned mother protecting her children. She was a student cramming for exams. She was a skilled amateur performer asked to appear on Broadway twice a day. She was the Alaska politician struck by a flood of stories coming from her home state with scraps of potentially juicy news about her life as far back as high school. She was the new national figure, who instantly attracted a host of excited supporters, got accustomed to family life with a Secret Service detail and to reporters calling her relatives and friends, while she prepared for interviews with the national press and a debate with my friend Joe Biden. It was a lot to ask of a more experienced politician. She had to be ready to debate Joe just over a month after she had been announced. If you haven't been a principal in the do-or-die intensity of a presidential or vice presidential debate, where a single mistake can doom your candidacy, you can't imagine the anxiety it produces. Yet Sarah acquitted herself well in her exchanges with one of the most experienced politicians in the country.

She stumbled in some interviews, and had a few misjudgments in the glare of the ceaseless spotlight and unblinking cameras. Those missteps, too, are on me. She didn't put herself on the ticket. I did. I asked her to go through an experience that was wearing me down, that wears every candidate down. I made mistakes and misjudgments, too. I said something wrong or inaccurate or poorly chosen from time to time. So did my opponent and his running mate, mistakes we attributed to the pressure and exhaustion of a national campaign. Ours were often overlooked or viewed less seriously than were Sarah's because reporters and pundits generally assumed Barack, Joe, and I were better than our screwups. Sarah wasn't given that allowance.

There's no use bitching about how you were treated in a presidential campaign after it's over, and I've always tried to resist doing that. We caught some breaks. We messed up sometimes. We took some lumps we deserved and some we didn't. On the whole, it was the privilege of a lifetime. I mean it. I'm a very competitive guy. I hate losing. But I knew the moment I had it and even in the moment I lost it that I had an opportunity granted to very few people in this world. I had a fair chance to lead the most important nation on earth. I had a full opportunity to persuade Americans they should trust me with the security and prosperity of our civilization. I didn't convince them.

But on the night of September 4, 2008, when I stepped out onstage to accept my party's nomination, looked out on the crowded arena and into the center teleprompter, I got to make my case. I haven't Barack Obama's eloquence, but I can convey how much this country means to me, which I tried very hard to do that night. I love this country. I want to do right by her always. Some critics believe my decisions and statements weren't always consistent with my "Country First" rhetoric. People draw the conclusions they expect from your mistakes, whether you've consciously done something wrong or made an inadvertent error or don't believe you did anything wrong at all. We all judge people through the lens of our beliefs and associations, and in politics that perspective can find more than disagreement in an opponent's statements and decisions. It can suspect bad faith. I know I've done and said things throughout my public life that I thought were right or at least arguable but others considered offensive. Sometimes they were right. But I have never thought to hurt this country to gain something for myself. Never.

I swore in my acceptance speech that I wasn't "running for president because I'm blessed with such personal greatness that history has anointed me to save our country in its hour of need." I was running because "my country saved me . . . and I can't forget it. And I will fight for her for as long as I draw breath." I meant it. I offered little more than implicit criticism of my opponent, and some praise. I assured him of my respect and admiration, and I meant that, too:

> Despite our differences, much more unites us than divides us. We are fellow Americans, an association that means more to me than any other. We're dedicated to the proposition that all people are created equal and endowed by our Creator with inalienable rights. No country ever had a greater cause than that. And I wouldn't be an American worthy of the name if I didn't honor Senator Obama and his supporters for their achievement.

I wanted to make the affirmative case for my candidacy. I wanted to convince Americans that whatever they might think of my politics, my views, my conduct as a public official, whether they thought I was right or wrong, they could trust that in my heart I believed I was fighting for our country. That's how I hope people will remember me. Others have fought more successfully than I have, and made fewer mistakes in the bargain. But I am grateful beyond expression to have had the opportunity to fight for her as best I can.

To the extent we had any surges in our campaign, we practically roared out of St. Paul. In the week after the convention a few polls had the race tied. Most gave me a small but not insignificant lead, and one, Gallup, had me ahead by ten points. There weren't many times before that moment when I thought the race might be mine to lose. Actually, the thought had never occurred to me before that week. We had big highs in the race for the nomination, New Hampshire, South Carolina, Florida, Super Tuesday. But I was usually behind in the polls in the general, and I was always aware that the country was extremely dissatisfied with the incumbent administration and with Republicans in general. That week, though, we let ourselves believe. We weren't celebrating or congratulating each other. Our days were too crammed with activity and worry for that. The debates were approaching, and almost every spare hour between campaign events was dedicated to preparing for them. We were probably a little more cheerful, I suppose, though I doubt anyone outside the campaign would have noticed a change in our demeanor. But optimism in a campaign, especially a campaign as beset with challenges as ours was, spreads quickly and creates energy if not exuberance, an extra something that drives everyone from volunteers to the candidate to hustle more, to fight harder. We were feeling all of that in the immediate aftermath of the convention. It didn't last long.

By September 11, as Senator Obama and I together laid a wreath at Ground Zero to commemorate the anniversary of that terrible day, our bump in the polls had receded. The race was tight again with some polls giving a slight advantage to my opponent. Four days later, Lehman Brothers filed for bankruptcy, the biggest casualty to date of the subprime mortgage crisis that had begun the year before and was now spreading like a forest fire. The week before Lehman fell, the federal government had taken control of mortgage giants Fannie Mae and Freddie Mac, which were overly invested in bad subprime loans. Merrill Lynch was sold, and insurance behemoth AIG had to be rescued by a government bailout or it would've fallen, too. The housing bubble burst spectacularly as the resulting liquidity crisis dried up financing for residential and commercial lending. Families who were relying on equity in their homes as a retirement fund, encouraged by the long boom in housing prices, were suddenly holding an underwater mortgage, owing more than their homes were worth.

At a campaign appearance the day after the Lehman Brothers news, I wanted to say something encouraging that wouldn't contribute to the spreading panic. I offered the assurance that "the fundamentals of our economy are strong." Whether or not that statement was accurate at the time, it proved colossally impolitic. The fundamentals sure didn't look strong to most voters, not with a flood of bankruptcies, a global credit crisis under way, a collapsing housing market, and the Dow Jones average shedding nearly 800 points in a single day.

We had struggled and clawed our way into a competitive position with less than two months to go to Election Day. We did it despite massive voter dissatisfaction with the direction of the country, and while being outspent four to one. We did it while our disciplined opposing campaign was rarely knocked off stride, owned most of the strategic advantages, and was branded with the "hope and change" message while we cast around for new ways to make the same claim, and made a few mistakes in the process.

We were in New York City for a fund-raiser the night of September 24, and spent the afternoon in debate prep. The crisis seemed to be spiraling beyond anything experienced since the bank runs of the Great Depression. Some of my economic advisors were worried that any day people would be unable to withdraw cash from ATMs. Beside my ill-timed "sound fundamentals" remark, all I had added to the national debate so far was a denunciation of greed and a call for a 9/11-type commission to investigate what had happened and who was responsible. That wasn't cutting it.

The Bush administration was working on a financial rescue plan, and my staff were hearing reports that House Republicans were reluctant to support it. We knew that this mounting disaster would likely doom us unless we could figure out some way to demonstrate that we were helping get it under control. We hatched a plan to propose to Obama that we suspend our campaigns for a week, and postpone the first debate scheduled for two days hence, while he and I, the White House, and both parties' congressional leadership worked out a rescue plan that could pass Congress. Senator Obama called that day to ask me to join him in endorsing the plan that Treasury Secretary Hank Paulson had put together. I countered with the suspension idea and a bipartisan meeting at the White House. He rejected the idea. I called Senate Majority Leader Harry Reid to see if I could get him to help. We'd known each other for years and were on friendly and informal terms. When he responded by reading clearly prepared talking points and calling me Senator McCain, I knew I wasn't going to get anywhere with our idea. The Obama campaign denounced it, insisting he would be at the debate as scheduled. He couldn't speak for me, he allowed, but he could campaign and discharge his Senate responsibilities at the same time.

We had the White House meeting. It was a waste of time. Harry and Speaker of the House Nancy Pelosi just stirred the pot, blaming the crisis on Republicans. Barack spoke briefly. I went in knowing the House Republican votes for the rescue package weren't there. Even though I was the party's presidential nominee, I had more than a few detractors in the House caucus. I had already met with their leader, my friend John Boehner, and I could see he didn't have the votes yet. I wanted whatever agreement we might work out to appear to be as much the product of House Republican concerns as mine or the White House's. When asked by President Bush to speak, I said I would defer to the House Republican leader. I should have hogged the floor a little. Minutes after the meeting ended, press accounts quoted anonymous sources claiming I hadn't had anything to offer.

We were stuck now trying to help whip House Republicans to support the Paulson plan, while I resumed debate prep, knowing that my suspension idea was a bust, and I would have to back down on my decision to postpone the debate. When it came time for the vote, most House Republicans voted against the plan, and it went down. A second attempt succeeded a few days later. Our gambit failed and that cost us support we couldn't afford to lose. I wish we hadn't tried it, but I'll be damned if I can think of anything else we might have done that could have gained us support or limited the damage the crisis was doing to our campaign, which we were pretty sure would prove mortal.

I showed up for the debate, in Oxford, Mississippi. It was originally supposed to focus on foreign policy, which should have favored my strengths. But given the extraordinary events of the last couple weeks, the first part of the debate concentrated on the financial crisis. I thought my strongest performance, surprisingly, was in our exchanges on economic policy. I was generally pleased with how I'd done. But snap polls gave the edge to Senator Obama, which was enough for most pundits to give him the win.

I thought my best debate was the third and final one, although I'm not sure any of them mattered all that much in the end. In the wake of the financial crisis, Obama gained a lead he never surrendered. Unless he made some monumental mistake in the debates, which he did not, nothing I said was likely to get the lead back. Sarah acquitted herself well in her debate with Joe Biden. The conventional wisdom expected Joe to beat her easily, with the only worry that he might so overwhelm her that he appeared a bully. That didn't happen. Joe had a good debate. I thought Sarah had a slightly better one. At worst, the contest was a draw.

Prior to the last debate, we had been alerted by press reports that supporters at some of our events had shouted vulgar or racist things about my opponent. It was hard for me to hear any individual remark from the crowd, just the general din of applause and cheers. But reporters heard some of them and wrote about it, and I knew I had to make a point of rebuking the next person I heard say something false or inappropriate about Obama. It happened during a town hall–type event in a suburb of Minneapolis, as I walked among the crowd taking questions. A white-haired, otherwise polite supporter expressed her concern that Obama couldn't be trusted because he was an Arab. I took the microphone from her. "No, ma'am," I corrected her. "He's a decent family man and citizen whom I happen to have disagreements with on fundamental issues. That's what elections are for."

Obviously, this was before our contemporary understanding of how the Internet is used to spread conspiracy theories and calumnies about candidates to people with an appetite for that sort of thing or an inability to discern what could be true from something spawned in the fever dreams of people who should probably seek psychiatric help. Today, of course, Internet nuts and haters find willing recipients for their "ideas" on certain cable news and talk radio shows. At the time, I didn't have any idea where that crap was coming from, and assumed it was a bigoted reaction to Barack's name. I'd had to correct the same kind of nonsense on a few previous occasions, so I really didn't think much of the exchange in Minnesota.

It turned out to be a bigger story than I had expected. I'm sure

I didn't change many hearts and minds, but the publicity seemed to discourage it from happening again or at least happening in a way noticed by me or the press. My response was met with general approval except in a few media quarters. The *New York Times* claimed I hadn't refuted the claim that Obama was an Arab. I guess because I hadn't said, "No, ma'am, he's not an Arab." Others criticized me for not making clear that there was nothing wrong with being Arab. I suppose I thought that was obvious. But national campaigns are a funny business, open to different interpretations. Many find it hard to remain impartial and open-minded, and give people the benefit of the doubt. Some are quick to find offense where none was intended, and others to assume benevolence in an obviously malicious act. But I can say with a clear conscience, we did everything we could to avoid taking advantage of people's prejudices.

There were twenty days left in the campaign after that last debate, and they were a blur. We crisscrossed the country, stopping wherever we thought we were still competitive, staging several rallies a day, making my closing argument four, five, six times a day, which meant shouting myself hoarse, firing up supporters to fight for me. They were the most crowded days of the campaign, with the longest hours in the air and on the ground. It takes a special fortitude to get through it, and an ability to live completely in the moment, not thinking ahead to when it will be over. All the more so if you know you're losing, as we did. We might not have abandoned all hope, but we were realistic. The odds were heavily against us. We were outspent, out-advertised, and out-organized and we knew it. But you can't phone in the end of your campaign. You have to appear to the world as if you believe you can win and are fighting like hell to do it. Down-ballot races depend on it. Staff depend on your example to find the wherewithal to do their jobs. The country expects it. I took every chance I had to make my case to the American people, campaigning in almost every competitive state in those last frenzied days, which included the morning of Election Day, when I made two last-minute campaign stops in Colorado and New Mexico, my shredded voice barely audible.

Oddly enough, I enjoyed the experience. I knew then I would likely never again hear a crowd roar their approval of me like that. It's pretty intoxicating, and I wanted to remember what it felt like, so I hit hard every line I knew brought people to their feet. You would have thought we were winning at some of those events. They were almost joyous. We tried to keep things light on the plane, too, teasing each other, relying on gallows humor, swapping old stories with Lindsey, Joe, and other friends who had come along for the last ride.

The end came swiftly. By five o'clock Arizona time, we knew we had lost. As soon as the polls closed in California, every news organization called the race for Senator Obama. I immediately took the stage with Sarah and our spouses to concede the race to the man who had been my opponent and would now be my President. As I mentioned, I don't like to lose. But I had a while to prepare for this loss, and I was ready to move on that night. Every defeated candidate says it, and some mean it, that the honor of running is much greater than the pain of losing. It is. I gave it my best shot. I did some things right and some things wrong. I had the rare privilege of being seriously considered for the job of commander in chief of the greatest armed forces in the world, and leader of the free world. I fought for it as hard as I knew how, and I lost. But who could resent any disappointment who had had such an opportunity? In a couple days, I would plan with friends and aides in the comfortable surroundings of our place up north my legislative agenda for the upcoming Congress, and the role I should play in national debates to come.

I felt, too, on that balmy Arizona night, that my opponent's election said something important about the country that my election obviously wouldn't have. I wanted my concession to underscore that point respectfully.

I've always believed that America offers opportunities to all who have the industry and will to seize it. Senator Obama believes that, too. But we both recognize that though we have come a long way from the old injustices that once stained our nation's reputation and denied some Americans the full blessings of American citizenship, the memory of them still had the power to wound.

A century ago, President Theodore Roosevelt's invitation of Booker T. Washington to visit—to dine at the White House— was taken as an outrage in many quarters. America today is a world away from the cruel and prideful bigotry of that time. There is no better evidence of this than the election of an African American to the presidency of the United States. Let there be no reason now for any American to fail to cherish their citizenship in this, the greatest nation on earth.

I thanked my supporters, friends, and family. I thanked Sarah and her family. I thanked Arizonans for letting me keep my day job. I thanked God for making me an American. Then I said goodbye, took Cindy home, and looked forward to regaining my freedom in the morning, and to all the wonderful days to come.

CHAPTER THREE

ABOUT US

I WAS IN MY SENATE OFFICE ON SEPTEMBER 11, 2001, AND watched in horror as the second plane struck the south tower of the World Trade Center. I had been alerted with thousands of others to flee the Capitol because another attack was imminent. I heard American Airlines Flight 77 slam into the Pentagon, and saw the destruction a few hours later. When a reporter asked me the next day if I had something to say to the terrorists responsible for the mass murders of the day before, I answered, "We are coming. God may have mercy on you, but we won't." I was angry and I wanted retribution. I understand why Americans responsible for protecting our country from new attacks in those terrible days after September 11 might have felt justified in taking extreme measures to track down those who murdered innocent people in the name of God. Bad things happen in war. Good people do things they would object to or even recoil from in peacetime. The CIA had received considerable criticism, some of it justified, some of it not, for failing to prevent the 9/11 attacks. So had other intelligence and security agencies. So had the Bush White House, which had been in office for less than eight months. There was a desperate quality to decision making at Langley and in the White House after three thousand Americans were killed in one day of terror, a desperate desire not to be caught unaware again, a desperate intention to leave nothing to chance, a desperate conviction to do whatever had to be done, even if forbidden by values we would otherwise uphold, to protect Americans from future atrocities of that magnitude or worse, and to bring our enemies to heel.

I understand the reasons that governed the decision to resort to interrogation methods that were assigned the banal classification "enhanced interrogation techniques (EIT)." I know that those who used them and those who approved them wanted to protect Americans from harm. I appreciate their dilemma and the strain of their duty. But as I have argued many times, they were wrong to do so, politically, intellectually, and morally wrong. It was a decision that gravely damaged the interests, reputation, and influence of the United States.

Abdel Hakim Belhaj is a civil engineer by training and an Islamist militant by calling. He fought the Soviets in Afghanistan in 1988 beside mujahedeen led by Osama bin Laden, whom Belhaj acknowledged meeting. With other Libyan veterans of the Afghanistan war, he helped organize an insurgent force in armed rebellion against Muammar al-Qaddafi's regime, the Libyan Islamic Fighting Group (LIFG), which tried and failed several times to assassinate Qaddafi. He became the group's emir in 1996. When Qaddafi's forces crushed the LIFG in 1998, the survivors fled the country, and many returned to Afghanistan. Belhaj did not have many potential refuges to choose from. The Libyan government had prioritized his capture, and pressured countries in the region not to admit him. He eventually made his way back to Afghanistan. Many LIFG exiles in Afghanistan formed alliances with the Taliban or joined al-Qaeda. Though there were reports to the contrary, and Belhaj admits to having met bin Laden again, he denies ever allying with either group, and claims to have rejected bin Laden's fatwas against Americans and his invitations to join his World Islamic Front. "We focused on Libya," Belhaj told a *New York Times* reporter. "Global fighting was not our goal."

He left Afghanistan after the September 11 attacks, stateless and a fugitive from an arrest warrant issued in Tripoli. Partly in response to Qaddafi's attempted reconciliation with the West and his pledge to surrender his weapons of mass destruction, the U.S. and U.K. declared the LIFG a terrorist organization. In March 2004, Belhaj and his pregnant wife, Fatima, were transiting through the Kuala Lumpur airport on their way to London, when they were taken into custody by American intelligence agents acting on a tip from Britain's MI6.

Seven years later, U.S. military and diplomatic officials met with Abdel Hakim Belhaj in his capacity as the commander of the Tripoli Military Council, the provisional rebel military authority in charge of keeping order in Tripoli in the wake of the Qaddafi regime's overthrow. He had commanded a battalion in the battle for Tripoli in late August 2011. His fighters had seen combat later than had other rebel militias in the NATO-supported Libyan revolution, especially those fighting in the east. The regime had arrested his father and brother in the early days of the revolution, and Belhaj had gone into hiding and escaped by boat to Tunisia. He arrived in Benghazi later that spring, and began organizing his militia with arms, supplies, and training provided by Qatar. They were in the fight by midsummer. His was one of the better-disciplined rebel forces, and they led the way in fierce fighting during the attack on Qaddafi's fortified Tripoli compound, Bab al-Azizia. He was the consensus choice of the other rebel battalion commanders to take command of the Tripoli Military Council, whose members were pledged to the authority of the provisional rebel governing authority, the National Transitional Council (NTC). But the NTC hadn't made Belhaj's appointment, and that heightened concerns among more liberal Libyan rebel factions about the growing Islamist role in the revolution.

It worried U.S. officials as well. The NATO intervention brought U.S. and allied air and naval power into the war in March 2011 as

Benghazi was about to fall to Qaddafi, who had threatened "no mercy" to its inhabitants. The decision would be harder to justify to the American public if the revolution ousted Qaddafi only to hand power to Islamists, some of whom might have once been associated with al-Qaeda, might be suspected terrorists, might even have been detained by U.S. officials. A week after Tripoli fell, Belhaj traveled with the NTC chairman to Qatar, where they met with NATO officials, I assume for the purpose of persuading them he wasn't a terrorist dedicated to the destruction of the West.

I was in Tripoli in September 2011, just a month after the capital had fallen. It was a confusing situation where few effective lines of authority controlling the chaos were apparent. The tension in the capital between civilians and the dozen or more heavily armed militias operating there and between the militias themselves was palpable. When I met with NTC members, I urged them to expand the council to include political representatives for the militias operating in the city, and get them under the council's full authority. I learned Belhaj had used his authority as head of the Tripoli Military Council to help stabilize the situation and encourage the militias to remove their heavy weapons from the city.

I was back in Libya in February 2012, and asked to meet with Belhaj to show my appreciation for the constructive role he was playing in Libya's political transformation and urge his continued efforts toward that end. I wanted to encourage him to make his own transition from revolutionary to politician, and assure him the United States wasn't his enemy, and didn't want to be. As long as he was committed to the democratic process, his religious views should not be an impediment to a good working relationship with us. This was a heady moment for political Islam. The Muslim Brotherhood, the main Islamist movement, had won power in Tunisia and Egypt. It was gaining strength in Libya and was generally ascendant throughout the Middle East. I thought it was urgently important for the U.S. to do what we could to encourage its proponents to embrace the rule of law in return for international recognition. Toward that end, and because it was owed him, I intended to offer Commander Belhaj my personal apology as an elected official of the government that was responsible for his torture.

After Belhaj and his wife had been seized in Kuala Lumpur, they were taken to a secret facility in Bangkok, where they were interrogated by CIA agents for several days. Belhaj cannot remember for certain the exact length of their detention in Bangkok. That's hardly surprising. He was stripped naked, and chained to the ceiling of his freezing-cold cell. He was also submerged in ice water and deprived of sleep.

When the Americans had finished with him they rendered him to Libya. Qaddafi's secret police held him at their headquarters prison for four years of torture and isolation before transferring him to the notorious Abu Salim prison, where he was tortured some more. He was kept in solitary confinement the entire time, six years, before the regime released him. "I was beaten, hung from the walls by my arms and deprived of food and sunlight," he recalled recently to a *Washington Post* correspondent.

I imagine the worst of it, though, was the knowledge of what the CIA interrogators had done to his wife, whom he would not see, nor the child she had been carrying, until his release from Abu Salim prison in 2010. They had taken a photograph of her in the interrogation room at the black site in Bangkok. She was seated in a chair, Americans surrounding her, duct tape wrapped around the lower half of her face, her wrists bound, and completely naked. She was six months pregnant at the time.

I had learned of his rendition and torture from Tom Malinowski, the Washington director of Human Rights Watch, with whom I had worked in the national debate over torture and on other human rights issues. Tom was working with the rebels and advocating on their behalf. He knew Belhaj and was impressed by him. He acknowledged he was an Islamist, but believed his war had been with Qaddafi not the West. He told me Belhaj had been instrumental in keeping Tripoli from descending into violent chaos and reining in human rights abuses by the rebels. I was disturbed by Tom's account of what had happened to Belhaj, and America's role in it. But I had heard worse stories about our mistreatment of prisoners, and I wasn't shocked. I learned about the photograph later, and that was a shock.

"Shocked the conscience" was the term used to identify practices that were indisputably cruel and unusual. The CIA and certain quarters of the Bush administration used the term to raise the bar on what constituted torture in order to rationalize forms of abuse they argued did not shock the conscience. The degradation of Belhaj's pregnant wife, for the purpose of humiliating her and her husband, shocked my conscience, and made me ashamed.

He received us in a hotel conference room with chairs arranged in a horseshoe and Belhaj seated at the center. He had brought a couple of aides with him. Our party numbered as many as ten, including U.S. embassy personnel and four Senate colleagues. We exchanged introductions, and I took a seat just to Belhaj's left. He was short and stocky, with a furrowed brow and erect bearing. He had a brisk and serious manner. He came across as very self-assured, having traded his combat fatigues for a dark business suit.

He spoke through an interpreter, but the discussion flowed easily. He acknowledged concerns I raised about the situation in Tripoli. He smiled but offered no assurances when I said I hoped he would make the transition from rebel commander to politician. Libya would need more talented politicians than soldiers, I argued, in what would surely be a difficult transition from a family-run kleptocracy to a nascent democracy. His commitment and the commitment of other devout Muslims to peaceful political change would be essential to building a functioning and lasting democratic polity. "We might have disagreements between us," I acknowledged, "about political issues and the future of the region. But as long as you're committed to the democratic process, we can have a good relationship."

At the end of the meeting, in a quieter voice, I mentioned I had recently learned that Americans had detained and interrogated him using tactics that should not have been allowed and were not allowed any longer. I knew about his rendition to Libya, and the years of torture he had suffered in prison. I assumed someone had briefed him on my military background and service in Vietnam, and I tried to relate to him as a former military officer who had entered politics and as one torture victim to another. I told him it had always been important to me that my country act honorably in war and peace, even when our enemies did not. "Some of us in the delegation have worked to outlaw mistreatment of our prisoners because it doesn't befit a great nation." He looked me in the eyes the entire time I was speaking, but I don't remember him nodding his head or in any other way acknowledging my words. But when I added that I knew his wife had been mistreated, his eyes welled with tears. "I'm sorry," I told him, "and as an elected representative of my country, I apologize for what happened, for the way you and especially your wife were treated, and for all you suffered because of it."

He leaned toward me and expressed through the interpreter his appreciation for the apology. "We regret all that happened," he said, "but we don't think of revenge. We will behave responsibly in Libya. Our actions will be governed by law and we will live up to universal standards." I thanked him for that assurance, and the meeting ended.

I never saw him again after our meeting. He did, in fact, become a leading Islamist politician in Libya, and, I've heard, quite a wealthy man. I don't for a moment assume his views and career decisions were influenced by my brief conversation with him. He'll have had his own reasons, political, religious, and personal, for the course he has chosen to follow. I do believe, though, that he genuinely appreciated the apology I offered him. And even if he hadn't, he was still owed one. Neither he nor I believed the apology was compensation for our cruel, inhumane, and degrading treatment of him. It was literally the least I could do. Whatever his private feelings about the U.S., in public he maintains that his views on Libya's relationship with the West aren't influenced by his personal experiences with United States intelligence officers. Of course, he believes, correctly, that he is entitled to an acknowledgment that what was done to him and his wife was wrong. He filed a lawsuit against government officials in Great Britain, who appeared to have been involved in his apprehension and rendition. But all he wanted from the U.S. was an apology. Not everyone at the embassy believed he was owed one, and some weren't pleased I had given him one. The CIA station chief took offense, insisting the Agency had nothing to apologize for. I disagreed.

The first formal step in the breach of American ideals was a decision by the national security principals in the Bush administration, who conferred in the spring of 2002 on the proposed "coercive" interrogation of Abu Zubaydah, a senior al-Qaeda operative captured in a shootout in Pakistan, and held by the CIA in various overseas black sites. The techniques discussed were likened to the harsh treatment U.S. military personnel were made to suffer in SERE school (Survival, Evasion, Resistance, and Escape). Prior to their decision, the principals received a memorandum signed by President Bush, prepared by White House counsel likely with guidance provided by the Justice Department's Office of Legal Counsel. The memo was titled "Humane Treatment of Taliban and al Qaeda Detainees." Its purpose was to offer a legal rationale for doing the opposite, to justify the inhumane treatment of captured enemies. Though the memo directed that detainees be treated humanely, it concluded that "none of the provisions" of the Geneva Conventions requiring the humane treatment of prisoners of war applied to al-Qaeda, and by inference to the Taliban, because it wasn't a signatory to the Convention. This included Common Article 3, which requires the humane treatment of combatants detained in armed conflict other than a war between nation-states.

After the principals approved the abusive treatment of Zubaydah, lawyers at the Department of Justice were tasked with providing additional legal justification for his aggressive interrogation. The so-called torture memos issued in August 2002 were written by the head of Justice's Office of Legal Counsel, Jay Bybee, and his deputy, John Yoo. In addition to the methods used against Zubaydah, the memoranda sanctioned a general program of torture against known or suspected terrorists in our custody. Among other rationalizations, the memos concluded that a federal statute prohibiting torture concerned only extreme acts of abuse that caused "serious physical injury, such as organ failure, impairment of bodily function, or even death." Further, for "prolonged mental harm" to amount to torture it must "last months or even years." The authors further maintained that even the criminal prosecution of interrogation techniques that met their definition of extreme would be an unconstitutional infringement of the President's authority to conduct war. They also contended "federal laws against torture, assault and maiming would not apply to the overseas interrogation of terror suspects."

In other words, Bybee and Yoo were arguing that the aggressive interrogation methods weren't torture, and if they were, so what, U.S. and international law are powerless to prevent the President from ordering them anyway.

For good measure, they provided an approved list of techniques to be used on Zubaydah that, according to their reasoning, were not torture. Among the techniques were some that were familiar to me, including stress positions and sleep deprivation. The North Vietnamese regularly employed those "techniques" on American POWs. They tied us in ropes with our arms behind our backs and stretched into quite uncomfortable stress positions. Even though the rope treatment was painful, we could, if left alone overnight as we often were, drift off to sleep for a few minutes in that position. It's amazing what you can get accustomed to if you don't have a choice. Of course, the guards checked us regularly and slapped us awake the moment we fell asleep. Other times, we were made to stand up for twenty-four hours or longer. It's harder than it sounds.

The most serious of the abuses authorized in the torture memos was waterboarding, the notorious practice where a cloth is placed over a restrained victim's face, and water is poured into his open mouth and nose until he suffers acute panic from the sensation of drowning. The victim believes he is drowning even if he realized in advance that his torturers did not intend to kill him. He experiences near-death. To my mind, it is no different than a mock execution, which is expressly forbidden by U.S. law and international treaties we are signatories to. Waterboarding can be very painful. It can cause lasting physical and mental damage from oxygen deprivation. And, of course, if not very carefully administered, it can end up drowning the victim for real. It was used in the Spanish Inquisition, by the Japanese in World War II, and by the Khmer Rouge in Cambodia. The U.S. military is believed to have adopted the practice in the Philippine-American War, although at least one officer was court-martialed for ordering it. Waterboarding was forbidden in the U.S. military in Vietnam, and a published report of its use there resulted in the court-martial and dishonorable discharge of the guilty party. Waterboarding is torture by any reasonable definition, and its use is a stain on the honor and reputation of the United States.

Zubaydah, who had been seriously wounded during his capture, was placed in CIA custody and held at the secret site in Thailand. An FBI team, headed by a top al-Qaeda expert, Ali Soufan, led his initial interrogation in the spring of 2002. At the time, Zubaydah was feverish, still suffering from his bullet wounds. Using traditional, humane interrogation methods to gain his confidence, Soufan and his associate managed within a few days to get him to identify Khalid Sheikh Mohammed as the mastermind of the September 11 attacks and to disclose Jose Padilla's ill-conceived plot to build and detonate a "dirty" bomb.

A CIA contractor, one of two psychologists who designed the CIA's program of abuse and would be paid tens of millions of dollars for their service, arrived on the scene and took charge of the interrogations. Zubaydah was stripped naked, kept in a cold isolation cell, deprived of sleep, and bombarded with loud music. Ali Soufan's angry objections to the abuse were disregarded. When the FBI agent noticed a small, coffin-like box had been constructed, presumably to confine the prisoner in what, considering his wounds, would be an extremely painful position, he contacted his superiors at the Bureau to protest that the CIA's mistreatment of Zubaydah amounted to torture. In reaction, FBI director Robert Mueller ordered Soufan and his associate home, and terminated the FBI's participation in detainee interrogations.

After the torture memos were issued in August, CIA contractors really went to work on Zubaydah. Held in a succession of black sites, he was subjected to constant abuse for weeks, some reports allege for months, much of it videotaped. The abuse included beatings, long periods in the confinement box, and the CIA's first use of waterboarding. Before they were finished with him, Zubaydah would be waterboarded eighty-three times, rendering him almost insensible. After one session, his torturers worried they had killed him. Somehow during these weeks of abuse, Zubaydah lost his left eye. A 2007 report by the International Committee of the Red Cross identified him as the only one of fourteen "high-value detainees" who had been subjected to all twelve of the enhanced interrogation techniques specified in the torture memos. After all that, and Jose Padilla's delusion of malevolent grandeur notwithstanding, Zubaydah gave his torturers nothing that helped the Agency uncover new terrorist plots.

The most senior officials at the CIA, including Director of Central Intelligence (DCI) George Tenet, maintained that the mistreatment of Zubaydah yielded important intelligence that he wouldn't have given up otherwise. President Bush and other senior members of his administration, relying on information the Agency provided them, made the same claim. Ali Soufan begs to differ:

> There was no actionable intelligence gained from using enhanced interrogation techniques on Abu Zubaydah that wasn't, or couldn't have been, gained from regular tactics. (Ali Soufan, "My Tortured Decision," *New York Times*, April 22, 2009.)

Zubaydah was transferred in 2006 to the Guantánamo Bay detention camp. The videotapes of his interrogations, along with recordings of the torture of other detainees, were ordered destroyed by the head of the CIA's clandestine service, Jose Rodriguez, despite standing orders from the White House Counsel's Office to preserve them. According to his attorney, Zubaydah, who remains in Guantánamo today, has "permanent brain damage," has suffered hundreds of seizures, and "cannot picture his mother's face or recall his father's name."

Some might read this and say to themselves, "Who gives a damn what happened to a terrorist after what they did on September 11?" But it's not about them. It never was. What makes us exceptional? Our wealth? Our natural resources? Our military power? Our big, bountiful country? No, our founding ideals and our fidelity to them at home and in our conduct in the world make us exceptional. They are the source of our wealth and power. Living under the rule of law. Facing threats with confidence that our values make us stronger than our enemies. Acting as an example to other nations of how free people defend their liberty without sacrificing the moral conviction upon which it is based, respect for the dignity possessed by all God's children, even our enemies. This is what made us the great nation we are.

My fellow POWs and I could work up very intense hatred for the people who tortured us. We cussed them, made up degrading names for them, swore we would get back at them someday. That kind of resistance, angry and pugnacious, can only carry you so far when your enemy holds most of the cards and hasn't any scruples about beating the resistance out of you however long it takes. Eventually, you won't cuss them. You won't refuse to bow. You won't swear revenge. Still, they can't make you surrender what they really want from you, your assent to their supremacy. No, you don't have to give them that, not in your heart. And your last resistance, the one that sticks, the one that makes the victim superior to the torturer, is the belief that were the positions reversed you wouldn't treat them as they have treated you. The ultimate victim of torture is the torturer, the one who inflicts pain and suffering at the cost of their humanity.

By November 2002, Abd al-Rahim al-Nashiri, the man responsible for the bombing of the USS *Cole* that killed seventeen U.S. sailors, was in CIA custody at the same facility where Zubaydah was being held. He, too, was waterboarded. He was also threatened with a gun and a power drill held to his hooded head. He was the last detainee whose treatment was videotaped by his torturers. That same month, Gul Rahman, a suspected Afghan militant, who no one thought was a "high-value" target, was held by the CIA at a notorious detention site in Afghanistan known as the Salt Pit, where the prisoners were described as looking like kenneled dogs. Rahman was dragged through the prison's corridors, slammed against walls, struck repeatedly, short shackled to the wall of his cell, where the temperature was kept in the mid-30s Fahrenheit, and left naked from the waist down to lie on the cold cement floor overnight. He died from hypothermia in the early morning hours of November 20, 2002. His death reportedly influenced the CIA's decision to discontinue videotaping abusive interrogations of detainees.

A classified review of CIA interrogations by CIA inspector general John Helgerson was completed in May 2004 but not released in redacted form until 2009. It found CIA interrogators were complicit in the deaths of three detainees, and referred eight instances of alleged homicides and severe mistreatment to the Justice Department. The report cast doubt on the reliability of the intelligence extracted from the mistreated detainees, and warned that some of the techniques used might have violated the United Nations Convention Against Torture. It also raised serious concerns about the professionalism and psychological stability of some interrogators, and found that in some instances the mistreatment of detainees had included methods that weren't on the approved list of techniques or that exceeded the guidance for their use.

Khalid Sheikh Mohammed (KSM), September 11 mastermind and probable murderer of *Wall Street Journal* reporter Daniel Pearl, was captured in Pakistan in March 2003 and placed in CIA custody at a secret prison in the Middle East. An utterly unsympathetic sociopath, KSM would become the poster boy for defenders of torture. They credit his harsh interrogation, including the 183 times he was waterboarded, with various intelligence breakthroughs, none of which, frankly, hold up to careful scrutiny. But even if they didn't get anything useful out of him, whose scruples are troubled by the treatment of a vicious, unforgivable killer? Mine are. His treatment was so extreme that it was among the cases the inspector general's report cited as probably criminal.

So was that of Manadel al-Jamadi, an Iraqi insurgent believed responsible for a number of high-profile bombings. He was captured by the U.S. military in November 2003 and turned over to the CIA, who held him at a soon to be notorious prison about twenty miles outside Baghdad. He was dead forty-five minutes after he had arrived at Abu Ghraib. Taken to a shower room for interrogation, a plastic bag placed over his head, and his arms shackled to the wall in a crucifixion pose, he suffocated. Though his homicide was one of the criminal referrals Helgerson made, the interrogator responsible for his death was never charged.

The inspector general's report motivated DCI George Tenet to ask the White House Counsel for explicit secret authorization for the enhanced interrogation programs, especially the use of waterboarding. The report also drew the disapproving attention of Vice President Cheney, who summoned Helgerson to his office for some not-so-friendly persuasion. One of Tenet's successors, General Michael Hayden, a vocal proponent of the interrogation program, ordered an investigation of the inspector general's office in response to criticism that Helgerson was on a "crusade" against the program.

The excesses identified in the report, as well as the questions it raised about the professionalism of some interrogators, remained classified for years. But worse abuses came to light suddenly around the same time and caused an international scandal that badly damaged U.S. interests and our reputation as a nation that acts consistent with our values even in a war. In the spring of 2004, the CBS news program *60 Minutes* and an investigative report in *The New Yorker* broke the Abu Ghraib story, a revolting account of the widespread torture, humiliation, and sexual abuse of Iraqi prisoners by American military police guards, complete with dozens of graphic photographs. The disclosures caused senior Bush administration officials, including President Bush, to express their disgust, apologize, and give assurances that the guilty parties would be prosecuted.

I was stunned, and I shouldn't have been. I confess that at the time, I wasn't as knowledgeable as I should have been about how we were treating enemy prisoners. I was a senior member of the Senate Armed Services Committee. I had supported the invasion of Iraq. I was a retired military officer, with personal experience of war, captivity, interrogations, and torture. And I was pretty well-versed in the provisions of the Geneva Conventions, having had cause to accuse my jailers of violating them. I should have made sure we were living up to those commitments. I was appalled to learn that we were not.

A few months earlier, Army Specialist Joseph Darby had discovered the photographs and reported them to his superiors. The U.S. commander in Iraq, Lieutenant General Ricardo Sanchez, ordered Major General Antonio Taguba to investigate misconduct by prison guards in the 800th Military Police Brigade. Taguba reported back to Sanchez in April 2004, finding that "between October and December 2003, at the Abu Ghraib Confinement Facility, numerous incidents of sadistic, blatant, and wanton abuses were inflicted on several detainees. This systematic and illegal abuse of detainees was intentionally perpetrated by several members of the military police guard force." I was shaken by what I learned. The guards' behavior exhibited a degree of perversion and glee in the sexual degradation of prisoners that I didn't want to believe American soldiers were capable of. The North Vietnamese could be cruel, and would inflict pain to get what they wanted from us. But they never did anything like this, and the thought of that, that my captors had, on the whole, treated prisoners more humanely than the American soldiers at Abu Ghraib treated prisoners, made me sick to my stomach.

The Senate Armed Services Committee convened a hearing on the scandal on May 7, 2004. Secretary Rumsfeld was called as a witness, as was the chairman of the Joint Chiefs, the chief of staff of the Army, the acting secretary of the Army, the deputy commander of the Central Command (CENTCOM), and the undersecretary of defense for intelligence. I had prepared what I thought was a straightforward question for Rumsfeld. I wanted him to explain the chain of command from the prison guards to the top military and civilian authorities. I wanted to know who supervised interrogations at Abu Ghraib and what instructions they had given the guards there. Rumsfeld answered that he had ordered a chart prepared outlining the chain of command, but that his aides had neglected to bring it. General Lance Smith, the deputy CENTCOM commander, volunteered to walk me through the chain of command. I interrupted him, and told him to submit it for the record, and asked,

"What agency or private contractor was in charge of the interrogations? Did they have authority over the guards? And what were the instructions that they gave to the guards?"

Some hemming and hawing ensued, some continued lamenting of the missing chain of command chart, then committee chairman John Warner referred my question to General Smith. "No," I interjected,

"Secretary Rumsfeld, with all due respect, you've got to answer this question. And it could be satisfied with a phone call. This is a pretty simple, straightforward question. . . . What agencies or private contractors were in charge of the interrogations? And what were their instructions to the guards? This goes to the heart of the matter."

What I wanted to know, as was apparent to the witnesses, was whether the sadistic behavior of the guards had been influenced by instructions from or the example set by the people interrogating detainees at Abu Ghraib. Again, General Smith intervened and after a little back-and-forth, informed the committee that the commander of the military intelligence brigade had authority over the interrogators and "tactical control over the guards." I asked Secretary Rumsfeld why he couldn't answer these "fundamental questions." When I pressed him on the instructions the guards had received, he punted, referring the matter to an ongoing investigation. When I reminded him again that it was a simple question he ought to be prepared to answer, he allowed that the guards had been instructed to adhere to the Geneva Conventions.

In the weeks after my questioning of Rumsfeld, which had been televised, my staff received a number of cold calls from people with knowledge of detainee interrogations, warning us that bad things were happening. Frequent revelations in the press that year exposed abuses at prisons other than Abu Ghraib, at the Salt Pit and at the Bagram Air Base prison in Afghanistan, where men were heard crying all night long. We heard stories about prisoners killed by interrogators because the interrogators were inexperienced and insufficiently trained and supervised. One Iraqi had suffocated to death when his interrogators had put him in a sleeping bag, zipped it over his head, and rolled him back and forth repeatedly. One of the interrogators had a brother who had done the same to him, and he thought it would be a good way to get the prisoner to talk. My foreign policy assistant at the time, Richard Fontaine, had previously worked at the National Security Council. He told me about the black site rendition program. In November 2005, the *Washington Post* would report the existence of these black sites in a story that would win a Pulitzer. Someone leaked a memo from Rumsfeld concerning interrogations at the Guantánamo detention facility, complaining that prisoners were only made to stand up for eight hours. Rumsfeld, who worked at a standing desk, observed that he stood up longer than that. Interrogation logs from Guantánamo also leaked, and revealed that one prisoner hadn't slept more than three hours in a single night for several months. The interrogators had made him do dog tricks.

Some of the dubious legal assertions proposed in the torture memos were leaked to the press in the wake of the Abu Ghraib scandal. Jack Goldsmith, a distinguished law school professor, who had previously worked in the Defense Department, succeeded Jay Bybee as head of Justice's Office of Legal Counsel. To much consternation in some White House offices, he rescinded the torture memos and began working on a revised legal opinion, believing the former were flawed legal analyses that appeared to give "official sanction to torture, and brought such dishonor on the United States." He resigned his office after just ten months, before he had finished writing a revised legal opinion, in part because of the distrust he was held in by senior administration officials.

With all these stories breaking about black site renditions and prisoner abuse, torture memos, and, although still a little murky, increasing reports of so-called enhanced interrogation techniques used by the CIA, it was clear that a problem the administration had blamed on a bunch of undisciplined knuckleheads at Abu Ghraib was more systemic than that and might be the product of a deliberate policy. I was already considering how Congress could ensure that core American values and our responsibilities under the Geneva Conventions were upheld in our treatment of all detainees. The undertaking acquired greater urgency after I received a letter from an Army officer, Captain Ian Fishback, confirming our suspicions.

Ian Fishback, a West Point graduate, and a veteran of combat tours in Iraq and Afghanistan with the 82nd Airborne Division, had conveyed reports about prisoner abuse by soldiers in the 82nd to his chain of command, and been mostly ignored. After nearly a year and a half waiting for a sign that the Army was taking his concerns seriously, and having seen my exchange with Rumsfeld at the Abu Ghraib hearing, he wrote a letter to me. He contacted Tom Malinowski at Human Rights Watch, as did two sergeants in his former battalion. Tom put him in touch with Richard Fontaine, to whom he sent a letter addressed to me. It was a sincere, convincing, and distressing appeal from a professional soldier who believed the honor of his service and his country was being stained. It's worth reprinting here in full.

Dear Senator McCain:

I am a graduate of West Point currently serving as a Captain in the U.S. Army Infantry. I have served two combat tours with the 82nd Airborne Division, one each in Afghanistan and Iraq. While I served in the Global War on Terror, the actions and statements of my leadership led me to believe that United States policy did not require application of the Geneva Conventions in Afghanistan or Iraq. On 7 May 2004, Secretary of Defense Rumsfeld's testimony that the United States followed the Geneva Conventions in Iraq and the "spirit" of the Geneva Conventions in Afghanistan prompted me to begin an approach for clarification. For 17 months, I tried to determine what specific standards governed the treatment of detainees by consulting my chain of command through battalion commander, multiple JAG lawyers, multiple Democrat and Republican Congressmen and their aides, the Ft. Bragg Inspector General's office, multiple government reports, the Secretary of the Army and multiple general officers, a professional interrogator at Guantanamo Bay, the deputy head of the department at West Point responsible for teaching Just War Theory and Law of Land Warfare, and numerous peers who I regard as honorable and intelligent men.

Instead of resolving my concerns, the approach for clarification process leaves me deeply troubled. Despite my efforts, I have been unable to get clear, consistent answers from my leadership about what constitutes lawful and humane treatment of detainees. I am certain that this confusion contributed to a wide range of abuses including death threats, beatings, broken bones, murder, exposure to elements, extreme forced physical exertion, hostage-taking, stripping, sleep deprivation and degrading treatment. I and troops under my command witnessed some of these abuses in both Afghanistan and Iraq.

This is a tragedy. I can remember, as a cadet at West Point, resolving to ensure that my men would never commit a dishonorable act; that I would protect them from that type of burden. It absolutely breaks my heart that I have failed some of them in this regard.

That is in the past and there is nothing we can do about it now. But, we can learn from our mistakes and ensure that this does not happen again. Take a major step in that direction; eliminate the confusion. My approach for clarification provides clear evidence that confusion over standards was a major contributor to the prisoner abuse. We owe our soldiers better than this. Give them a clear standard that is in accordance with the bedrock principles of our nation.

Some do not see the need for this work. Some argue that since our actions are not as horrifying as Al Qaeda's, we should not be concerned. When did Al Qaeda become any type of standard by which we measure the morality of the United States? We are America, and our actions should be held to a higher standard, the ideals expressed in documents such as the Declaration of Independence and the Constitution.

Others argue that clear standards will limit the President's ability to wage the War on Terror. Since clear standards only limit interrogation techniques, it is reasonable for me to assume that supporters of this argument desire to use coercion to acquire information from detainees. This is morally inconsistent with the Constitution and justice in war. It is unacceptable.

Both of these arguments stem from the larger question, the most important question that this generation will answer. Do we sacrifice our ideals in order to preserve security? Terrorism inspires fear and suppresses ideals like freedom and individual rights. Overcoming the fear posed by terrorist threats is a tremendous test of our courage. Will we confront danger and adversity in order to preserve our ideals, or will our courage and commitment to individual rights wither at the prospect of sacrifice? My response is simple. If we abandon our ideals in the face of adversity and aggression, then those ideals were never really in our possession. I would rather die fighting than give up even the smallest part of the idea that is "America."

Once again, I strongly urge you to do justice to your men and women in uniform. Give them clear standards of conduct that reflect the ideals they risk their lives for.

With the Utmost Respect,

—Capt. Ian Fishback
1st Battalion,
504th Parachute Infantry Regiment,
82nd Airborne Division,
Fort Bragg, North Carolina

"I would rather die fighting than give up the smallest part of the idea that is 'America.'" If there is a finer declaration of an American soldier's duty and sense of honor, I haven't heard it. I met with Captain Fishback, and was as impressed with his genuineness and professionalism in person as I had been with the qualities evident in his letter. I assured him he was right to have reached outside his chain of command to bring his legitimate concerns to responsible public officials, and that I and others in Congress were already working to make sure that, as he affirmed, the United States would "confront danger and adversity in order to preserve our ideals."

Our first effort to do just that was the Detainee Treatment Act of 2005, which Senator Warner and Lindsey Graham and I offered to that year's defense appropriations bill. It had two main provisions: first, that interrogations of detainees by U.S. military or civilian Defense Department officials must adhere to the strict guidance for treating enemy prisoners provided in the Army Field Manual; second, that all other agencies of the federal government, including the CIA, are prohibited from the "cruel, inhuman or degrading" treatment of any prisoner "regardless of nationality or physical location."

White House opposition to the resolution was initially fierce, spearheaded by the vice president and his staff, and the new CIA director, Porter Goss. Before they had seen the text of the resolution the administration had put out a statement opposing it. Cheney and Goss came to see me in a secure room in the Capitol and laid out what they claimed was valuable intelligence obtained through enhanced interrogation techniques that had prevented new terrorist attacks. They walked me through the techniques, downplaying their actual severity. At one point, we got in a back-and-forth over sleep deprivation. "How long are you keeping them awake?" I asked. They eventually acknowledged that some detainees had been deprived of sleep for as much as 120 hours. "I had a friend, a Marine, who was kept awake for a week," I observed. "It almost killed him."

They also intimated that if our resolution passed the techniques would be discontinued and I would have American blood on my hands. That was a misjudgment on their part. All their crude attempt to shame me did was anger me, and make me deeply suspicious about the credit they were giving torture. I knew from personal experience that every man has his breaking point, and would yield to torture at some point. But I knew, too, that information extracted by torture is unreliable. You say anything to make it stop, true, false, or just fed to you by your torturers. An aide to the vice president, David Addington, handed me an amendment to the resolution he had prepared that would have excluded the CIA from the prohibition against cruel, inhuman, and degrading treatment. That would have been worse than doing nothing.

There were additional meetings with Vice President Cheney and his staff for the Republican senators supporting our resolution; a few got wobbly, but only nine Republican senators ended up opposing it. We also discouraged Senate Democrats, all of whom supported the resolution, from formally co-sponsoring it. We wanted the effort to be seen as a revolt of Republican hawks, which we believed would have a greater restraining impact on the administration.

The lobbying by the vice president and associates was persistent and intense, and it provoked unflattering attention on the editorial pages of the nation's newspapers. Eventually, in a sign that the President wanted the matter resolved, his national security advisor, Steve Hadley, contacted us. Richard Fontaine had once worked for Hadley, and he advised me that when Hadley took the lead in negotiations it was an indication the President wants a deal. The discussions dragged on a few more weeks. We eventually agreed to some fairly minor language changes that left the major provisions intact.

In the end, the resolution passed the Senate by 90 to 9. After the President signed the underlying bill into law, the White House released a statement that the President as commander in chief would construe the detainee protections consistent with his duty to protect "the American people from further terrorist attacks." In other words, administration officials refused to acknowledge they were absolutely bound by the prohibitions. We would have to find another way to convince them they were.

An opportunity to do so was presented by the Supreme Court's decision in *Hamdan v. Rumsfeld*, which found, among other things, that Common Article 3 applied to our treatment of al-Qaeda prisoners, and that their detention must comply with the Geneva Conventions. The administration determined that the only way around the decision's ramifications for the legality of the EITs was to water down the meaning of Common Article 3, an idea that was, to say the least, abhorrent to me. They proposed to weaken the Article's protections so they could continue abusive interrogations and still claim they were legal. The notion that abuse that included waterboarding was permitted by the Geneva Conventions was as bizarre as it was unacceptable.

I was worried that Congress, needing to act in response to the *Hamdan* decision, would go along with the administration's wishes. So I was willing to talk. Initially, our discussions were focused on using military commissions to adjudicate the cases of detainees held at Guantánamo. During the course of examining the bill language they proposed, we noticed the changes to Common Article 3. Fontaine conveyed my objections to the NSC, and a succession of high-profile officials including DCI Mike Hayden, NSA Steve Hadley, and the new head of the Justice Department's Office of Legal Counsel, Steven Bradbury, who had been involved in preparing parts of the torture memos, were dispatched to change my mind. It was clear that Hayden wanted legal cover from Justice that would allow the continued use of the EITs, and, perhaps more important, that protected the CIA from legal jeopardy for their past use. Bradbury was willing to provide it but only if Congress gave him cover. Hadley wanted to find a deal.

Efforts were made again to persuade me that the EITs, including waterboarding, were not torture. They included a briefing with a young officer who had waterboarded detainees and assured me it was done safely and did not do lasting harm to the victims. Hayden and company met with my staff, too, namely Fontaine and Salter, who weren't persuaded, and explained that it wouldn't matter if they were because I was unmovable. Eventually we began negotiating provisions of what would become the Military Commissions Act of 2006. Lindsey, an Air Force Reserve lawyer, and my Arizona colleague Jon Kyl, took the lead on working out the terms of the military commissions. I focused on protecting the Geneva Conventions. Our bottom line demand was that the clear intent of the Conventions could not be altered, and any language we agreed to must have the effect of prohibiting the continued use of waterboarding and other extreme practices. After weeks of talks, we reached a compromise.

There are two kinds of breaches of Common Article 3, grave and nongrave. Grave breaches are prosecutable under the war crimes statute. Nongrave breaches are not prosecutable as war crimes. The administration position was that the Article was vague on what constituted grave and nongrave breaches. They wanted the President to proclaim those definitions. Eventually, we agreed to let the President enumerate nongrave breaches so long as the standards he promulgated were higher than those that currently existed. To my regret, the administration did not adhere to the clear intent of the agreement. They never enumerated nongrave breaches or established higher standards.

Grave breaches were already enumerated in the War Crimes Act of 1996, and it was there that I wanted to restrict the administration from resuming the worst abuses. In fairness, the administration had not to my knowledge waterboarded another detainee since passage of the Detainee Treatment Act the year before and had refrained from some of the other techniques as well, believing, I assume, that they would likely violate the act's prohibitions. Still, no one in authority had ever conceded that waterboarding or any other interrogation technique was torture and thus prohibited, and I wanted more certainty that the CIA would not resort to using such techniques in the future.

In the last week of September 2006, Salter, Fontaine, and I joined in marathon negotiating sessions with administration officials, including Hadley and Bradbury, in a hearing room in the Dirksen Senate Office Building. Having agreed to allow the President to enumerate nongrave breaches, we searched for a way to define grave breaches that would prevent the resumption of waterboarding and other abuses.

The solution we arrived at involved amending the War Crimes Act of 1996 to define nine offenses that constituted grave breaches of Common Article 3, prosecutable as war crimes and punishable by imprisonment or death. The first offense was "torture," the second, "cruel and inhuman treatment." Torture included acts that were "intended to inflict severe physical or mental pain and suffering." The prohibition against cruel and inhuman treatment added the descriptor "serious" to "physical and mental suffering." Serious mental pain and suffering was defined in the act as "prolonged." That adjective was easy to exploit, as the authors of the torture memos had, interpreting it to mean months and years of suffering. They had used its vagueness to allow waterboarding. I asked Hadley and Bradbury to remove the word from the definition, and recommended a substitute, "non-transitory," and lest that be interpreted as synonymous with "prolonged," we added in parentheses "which need not be prolonged." They said they could accept the former but not the latter. We insisted, and eventually they acquiesced, but only if we agreed that the new definition would not be retroactive, that it would apply only to conduct after the bill's date of enactment.

The reason was obvious: they felt the new definition of cruel and inhuman treatment made waterboarding and likely some of the other EITs prosecutable as war crimes. With that in mind, I asked Bradbury if he believed the new definition would prohibit waterboarding in the future. He answered that he believed it would. Hadley concurred. And although neither man nor anyone else in the administration ever acknowledged publicly that the revised statute made waterboarding a war crime, I am confident that it did, and so were they. The practice was not used again. I believed that whatever protection from legal jeopardy the date of enactment condition gave the Agency was acceptable in exchange for preventing the resumption of the worst practices.

Throughout our negotiations with the administration, we kept in close touch with Tom Malinowski at Human Rights Watch and Elisa Massimino, the president of Human Rights First. We had good working relationships with both of them based on mutual trust. The human rights community, including Tom's and Elisa's organizations, opposed the Military Commissions Act, although their biggest objection to the bill was the denial of habeas corpus in the provisions establishing the commissions, which I had not been involved in negotiating. The critics had a point, as was evidenced by the Supreme Court's 2008 decision in *Boumediene v. Bush*, which held that the suspension of habeas was unconstitutional.

Their principal concerns with our efforts were our agreement that the Bush administration could define nongrave breaches of Common Article 3 and that our revisions to the War Crimes Act weren't retroactive, making the use of EITs before the MCA harder to prosecute. Despite those concerns, I think Tom and Elisa recognized we had prevented the Geneva Conventions from being weakened, and had imposed a formidable legal obstacle to the worst interrogation practices. The MCA passed both houses of Congress easily but without much Democratic support, and to little applause and a fair amount of criticism. In July 2007, President Bush signed an executive order that, instead of establishing higher standards for nongrave breaches, stated that the CIA's detention and interrogation program "fully complies with the obligations of the United States under Common Article

Three." That was predictable, critics in the human rights community argued. Perhaps so. In December of that year, the *New York Times* reported that tape recordings of CIA interrogations had been destroyed on Jose Rodriguez's order. That, too, angered me, and eroded further my already diminished store of trust in the good faith of the Agency's leadership.

Nevertheless, I believed I had achieved what I had set out to achieve—protecting the Geneva Conventions and stopping water-boarding, and I honored my end of the bargain by not restricting the CIA interrogations more than I already had. In February 2008, I voted against a Senate resolution that President Bush had promised to veto, which would have limited CIA interrogators to the practices approved in the Army Field Manual. I received a fair amount of abuse in the editorial pages for that vote and from human rights advocates, even some with whom I worked closely. I was the front-runner for the Republican presidential nomination at the time of the vote, which drew a bigger crowd of Democratic critics than it normally would have. But on this issue, I don't need any more approval than a quiet conscience.

With the death of Osama bin Laden in May 2011 came fresh reminders that the torture debate had not ended. As long as serious men and women argued for torture's efficacy the United States would be at risk of staining our honor again by resorting to the abuses that our enemies could use to encourage mistrust of our leadership and cynicism about our values.

In one of his first acts as President, Barack Obama rescinded President Bush's executive order claiming the CIA had acted in full compliance with Common Article 3, and he withdrew the Agency's authority to hold detainees and restricted their interrogations to those approved in the Army Field Manual. He and Attorney General

Eric Holder would eventually decide not to prosecute interrogation abuses during his predecessor's administration. But when bin Laden finally met the fate he deserved, the apologists for torture appeared in numbers on cable news shows and in the newspapers claiming bin Laden wouldn't have been found without intelligence gained through the use of EITs. Article number one in their reinvigorated apologia was information coerced from Khalid Sheikh Mohammed after he was waterboarded repeatedly. No less an authority than former attorney general Michael Mukasey stepped forward to claim in the *Wall Street Journal* that:

> The intelligence that led to bin Laden ... began with a disclosure from Khalid Sheikh Mohammed, who broke like a dam under the pressure of harsh interrogation techniques that included waterboarding. He loosed a torrent of information—including eventually the nickname of a trusted courier of bin Laden.

Virtually nothing in that statement is true. But as angered as I was at the time by Mukasey's disingenuousness, I would learn later that he wasn't entirely to blame. CIA officials had misled him as they had other Justice officials, and, as it turns out, as they misled senior White House officials, including President Bush and Vice President Cheney.

The first mention of bin Laden's courier's pseudonym, Abu Ahmed al-Kuwaiti, came from a detainee held in another country, who was not waterboarded or otherwise tortured, and who identified Kuwaiti as an important figure in al-Qaeda. When interrogators confronted KSM with the name, he claimed Kuwaiti wasn't active in al-Qaeda, had married, and had moved to Peshawar in Pakistan, none of which was true. The best intelligence on Kuwaiti's real role in al-Qaeda and his relationship to bin Laden came to us from a detainee who was questioned using standard, noncoercive means by interrogators who had done the most essential thing in questioning a suspect. They had gained his trust. In truth, most of the CIA's claims that abusive interrogations of detainees had produced vital leads to help locate bin Laden were exaggerated, misleading, and in some cases, complete bullshit. We would learn the truth from the same investigation that revealed how the CIA had misled Bush administration officials. We learned it from the persistent, scrupulous, determined investigation of the CIA's use of enhanced interrogation techniques by the Senate Select Committee on Intelligence, chaired by Senator Dianne Feinstein.

Begun early in 2009, partly out of concern that Jose Rodriguez's destruction of interrogation video recordings might be part of an effort to cover up the unlawful torture of detainees, the investigation would examine millions of emails, cables, communiqués, and other documents related to the CIA's detention and interrogation program between the years 2001 and 2006. After 2006, the Agency was believed to have stopped using most of the techniques in question. After nearly four years, tens of millions of dollars, countless man hours of dogged inquiry, examination, and analyses, unexpected good luck, a lack of bipartisan cooperation, and an attempt by the Agency to spy on committee investigators, the committee approved a six-thousand-page report almost on a strict party-line vote, with Susan Collins the only Republican voting with the committee majority. Two years later, over the furious objections of the CIA and senior officials in the Obama administration, the committee publicly released a 525-page, unclassified, overly redacted, meticulously footnoted, and damning summary. The following are some of its findings.

The CIA's enhanced interrogation techniques were ineffective at acquiring good intelligence. Interrogations of detainees were much more brutal than the Agency had acknowledged. Some detainees were subjected to abuses not authorized by CIA leadership or the Justice Department. The CIA made inaccurate claims for the effectiveness of the techniques. It misled the Department of Justice and other executive branch offices. It impeded congressional oversight, the CIA inspector general's investigation, and White House oversight and decision making. DCIs George Tenet, Porter Goss, and Michael Hayden misled the White House, Congress, and the Director of National Intelligence about the program's effectiveness. The CIA planted false stories in the press. It lied about the value of intelligence extracted from abused detainees. At least twenty-six of the 119 detainees held by the CIA were subsequently found to have been innocent. Many of them were tortured. Torture inflicted on detainees included force-feeding and hydrating prisoners anally, and rectal examinations using "excessive force"; mock executions and at least one instance of forcing a prisoner to play Russian roulette; prisoners kept awake for a week, and one kept in a coffin-sized confinement box for eleven days; forcing a detainee to stand and stay awake for nearly three days; prisoners denied waste buckets; kept short-shackled and naked in darkened cold cells, with constant white noise; prisoners slapped, punched, slammed against walls and cement floors.

These were just the detainees held by the CIA. God have mercy on those the Agency rendered to other countries.

Evidence for all the above charges and more was found in communications the Agency provided the committee voluntarily, and much of it was confirmed in a document the CIA accidentally provided and wished it hadn't, the report of an internal review ordered by Leon Panetta, whom President Obama had appointed director of Central Intelligence. Panetta's successor, John Brennan, accused committee investigators of improperly accessing the Panetta Review and removing it from the CIA, and had filed a criminal referral at Justice against lead investigator Dan Jones, a former FBI officer. It was an ass-covering feint. In truth, the Agency had inadvertently included the Panetta Review in a massive data dump to the committee, a tactic often used to hide embarrassing disclosures in a haystack of unimportant and dull information. When they realized the committee now possessed it, CIA personnel hacked the investigators' computers, an unlawful act, and a violation of the separation of powers, which should have resulted in the firing of officials who had ordered it. I denounced the hacking as "clearly unconstitutional, and in some ways, worse than criminal."

There were references to me in some of the cables and emails committee investigators reviewed. One memo from the Office of Legal Counsel reported that DCI Hayden had briefed several members of Congress including members of the House and Senate intelligence committees and Senator McCain on six of the enhanced interrogation techniques. "None of the members expressed the view that the CIA interrogation program should be stopped, or that the techniques at issue were inappropriate." A memo prepared by the CIA about the briefing contradicted that assertion, acknowledging that after the briefing, "Senator John McCain informed the CIA that he believed the CIA's enhanced interrogation techniques, including sleep deprivation and the waterboard, were 'torture.'" In another amusing exchange, one of the officers who had briefed me was asked by a colleague if I was "on board." He replied, "Not totally."

"If he's moved in our direction at all, you're a miracle worker . . . was it painful?"

"Very much so."

"Is the issue the EITs still?"

"Yep."

The committee's investigation, in my opinion, was as professional as any I've observed by a congressional committee, and a credit to Dianne Feinstein's leadership. It was ably managed by Dan Jones, an indefatigable, fair-minded, and conscientious seeker of the truth. I regretted the decision by most committee Republicans not to cooperate in the investigation, and to publish their own dissenting report. Although many of them are friends of mine, I fear their actions were a product of an ill-conceived priority to protect CIA officials from repercussions for their breach of core American values, and not a sincere effort to find the truth. Senior officials in the Obama administration, who opposed the release of the report, including, among others, the White House chief of staff and secretary of state, shared the same mistaken purpose.

As chairman of the Armed Services Committee, I am an ex officio member of the Intelligence Committee. As an ex officio member, I do not have a vote in the committee's decisions. But before the vote to approve the report, I sent a letter to every member of the committee urging their support for it. I joined Dianne and committee Democrats as they resisted a two-year campaign by the Obama administration to prevent publication of an unclassified version of the report, and in pitched battles over unnecessary redactions they insisted on making to it. No protest from the Agency, the White House, or Republicans was complete without the dark warning that we would have "blood on our hands" if we went through with publishing the report, as it would result in the death of Americans.

Undaunted, on December 9, 2014, the committee released the unclassified report to the American public. Many of my Republican colleagues denounced it as a partisan smear. Former DCIs Tenet, Goss, and Hayden did the same in an op-ed for the *Wall Street Journal*. DCI Brennan disagreed with some of the committee's conclusions. Dick Cheney called it "hooey." And any number of hard-charging Washington tough guys repeated the same old false claims for the efficacy of waterboarding and all the other abuses the report had so thoroughly discredited.

I spoke on the Senate floor in support of the report's release. "I believe the American people have a right," I contended,

> —indeed, a responsibility—to know what is done in their name; how these practices did or did not serve our interests; and how they comported with our most important values. . . . The truth is sometimes a hard pill to swallow. It sometimes causes us difficulties at home and abroad. It is sometimes used by our enemies in attempts to hurt us. But the American people are entitled to it nonetheless.

I ended my remarks by calling on all Americans to live our nation's ideals, to remember that "we are always Americans, and different, stronger and better than those who would destroy us."

In the following presidential campaign season that was soon to begin, the eventual Republican nominee and next President of the United States insisted torture "absolutely works" and swore he would bring back waterboarding "and worse." His statement was made out of ignorance, attributable to his lack of experience in a role related to the defense of this country. It also exposed his apparent lack of appreciation for the importance of our values to our security, and for the understanding that simple human decency is as essential to the souls of nations as it is to the souls of people. There isn't anything he can do about it, though. Dianne Feinstein and I offered an amendment to the defense bill in 2015 that mandated the CIA and all government agencies abide by the restrictions in the Army Field Manual in their interrogation of any detainee. President Trump would need congressional approval to resort to these techniques again, and I'm confident enough members of Congress, shamed by the abuses of the last decade, would refuse.

One critic of the committee's report wrote in a column for the

Washington Post that the Democrats had "lost the torture debate" because public polling showed that despite all the negative publicity about enhanced interrogation techniques, a majority of Americans still supported them. Democrats had failed to make the case that they were ineffective, unwarranted, and immoral, he argued.

You can fail to tell the truth. But the truth cannot be a failure even if it's ignored or rejected. The report told the truth. And those who claim it did not are not telling the truth any more than they did when the practices were in use. They didn't tell the truth to the American people then and they are not telling the truth to the American people now. They didn't tell the truth to the most senior officials in the government they served in. They didn't tell the truth to themselves. But the truth, or at least the closest, most thorough approximation of it that can be discovered and assembled in a coherent fashion at this time, exists in the classified and unclassified Senate Intelligence Committee's report despite all the delays, all the attempts at obfuscation, all the unnecessary redactions, all the false claims by people who felt the truth was a threat to them. It exists and is accessible to the American people. Some Americans might not believe it. Some might read it and forget it. Some might not care that we tortured people. But their moral failure isn't the truth's failure. The moral values and integrity of our nation, and the long, difficult, fraught history of our efforts to uphold them at home and abroad, are the test of every American generation. Will we act in this world with respect for our founding conviction that all people have equal dignity in the eyes of God and should be accorded the same respect by the laws and governments of men? That is the most important question history ever asks of us. Answering in the affirmative by our actions is the highest form of patriotism, and we cannot do that without access to the truth. The cruelty of our enemies doesn't absolve us of this duty. This was never about them. It was about us.

CHAPTER FOUR

IN THE COMPANY
OF HEROES

I MADE MY FIRST TRIP TO AFGHANISTAN IN JANUARY 2002. We were the first congressional delegation to travel there since the start of Operation Enduring Freedom three months earlier. There were nine of us, including some of my closest friends in the Senate at the time, Joe Lieberman, Chuck Hagel, Fred Thompson, and Susan Collins. We had spent the day in Tajikistan, waiting for dark and a specially equipped C-130 that normally ferried Special Forces and their supplies. I was anxious to go. I doubt the U.S. military command in Afghanistan was excited to see us. Kabul had fallen in November and Kandahar in December. The Battle of Tora Bora had been fought only a few weeks earlier. While many Taliban and al-Qaeda had fled to Pakistan, there was still hard fighting in the south, and large swaths of the country were mostly ungoverned and very dangerous. We were likely considered a distraction and a security headache. British prime minister Tony Blair was scheduled to make a visit the same day, complicating the situation. We weren't allowed to spend the night, and would be in country for six hours or less. We boarded the C-130 accompanied by a guy dressed in black with a suitcase handcuffed to his wrist containing $10,000 in cash to pay for our fuel. Evidently, Bagram Airfield didn't take plastic. We flew without lights, with only glow sticks for illumination. Our pilots, fearing we would be fired at as we approached, took evasive measures. We arrived at Bagram at midnight. As we disembarked we were warned not to wander off the tarmac, as the surrounding ground was mined.

We drove through the ramshackle base in a Humvee as men with long beards dressed as mujahedeen and carrying arms observed us. They looked threatening. "Who are they?" my foreign policy aide, Dan Twining, asked. "They're our guys," someone replied. "Special Forces." We were taken to a tent, seated on sandbags, and briefed on the war's progress and the coalition's efforts to help set up a functioning national authority. Hamid Karzai was brought in to meet with us. An Afghan assembly representing all districts in the country, a *loya jirga*, would select him as president of a transitional government in June. He hadn't a title when we met him that first time, but he was clearly the U.S. and Britain's preferred choice for the national government's leader. He made an impression that night in his robes, captivating manner, and idiomatic English. I got along well with him, and continued to get along with him in the years to come though he would prove to be a corrupt and insecure leader, and difficult to deal with. That night he seemed the right man for the job, and we talked at length about his vision of a modern, democratic Afghanistan before Karzai had to leave to meet with the just arrived Tony Blair. It was a fascinating discussion, and meeting like that, under a tent in the desert night, was evocative, to say the least. We met briefly with Blair, too, before we departed for Pakistan in the early morning, all of us fairly optimistic that coalition authorities and enlightened Afghans had a decent shot to pacify the turbulent country once known as the graveyard of empires, and rid the world of one of the most inhumane regimes on earth. On my next trip to Afghanistan, I went with Twining to Bamiyan to see the ruins of the thousand-year-old Buddhist statues destroyed by the Taliban. Quite a metaphor for Taliban rule, I thought. The statues had survived

Genghis Khan and the Mongol horde and the Soviet invasion, but not this crew of annihilating fanatics.

We paid a visit to the carrier USS *Theodore Roosevelt*, on station in the Arabian Sea, after that first visit to Afghanistan. Responding to the enthusiasm of a gung ho crowd of sailors and aviators, I said something I later regretted. "Next up, Baghdad!" I shouted, and was cheered. I was an advocate for invading Iraq, not because I believed that Saddam Hussein, like the Taliban in Afghanistan, was harboring al-Qaeda, but because I believed the U.S. intelligence community assessment that he had weapons of mass destruction, which he had proven willing to use in the past. He had refused to allow U.N. inspectors the access necessary to ascertain whether or not he had them. He was also as brutal a tyrant as any who lived, guilty of numerous atrocities, some of which he had committed when he believed the United States would not react. He routinely ordered his air defenses to shoot at U.S. overflights of Iraq. I also believed the overthrow of his regime and the establishment of an Arab democracy would strike as great a blow as any force of arms against extremism and despotism in the Middle East.

But the principal reason for invading Iraq, that Saddam had WMD, was wrong. The war, with its cost in lives and treasure and security, can't be judged as anything other than a mistake, a very serious one, and I have to accept my share of the blame for it. None of that was known, of course, that day on the *Roosevelt*, when I was firm in my convictions, and self-assured. Even if we had been right about Saddam's weapons program, I shouldn't have used the occasion to cheer the prospect of war. All wars are awful. My exclamation would have been appropriate had I been an officer rallying troops to arms. But I wasn't. I was a politician, and I had other responsibilities, one of which was to make certain there was a valid purpose for ordering Americans into harm's way, and an achievable mission.

This isn't to say that the overthrow of Saddam Hussein's atrocious regime, and the effort to replace it with a rudimentary democracy, wasn't a just cause. It was. And the hundreds of thousands of Americans who have risked their lives to achieve those ends are owed the eternal gratitude of Iraqis and Americans for the sacrifices they made for people who were strangers to them. But for all the justice they served, for all their courage and professionalism and endurance, they wouldn't have been asked to make such sacrifices if we hadn't believed Saddam had WMD. But we did, and we sent them to war in Iraq. Every public official involved in that decision has to accept responsibility for it. And we also had to accept responsibility for making sure that, mistake or not, the sacrifices made by Americans in that conflict wouldn't end in our defeat.

Unlike my initial visit to Afghanistan, my first trip to Iraq didn't leave me optimistic about our prospects for success. On the contrary, I thought we were heading in a direction that would almost certainly result in failure. It was August 2003, a few months after President Bush had announced on the USS *Abraham Lincoln* that major combat operations in Iraq were over. He never said "mission accomplished." That unfortunate declaration was printed on a banner hung in the background by the ship's crew. And he acknowledged that there was still fighting ahead in Iraq. But the event gave Americans the impression that we were just mopping up in Iraq, that our effort there was nearing a conclusion. It fit with the theory advanced by Defense Secretary Donald Rumsfeld, that the armed resistance coalition forces were still encountering amounted only to a few "dead enders." That was a very mistaken point of view, which was quite evident in August 2003.

We were a large, bicameral delegation, and on the ground for only thirty-six hours in total. My Arizona colleague, Jim Kolbe, was there, as was Lindsey Graham, a newly elected senator then. As in Afghanistan, we couldn't remain in the country overnight. We made stops in Baghdad, Kirkuk in the north, and Basra in the south, and returned to

Kuwait City at the end of each day. We met with Coalition Provisional Authority (CPA) administrator Paul Bremer, who a few months before had dissolved the Iraqi army and banned Baathists from serving in military or government positions. Even teachers who had to register with the Baathist Party in order to work, lost their jobs. Hundreds of thousands of armed and angry Sunni men had a lot of time on their hands, and scores to settle.

Lieutenant General Ricardo Sanchez was commanding coalition forces then, and was rumored to have opposed Bremer's de-Baathification policy, as had most field commanders in Iraq, believing correctly that it was a primary cause of the incipient Sunni insurgency that had started causing trouble in the Sunni Triangle and elsewhere, and would ally with terrorist groups. We were meeting with Bremer and Walt Slocombe, a well-regarded senior Defense Department official, when Sunni jihadists struck their first hard blow. A suicide bomber enlisted by Jordanian terrorist Abu Musab al-Zarqawi and his al-Qaeda affiliate, al-Qaeda in Iraq, drove a truck bomb next to the Canal Hotel and detonated it. The blast could be felt a mile away. We heard a thud, and a minute later an aide handed Bremer a note. He glanced at it, apologized, and cut short our meeting. The Canal Hotel housed the headquarters for the United Nations Mission in Iraq, which was led by one of the U.N.'s most accomplished diplomats, Sergio Vieira de Mello, who died in the blast along with twenty-one other U.N. staff and international and Iraqi aid workers. A second bombing in September would result in the U.N. effectively shutting down its Iraq mission, leaving the U.S. and its allies with even more responsibilities to rebuild the shattered country while we dealt with the spreading insurgency.

Security precautions in Baghdad were less restrictive in subsequent visits than they were on that initial one, but then got worse with each passing year. I've made over twenty trips to Iraq and Afghanistan. In 2004, we could have dinner in a Baghdad restaurant, and walk unmolested at night back to the Al Rasheed Hotel. We moved around the city in SUVs. If we had a little spare time, we could poke around in the local markets. Two years later, our plane touched down after a corkscrew landing to avoid missiles, we traveled in armored vehicles through deserted streets, were mostly confined to the Green Zone, the heavily protected government district in central Baghdad, and wore Kevlar vests if we were going to spend even a few minutes in a public space.

Something else I noticed, too, even on that first trip. Iraq was a grimmer, more oppressive place than Afghanistan, where we had stopped before coming to Iraq. It didn't feel liberated from tyranny so much as hungover from the experience, whereas with Afghans you generally had the sense that they were relieved to be out from under the Taliban. Afghans also appeared more disarming and open, whatever ulterior motives they might possess. Most Iraqis we met in an official capacity or in public encounters appeared reticent and suspicious, even angry. You never felt anyone trusted anyone else. Things were different in the north with the Kurds, who were more engaging and cooperative, and where I've managed to cultivate more than a few trusting relationships. But meetings in Baghdad and elsewhere with Shia or Sunnis could be dour affairs, and it was hard to get a sense of whom to trust.

The most impactful meeting I had on that first visit, the meeting that convinced me our strategy in Iraq was the opposite of what we needed there, was a briefing we received from British soldiers in Basra. Basra should have been friendly country for the U.S. and British liberating forces. This wasn't the disenfranchised Sunni Triangle. It was our part of Iraq, the Shia south, oppressed and terrorized by Saddam and the Sunni minority, people who had longed for Saddam's overthrow. It was a mess. Local government was completely ineffectual. Lawlessness was rampant. It was hotter than hell and water was scarce. There were frequent power outages. The sewage system wasn't working. Canal beds were dry and filled with uncollected garbage. The Brits, who had authority over the place, were headquartered in a heavily barricaded base. But they would go out every day and engage the Shia population, wearing berets and no body armor. Muqtada al-Sadr, the Shia militia leader, was starting to mobilize and had already denounced the CPA in Baghdad as imperialists. Although he wasn't yet as powerful as he aspired to be, he had figured out that the way to win friends and influence people was to inveigh against Western imperialists. In Basra and throughout the south, the Shia population wasn't in rebellion against the occupiers yet, but things were heading in that direction.

The British had a long history with Iraq, having occupied the country a century earlier. The British officers posted in Basra in the summer of 2003 had a sense of history and an acute appreciation for local attitudes and the broader challenges facing the coalition. One of them, a no-nonsense colonel, whose name I wish I could remember, took it upon himself to give us the unvarnished truth about our situation as he saw it. They met with us at the local airfield that had been built by the Germans. After introductions were made, the British colonel got down to business, prefacing his briefing by declaring, "I'm going to tell you the truth," and his tone and demeanor instantly conveyed the impression that the truth was going to be distressing.

"No one with stars on their shoulders will tell you what I'm going to tell you. No one at CPA or the coalition headquarters. You're in their chain of command. You're not in mine. I probably won't see any of you again. So, I'm going to tell you the truth." He then proceeded to explain very frankly, brutally so, all the ways in which the occupation, and not just in the south, was failing. "We are not winning. These people are prepared to give us the benefit of the doubt for a limited period of time if we improve their lives. If we don't, they'll turn against us like they've turned against everybody else who's occupied this country. They're already starting to."

He was emphatic that the key to turning things around was taking responsibility for protecting the security of local populations and improving their living conditions right now, essential counterinsurgency methods. They were objectives just as important if not more so as standing up a new Iraqi army, and measuring the metrics that went with it, how many units trained, how many enlistments, etc., that Washington was using as benchmarks to determine when we could get the hell out of there. "When they stand up, we stand down" went the mantra.

What this British colonel told us is that to prevent further chaos and curtail the growing insurgency, and prevent the entire country from turning against the occupation, we had to give people hope we could keep them safe, that infrastructure and commerce functioned well enough to support them, that their future would be better than their past. If you do that you'll prevent the insurgency from catching fire, and the locals will help you defeat it. But you don't encourage hopes by staying hunkered down on your base all day, while families sweltered in the heat without water, electricity, and plumbing or when your patrols raced through the city at night looking for doors to knock down, terrorists to kill, and arms caches to seize. "You have four to six months to turn this around," he advised. "After that, you'll lose."

It was a pretty bracing presentation, very different from what we had received at coalition headquarters and the CPA. It added to my concerns that however astute prewar planning had been for the invasion, there had been little thought, and far too few resources, men and material, devoted to postwar needs. That deficiency had been mandated from the top, from Rumsfeld, and it was the first of many mistakes in judgment the defense secretary would make.

When we returned to the States, I began reading and meeting with strategists who were calling for changing our strategy and tactics in Iraq. Some experienced observers worried that the Iraqification of the conflict, giving hastily trained Iraqi militias and the Iraqi army we were building from scratch the main responsibility for suppressing the insurgency, was doomed to fail. They began advocating for a coalition-led, sufficiently resourced counterinsurgency, which meant sending more U.S. troops to Iraq, not drawing down the force in place now. I was convinced that our plan to transfer military responsibilities to the Iraqis was too hasty while our plan to return political control of the country to them was too attenuated, and I began saying so in speeches and interviews. I wrote an op-ed for the *Washington Post* just after we had returned to the States, echoing the dire prediction of the outspoken British colonel. "Having liberated Iraq, we must demonstrate the tangible benefits of occupation, which the Iraqi silent majority will tolerate if it successfully delivers services, law and order and a transition to Iraqi rule," I argued.

> The danger is that our failure to improve daily life, security, and Iraqis' participation in their own governance will erode their patience and fuel insurrection. We do not have time to spare. If we do not meaningfully improve services and security in Iraq over the next few months, it may be too late. We will risk an irreversible loss of Iraqi confidence and reinforce the efforts of extremists who seek our defeat and threaten Iraq's democratic future.

I recounted our briefing from the British colonel to almost everyone I met with to discuss Iraq. Word must have gotten back to Baghdad that there was a British officer in Basra who was decidedly off script, and causing consternation among visiting congressional delegations. I heard later that the colonel's tour was abbreviated and he had gone home, and that Bremer or Sanchez or someone in Baghdad had issued an unwritten edict forbidding future British briefings of American politicians.

In November, I wrote another piece for the *Post* that specifically called for a U.S.-led counterinsurgency in the Sunni Triangle. Noting that attacks on coalition forces had doubled since we had been there, and were increasingly lethal, I warned against accelerating the timetable for training an Iraqi army in order to shift the burden of defeating the insurgency to Iraqis before they were ready to do it. We had to do it, I argued. We had accepted the responsibility for securing the country when we invaded. Deluding ourselves into believing the Iraqis could be ready right then to defeat an insurgency was an evasion of that responsibility. "The number of American forces in Iraq has not increased," I objected. "Our overall troop level in Iraq doesn't reflect a careful assessment of what it takes to achieve victory. It reflects the number of forces who were in Iraq when the war ended." Then I got to the point that was anathema to Secretary Rumsfeld and the commander of coalition forces in Iraq.

> I believe we must deploy at least another full division, giving us the necessary manpower to conduct a focused counterinsurgency campaign across the Sunni Triangle that seals off enemy operating areas, conducts search-and-destroy missions and holds territory.

I criticized the reluctance of the CPA to transfer political authority to Iraqis quickly. "The United States is treated as an occupying force in Iraq," I argued, "partly because we are not treating Iraqis as a liberated people."

Little of my criticism made a favorable impression on the most senior officials running the war. Those like Rumsfeld, and Rumsfeld loyalists who presumably included his White House sponsor, Vice President Cheney, persisted in doubting the insurgency was anything more than the last gasp of a dead regime, and adamantly refused to entertain the idea that the "they stand up, we stand down" formula was contributing to the spreading insecurity and instability. I wasn't certain that General Sanchez was in that camp. He had seemed to me to be mindful that his force level could be overwhelmed by the proliferating challenges in Iraq. But his successor, General George Casey, was as adamant as Rumsfeld. He never once, as far as I know, in his nearly four years in the job, felt he needed more forces in country, despite it all going to hell over the course of his tenure. Others could see the strategy was failing, but wanted to preserve it as a pretext to get out of there sooner rather than later. And there were those who didn't know what to believe or what to do. But there was a growing number of people who believed that only a counterinsurgency that took and held territory, and maintained security and law and order for the affected populations, had a chance of rescuing victory from the trajectory of defeat. And that would take more troops, not fewer. American troops. We looked to the example of innovative officers in Iraq who, more or less on their own, had employed counterinsurgency tactics in their area of responsibility, including a colonel in Tal Afar, H. R. McMaster, and a two-star general in Mosul, David Petraeus, whose focus on the local population's security, governance, and reconstruction would be the template for all of Iraq in 2007. In 2005, when Petraeus headed the Command and General Staff College at Fort Leavenworth, he and another enterprising general officer, Marine Lieutenant General James Amos, worked with a team of officers, international development assistance experts, human rights advocates, journalists, and others to produce *Counterinsurgency*, the Army field manual that explained the fundamental principles of counterinsurgency.

I traveled to Iraq at least twice a year between 2004 and 2007, and watched with growing distress what can only be described as a persistently reinforced failure of leadership caused for the most part by a refusal to face facts and abandon a strategy that wasn't working and couldn't work. Sunni insurgents launched an offensive in the spring of 2004, involving secular and religious extremist elements, native Iraqi and foreign fighters. Marines attempted to pacify Fallujah, an insurgent stronghold in Anbar Province, in early April. News accounts of the difficult urban fighting and high civilian casualties brought protests from Iraqi leaders and the public, and necessitated a cease-fire after five days of fighting, disrupted repeatedly over the next several weeks by attacks on the Marines, and air strikes called in response, until the Marines withdrew in early May. At the same time, we were engaged with Muqtada al-Sadr's Mahdi army in Baghdad's Sadr City, in Najaf, and in other Shia strongholds. Insurgents took advantage of the situation, and launched attacks against U.S. forces in a dozen or more Anbar cities and villages, including Ramadi, Anbar's capital, and in Samarra and other cities located in the Sunni Triangle. We turned over peacekeeping duties in Fallujah to an Iraqi army brigade, which promptly switched sides to join the insurgents. By the summer, insurgents effectively controlled most of Anbar and much of the Sunni Triangle.

In November, U.S., British, and Iraqi forces fought a second, even bloodier battle for Fallujah, which ended with its liberation, for lack of a better word, at the cost of high casualties on all sides and the city in ruins. At the same time in the north, we fought to clear Mosul of insurgents. The CPA had turned over governing authority to an interim Iraqi government in June, and Paul Bremer went home. In December, General Casey ordered coalition forces to concentrate on training the Iraqi security forces, and leave more of the fighting to them. The insurgents were happy to oblige, and concentrate more of their attacks on Iraqi troops. Two thousand four was also the year that the prisoner abuses at Abu Ghraib were revealed, which provided more fuel for the insurgency. As I sat in Washington reading news accounts of the fighting, it seemed that in most engagements with insurgents the Iraqi forces broke first, an impression that persisted for years. By

December of that year, I was certain we would fail in Iraq unless we changed strategies and changed the military and civilian leaders who had orchestrated the failure. I repeatedly volunteered that I had "no confidence" in Secretary Rumsfeld, hoping others would publicly and in the White House privately join the choir. His tenure would continue for another two years, as would General Casey's command.

I went less often to Afghanistan during those years. The situation there wasn't as dire as it was in Iraq. The smaller force we had there and the less attention it received from the media reflected the lower priority it was accorded while Iraq was descending into a dystopian nightmare. In comparison, Afghanistan, blessedly, seemed somewhat anticlimactic. By 2005, I had become single-minded in my advocacy of a revised strategy in Iraq, and a big increase in the number of troops there. I knew what that meant for Afghanistan. We would have to maintain our position there with less force than desirable. That wasn't fair to the soldiers who were holding the line in Afghanistan. But there wasn't much of a choice. As tough as it was there, it wasn't as bad as Iraq. We would have to muddle through until we had salvaged the disaster that Iraq had become.

I went to Iraq and Afghanistan in February 2005 with Lindsey and Senators Russ Feingold, Susan Collins, and Hillary Clinton. It was my second experience traveling with Hillary, whose company I enjoyed very much. She was a hardworking and intelligent senator, which wouldn't surprise anyone to learn. But she is also, contrary to the negative public image promoted by her detractors, very warm, engaging, and considerate in person, and fun. I had traveled with her for the first time the year before on a trip to the Baltics and Norway, and she had been a valuable addition to the delegation and good company. That was the trip that saw a pleasant evening's repast become an urban legend that recounted a vodka-drinking competition she and I are alleged to have had in Tallinn. I don't drink very much, and I never have.

I have one or two drinks on the weekend or when I'm out to dinner with friends, and my drink of choice is vodka. We did go out to dinner in Tallinn, Hillary, Lindsey, Susan, and I, and we did have vodka. But the rumored multiple-bottle contest, in which Hillary is reported to have drunk me under the table, is fiction. There was a bottle on the table that we did not finish. She and I had a few glasses. Lindsey, who I suspect is the author of the legend, was furtively emptying his glass into a vase or some other handy receptacle. We had a pleasant evening, and we left the table no worse for wear, steady on our feet, and in good shape to keep our busy schedule the next day. As I said, I suspect my friend from South Carolina had a hand in turning an enjoyable evening into a more colorful experience than it had been. He's a good storyteller, old Lindsey, and stretching the truth a little in the service of a funny tale is no crime in his book or mine.

Hillary is also a very diligent person, who pays close attention to detail. We had arranged in Afghanistan to be briefed by the minister in charge of counter-narcotics. He was former mujahedeen, and had lost a leg fighting the Soviets. He was probably a fascinating guy. Unfortunately, his wasn't the most fascinating briefing I'd ever received. Someone must have advised him that Americans like PowerPoint presentations (personally, I hate them). He had prepared maybe the longest PowerPoint in the history of PowerPoints, with slide after slide after slide on the structure and legal framework of the government's counter-narcotics policies, on the progress of the poppy crop eradication effort, and various prosecutions the government had brought. Don't get me wrong, it's an important subject. But, my God, the presentation was just interminable, an hour and a half at minimum. That's far too long and detailed for a bunch of generalists, which describes most senators, except, perhaps, the senator from New York. She was positively riveted. Our schedule had been exhausting. After twenty minutes, I was struggling to stay awake. I turned to my aide, Richard

Fontaine, and whispered that I thought I was going to die, and asked him to figure out some way to get us out of there. As he pondered how, the minister carried on, and I continued to wilt. But not Hillary. She was gathering strength with every slide, asking lots and lots of questions, referring back to earlier slides, and extending the experience beyond my limits of endurance. Finally, mercifully, the briefing sputtered to its end. I turned again to Fontaine to whisper that it had been, without doubt, the worst PowerPoint of all time, just as Hillary volunteered to the gratified minister that it had been one of the best briefings she had ever received, and might she have a hard copy to take back to the Senate to share with colleagues?

I met David Petraeus on that 2005 Iraq trip. He and the 101st Airborne Division he commanded in Mosul had returned to the States in early 2004. They had been replaced by a Stryker brigade, a much smaller force that did not continue their predecessors' population-focused policies, and were seen as occupiers. As the Sunni insurgency gained strength, things fell apart in Mosul as they had in Tikrit, Fallujah, and elsewhere in the Sunni Triangle. Petraeus had been ordered back to Iraq in the summer of 2004 to take command of setting up and training Iraq's security forces. It was in that capacity that he briefed our delegation during that February 2005 trip. He's a good briefer, insightful and well-spoken, and he had a lot of encouraging statistics for how many Iraqis had been trained and how many more coalition forces were involved in their training. But even then, and even with an innovator like Dave Petraeus, whom I admire immensely, I was frustrated with the emphasis placed on building an Iraqi army rather than the deteriorating security situation facing our troops and the Iraqi people. "General," I interjected, "I'd like to know when you think the violence will go down, not when the trainees and trainers will go up, but when will the violence go down." I know he appreciated the question, because I know that was the question his tactics as a field commander

were most concerned with addressing. But as the commander oversee-
ing the building of the Iraqi army, it wasn't his job to second-guess
General Casey and the Pentagon to a U.S. senator asking a subversive
question. He hemmed and hawed a little. "Best guess?" I asked again.
"How long will it take to get the violence down? A day? A week? A
month? Six months? A year? A century? What do you think is closest to
the right answer?" He relented, and said he thought the violence would
come down by the end of the year. But it didn't. It got worse.

Back in Washington, it was hard to ignore how badly Iraq was deteriorating. The news was full of it. The judgment was inescapable,
and I began worrying that the situation might not be salvageable. In
January 2005, Iraqis had elected a temporary government to write a
new national constitution. Sunnis had mostly boycotted the vote. Still
it was encouraging to see Iraqis want to take charge of their country's
future while facing down threats of violence, and to see them do it
again at the end of the year when they elected a National Assembly,
and the new Iraqi government formed with Nouri al-Maliki, a Shia,
as prime minister and Jalal Talabani, a Kurd, as president. But what
small ember of hope the election might have kindled would be mostly
extinguished the following year, 2006. Al-Qaeda in Iraq bombed the
al-Askari mosque in Samarra, one of the holiest Shia sites in Iraq, an
atrocity that lit the growing sectarian conflict into a blazing conflagra-
tion. Shia death squads targeted Sunni clerics and civilians for assas-
sination in retaliation, including the mass murder of nearly fifty Sunni
civilians, the bodies heaped in a ditch, broadcast by the media to the
world. Scores of Sunni mosques were attacked. Sunni insurgents and
al-Qaeda fighters returned the savagery. Within a week it looked like
a religious civil war could destroy the U.S. effort there and leave the
country worse off than it had been under Saddam and ignite sectarian
violence throughout the Middle East, an intolerable defeat for U.S. interests and ideals. But by the end of the month, Shia leaders, including

even Sadr, were calling for no further retaliations, and the lid was kept on the catastrophe just barely. Sectarian killings still occurred regularly, and the continuing persecution of minorities in certain Baghdad neighborhoods and elsewhere amounted to ethnic cleansing. The end times hadn't quite arrived yet, but we had a glimpse of what it would be like when they did.

The new Iraqi government took office in May, and coalition forces, officially designated Multi-National Force-Iraq under General Casey, with U.S. ambassador Zal Khalilzad's concurrence, began turning over the authority for entire provinces to the Iraqi government and army. No one took authority for Anbar Province, however, as it was effectively controlled by the Sunni insurgents. Al-Qaeda in Iraq had declared Ramadi the capital of its caliphate. The battle for Ramadi, involving the U.S. Marines, Army, and Navy SEALs, and Iraqi troops under the command of another innovative officer, Army Colonel Sean MacFarland, began in June and difficult house-to-house fighting continued most of the year. The streets of the nation's capital, Baghdad, routinely echoed with explosions of IEDs and suicide bombers, the gunfire of death squads, and the cries of their victims. An assessment by the Marines' chief intelligence officer in Iraq, Colonel Peter Devlin, had leaked in September. It concluded that "The U.S. military is no longer able to defeat a bloody insurgency in western Iraq or counter al Qaeda's rising popularity there."

I went twice that year to Iraq, in May and December, and the most important of those visits, the pivotal one from my perspective, was in December. Congressional elections that November had returned big Democratic majorities in both houses, a Republican defeat blamed almost entirely on public dissatisfaction with the war. The day after the election, President Bush accepted Secretary Rumsfeld's resignation and announced his intention to nominate Bob Gates as his successor.

For two years, I'd been having regular discussions with critics of the Iraq strategy, principally, Lindsey Graham and Joe Lieberman; retired Vice Army Chief of Staff General Jack Keane; two military historians, Fred Kagan and his wife, Kim; Ken Pollack, a former CIA Middle East analyst; and Andy Krepinevich, who authored an essay in *Foreign Affairs* that argued for the application in Iraq of counterinsurgency principles that had been employed in the latter years of the Vietnam War. I wanted to get an understanding of how a counterinsurgency could succeed in Iraq at this late date, and how big a force was needed to execute it. Jack Keane with other retired flag officers had been making the case to the White House for the surge, as had the Kagans, and a growing number of other prominent national security figures. Before his resignation, Rumsfeld had routinely managed to cut off all interagency debates about transitioning to a counterinsurgency and sending more troops to Iraq. Those discussions were happening now, and I was guardedly optimistic that the President would make the politically difficult but militarily necessary decision to change strategies and commanders in Iraq, and send enough troops to prevent what I believed was our looming defeat.

General Casey and his number two, the commander of U.S. ground troops in Iraq, Lieutenant General Peter Chiarelli, had devised a plan to consolidate U.S. forces in a few bases in Iraq, increase the numbers of Americans training and embedding with Iraqi units, and leave most combat to the Iraqis. As far as I was concerned the plan would have continued to reinforce failure and accelerate our defeat. I was traveling with Lindsey, Joe, and Susan. John Thune of South Dakota had joined us, as had several members of the House. As our C-130 landed at Baghdad International, we heard the first loud explosion, a bomb detonated somewhere in Baghdad. As we disembarked down the mobile staircase, we heard a second boom, and gunfire as well. We flew by helicopter to the city. We didn't see any cars and very few people on the streets below. The only people who ventured out of their homes were those doing the shooting and bombing. No commerce, no security, nothing that appeared to indicate even a rudimentarily functioning society was visible. It was a bleak scene.

Our first meeting was with General Chiarelli, who had spent the last two years in Iraq, and his newly arrived replacement, Lieutenant General Ray Odierno, who would assume the command later that day. It was a coincidence of timing that revealed the wide gulf between their opposing philosophies. I began as I began most discussions with military commanders in Iraq by noting that they needed more troops. Chiarelli insisted he did not, and another frustrating exchange commenced as I noted rising levels of violence and the fact that large swaths of the country were under insurgent control. Chiarelli, echoing the views of General Casey, maintained that we shouldn't do what Iraqis could do for themselves. The mission of the U.S. was to train more, not fight more. When more Iraqi units are trained, the violence will go down. "I doubt that, General," I responded. "They're fighting now, and the violence is worse." I asked Odierno what he thought, expecting him to repeat Chiarelli's argument. To my surprise, he did not.

"I think we need more troops in this country," he acknowledged. "If I had five more brigades, I'd send two to Baghdad, two to the Baghdad Belt, and one to Anbar Province." Clearly General Odierno had been doing a little planning in the hope that the President would decide to surge troops to Iraq. He had contradicted about as directly as possible the officer he was succeeding, and his boss, General Casey, who would leave Iraq early the following year to become chief of staff of the Army. He did it without blinking an eye. An officer who worked for Odierno later told Richard Fontaine that they knew Casey would kill any proposal they presented for more troops, and Odierno had been so blunt with me knowing that when I got back to Washington I would make the case for the additional brigades, and be certain to repeat what he had told me.

We met with Casey after my meeting with Chiarelli and Odierno. He and I had had quite a few back-and-forths over the last few years. This one was the most frustrating, and I got pretty heated. Casey had just made a statement proclaiming we were winning, and my first question to him was how he could say that. He repeated, "We are winning in Iraq."

"What are you talking about?" I asked incredulously. "There's like a thousand bodies showing up every week on the streets of Baghdad. There's no political activity, no economic activity. People are afraid to leave their homes. Our guys are getting killed every day." To which Casey replied, "Every day we're taking steps to meet our strategic objective, which is to turn control of this country over to the Iraqi security forces, and we're doing that because every day we are training more units and doing more operations with them." Casey's strategic sense of the U.S. military's mission in Iraq was to hold the line until the country's politics matured and its leaders made the compromises necessary to end the violence. The view of counterinsurgency advocates was the opposite. We had to protect the population and get the violence under control before genuine political progress could occur.

I asked Casey for the most recent casualty figures for our troops. "I've got them here somewhere," he responded, and made a brief show of looking for them without actually producing them. "We're not winning, General," I concluded. "We're losing." While we were meeting, there was another suicide bombing in the city, killing over sixty people. We were told about it as we left Casey's headquarters. "This is winning," I said to Lindsey and Joe.

We had arranged to meet with an assortment of people who had been in country awhile and were outside the bubble of official dogma, including a guy who ran a Coca-Cola bottling plant in Basra, and some German diplomats. They all had the same message: "Don't leave." They argued that the U.S. was the only authority capable of imposing any order in this country. If we left it would be chaos and killing all the time.

I had been relieved to learn Odierno's view of the situation was the same as mine, but the most encouraging experience I had on that trip was a visit to Ramadi the next day, and a meeting with the resourceful American in charge there, Sean MacFarland. Ramadi was quite a scene. It had been the heart of the insurgency, and the battle for the city had lasted nearly seven months. All told, about fifty-five hundred Americans had fought there, Army, Marines, Navy, infantry, armored, Special Forces, and two Iraqi brigades. MacFarland had established outposts around the perimeter and inside the city, little Fort Apaches, surrounded by enemies. He ordered constant patrols of the city, showing the population this wouldn't be one big show of force that ended with Americans returning to a base somewhere else. Americans were there to stay. They were going to take control of the city, destroy anyone who fought them, and protect those who didn't want to fight. They cleared Ramadi one building at a time. It had been a very violent, deadly enterprise. Casualties on both sides were high. The heaviest fighting had ended the month before our visit. Many insurgents had fled the city by December, but a good many were entrenched in central Ramadi, and sporadic fighting still occurred there and outside the city.

As MacFarland briefed us on his operations, it became clear he had done, mostly if not entirely on his own initiative, what I and others had been arguing was necessary for all of Iraq. He had run a counterinsurgency and he had a big enough force to do it successfully. I had been to the country often enough and talked to enough junior officers and enlisted soldiers to have gained a ground-up understanding that what we were doing wasn't working. Our forces were confined to large bases. They would dash out to fight somebody, kill some people, and dash back, while the population stayed in their homes in fear of their lives. But the transition to a counterinsurgency was still a theoretical framework. I hadn't seen it tried until I went to Ramadi. I wanted to understand exactly how dangerous counterinsurgency operations would be, and how costly. And so I pressed MacFarland about the forward deployment of his forces and the constant patrols he ordered to protect the population. I told him what he was doing was admirable, and that the force under his command was fighting bravely and effectively. "But you're holding memorial services every day." I remember his response almost word for word. "This is what our country decided we needed to do in Iraq," he began, "and this is the only way we have a chance of doing it." Then he ran the numbers for us. American and Iraqi forces had taken a lot of casualties in the beginning and for a number of months after, but they had come down as they had reclaimed more of the city. Insurgent activity was down, violent incidents down, dislocated civilians were returning to their homes. It was the first validation I had that counterinsurgency tactics worked in Iraq. I was relieved and so impressed with MacFarland and the Americans and Iraqis he commanded. He had tested them and his ideas without asking permission from Baghdad and they proved successful.

MacFarland also informed us of an unexpected political development in Anbar. In August, he had received a call from a local sheikh, Abdul Sattar Abu Risha, who explained that he and other Sunni sheikhs in the area wished to break with al-Qaeda. They couldn't bear any longer the foreign jihadis' religious fanaticism, oppressive rule, and terror tactics, and they were willing to risk their lives to side with the coalition against al-Qaeda and the insurgency if the U.S. would give them some protection. MacFarland hung up the phone and immediately dispatched a tank to the sheikh's house. The Anbar Awakening had begun. Abu Risha would be assassinated by al-Qaeda less than a year after his fateful call to MacFarland, but it was too late by then to curtail the movement he had started. The growing support of Anbar tribal leaders not only helped defeat the insurgents in Ramadi, but would prove critical to the success of the surge, which President Bush would announce a few weeks later.

A month before, the Iraq Study Group, authorized by Congress and chaired by two respected statesmen, former secretary of state Jim Baker and retired congressman Lee Hamilton, had announced its recommendations for Iraq: accelerate Iraqi military and police training and begin the phased withdrawal of coalition forces. President Bush had decided to do the opposite at a point of widespread public and congressional opposition to the war. I believe it was the finest moment of his presidency, and it included two of the best appointments he had made. He selected David Petraeus, the man who wrote the book on counterinsurgency, as the new commander of Multi-National Force-Iraq, and Ryan Crocker, an extraordinarily talented career diplomat, as the new U.S. ambassador there. As it turned out, the size of the surge and its distribution would closely approximate General Odierno's prescription; five combat brigades and supporting troops, and four thousand Marines in Anbar had their tours extended. The coming months would be the deadliest of the war for our forces.

As I discussed in an earlier chapter, I was running for President at the time, and not doing particularly well at it as I was closely identified with the unpopular war. I won't reiterate that saga here, except to say that Iraq was always on my mind every day of that campaign. I went three times to Iraq in 2007 to see the surge's progress for myself, and once in 2008 after I had effectively won the nomination. The first trip was in March 2007, very early days, of course, but even then you could see signs of encouragement that the surge was working, which both Petraeus and Crocker were quick to point out. Petraeus wanted to take us to a market area of downtown Baghdad, where we couldn't have gone the previous December. We would have come under fire, and there weren't any merchants doing business there anyway. By March, economic activity had returned to the area. People felt safe enough to shop there. I was impressed by the progress, and said so. But because we were wearing Kevlar vests and were protected by soldiers and helicopter gunships, I was criticized by a CNN reporter in Baghdad, and by pundits at home. I didn't like it, but I should have seen it coming.

For weeks afterward, I swore I would insist on my next trip that I be allowed to wander the area in my shirtsleeves and without a security detail. That was never going to happen. Even my own staff didn't take me seriously. The point that got lost in the attention accorded me was that while I had extra protection, the shopkeepers working there and their customers did not. They were there because the surge had begun to improve security in Baghdad, and they felt safer going about their business. We all knew there was a long, hard road ahead, and that as our forces engaged more of the enemy in more places, our casualties would increase. But even less than two months into the surge, there was evidence that the theory might prove correct in practice. That judgment would have to wait for more evidence, of course, to substantiate it. But there was good reason to hope. There was at least that. And hope had been in very scarce supply in Iraq the last few years.

Petreus and Crocker returned to Washington in September to testify before Congress after issuing a progress report on the situation in Iraq. They appeared before committees in the House and the Senate, including mine, the Senate Armed Services Committee. "The military objectives of the surge are, in large measure, being met," Petraeus claimed, and he had the statistics to back it up. Sectarian violence had declined, as had al-Qaeda attacks. Coalition forces were reestablishing their authority in the most dangerous parts of the country. He was confident that MNF-I could return to pre-surge levels by the summer, and it would. Crocker maintained that "a secure, stable, democratic Iraq at peace with its neighbors is attainable." Both were cautious in their presentation, acknowledging, in Crocker's words, "the process will not be quick, it will be uneven, punctuated by setbacks as well as achievement, and it will require substantial U.S. resolve and commitment." It was an impressive performance, and encouraging. I was already aware of the progress, and determined to use my statement and questions at the hearing to emphasize it. Many of the Democrats, especially those who were, like me, running for President at the time, were equally determined to dispute it. Hillary, who was a member of the committee, said about Petraeus's testimony that it required "a willing suspension of disbelief." Obama's campaign dismissed it as illogical. Harry Reid and others insisted the presentation had been dictated by the White House though Petraeus and Crocker protested otherwise. The leftist activist group MoveOn.org bought an ad in the *New York Times*, accusing Petraeus of "cooking the books," and labeled him "General Betray Us." The offensiveness of that accusation and the stupidity of the people who had dreamed it up hurt their side's argument more than mine. But it outraged me just the same.

When I went back in March 2008, the surge's effects were undeniable, though politics being what it is, there were still plenty of critics who insisted on denying it. Most of the surged forces were still in country, and no one was claiming victory, but there had been a complete transformation from what the country had looked like in December 2006, and almost everyone in Iraq appreciated it except the bad guys. No one more so than me. I believed I could even turn Iraq to my advantage, and highlight my judgment on the surge against Hillary's and Barack's opposition to it. I sure tried. Alas, as we know, it wouldn't be enough, and my next trip to Iraq and to Afghanistan would be as a defeated presidential candidate just a few weeks after the election, returning again with two friends who had stayed close by my side throughout the campaign, Lindsey Graham and Joe Lieberman. No one was making much of an argument about the surge by then. It had succeeded. Not everyone wanted to credit it, but few wished to dispute it. The two men who had led the successful effort to snatch victory from the jaws of defeat had both been promoted. David Petraeus had been selected the commander in chief of Central Command, and Ray Odierno had succeeded him as commander of Multi-National Force-Iraq.

While we were there, the Iraqi government approved a new Status of Forces Agreement (SOFA) negotiated with the Bush administration, which called for coalition combat forces to withdraw from most Iraqi cities by June 30, 2009, and from the country entirely by the end of 2011. There was a provision in the SOFA for a possible extension and renegotiated status, which presumably would be employed to keep a U.S. military presence in country to continue training the Iraqi security forces and help preserve Iraq's hard-won stability. That wasn't a universal expectation, however. Some Iraqis objected to the SOFA as written. And some Americans were adamant that an election mandate had been delivered, and its first command was to get all U.S. forces out of Iraq as quickly as possible. I hoped and believed that the new President wasn't among them.

President Obama had campaigned on his early and consistent opposition to the Iraq War. He had argued that the necessary war had been in Afghanistan, which the war in Iraq had deprived of resources and attention. He mostly declined to acknowledge that the surge had achieved its objectives. But I put that down to politics. He's an intelligent man, reasonable and cautious. He knew how much progress had been made in Iraq at such a high cost. I didn't think he would want to risk squandering it, and that he could be persuaded to keep a force in Iraq after the SOFA mandate expired. Ten thousand or so, many knowledgeable military observers believed, would be sufficient to help the Iraqis keep the bad guys at bay, exert a positive influence on the government and the main factions in the country, and prevent a political vacuum Iran was likely to fill. I thought I should make a public case for it, and help the Iraq government and the Obama administration come to that conclusion, too.

My post-election trip to Iraq was an opportunity to begin that campaign. But I had another, personal reason for going. Right after my defeat, I had a strong desire to have Thanksgiving dinner that year with the Marines in Iraq, and with one Marine in particular. We weren't able to get there in time for the actual holiday. Nevertheless, I traveled alone one day to a Marine base in Anbar, Camp Habbaniyah. I met in a conference room there with the camp's senior officers, and after a while I noticed we had been joined by a young, skinny lance corporal, carrying his weapon as all Marines in Anbar were obliged at all times to do. Eventually my hosts excused themselves, and my son Jimmy and I sat down to a belated holiday dinner, and gave thanks for all our blessings.

I didn't have much success in the first year of the Obama administration. I had opposed and voted against the administration's first ambassador to Iraq, Chris Hill. He was a veteran diplomat but had no experience in the Middle East. He had succeeded the peerless Ryan Crocker, who had been an ambassador in Lebanon, Kuwait, Syria, and Pakistan, spoke fluent Arabic, had been a very active representative of our interests in Iraq, and influential with every major political player in the country. I felt the same about Ryan as I did about Petraeus and Odierno. I admired them, I learned a lot from them, and I felt privileged to have worked with them. Ambassador Hill and I didn't have that kind of relationship. It wasn't anything personal, just our differing views about Iraq. Hill appeared to be Crocker's opposite. He took a more hands-off approach to helping Iraqis sort out their differences collaboratively. Hill believed the more of a role we played in Iraq's national affairs, the more dependent on us Iraqis were, the longer we would be stuck with responsibility for the country. He wanted Iraqis to sort things out for themselves now. I appreciated his position theoretically, but not practically. Iraqis had too little experience with democratic politics, and were too captive to their sectarian identities to realize the vision of a stable, democratic Iraq in the heart of the Middle East without our continued influence, not to mention Iraq's susceptibility to the machinations of their neighbor and our adversary, Iran. As the sectarian and tribal factionalism that always plagued Iraq's politics intensified, I thought the American ambassador's excessive restraint was counterproductive.

Hill didn't strike me as overly interested in negotiating a new SOFA, either. Prime Minister Maliki had demanded that were American forces to remain in Iraq after 2011, the U.S. would have to assent to surrendering the immunity from local prosecution our troops currently had should they be accused of crimes. That was, of course, a nonstarter for the U.S. government and military. And while his position was politically correct in Iraq, I believed Maliki could be persuaded to drop or alter it enough that it would be acceptable to us. I didn't get the impression that Hill felt similarly. Our exchanges on my trips to Iraq during his tenure were often contentious.

New parliamentary elections in March 2010 ended in a political stalemate, preventing the formation of a new government. Ayad Allawi's party had won two more seats than Maliki's. By rights he should have been allowed to form a government, but the problem was that Allawi, who spent much of his time abroad, wasn't nearly the political infighter Maliki was. Both sides seemed to prefer the impasse to a compromise. When Hill left Iraq in August 2010, the sides were no closer together. Hill's successor, Jim Jeffrey, was an experienced Middle East diplomat, and we got along well. In addition, President Obama had recalled Brett McGurk, a skilled Iraq hand who had served in the Bush administration with distinction, back into service to help broker an agreement between the competing factions. When Lindsey and I came to Iraq in November 2010, Jeffrey and McGurk enlisted us in an administration plan to propose a compromise. Since the first parliamentary elections in Iraq, political spoils had been divided between the three main factions, Shia, Sunni, and Kurd. A Shia, Maliki, was given the prime minister's job, the most powerful post. A Sunni was speaker of the parliament, and a Kurd, Jalal Talabani, was Iraq's president. To break the current impasse, the Obama administration wanted to propose an alteration of that arrangement. Maliki would remain as prime minister, but Allawi would be president. A Sunni would remain as speaker, and a new position, head of the National Security Council, would be given to Talabani or another Kurd.

We were scheduled to stop in Irbil, the capital of the Kurdistan region of northern Iraq, and meet with Masoud Barzani, the president of Iraqi Kurdistan and leader of the Kurdistan Democratic Party (KDP). I had gotten to know Barzani well over the years, and we were on very friendly terms. He had once shown me the cave where he had hidden when he was on the run from Saddam's goons. On another visit, when he was running for president, which is not quite the retail enterprise there that it is in the U.S., I suggested we "do a little campaigning." We went to a shopping district in Irbil. His aides and security looked nervous, but Barzani seemed to enjoy it. We went into a shop, where I bought some spices, while the sidewalk outside filled with people waiting for us to emerge. I waded into the crowd, shaking hands, posing for pictures, and motioned for Barzani to do likewise. It had been fun.

In advance of our November meeting, Ambassador Jeffrey had given Lindsey a letter from President Obama addressed to Barzani, proposing the political rearrangement in Baghdad the administration hoped would end the stalemate. We only discussed it for a few minutes, but we said we'd support it and agreed that Lindsey would give it to the Kurdish leader. Barzani was the godfather of Kurdish politics. If he went along with a new division of power and told Talabani to relinquish the presidency, it would happen. But we could tell as Barzani read the letter Lindsey had handed him, frowning as he did so and shaking his head, that he was put out by it. He and Maliki were estranged at that time, and he wasn't disposed to help him stay in power. He said curtly that he would consider it, perhaps he could put another Kurd in the job, although he had promised Talabani his support. We knew he wasn't going to agree to give Allawi the job, and both Lindsey and I regretted even raising it with him. I don't think Jeffrey or McGurk had much hope that he would. But a few days after our meeting, Barzani relented, and a government was formed. Maliki remained prime minister, Talabani stayed in the presidency, and Allawi was made the head of the new National Security Council.

I would have another request to ask of Barzani when I was next in Iraq in May 2011. Lindsey and I had planned to go back then, but weeks before we left, Hillary Clinton, who was now secretary of state, talked with Lindsey and asked that we raise with the Iraqis the idea of a new SOFA that would keep U.S. forces in country after the end of the year when the existing SOFA mandated their complete withdrawal, and to try to gauge whether Maliki would relent on his insistence that U.S. soldiers in Iraq accused of felonies be tried in Iraqi courts. A little more than a month after his inauguration, President Obama had reiterated in a speech to Marines at Camp Lejeune that the U.S. combat mission in Iraq would conclude by the end of August 2010. We had already handed over authority for the Green Zone to the Iraqis, as well as Saddam's al-Faw Palace, where coalition forces had headquartered. We had withdrawn U.S. forces from Baghdad, and handed over dozens of bases to the Iraqi security forces. The last British and Australian units had left the country, and Multi-National Force-Iraq was now the United States Forces-Iraq. The last combat brigade had left Iraq in August 2010. Fifty thousand U.S. troops continued training Iraqi units and conducting counterterrorism operations. The deadline for withdrawing the last of them was looming, and the country was suffering from renewed sectarian violence, a resumption in insurgent activity, and terrorist attacks by the successor to al-Qaeda in Iraq, the Islamic State of Iraq. Through its growing company of proxies in Iraq's Shia community, Iran was insisting on a complete withdrawal.

We met with Allawi first. He spent much of the time complaining about Maliki and the people around Maliki, and that the U.S. wasn't doing enough to support him. But he was all in on a new SOFA. He wanted closer relations with the U.S. and saw support for a continued American military presence as instrumental to that end.

The meeting with Maliki was trickier. Ambassador Jeffrey was there, as was Lieutenant General Lloyd Austin, Ray Odierno's successor, a very capable commander, whom I trusted. We were direct, and Maliki was evasive. The politics were difficult for him. He would take most of the heat from Iran, and anger his own political base, the Shia. I spoke first and then Lindsey, both of us making the same points. We told him Allawi had offered support for the idea. We stressed the security challenges facing Iraq and the need for a stabilizing force that could help Iraq fight terrorists. We expressed confidence that a solution to the immunity impasse could be found. The discussion had gone on quite a while with Maliki listening more than arguing a position. Finally, in answer to a question from Lindsey about what he needed to agree, Maliki indicated receptivity to the idea, and asked the obvious question. How big a force are you talking about? Lindsey turned to General Austin, and asked him to answer. He demurred and looked at Jeffrey, who answered that he didn't have guidance on that. Then Austin interjected that they were still working on a number.

What was clear to me in that instant was that the administration hadn't made up its mind about a residual force. I knew the number the military wanted. I had talked to scores of senior officers over the last couple years, and they all agreed that you would need ten to fifteen thousand troops for the force to be effective. That seemed a reasonable number to me, and I bet it did to Maliki, too. I think some of Obama's civilian advisors, and probably Obama himself, had been entertaining a much smaller number, a few thousand, perhaps. We were asking Maliki to do a very hard thing, and he was going to catch hell for it. He wasn't going to do that for a force too small to do him or us any good. I wasn't happy to be surprised by the administration's indecision in the middle of our discussions. But I didn't make a fuss about it. Instead, we went home to let the administration know that a deal was reachable, and to start pushing for a force level sufficient to make the deal worthwhile. Our last stop was Irbil, and though Barzani acknowledged that he and Maliki hadn't been on speaking terms for months, he promised to go to Baghdad in support of the idea.

If memory serves, I put a call in to the White House as soon as we got back, and asked to speak with the President. I ended up talking several times with National Security Advisor Tom Donilon. I talked to his deputy, too, Denis McDonough. Lindsey reported to Hillary. We both insisted there was a deal to be had, including an accommodation on the immunity question. Donilon and I had one exchange about how big a force to keep there. I posited the ten to fifteen thousand estimate, and he said something like, "You know, Senator, the military always asks for more than they really need," which kind of stuck in my craw. Nevertheless, we were encouraged. We assumed a deal would be negotiated, and we were pleased to have lent a hand. I talked during the summer to friends in the administration and at the Pentagon. I didn't get the sense that there had been a lot of progress made on a deal, but I assumed it was probably in the hands of a small, tight-lipped circle, and they would close it before the end of the year.

In late October, I saw a news report that the President had abandoned the idea of negotiating a residual force, and that all U.S. troops in Iraq would be out of the country by January. The next day, the President made the announcement in the Rose Garden. I watched it on television. No one in the administration had warned Lindsey or me that the announcement was coming. Administration officials attributed the decision to the Iraqi government's intransigence on the immunity question. That was bullshit. Maliki would have relented. More likely, the administration hadn't wanted to keep a force in Iraq big enough to make the political pain it would cause the Iraqi government worth it.

I was furious. I believed then and I believe now that a modest but capable American military force in Iraq that wasn't involved in day-to-day combat operations was indispensable to preventing resurgent terrorist activity, intensified sectarian divisions, a spreading Sunni insurgency, and a growing Iranian influence over the Iraqi government. I issued a harshly worded statement that predicted dire consequences for a decision I considered a failure of leadership on the part of both governments.

Today marks a harmful and sad setback for the United States in the world. I respectfully disagree with the President: this decision will be viewed as a strategic victory for our enemies in the Middle East, especially the Iranian regime, which has worked relentlessly to ensure a full withdrawal of U.S. troops from Iraq. It is a consequential failure of both the Obama Administration—which has been more focused on withdrawing from Iraq than succeeding in Iraq since it came into office—as well as the Iraqi government.

I share the desire for all of our troops to come home as quickly as possible. But all of our military commanders with whom I have spoken on my repeated visits to Iraq have told me that U.S. national security interests and the enduring needs of Iraq's military required a continued presence of U.S. troops in Iraq beyond 2011 to safeguard the gains that we and our Iraqi partners have made. I am confident that no U.S. commander of any stature who has served in Iraq recommended the course of action that has now been taken.

On December 18, 2011, five hundred American soldiers crossed the Kuwait border, the last of U.S. Forces-Iraq. "Nearly 4,500 Americans have given their lives for our mission in Iraq," I concluded in my October statement.

Countless more have been wounded. Through their service and sacrifice, the possibility of a democratic state in the heart of the Middle East has been opened to millions of Iraqis. I fear that all of the gains made possible by these brave Americans in Iraq, at such grave cost, are now at risk.

It started falling apart almost immediately. On December 22, eighty Iraqis were killed in a series of bombings and hundreds were wounded. Suicide bombings, insurgent attacks, and crime spiked in the weeks and months after our withdrawal, and were regular facts of life in Iraq for years to come. Maliki cracked down on the Sunni opposition and concentrated power in his hands. The last American soldier had just left the country when Maliki had an arrest warrant issued for a prominent Sunni politician, Vice President Tariq al-Hashemi, who fled to Qatar. Arab Spring protests in Egypt and elsewhere in the Middle East encouraged Sunni protests in Iraq, and Sunni politicians were boycotting parliament by the end of 2011. A government-ordered raid on the home of another prominent Sunni official, Finance Minister Rafi al-Issawi, triggered protests in Fallujah that rapidly spread to all Sunni communities in Iraq. Even Muqtada al-Sadr blamed the unrest on Maliki, whose supporters staged protests in response. In December, Maliki ordered the military to break up a camp of protesters in Ramadi and violence ensued. The Kurds, too, were increasingly alienated by the Maliki government. Iran's influence over the Baghdad government grew. It was starting to look like Iraq might split into three countries.

The civil war in neighboring Syria began to engulf Iraq in 2012. In the summer of 2013, ISIS attacked Abu Ghraib and another prison, liberating five hundred jihadis. By January 2014, ISIS was in control of Fallujah, much of Ramadi, and most of Anbar Province. In June, they attacked an Iraqi army camp, and massacred 1,700 Shia soldiers. That same month, they overran Mosul, Iraq's second-largest city. The Iraqi security forces, poorly led, fractured by sectarian politics, abandoned the defense of the city. The Kurdish military, the Peshmerga, offered to help take it back. Maliki declined the offer. Iran began supplying Shia militias with weapons and supplies, even aircraft, and Iranians assumed leadership roles in planned counterattacks. By August, Iran's Islamic Revolutionary Guard Corps (IRGC) had sent Quds Force fighters to Iraq. ISIS conquered Sinjar in Nineveh Province, and massacred five thousand Yazidi men, enslaved Yazidi women, and forced fifty thousand Yazidis to flee to nearby mountains. President Obama gave a live address on August 7, announcing that he had ordered U.S. air strikes against ISIS positions in Sinjar and around Irbil to protect the Kurds. He had dispatched eight hundred soldiers to Iraq the month before. General Austin took command of all U.S. efforts against ISIS in Iraq and Syria. The U.S. was soon coordinating air strikes with Iraqi army offensives. By December, American soldiers were fighting alongside Iraqi units to repel an ISIS attack on a base where U.S. advisors were stationed. The U.S. appealed to its allies to send warplanes to help dislodge ISIS, and nine countries did. By the end of September, U.S. Navy and Air Force planes had flown a few hundred sorties in Iraq and Syria. In December, a Kurdish offensive in Sinjar with close U.S. air support stemmed the tide of ISIS's advance, and began to push them back. Another inconclusive election left Maliki in power for another several months, but from within and without Iraq, including the U.S., pressure mounted on him to relinquish power. In September 2014, a new prime minister, Haider al-Abadi, took office. In March 2015, the long campaign to retake Mosul began, spearheaded by Kurdish forces and U.S. and allied airpower.

The war against ISIS in Iraq was a long, hard slog, and for a time the administration was as guilty of hyping progress as the most imaginative briefers at the old "Five O'Clock Follies" in Saigon had been. In May 2015, an ISIS assault on Ramadi and a sandstorm that grounded U.S. planes sent Iraqi forces and U.S. Special Forces embedded with them fleeing the city. Thanks to growing hostility between the Iraqi government and Iranian-supported militias in the battle, the city wouldn't be taken until the end of the year.

Before it was over we had sent well over five thousand military personnel back to Iraq, including Special Forces operators embedded as advisors with Iraqi and Kurdish units. A Navy SEAL, a native Arizonan whom I had known when he was a boy, was killed in northern Iraq. His name was Charles Keating IV, the grandson of my old benefactor, with whom I had been implicated all those years ago in the scandal his name had branded. He was by all accounts a brave and fine man, and I mourned his loss. Special Forces operators were on the front lines when the liberation of Mosul began in October 2016. At immense cost, Mosul was mostly cleared of ISIS fighters by the end of July 2017, though sporadic fighting continued for months. The city was in ruins, and the traumatized civilian population was desolate. By December ISIS had been defeated everywhere in Iraq.

I believe that had U.S. forces retained a modest but effective presence in Iraq after 2011 many of these tragic events might have been avoided or mitigated. Would ISIS nihilists unleashed in the fury and slaughter of the Syrian civil war have extended their dystopian caliphate to Iraq had ten thousand or more Americans been in country? Probably, but with American advisors and airpower already on the scene and embedded with Iraqi security forces, I think their advance would have been blunted before they had seized so much territory and subjected millions to the nightmare of ISIS rule. Would Maliki have concentrated so much power and alienated Sunnis so badly that the insurgency would catch fire again? Would Iran's influence have been as detrimental as it was? Would Iraqis have collaborated to prevent a full-scale civil war from erupting? No one can answer for certain. But I believe that our presence there would have had positive effects. All we can say for certain is that Iraq still has a difficult road to walk, but another opportunity to progress toward that hopeful vision of a democratic, independent nation that's learned to accommodate its sectarian differences, which generations of Iraqis have suffered without and hundreds of thousands of Americans risked everything for.

I had made more trips to Afghanistan than I had made to Iraq these last seven years. I spent Christmas there in 2014, and managed another holiday meal with Jimmy, who had deployed to another combat zone, this time as a corporal in the Army National Guard. With Afghanistan, too, I had a profound difference with the President's decisions. He had campaigned on disengaging in Iraq, and though I thought his decision to get out was a disaster, I have to acknowledge that at least it was consistent with his campaign pledge. He had also promised to get Afghanistan right, and I welcomed his decision in February 2009 to surge seventeen thousand desperately needed troops to Afghanistan to confront a resurgent Taliban and al-Qaeda that required, in his words, "urgent attention and swift action." He ordered another four thousand troops there the next month after completing an Afghanistan policy review, along with a surge of civilian aid workers for what was clearly a counterinsurgency strategy rather than one focused more narrowly on counterterrorism. I welcomed that as well.

And I was enthusiastic about his subsequent choice to command the effort. General Stanley McChrystal was a brilliant and inspiring officer, who had commanded the Joint Special Operations Command (JSOC), a strong advocate of a counterinsurgency plan for Afghanistan, and an ideal choice to command the allied effort there, blandly named the International Security Assistance Force (ISAF). He assumed command in June and after a top-to-bottom review of our war policy reported to Defense Secretary Gates and to President Obama that "Failure to gain the initiative and reverse insurgent momentum in the next . . . [twelve months] . . . risks an outcome where defeating the insurgency is no longer possible." To run an effective counterinsurgency, he needed more troops. Forty thousand was his preference but the minimum he needed was thirty thousand. Either figure was more than the White House wanted to hear. He had been instructed not to present a plan for destroying the Taliban but for degrading them. The report leaked. Purportedly, an angry Obama felt he had been boxed in by McChrystal and by the chairman of the Joint Chiefs, Admiral Mike Mullen, into making a bigger investment in Afghanistan than he wanted to. But, in truth, there were not many senior officers who would have advised any other policy. If you're going to commit American lives to a conflict, you must give them a mission they can win and the support they need to do it.

The situation in Afghanistan was indeed dire, the cost of mistakes by the previous administration and commanders. I had a general idea what McChrystal would report, but I was anxious for it to reach the President's desk and for the President to make a decision. Lindsey, Joe, and I bylined an op-ed for the *Wall Street Journal* that September arguing that "only a decisive force can prevail." The three of us had last been in Afghanistan the month before when we could see the changes made since our visit nine months earlier when we had been alarmed by the direction of the war and the strategy then employed there.

"Our mistakes are infuriating, but they are also reversible," we continued. "A significant shift in our strategic leadership and focus has taken place." But we would need a further significant increase in the force level there and warned against deciding on a number that would represent a middle path between the force level needed to win and no further increases. That was the kind of split-the-difference thinking that had sunk us in a quagmire in Iraq before the 2007 surge decision. We urged the President to do the hard thing and assured him of our support in "the tough months ahead."

The President chose the lower number McChrystal had presented, and announced the decision in a speech to the cadets at the U.S. Military Academy at West Point. He had ordered thirty thousand more troops to Afghanistan to "bring this war to a successful conclusion." Then, to my intense disappointment, he set a nineteen-month deadline for beginning to withdraw our forces from Afghanistan. I issued a statement welcoming the surge of troops, and blasting the utterly arbitrary deadline for ending their mission.

What I do not support, and what concerns me greatly is the President's decision to set an arbitrary date to begin withdrawing U.S. forces from Afghanistan. A date for withdrawal sends exactly the wrong message to both our friends and our enemies—in Afghanistan, Pakistan, and the entire region—all of whom currently doubt whether America is committed to winning this war. A withdrawal date only emboldens Al-Qaeda and the Taliban, while dispiriting our Afghan partners and making it less likely that they will risk their lives to take our side in this fight.

The President hadn't been in office that long, and I don't think he understood warfare at that point. All warfare, even a counterinsurgency, is ultimately about breaking an enemy's will to fight. You won't do that by telling the enemy, We're going to send more troops to the fight, but we'll bring them back in less than two years. You're incentivizing him to wait it out. The way to shorten a war is to make clear to the enemy you're going to do whatever it takes for as long as it takes to defeat them. The Afghanistan war has lasted more than sixteen years. It seems paradoxical to suggest that we can only win by committing to stay indefinitely, but that is the reality. Obama was signaling to the enemy the limit of our resolve, and the enemy calculated they could endure it. Additionally, insisting on the lower number, lower than the one most of his generals were recommending, meant that we would have to fight the Taliban sequentially, surging troops to one part of Afghanistan and turning back the insurgency there, then deploying to another part of the country, leaving the area you had just cleared vulnerable to a resurgent enemy. I don't think any President should ever accept his military commanders' recommendations without challenge. But I kept hearing stories that White House skepticism was becoming dismissiveness. And I heard them again in 2011 when we started to draw down in Afghanistan and the military was warning that they were risking a disaster. The White House would phrase the question, What could you do with five thousand troops? Ten thousand? The right question is What do you need to succeed?, and challenge them on why. Even as a political decision it was dubious. Whatever criticism you got from opponents of the war for increasing the force level, it wouldn't be appreciably more or less if you deployed forty thousand rather than thirty thousand.

The President relieved General McChrystal in June 2010 after some of his subordinates had criticized administration policies and personnel and claimed they were the general's views to a reporter for *Rolling Stone*. I admired General McChrystal a great deal, and I believed his departure to be a serious setback for our efforts in Afghanistan. I was also not certain that the reporter's story was entirely credible. But McChrystal hadn't denied it, at least not publicly. And so, I released a statement criticizing his alleged comments as "inappropriate," and signaled that I would support whatever decision the President made about his future. I also expected the loss of this intelligent and inspirational commander would be a setback for our efforts in Afghanistan, and I was much relieved when the President appointed General Petraeus to replace him. He would command ISAF until the President's scheduled drawdown commenced in the summer of 2011, when another exceptional commander relieved him, Marine Corps General John Allen, a Naval Academy graduate and a blunt, honest leader who never evaded difficult questions about his mission and what he needed to achieve it. After the leaked McChrystal report, the administration never again asked military commanders to provide a number of troops they thought they needed to achieve their mission, but would ask them to respond to proposals they suggested, the what-could-you-do-with-X-number approach. I heard that Allen would answer something like, "I've been asked to respond to the following numbers, but before I do let me say that my best military advice is we need X number of troops here. Now I'll respond to your homework assignment." I also heard that General Joe Dunford, who succeeded Allen as commander of ISAF, while perhaps not as blunt as his predecessor, also chafed at White House micromanagement.

The President announced the beginning of the phased drawdown of U.S. forces in June 2011. The "tide of war is receding," he declared, justifying his decision to withdraw ten thousand troops by the end of the year, and another 23,000 within a year, and continuing on "a steady pace" until all forces were out of the country in 2014. Sixty-five thousand American troops would remain after the first two drawdowns. Secretary of Defense Leon Panetta declared in 2012 that the U.S. would cease combat operations in Afghanistan in 2014 but the administration was still considering the structure of the phased drawdown and how many trainers and Special Forces would stay to conduct counterterrorism operations after 2014. In his 2013 State of the Union address, the President announced that the number of troops in Afghanistan would be reduced to 34,000, after which military commanders would determine the pace of the rest of the drawdown. In May 2014, he announced all U.S. combat operations would end by December of that year. Fewer than ten thousand troops would remain in country, and they would be reduced by half by the end of the following year, and the rest of the force would be out of the country by the end of Obama's term.

I knew these numbers were lower at every phase than the numbers military commanders believed were necessary. And I knew, too, that every date, every announcement, encouraged the Taliban to keep fighting, not to negotiate, but to keep pressing and wait us out. Before he left office, President Obama had decided to keep more than eight thousand troops in Afghanistan. The security situation had so deteriorated, and the Taliban had made so many gains, that the Trump administration wisely announced that henceforth, conditions on the ground would determine troop levels and has to date increased the force to fourteen thousand. I am glad that they did, although it is not clear to me what exactly our strategic plan is for Afghanistan. I am encouraged that Secretary Jim Mattis, with the President's support, recognizes the folly of substituting arbitrary dates for an exit strategy, and I expect the Taliban see the overdue change in approach in how we make decisions about force strength as detrimental to their interests.

As I mentioned earlier, I traveled to Afghanistan frequently over the last seven years, more than once a year on average. I have a great many powerful memories from my visits there, some of them quite unusual. On a trip in 2011, Petraeus, who had really ramped up the village stabilization effort in Afghanistan as he had in Iraq, wanted Lindsey and me to visit one of the projects in the middle of nowhere in northeastern Afghanistan. We flew by helicopter. It was a very austere, ominous place, and you could sense the danger. A Special Forces major, Jim Gant, ran the show, and he was quite a character. He had gone full mujahedeen in his appearance, long beard, native attire, baggy pants, vest, headgear, the works. He had made friends with the village leaders and a lot of the locals, who appeared as amused by him as we were. He would provoke the Taliban on the radio and leaflet their areas, questioning their manhood, taunting them to come out and fight. Reportedly, he had a girlfriend, an American reporter who came to interview him one day, and never left, or something like that. He was quite an operator, and brave as hell.

Of all my memories of Afghanistan, I treasure most of all the many reenlistment ceremonies I've attended there. Some were big events in a Bagram hangar or in an ISAF headquarters courtyard. Others were smaller and more subdued affairs in a Forward Operating Base in some remote part of the country. They all meant so much more to me than they could have possibly meant to the soldiers there. I mean it. There they were, many of them after multiple combat deployments, aged beyond their years, having seen the worst and the best of humanity, having risked everything for our country and its causes, signing up to do it some more. My God, they are a blessing to this nation, a living rebuke to cynicism and empty patriotism.

For many years, I often told the story of a friend of mine from prison, a man who epitomized to me the soldier's strained and selfless valor. But I had mostly stopped recounting it after 2008 because I thought by that time there weren't many Americans who hadn't heard me tell it. I told it for the first time in a long time at a reenlistment ceremony in Jalalabad in 2012. There were hundreds of soldiers there. As I looked out on their tired faces, I couldn't think what else to tell them, other than I'd seen such perseverance before and that it had inspired me forever after.

In 1971, the North Vietnamese moved us from conditions of isolation into large rooms with as many as thirty to forty men to a room. This was, as you can imagine, a wonderful change. One of the men moved into my cell was Mike Christian. Mike came from a small town and a poor family near Selma, Alabama. He didn't wear a pair of shoes until he was thirteen years old. At seventeen, he enlisted in the U.S. Navy. He later earned a commission, and became a flying officer. He was shot down and captured in 1967. Mike had a keen and deep appreciation for the opportunities this country—and our military—provide for people who want to work and want to succeed.

The uniforms we wore in prison consisted of a blue short-sleeved shirt, trousers that looked like pajama trousers, and rubber sandals that were made out of automobile tires. I recommend them highly; one pair lasted my entire stay.

As part of the change in treatment, the Vietnamese allowed some prisoners to receive packages from home. In some packages were handkerchiefs, scarves, and other items of clothing. Mike got himself a piece of white cloth and a piece of red cloth and fashioned a bamboo needle. Over a period of a couple months, he sewed the American flag on the inside of his shirt.

Every afternoon, before we had a bowl of soup, we would hang Mike's shirt on the wall of our cell and say the Pledge of Allegiance. I know that saying the Pledge of Allegiance might not seem the most important or meaningful part of our day now, but I can assure you that for the men in that stark prison cell, it was, indeed, the most important and meaningful event of our day.

One day, the Vietnamese searched our cell and discovered Mike's shirt with the flag sewn inside and removed it. That evening they returned, opened the door of the cell, called for Mike Christian to come out, closed the door of the cell and, for the benefit of all of us, beat Mike Christian severely for the next couple of hours. Then they opened the door of the cell and threw him back inside.

He was not in good shape. We tried to comfort and take care of him as well as we could. The cell in which we lived had a concrete slab in the middle on which we slept and four naked light bulbs in each corner of the room.

After things quieted down, I went to lie down to go to sleep. As I did, I happened to look in the corner of the room. Sitting there, beneath that dim light bulb, with a piece of white cloth, a piece of red cloth, another shirt and his bamboo needle, his eyes almost shut from the beating, was my friend, Mike Christian, sewing another American flag.

He wasn't doing it because it made him feel better. He was making that flag because he knew how important it was for us to be able to pledge our allegiance to our flag and country.

It seems that I won't be returning to Afghanistan anytime soon. I regret that very much. I think we have all had over the last year or so reason to wonder about the direction of our country and some of the people leading it. I would like to be again in the company of Americans who embody our nation's greatness, and who know it is something more profound and dearer than a politician's campaign slogan.

CHAPTER FIVE

ARAB SPRING

MOHAMED BOUAZIZI WAS BORN POOR AND WITHOUT rights, and he died in the same condition. He lived his entire life in Sidi Bouzid, a city in central Tunisia. He had worked as a street vendor since he was a child to help support his family. He sold produce from a wheelbarrow. He was routinely harassed by the city's notoriously corrupt police for bribes he could not afford to pay, and his goods were frequently confiscated. He was accosted by a female municipal official on the morning of December 17, 2010, purportedly for not possessing a vending permit. His vegetables and weighing scales were confiscated. The woman is alleged to have slapped Bouazizi in the face, humiliating him. He went to the provincial government headquarters to file a complaint and ask that his scales be returned to him. He was turned away. He returned a short while later with a can of gasoline, drenched himself in it outside the building's entrance, and lit himself on fire. He would die of his burns eighteen days later. He was twenty-six years old.

That evening, Bouazizi's mother demonstrated outside the government building where he had staged his fatal protest. A relative posted a videotape of the grieving woman on Facebook. Al Jazeera picked it up and aired it that evening. Outraged protesters, fed up with the endemic corruption, lack of opportunity, and oppression under Tunisia's autocratic president, Zine el-Abidine Ben Ali, took to the streets. The police attempted to confront the protesters, who rioted in response. Word of the protests in Sidi Bouzid spread rapidly through social media, and Tunisians in other cities, predominantly young men and women, started protests. After Bouazizi died and five thousand people marched in his funeral procession, the protests spread nationwide and to other autocratic regimes in the Middle East. The Arab Spring had begun.

Democratic internationalists had predicted for years that the autocracies of the Middle East would come undone when generations of young people without jobs, without hope, and without recourse had finally had enough and revolted. And in early 2011 that's exactly what seemed to be happening. Ten days after Bouazizi's death, the Tunisian military refused to crack down on the protests and Ben Ali fled to Saudi Arabia, where he was given asylum. Mass protests began in Cairo's Tahrir Square on January 25. Seventeen days later, on February 11, Hosni Mubarak, who had ruled Egypt for more than three decades, was forced out of office when Egypt's armed forces, like Tunisia's, refused to intervene to save him. Protests against Muammar Qaddafi's regime began in Libya four days later, and quickly triggered a civil war when the regime tried to suppress them. Within a few days, regime opponents were in control of Benghazi. By March, the United States and its NATO allies had intervened militarily on the side of the rebels. Widespread protests against President Ali Abdullah Saleh erupted in Yemen in mid-January, and confrontations with the regime turned immediately violent. The majority Shia population of Bahrain demonstrated against the Sunni monarchy in mid-February, and within a month the king had declared martial law and Saudi Arabia and the Emirates had dispatched troops to violently suppress the protests. The first big protests in Syria began outside the capital of Damascus and other major urban areas in March, but soon spread everywhere. The response from Bashar al-Assad's regime was so brutal it started one of the most barbarous, destabilizing civil wars in living memory, a shocking humanitarian crisis that persists to this day. In all but Tunisia, winter would follow spring, and another Middle East generation desperate for change would see their hopes lost to a restoration of despotism or worse.

As some of the ancien régimes under duress, in particular Tunisia, Bahrain, and especially Egypt, were U.S. allies, the Obama administration's response to the regional wave of democratic uprisings would be tugged in different directions by the demands of security interests and the moral appeal of political ideals. That conflict was complicated by the fact that in many of these oppressed societies, Islamists provided the most potent opposition, particularly where the Muslim Brotherhood, accustomed to decades of persecution, had the organizing skills and cunning to dominate the politics of the revolution, if not in the first sudden explosion of exuberant youthful rebellion, then in the complex maneuvering and militancy that followed.

I would criticize many of the administration's decisions concerning these revolutions, but I recognized what a daunting array of challenges the Arab Spring presented to American policymakers. I thought it right to support the protests, and urge a peaceful transition of power and the creation of new political processes that welcomed the participation of all parties committed to democratic principles and the rule of law. I thought that welcome would have to include parties that were expressly Islamist if their democratic commitment was not just to one or two free elections or however many it took for them to come to power, and their commitment to justice applied the protections of the law equally to all. Middle Eastern societies, misruled and corrupted decade after decade, where political, religious, and personal differences are often violently prosecuted, have pathologies that aren't easily tamed. But I don't believe there is any way to get rid of them other than to open those societies to democratic political habits that in time lead to a broader distribution of economic opportunity, equal justice, and the government's accountability to the governed.

Joe Lieberman and I made plans to travel to the Middle East in February 2011. We would meet in Tunisia, before traveling on to Lebanon, Jordan, Israel, and finally to Egypt. We arrived on different flights, and rendezvoused at a cemetery on the Mediterranean to pay our respects to the Americans killed in North Africa in World War II. It is a beautiful and serene place, one of the most beautiful of the many plots of land in all the far-flung foreign locations where Americans rest who gave their lives for their country and someone else's.

Following Ben Ali's exile, Tunisia entered a protracted period of political uncertainty. The prime minister, Mohamed Ghannouchi, had formed a caretaker government with holdovers from Ben Ali's party, as well as opposition representatives, although no one from Ennahda, the main Islamist party, which had been banned by Ben Ali, had been included. We met with the prime minister and his defense minister. They would both be out of office the next week. Protest rallies had continued across the country and had intensified in recent days. Ghannouchi was forced to resign on February 27.

The most interesting exchanges we had were with civil society activists, mostly young idealists, who were guiding the revolution on the streets and online. We had dinner with them at the ambassador's residence. To an old geezer, they seemed impossibly young and energetic, and to an old cynic, very self-assured. But they fascinated me. We told them we admired their courage, and we hoped they might be the start of the Arab world's transformation. I sensed that their ambitions weren't quite that grand. They wanted an accountable government and economic opportunities. But of such desires sweeping revolutions can be made. They explained how they had used social media to communicate and coordinate their protests. The Internet was heavily censored by Ben Ali's government, but not, curiously, Facebook, which became their main communication platform. I asked what assistance we could provide them and if there was anyone in the U.S.

they wanted to speak to that we might be able to connect them with. It was unanimous. Mark Zuckerberg was their man. "If it wasn't for Facebook," one of them said, "there would've been no revolution." They wanted to invite Zuckerberg to come to Tunisia, and asked me to intercede on their behalf. I told them I'd try to get in touch with him when I was back in the States. I did, too. I put in a call to him right after I returned, and told him that he was a hero to a group of extraordinary kids who were trying to change the Middle East, and were using his creation to do it. They wanted very much for him to come to Tunis, and I offered to put him in touch with some of them if he was so inclined. Alas, he didn't appear to be, and I didn't hear from him again.

The other fascinating encounter we had was with a Tunisian businessman, Mondher Ben Ayed, whom we had been advised was one of the shrewdest, best-connected people in the country. He did have an insightful view, given the confusing scene it appeared to us, of where Tunisia was headed. A period of instability would continue until a new constitution was drafted, but he believed the prospects were good for Tunisia's successful transition to a modern representative democracy as long as the economy along with the political system was opened to ordinary Tunisians. Economic reforms were essential to ensuring the success of political reforms. He also seemed rather sure that Ennahda would figure prominently in that transition, and would not, as some in the West feared, subvert it.

That is what happened. Ennahda was sort of the Tunisian chapter of the Muslim Brotherhood, but it is more committed to the conviction that democracy and Islam are compatible. Ennahda won the most seats in parliamentary elections in October, though not an outright majority, and governed in a coalition with secular parties. A longtime dissident who'd been living in exile, Moncef Marzouki, was selected president in December, and he appointed the leader of Ennahda, Hamadi Jebali, prime minister. Some months before the election, Jebali came to Washington under the auspices of an organization that promoted democratic norms in Islamist political movements, and met with Joe and me to assure us of his party's commitment to democracy. Ennahda is everything that democratic internationalists ask of religious parties. They reject sharia law and accept the secular character of government, which alienated the more militant Islamists in Tunisia. Although analogies to American political models aren't really apt, if we explained Ennahda's issue positioning using our references, we would probably describe them as socially centrist and economically liberal. The next time we saw Mr. Ayed, on a subsequent visit to Tunisia in 2012, he was a senior advisor to Prime Minister Jebali.

We traveled to Lebanon after our stop in Tunis, and from Lebanon to Jordan. It was on our flight to Amman that Joe and I discussed whether we should call for the U.S. and our NATO allies to intervene militarily in Libya. The uprising against the regime began in Benghazi, and Qaddafi's security forces had cracked down as soon as the first protesters had taken to the streets. Six demonstrators were killed in Benghazi on the second day of protests. Opposition groups called for a "Day of Revolt" the following day. Police snipers and helicopter gunships had fired into the crowd. Demonstrators marched in cities across eastern Libya, and were met with violence. The first protests in Tripoli started on February 20. By then, hundreds of demonstrators had been killed in Benghazi, but the opposition was now in control of most of the city, and some military units stationed in eastern Libya began changing sides. Prominent Libyan diplomats defected and called on the U.N. Security Council to impose sanctions on the regime. They would soon be joined by Libya's ambassador to the U.N., who had defended the regime for more than a week before breaking with it in an emotional speech. "They are asking for their freedom," he said, referring to the protests. "They are asking for their rights. They did not throw a single stone and they were killed. I tell my brother, Qaddafi, leave the Libyans alone."

Violence was now general everywhere in the country including the capital. A civil war was under way. Rebels were in control of most of eastern Libya, but Qaddafi still held most of the rest of the country. Claiming he had "brought glory" to Libyans, he refused to relinquish power, and threatened a Tiananmen-like response. He called on supporters to attack the "cockroaches" opposing him and promised to "cleanse Libya house by house." Libyan air and naval power bombed and shelled rebels, defecting army units, and civilians. The opposition beseeched the West for help. Joe and I discussed the pros and cons of endorsing the request. The situation was confused and fast-moving, and we wondered if, for all his vitriol, Qaddafi wasn't just days away from fleeing the country. We were also mindful about getting too far out ahead of the U.S. and allied governments, but by the time we landed we had decided to take Qaddafi at his word, that the threat of wholesale slaughter at the hands of a dying tyranny was too great to ignore. We issued a statement that day. We were the first members of Congress to take a public stand for intervention. "We are appalled by what appear to be crimes against humanity occurring in Libya," we declared. "The Qaddafi regime's ongoing slaughter and oppression is deplorable and must end." We called on other Libyan government and military officials to break with the regime, and for the international community to intervene.

There is an array of measures that the United States and our global partners, including the European Union and African Union, should immediately pursue. Some Libyan diplomats have bravely called for a no-fly zone to stop the Qaddafi regime's use of airpower to attack Libyan civilians. We support this course of action.

After Jordan we spent Shabbat in Israel and flew to Egypt Saturday night. The crowds in Tahrir Square had thinned by then, and the place was cleared of debris after the nearly three-week protest had achieved its principal aim. Mubarak was gone and the Supreme Council of the Armed Forces had assumed temporary control of the government. We walked through the square. There were still protesters there but in reduced numbers. The streets were mostly quiet, and there were tanks on every corner. We had one full day in country and it was a busy one. We met with the head of the Supreme Council, Field Marshal Mohamed Hussein Tantawi, whom I had known for decades, and with the foreign minister and prime minister. We talked with Amr Moussa, the longtime Arab League secretary-general, who had stepped down presumably to run in Egypt's presidential election. It was Sunday, so I indulged my regular Sunday habit. I did an interview with *Meet the Press* from Tahrir Square, where I repeated our call for a no-fly zone in Libya. Qaddafi was "using airpower and helicopters to continue these massacres," I noted. "We've got to get tough." I made clear that I wasn't advocating U.S. ground troops, but using U.S. and allied airpower to stop Qaddafi from murdering his own people. "Qaddafi's days are numbered," I contended. "The question is how many [people] are going to be massacred before he goes."

Again, our most interesting encounter was with the mostly young people who had been in the vanguard of the revolution. They were part of a group of opposition leaders the U.S. ambassador had convened to talk with us. We were no doubt regarded by the assembly, as most American politicians would've been, as patrons of the Mubarak regime. That was understandable. A close relationship with Mubarak had long been considered an essential instrument of U.S. interests in the Middle East. Joe and I had met numerous times with the deposed Egyptian president. But we also had an open-door policy for meeting Egyptian dissidents, and regularly stressed with Egyptian officials the need for political reform. I had given a speech at the Munich Conference in 2005 urging regimes in the Arab world, particularly Egypt's, to liberalize. We had co-sponsored in 2010 a resolution offered by Russ Feingold that called on Mubarak to allow international observers to monitor the presidential election scheduled for the following year. We were informed by Egypt's ambassador that we had hurt the president's feelings. The people raising concerns about the election, the ambassador insisted, "are all terrorists. President Mubarak values your friendship, and is shocked you signed on to this misguided resolution." Mubarak was deep in the bunker then.

The opposition leaders were a mixed bag of older, longtime Mubarak critics who had been marginalized over the years, a few retired diplomats who hoped to be summoned back into service in the country's hour of need, and then these young people with their colloquial English and high-tech sophistication. At one point, a former Egyptian ambassador, elegantly dressed in pinstripes, was belaboring the fact that the U.S. had been Mubarak's ally. While he appreciated our interest in their movement, he continued, honesty required him to point out that there couldn't be any rapprochement between the Egyptian people and the U.S. government until we dealt with the plight of the Palestinians. That is a complaint any American official traveling in the Middle East will hear repeated constantly. I sank back in the chair I was sitting in, a little bored, I suppose, and subconsciously disappointed that in this moment of promise, this little glimmer of hope that the maladies of the Middle East, most of which had little if anything to do with the plight of the Palestinians, might be improved by the political transformation of afflicted societies, we were going to get wrapped around the axle by another anti-Zionist rant from another Arab statesman. Then, to my relief and intrigue, one of the young men present interrupted the well-dressed bore. "Ambassador, with respect," he began. "We're not here to discuss the Palestinians. We're here to talk about the Egyptian people. We want to focus these senators on our needs in this next period of our history."

Alas, that period of Egyptian history will be a chronicle of disappointments, an uprising against authoritarianism and injustice that opened a path to power for an Islamist party, the Muslim Brotherhood, which wouldn't manage the transition to secular politics and brought disorder, intolerance, and another upheaval, which ended with a popularly supported military coup and a return of authoritarianism. But for a moment, in that abrupt dismissal by the young of the failed conventions of the old, we could glimpse what could have been, what should have been, and what I believe one day will be. We left for home encouraged by a genuine sense of promise, and eager to go back.

We hadn't met with any Muslim Brotherhood representatives on that first post-Mubarak visit, though I would in subsequent trips to Egypt, six more in total over the next two years. At the time, I was skeptical the Muslim Brotherhood could be trusted to adhere to democratic norms no matter what promises they made. I raised those doubts in interviews, observing that revolutions can go bad, and often do. I would eventually come to the view that the Muslim Brotherhood should be allowed to run in the election. They had renounced violence, and pledged to play by the rules. I was still skeptical, and didn't like the views they espoused, but I was open to the idea that this might be a phase democratizing Arab societies had to go through before embracing a more secular politics.

I went back to Egypt twice over the next four months, the first trip on my own and the second with John Kerry, who chaired the Foreign

Relations Committee. Although the Supreme Council of the Armed Forces was regarded by many, if not most, Egyptians as a legitimate temporary governing authority, public protests demanding an end to military rule continued until elections for a new parliament were held at the end of the year, and a presidential election was held in June 2012. I met again with my old acquaintance Field Marshal Tantawi, who stressed the military's firm intention to turn the country over to civilian rule at the earliest practicable opportunity. I met with scores of Egyptians engaged in building the institutions of civil society, at leadership positions and at the nuts-and-bolts level, and with business community leaders to get an appreciation for their progress. I solicited their views on whether they trusted the military to keep its commitment, and which politicians and political parties were in the best position to form a civilian government. Most expected the armed forces to follow through on the commitment, and more than one of my exchanges included the observation that the Muslim Brotherhood would do well in any fair election.

And they did. They won a plurality of the seats in parliamentary elections held at the end of 2011 and beginning of 2012, and in coalition with another Islamist party controlled almost 70 percent of the parliament. It seemed likely that the Brotherhood would win the presidential election, too, if they chose to run a candidate, which they had announced they would not do. I assume their initial position was taken out of fear that the military would reconsider its acquiescence to a civilian government. I brought another Senate delegation to Egypt in February 2012 just as the last of the parliamentary runoff elections were concluding. I hoped to use the trip to begin establishing a dialogue between members of Congress and leaders of the ascendant power in Egypt.

But I had another, more immediate responsibility to take up with my friend Field Marshal Tantawi. In December, just before the start of the elections, Egyptian security services had launched an armed raid on the offices of seventeen human rights and pro-democracy NGOs, including three American organizations, Freedom House, the National Democratic Institute (NDI), and the International Republican Institute (IRI), whose board of directors I chair, confiscating records, computers, and cash, none of which were ever recovered. NDI and IRI staff were prohibited from leaving Egypt, including IRI's Egypt director, who was the son of an old friend, former Illinois congressman Ray LaHood, who at the time was President Obama's transportation secretary. The Americans had to seek sanctuary in the U.S. embassy, where they had been living ever since, while our very dedicated ambassador, Anne Patterson, worked to get the travel ban lifted. I had already released a statement blasting the unexpected assault on American humanitarians, warning that it "could set back the long-standing partnership between the United States and Egypt." A week before we arrived, the Egyptians had escalated the crisis and filed criminal charges against forty-three of the aid workers, nineteen of them Americans, including Sam LaHood.

A Mubarak crony and minister for foreign aid organizations under Tantawi (and currently national security advisor to President Abdel Fattah el-Sisi), Faiza Abou el-Naga, had instigated the raids and prosecution. She's a longtime antagonist of democratic internationalists involved in party training, election monitoring, and other civil society efforts in Egypt. Most observers assumed she would lose power with Mubarak's departure, but she actually became more influential with the military. She blamed the NGOs for Mubarak's downfall, which is ridiculous, but she is unpersuadable on the subject.

My first task was to help Anne get the Americans out of Egypt before Abou el-Naga did something even more stupid. To do that, I had to suppress my natural outrage over the mistreatment of Americans, who had done nothing more nefarious than work to help Egyptians decide for themselves who would govern them. I had to adopt a tone and approach that could defend the work of the NGOs without jeopardizing efforts to get the victims safely out of the country. Joint Chiefs chairman General Martin Dempsey had appealed directly to Tantawi the week before to no apparent avail, as had Central Command CinC General Jim Mattis. A delegation of generals from Egypt visiting Washington had been ordered to return to Cairo before they could be harangued about the aid workers by members of Congress. I had stated in advance of the trip that it wasn't my intention to negotiate their release, but only to underscore to Egyptian authorities how seriously the U.S. Congress was taking the matter. As a rule, Egyptian generals, as political as any political party in Egypt, don't like to be perceived as making concessions to Americans immediately after they've been asked to make them. Standing up to the Americans was good politics in that fraught moment of Egyptian history. There was much lingering resentment, not just in Abou el-Naga's aggrieved attitude, but among the generals, too, over the U.S. government's lack of support in the crisis for Mubarak considering Mubarak had often been accused of being Washington's lackey. I had to be diplomatic. But I would struggle to keep my anger in check when my appeals were met invariably with references to laws that hadn't been broken and a judicial process that was clearly prejudicial.

I made the case I could—that U.S. and Egyptian relations were too important to be undone by a misunderstanding—to everyone we met with on that trip, starting with Tantawi, who was inscrutable in response. We met with parliament representatives, including the speaker, who was a member of the Muslim Brotherhood's party. I didn't make overt demands, just pleaded with each host to help defuse a crisis that was in neither country's interests. To Tantawi, I allowed that the Americans in jeopardy were "my people," as IRI chairman, and I had a personal interest in getting them home. They were mostly young and idealistic and there to do good. They shouldn't be treated as criminals. We need to resolve this, I said, and until we do our relationship isn't going to return to normal.

Our first meeting with a Muslim Brotherhood official was at the Brotherhood's headquarters with the deputy leader of the organization, Khairat el-Shater, a tall, imposing man but with a relaxed and open manner that put the delegation at ease. He had an interesting conversation with Jeff Sessions about the religious character of the Brotherhood's positions, in which he suggested there wasn't as much difference between their views and the way Americans viewed the role of religion in a democracy. Americans, he observed, are free to invoke their religious beliefs in official settings. Benedictions are given at your official ceremonies. God is referred to on your currency, and in your Pledge of Allegiance. There is a role for religion in public life in Egypt just like there is in America. Jeff couldn't have agreed more. The connection between a Muslim Brotherhood leader and one of the most conservative members of the U.S. Congress was an unexpected, to say the least, cultural appropriation.

Curiously, it was the Brotherhood representatives we met with who indicated the most willingness to be helpful. They made no promises, but emphasized they had played no role in the decision to initiate the prosecution, and agreed it would be a mistake to let it cause a serious breach in relations. Obviously, they had self-interested motives in appearing to Americans as less instinctively anti-U.S. than we had good reason to believe they were. But that didn't matter to me if it resulted in their assistance in getting our people safely out of Egypt.

That happened a couple weeks after we left Egypt just after the Americans' case had gone to trial. Some of the judges presiding over the trial had resigned. A few days later the Americans were on a chartered plane out of the country, except for one individual on the NDI team, who insisted on remaining in Egypt as an act of solidarity with his Egyptian colleagues. The popular reaction in Egypt was quite negative and contradictory. Angry protesters accused the government of inventing a case against the Americans only to cave to American pressure and injure the nation's pride. The Muslim Brotherhood released a statement insisting they had played no role in their release. The defendants were subsequently tried in absentia that summer, and convicted. That angered me, and the fact that our people were safely home meant that in future meetings with Egyptian officials I could allow myself to be more demonstrative in my protests over the injustice. A few weeks after their wrongful conviction, Mohamed Morsi, the Brotherhood's candidate selected after Khairat el-Shater had been disqualified, won Egypt's presidential election. The Supreme Council of the Armed Forces acquiesced to his inauguration but demanded the dissolution of parliament and reserved certain political powers for itself.

Morsi would govern for a year before protesters were back in the streets in full force, demanding his removal from office. He would be deposed in a military coup the next month. In the fall of 2012, he had given himself powers to legislate in the absence of parliament without judicial review, and to control, also without judicial review, the writing of a new constitution for Egypt. Protests erupted immediately as secularist politicians accused Morsi of "presidential tyranny." The new constitution ratified by a Brotherhood-controlled constitutional assembly confirmed their fears. Morsi had refused to make concessions to secularists, liberals, moderates, or the courts. The constitution gave greater powers to the president at the expense of the judiciary, and extended them to areas that had been the purview of the military. It declared sharia law as the basis for all laws and gave the government responsibility to "ensure public morality." More protests ensued.

The situation was rapidly deteriorating when I went back to Egypt with a large delegation concerned about the recent turn of events for the primary purpose of meeting with Morsi to state our concerns. In addition to his aggregation of powers and the decidedly Islamist constitution he had secured, attacks on Egypt's Coptic Christian community by Islamist extremists were multiplying, and would escalate the following year. Compounding the problem was the recent disclosure of anti-Semitic remarks Morsi had made a couple years earlier. He had called Israelis "bloodsuckers" and the "descendants of apes and pigs." Morsi claimed he had been quoted out of context. It was hard to imagine what an appropriate context might have been. The meeting was long and did not prove particularly productive. We had to explain to him why Americans were upset over his anti-Semitic statements, and that provoked an extended monologue about the Muslim Brotherhood view of Israel. Morsi had pledged as a candidate that he would keep the peace with Israel and honor Egypt's Camp David commitments, but it was clear he was more accustomed to the Brotherhood's militant view of Israel. We emphasized, too, the necessity of compromise and concession to successful governance. But I left the meeting with a strong feeling that the Brotherhood's hold on power was going to be very brief. Before we left Egypt, we met with the new defense minister who had replaced General Tantawi. I didn't know Abdel Fattah el-Sisi as well as I had known Tantawi. I'm certain we had met once or twice on my many trips to Egypt, but I couldn't recall any exchanges of interest we might have had.

I would see Sisi again in August a month after public protests had exploded, millions of demonstrators in Cairo had demanded Morsi's ouster, many of them surrounding the presidential palace, and the military had stepped in to enforce the people's will. Pro-Morsi demonstrators took to the streets to demand his restoration and clashed with anti-Morsi crowds. The violence that ensued looked like it might plunge the country into a very dark time. Lindsey and I flew there to appeal to both sides to step back from the brink. The army had already jailed Morsi and many other senior Brotherhood figures. Protests were still raging for and against Morsi.

Our message to the Muslim Brotherhood was, You were forced out by widespread popular demand that gave the military the opening because you dug in your heels and wouldn't make concessions. Don't compound the mistake by turning to violence. Let the Egyptian people see you call for reconciliation and cooperation. You can't win an armed confrontation. Our message to Sisi was, Be magnanimous in victory, the country can't continue in this direction, it will become ungovernable. You've got the upper hand, reach out and try to separate the Islamists you can work with from the intractable extremists. We asked his permission to meet with Morsi. He didn't say no explicitly, but he made it clear he wasn't going to allow it. He gave the impression of being a pretty cold-blooded individual, and there was a lot of ego inside the uniform he was wearing. In his view, the country was going off the rails and he had stepped in, heroically, to rescue it. He was the nation's savior, and now he was going to do what was necessary to end the chaos and insecurity. He didn't say, I'm going to arrest every Muslim Brotherhood member I can get my hands on, and kill a lot of people in the process. But he communicated clearly to us that the country needed order, and he was going to accomplish that, and he didn't really care who he had to destroy to do it or what we thought about it. It was an ominous exchange and it was clear in which direction things were heading. Deputy Secretary of State Bill Burns, one of the most capable members of the Obama foreign policy team, was in Egypt at the same time, and agreed with our assessment.

We discussed with our ambassador, Anne Patterson, how we should answer the inevitable question we were going to get at a press availability we had scheduled: "Do we consider the military's intervention a coup?" We both thought, as undiplomatic as that would sound to the generals, there really wasn't anything else we could call it. Anne worried that no one would hear any other part of our message, including our calls for dialogue and national reconciliation. They would just hear the word "coup." One side would be offended and the other incited. There was truth in her concern. But there really wasn't anything else we could call it. The Egyptian armed forces had removed an elected president from office, arrested him and his associates, and assumed governing authority. That's a textbook definition of a military coup, and calling it a banana would only sacrifice our credibility. So we called it a coup, and as predicted our comment blew up in the Egyptian and international media. There were no more meetings with officials in the new regime. We managed to meet with a couple Muslim Brotherhood representatives who weren't in jail yet, and then we left the country.

I haven't been back since. Sisi did ask to see Lindsey and me when he was in Washington last year to meet with President Trump. We went to his suite at the Four Seasons. Before the meeting, a Sisi aide had communicated that the President did not wish to discuss the continuing liability of the NDI and IRI staffers. Their convictions had never been overturned, and I regularly remonstrated with Egyptian officials, including Sisi, over that injustice. As long as their convictions stood, any one of them could be subject to an Interpol arrest warrant. It is a damn disgrace, and not the act of an ally. But the purpose of Sisi's trip was to reestablish his legitimacy in the eyes of official Washington. Trump had obliged him. Now he expected Lindsey and me to do the same. To that end, he was pleased to discuss other subjects of mutual interest, but not a matter that would cause him political discomfort for no appreciable gain. As soon as we were ushered into his suite and exchanged greetings, I began to lobby him on the forbidden subject as did Lindsey. He listened for a while, one of his aides tried to change subjects unsuccessfully, and then Sisi brought the encounter to an abrupt halt with something that sounded vaguely like a threat. "Don't damage this relationship, Senators. If you do this it will be on you. I am a stubborn and hard fighter." Needless to say, we left the Four Seasons with little expectation either of us would be going back to Egypt for a while.

I made my first trip to Libya in April 2011, over the initial objections of the Obama administration. I had wanted to go to Benghazi since Joe and I had endorsed U.S. military intervention in the civil war. The administration, understandably, was reluctant to have a U.S. senator in the country while a civil war was raging, even if Benghazi was in rebel hands. Chris Stevens, the administration's special envoy to the provisional Libyan rebel government, the National Transitional Council (NTC), was there as was a USAID team. So there was something like an official U.S. diplomatic presence in Benghazi that could coordinate my visit and see to it that I didn't wander into any real harm. Nevertheless, my repeated insistence that I be allowed to go was met with repeated resistance until the Qataris offered to fly me into the city. I informed the administration I would be traveling to Benghazi courtesy of the Emir of Qatar, at which point they relented, and arranged to fly me from Crete to Benghazi. I spent a night in Crete, where, at the insistence of the administration, my Navy escort officer, Captain Jim Loeblein, remained behind. The President had maintained since the announcement that the U.S. would fly air strikes that no American ground troops would be deployed to any operation in Libya. Apparently, the prohibition extended to a surface warfare naval officer assigned to staff a U.S. senator. We flew to Benghazi without him early the next morning on an old Dash 8 turboprop that belonged to our embassy in Baghdad.

I should be more specific. This was my first visit to Libya since the rebellion began, and I would make five more trips there over the next

three years. But it was not my first trip ever to Libya. That had been
a visit I made to the country two years before, when I had one of the
more unusual meetings with a head of state I have ever had, a 'round
midnight discussion with Muammar Qaddafi in his desert compound
outside Tripoli. Joe, Lindsey, Susan Collins, and I had been scheduled
to depart the hotel for the meeting at four o'clock, but were informed
by our Foreign Ministry minder that "Brother Leader" wasn't prepared to meet with us yet, and that we should delay our departure
a little while. Five o'clock arrived, and we were instructed to wait a
bit longer. Six o'clock, still not ready. Seven o'clock, the same, and
again at eight o'clock. Finally, as nine o'clock arrived, I announced
to my colleagues, our embassy officials, and our Libyan hosts that
unless we left within the hour, I was going to bed. Since we were leaving Libya in the morning, we would have to forgo the pleasure of
Brother Leader's company on this visit. That seemed to have an effect
on the Libyans, and a little before ten o'clock we were in a motorcade
speeding through the desert on a deserted highway in total darkness
for forty-five minutes en route to the Bab al-Azizia compound. We
learned later that we had taken a circuitous route to delay the meeting
until Qaddafi was at last ready to receive us. Finally, we approached
an army base where bright stadium lights had turned night into day,
illuminating a polo match under way, and not the water sport variety,
but the one with riders and ponies and mallets. It was an unusual
sight given the circumstances. We passed the polo field and turned
down a road that led to a dirt track, which we continued on for about
a mile until we reached Qaddafi's "tent," which, to my eyes, appeared
to be a Winnebago RV.

We met with Qaddafi's son first, who served as his national security
advisor, and two other aides. The discussion continued for a half hour
or so until, at long last, our night-owl host entered the room, wearing white jeans and a black shirt with little green maps of Africa on

it. He gave a rambling presentation that included references to a plot by Bulgarian nurses to infect Libyan children with the HIV virus. He began with an observation that had I not supported the surge in Iraq, I would have been elected President. Qaddafi had voluntarily surrendered his weapons of mass destruction in 2003, including a nuclear program, and there had been intermittent efforts since then to have something like normal relations with his government. There was some talk about improving security cooperation, but the only topic that gained any traction with the mercurial dictator concerned one of the bombers who had destroyed Pan Am Flight 103 over Lockerbie, Scotland. Britain was about to release him from prison for medical reasons, and we warned Qaddafi that were he given a hero's welcome in Tripoli it would have a very bad effect on public opinion in the U.S. Qaddafi responded that he could not control the Libyan people's reaction, to which Joe responded, "That may be, but then we won't be able to control the American people's reaction, either." Qaddafi ended the meeting not long after that exchange. We drove back to the hotel in half the time it had taken us to get there.

I hadn't known Chris Stevens before I met him in Benghazi, although he had worked on the Senate Foreign Relations Committee as a Foreign Service fellow. He was a talented diplomat, and an exceptional human being. He believed in what he was doing, supporting the Libyan people's rights to freedom and justice, and helping them build an open society, and he was effective. I was bound to like the guy. We had the same hopes for Libya, and the same faith and optimism they could achieve them. He was a go-getter, a risk-taker, who didn't wait on events but tried to shape them. He was positive, good-humored, and fun to be with. I liked and admired him a great deal, and I miss him very much.

The NATO air campaign was then about a month old. It had begun after the head of the provisional government, the National Transitional Council, had implored the West to establish a no-fly zone in eastern Libya and protect civilian populations. Qaddafi, who was moving armored and infantry columns to Benghazi from the south, had threatened to show Benghazi "no mercy." He swore he would go "door to door" to "snuff out the rats." When Joe and I had returned from that first trip to Egypt, we worked with John Kerry to get an understanding from the Pentagon of what enforcing a no-fly zone in Libya would entail, and to build support for it in the Senate and the White House. Toward that end, Kerry and I sponsored a bipartisan resolution authorizing the use of military force in Libya for a year. Inside the administration, U.N. Ambassador Samantha Power, National Security Advisor Susan Rice, and Secretary of State Hillary Clinton were the strongest advocates for intervention.

France and the U.K. were the first NATO countries to call for air strikes. They introduced a resolution in the U.N. Security Council approving a no-fly zone, and authorizing all necessary means to protect civilians, but expressly ruling out the use of ground forces. In response, and hoping to head off the inevitable, the Libyan foreign minister announced a cease-fire the next day. It was seen as an obvious ruse as the regime continued operations against a rebel-held city in western Libya, Misrata, and armor and ground troops were still approaching Benghazi. The French struck first on March 19, hitting regime forces converging on Benghazi. The U.S., U.K., and seven other countries also struck targets that day, with the U.S. planes concentrating on Qaddafi's air defenses and airfields, while the U.S. Sixth Fleet imposed a blockade of Libya's ports.

The U.S. Africa Command commanded the operations that first week. But by March 25, President Obama made the decision to transfer control of the campaign, which had expanded to include nineteen nations, to NATO under the command of a Canadian Air Force general. He explained his reasoning for intervening in Libya in a speech to the nation on March 28, announcing at the same time that NATO had assumed command, and the U.S would from that point on play "a supporting role." Our allies would take the "lead in enforcing the no-fly zone and protecting civilians." The U.S. would provide arms and supplies and fly most of the aerial refueling missions, but France, the U.K., and our other partners would fly the ground attack sorties. A couple days before the speech, my foreign policy aide, Chris Brose, told me he had received a call from a contact in the French embassy alerting him that the U.S. was withdrawing from a combat role. "They're giving command to NATO," Brose explained. I had a flashback to a point in the Balkans crisis in the 1990s, when the U.N. had authority over NATO air operations in Bosnia, and things had gotten thoroughly screwed up until we intervened and took command. At an Armed Services Committee hearing that day, I asked one of the witnesses to confirm the U.S. role in the operation. "We're acting in support of NATO," he explained. "In support of NATO," I repeated incredulously. "We are NATO." An anonymous White House staffer defending the decision described the administration approach as "leading from behind," a phrase that would come back to haunt them as it became shorthand for the general retrenchment and risk-averse nature of Obama's world leadership, and the power vacuums it created. I would make mocking reference to the term more than once over the next several years.

The NATO air campaign was ongoing when I arrived in Benghazi and would continue until Qaddafi was captured and killed in October. He hadn't been able to lay waste to the city as he had threatened, and Benghazi looked to me like any other run-down Arab city. Chris and his team had commandeered a dilapidated hotel as their headquarters, and he brought in a rotating cast of rebel leadership to meet us there. I was impressed by Mahmoud Jibril, who headed the NTC, essentially as provisional prime minister. He was a technocrat, sophisticated and widely traveled, with a doctorate from the University of Pittsburgh. He was a prominent moderating voice in rebel councils. Hillary Clinton had met with him in advance of the President's decision to intervene, and, reportedly, the impression he had made had helped convince her to support the decision.

I went to a local hospital to visit wounded rebels, and met with the folks from Human Rights Watch and the Libyans they were helping build a civil society. Every Libyan I encountered was excited and positive that their deliverance from decades of oppression and corruption was at hand. If there was a spirit of the Arab Spring that Americans could relate to—a people's confident belief in their ability to shape their own destiny—it was present in Benghazi. The Libyans I met were certain they were up to the challenge of defeating the regime, and ready for the difficult task of building a modern, free, and just society that would realize the most hopeful visions of the Arab Spring. They were thankful, too, for the help that had come from the West. I walked around Benghazi's Freedom Square with one of the rebel leaders. I looked at photographs of Libyans killed by the regime or missing in action that covered a wall of a nearby government building. A crowd of a hundred or so chanted, "Thank you, McCain! Thank you, Obama! We need freedom." I suspect the NTC had played a role in organizing the cheerleaders, but I enjoyed the experience just the same, noting to my guide that I hadn't had many occasions to hear my name and the President's chanted by the same people. "It's usually just one or the other of us," I explained. "We don't always have the same fans."

I had agreed that I wouldn't remain overnight in Benghazi. I departed for Cairo that evening certain we were right to have intervened, and more hopeful than I had been before I arrived that a better Libya could emerge from the destruction of Qaddafi's regime. Before I left, I agreed to hold a press conference. "We have prevented the worst outcome," I said.

Now we have to increase our support so that the Libyan people can achieve the only satisfactory outcome to this mass protest for universal rights—the end of Qaddafi's rule and the beginning of a peaceful and inclusive transition to democracy that will benefit all Libyans.

By the time I returned to Libya in September, Tripoli had fallen. We had just reopened our embassy, although it had been moved to temporary quarters because Qaddafi's forces had ransacked the building. We met with our ambassador, Gene Cretz, a career Foreign Service officer, who had been forced to leave Libya even before NATO operations had begun. Cables he had written documenting Qaddafi's corruption were disclosed in a massive WikiLeaks dump, which had also incidentally disclosed a cable reporting our strange encounter with Qaddafi in 2009. I asked to inspect a prison, where fifteen hundred Libyans were detained after they had been arrested by rebel militias. Human Rights Watch had recently conducted interviews with some of the prisoners and found many had been arrested for dubious reasons and held without trial. Many had also been physically mistreated. In the days just after Tripoli's fall, there wasn't a central authority directing militias. They were acting on their own more or less. The NTC had been based in Benghazi. I was encouraged that I had been allowed into the prison, but it was clear that militias were still acting independently from the NTC. When we met with Mahmoud Jibril, he acknowledged the difficulties in controlling the militias, and promised the Council would get control of the situation. We had again been requested not to remain in Libya overnight, and before we left that evening we walked around Green Square, renamed by the rebels Martyrs Square. It was crowded, militias were everywhere, and lots of folks were selling stuff on the street. No one knew we were coming this time. But as soon as we got out of our vehicles, they started chanting, "Thank you, America! We love America! Thank you, Obama! We love Obama!" and Lindsey quipped to one effusive Libyan, "I love America, too."

Qaddafi was making a last stand in his hometown of Sirte. In a month, rebels found him hiding in a drainpipe, and killed him as he begged for his life. NATO operations ceased at the end of October. I was proud of what we had accomplished. At the point when Qaddafi's forces had been retaking control of the country, while a vanguard of armor and infantry approached the outskirts of Benghazi, which would have ended in a massacre, NATO airpower had intervened and reversed the tide. Over seven months, NATO had acted as the revolution's air force, obliterating the regime's advantage in armor and heavy weaponry. The rebel forces improved and fought well as the war went on, but it was NATO that had ensured regime change, irrespective of official insistence that it had not been the purpose of our intervention. Protecting Libyan civilians, which had been the Security Council's mandate, required overthrowing Qaddafi, and it was sophistry to pretend otherwise.

I came back again for another brief visit in February. That was the trip when I had asked to meet with Abdel Belhaj, the Libyan militia leader whose wife had been abused by the CIA. But the most memorable of all my experiences in Libya were the two days I spent in Tripoli in July 2012. I had come to observe Libya's first free election. It was just Chris Brose, Captain Loeblein, and me on that trip, no other senators came with us. We stayed at Chris Stevens's residence. He had succeeded Gene Cretz as ambassador a couple months earlier. He and some other embassy personnel were still living in temporary quarters while the embassy and Chris's official residence were repaired after being torched and painted with anti-American graffiti. They had rented a compound with several villas from an oil company. Each villa had a swimming pool, and strikingly exotic decor of leopard skins and couches shaped like lips. No congressional delegation had been allowed to remain in

Libya for more than a day, out of concern for their safety. But I had insisted on this trip that I would stay for two days and nights, and the State Department had relented.

I had been in regular contact with Chris since our first meeting in April of the previous year. We saw Libya the same way. We were both enthusiastic about its prospects even though it had been ruled by a tyrant for four decades and hadn't national institutions that survived his downfall. Libyans would have to build everything from scratch while rival militias and political factions competed for turf. We both believed it was essential for the U.S. to be engaged in that project, using the relationships we had made in Libya over the last year, and our soft power resources to support national reconciliation and the rule of law. Chris was a California native, with the stereotypical Californian's sunny disposition. He had graduated from Berkeley. He had been a Peace Corps volunteer in Morocco. His politics were decidedly liberal, but we didn't discuss American politics much. He was good company and a gracious host. The morning of the election, he made us cappuccinos, knowing it was my preferred variety of caffeine. I've kept a picture that Brose took of Chris making us the coffees. We spent all day visiting polling sites, watching Libyans cast votes that actually mattered for the first time in their lives. They had showed up in encouraging numbers. There were long lines at all the polls we visited, and despite the huge turnout it appeared to be a very orderly election. Embassy staff and international observers had fanned out across the country. There were a few isolated instances of problems and boycotting here and there by some rebel factions, but on the whole they reported the same good turnout, well-run process, and enthusiastic voters we were finding everywhere we looked in Tripoli. It was awesome.

Mahmoud Jibril's party would win the most seats, which I took as an encouraging sign. We had dinner that night on the patio of a restaurant adjacent to the Marcus Aurelius Arch that the Romans had built in AD 165 to commemorate their victories over the Parthians. We went for a walk after dinner. Everywhere Libyans were celebrating their freedom, hanging out car windows waving flags, honking their horns, shooting off fireworks, cheering us. I don't know how many of the people who cheered and thanked us or stopped to pose for a picture with us knew exactly who we were. They just seemed to know we were Americans, and had helped make this day possible. It was a lovely, hopeful evening, and one of my favorite memories.

Two months later, Chris was dead. Most readers know the story, so I won't go into detail here. He went to Benghazi on September 11. He had worried about the deteriorating situation there as rival militias clashed and reports warned of a growing al-Qaeda presence. The central government, in office for a month, appeared too weak to do much about it. Al-Qaeda had recently called for attacks on Americans as the anniversary of 9/11 approached. Chris had asked the State Department for more security for the Benghazi mission, but it had been denied. On the evening of the 11th, an al-Qaeda offshoot attacked the main U.S. mission compound in Benghazi and a CIA annex about a mile away with grenades, RPGs, mortars, and automatic rifles. The attackers entered the building where Chris was hiding, poured gasoline, and torched it. Chris was killed as was an embassy information officer, Sean Smith. Two former Navy SEALs helping to evacuate Americans at the CIA annex, Glen Doherty and Tyrone Woods, were subsequently killed. Libyans discovered Chris's body, believed him to be alive, and tried to rescue him. He was pronounced dead at the hospital from smoke inhalation.

I heard about what had happened the same way most Americans did, from news reports. In those first days after his death, I was just terribly saddened by it. I wasn't angry with the administration. I remember listening to Secretary Clinton's memorial remarks about him, and being very moved by them, and I asked Chris Brose to send her a note of thanks. I started to get angry when it appeared administration officials were knowingly misleading us about the attack, attributing it to a video that some idiot had made mocking Islam that incited a spontaneous mob that turned violent. It took more than a week for the White House to acknowledge it had been a planned terrorist attack. The uproar that ensued became a lasting political controversy that's still debated. I was one of the most vocal critics, calling the administration's analysis "willful ignorance or abysmal intelligence," and a "massive cover-up or incompetence." I demanded that a special committee investigate it. In the end, all it established is what could have been presumed at the beginning, bureaucratic incompetence and ass-covering, two common conditions in Washington. Anger subsides, politics moves on, but sadness remains. Chris Stevens deserved better from all of us.

And what of the country he died trying to help? It disintegrated into anarchy as warring militias clashed, politicians feuded, rival legislatures contested for control, and ISIS exploited the chaos to establish a franchise operation in the country. Libyans who were ecstatic over their enfranchisement in 2012 showed up in reduced numbers to vote in 2014, half as many as two years before. The U.S. and Europe, having intervened to change the regime, disengaged from the urgent, complex task of transforming a terrorized nation into a functioning civil society, of helping Libyans build national institutions where none existed. A U.N.-brokered agreement in 2015 called for a new "Government of National Accord," and a new constitution and election that various warring factions continued to hinder. ISIS lost its territory but remains a presence. Last September, a new U.N. reconciliation plan was announced. A little hopefulness flickers in the embers that the worst might be behind. The memory of the heady optimism of 2011 that gave way quickly to resignation and despair cautions against great expectations. But that's not to say there are no Libyans left who believe in the promise of 2011. There are many who still have faith they are capable of building a modern democracy. I do, too. I have met them, and been inspired by them, and believe in them. They need other Libyans to believe in their future, too, and assistance from the West to help them build it. They need guidance and resources and security. They need time. They need the generosity and vision of Chris Stevens, reflected in the efforts of those who emulate the example of that good man.

As NATO contemplated whether to intervene in Libya in March 2011, the first large protests in Syria began in provincial towns. Fifteen kids were arrested in Deraa in the southwest corner of the country for scrawling anti-regime graffiti on school walls. Protesters marched to demand their release. Government security forces opened fire on them, killing several. More protesters marched in response, and police fired on them, too, killing scores. Protests proliferated nationwide, as did demands for Bashar al-Assad's resignation. The regime responded to the demonstrations with force, and casualties climbed, as Alawite Assad made war on the majority of his countrymen, who were Sunni. One hundred thousand demonstrated in Homs, the country's third-largest city. By the summer, as many as a million Syrians were marching. The regime was using tanks to put down the protests. The U.S. and Europe imposed sanctions on the regime. President Obama called for Assad to step down. Syrian army officers defected and formed the Free Syrian Army (FSA), and civil war ensued. In January 2012, they were fighting in the Damascus suburbs. In February, the army began shelling Homs, starting the offensive to retake the city that would kill thousands, and was described by an evacuated British journalist as a scene of "medieval siege and slaughter." In May, pro-regime forces executed over a hundred Syrians, most of them women and children, in the town of Taldou in the Houla region of Syria.

Syria's descent into hell was nearing the point of no return when I spoke on the Senate floor in March 2012 to argue for arming the Free Syrian Army and call for air strikes by the U.S. and our European and regional allies to ground the Syrian air force, which was indiscriminately bombing population centers. I proposed creating safe havens for opposition forces and refugees.

We had reached a "decisive moment" in the conflict, I began. Seventy-five hundred lives had been lost, and the regime was committing crimes against humanity. Most of the world had turned against Assad. The Arab League had expelled Syria and the U.N. General Assembly had rebuked the regime, though Russia and China used their vetoes to protect Assad in the Security Council. The Russians hadn't yet intervened militarily, though Moscow and Beijing were supplying arms and other assistance to the regime. Syria is Iran's only ally in the Arab world, and Iran's proxy, Hezbollah, had deployed fighters to the conflict. There were already Revolutionary Guard officers in Syria, but the full extent of Iran's involvement was a year away. ISIS hadn't yet exploited the conflict to establish the center of its caliphate. Had the U.S. and Europe intervened in that first year of the conflict, eliminated Assad's airpower advantage, and provided the FSA arms and munitions, including antitank weapons, I believe it would have been decisive. The regime would have collapsed and Assad, if he had survived, would likely have fled the country. Hundreds of thousands of lives might have been spared.

I commended the administration for leading international diplomatic and economic pressure on the regime, and I recognized their legitimate concerns "about the efficacy of military options in Syria." But the conditions on the ground in Syria were dire, and the "administration's approach is starting to look more like hope than a strategy." I criticized the insistence that Assad's collapse was inevitable. "Claims about the inevitability of events can often be a convenient way to abdicate responsibility." I argued that in addition to humanitarian concerns, we had important geopolitical interests at stake. As Iran's only Arab ally, Syria serves as "a forward operating base" for our adversary, and the supply route for arms to Hezbollah and Hamas, as well as the gateway to Iraq for foreign extremists.

"The time has come for a new policy," I contended. America and our allies should support both political and military opposition groups. "What opposition groups . . . need most urgently is relief from Assad's tanks and artillery sieges in the many cities that are still contested." The only realistic way to do that "is with foreign airpower."

Our goal should be to establish and defend safe havens in the north, "where opposition forces can organize and plan . . . [and] could serve as platforms for humanitarian and military assistance." I acknowledged we would have to destroy Assad's air defenses in most if not all of the country before we could ground his air force. But that wouldn't have been as great a challenge as some in the administration were suggesting it would be. We had to act now. With Iran's and Russia's backing, Assad had regained the momentum. The world was hedging their bets on Syria waiting for our leadership. The President had to make clear by word and deed that Assad "will not be able to finish what he started."

Are there dangers and risks and uncertainties in this approach? Absolutely. There are no ideal options in Syria. All of them contain significant risk. . . . [But] none so much that they should keep us from acting.

And the risks get worse the longer we wait. "The surest way for al-Qaeda to gain a foothold in Syria is for us to turn our backs on the Syrians fighting to defend themselves. . . . Sunni Iraqis were willing to ally with al-Qaeda when they felt desperate enough. But when America gave them a better alternative they turned their guns on al-Qaeda." Concerns that the civil war was a sectarian conflict and our intervention would allow Sunnis to take bloody revenge against their Alawite persecutors were legitimate, too. But that threat would only grow worse the longer the conflict lasts. "As we saw in Iraq, or Lebanon before it, time favors the hard-liners in a conflict like this." The worse the Sunnis suffered, the stronger the calls for revenge become, and the more it incentivizes the Alawites to keep fighting. And to those who argued all our intervention would do is further militarize the conflict, I noted that Iran and Russia were doing just that and could be counted on to continue strengthening Assad's "killing machine."

These warnings all came to pass, I'm sorry to say. Every concern raised as an argument against U.S. intervention became reality in the absence of our action. Al-Qaeda's role in the opposition grew stronger as nonextremist militias were compelled by necessity to join forces with it. Foreign jihadis flooded into Syria and ISIS claimed a huge swath of Syrian territory for its barbarous caliphate. The role Iran and Russia played in Syria escalated with every passing month, until the regime's dependence on them was total. And the slaughter surpassed imagination. By the summer, fighting had spread to Aleppo, Syria's then largest city. The regime ordered fixed-wing air strikes on rebel positions there and in Damascus, indiscriminate bombing that killed as many civilians as rebels. By the end of the year, another fifty thousand Syrians had perished in the conflict. The United Nations High Commissioner for Refugees estimated that over three-quarters of a million Syrians had fled the country, and hundreds of thousands more were displaced within Syria. Citing concerns that they could fall into the hands of terrorists, the administration continued to reject calls to intervene and to arm the Free Syrian Army with anything more than light arms and nonlethal assistance when they desperately needed antitank and antiaircraft weapons. Obama did announce in August that one thing could change his mind about intervening. "We have been very clear to the Assad regime," he stated, that a red line for us is we start seeing a whole bunch of chemical weapons moving around or being utilized. That would change my calculus. That would change my equation.

By February 2013, the U.N. Security Council estimated that over seventy thousand civilians had been killed directly and indirectly by the war.

For a year now, Lindsey, Joe, and I had continued our appeals to arm and train the opposition and for a no-fly zone. In response to administration reluctance to expose U.S. pilots to Syria's air defenses, I recommended using Patriot missile batteries in Turkey to shoot down Syrian warplanes. In every conversation, every committee hearing, every private discussion with senior members of the administration, I was told over and over that a no-fly zone was practically impossible. We would have to roll back all Assad's air defenses, destroy his command and control, bomb all his airfields, crater all his runways. It would take months before we could safely defend safe havens. In essence, the administration's pushback was that grounding Assad's air force and defending a no-fly zone was too complex and dangerous for the greatest airpower in the world to manage safely and quickly. And this was more than two years before Russia's first air strikes in Syria. It was a ridiculous assertion.

Rebel forces had gained the momentum by early 2013, and were advancing on multiple fronts. But Hezbollah fighters rushed to Assad's aid. In April, the regime launched an offensive and the opposition's advance had stalled. I had made a few trips to Turkey by then to meet with members of the Syrian political opposition, and with humanitarian workers, including a young Syrian from Homs, Abu Salim (a nom de guerre), who regularly ran arms and nonlethal assistance across the border to the FSA. He was an impressive young man, not an Islamist, who appeared to have ample resources and extensive contacts. I met with him several times, including twice in Washington, when he brought members of a Syrian volunteer group he was helping finance to meet me. They would eventually be widely known and admired as the White Helmets. I don't know where Abu Salim is these days or even if he's still using that name. I remember him as someone I hoped would be around when the war was over to help put the country back together. He wasn't a zealot, just a guy who wanted to help his country and took risks. I hope he's well, and if by some coincidence he should ever have an occasion to read this, I want him to know I admired him and wished him and his country well.

From my meetings in Turkey, I grew increasingly worried over reports that Syria might be using chemical weapons, that Iranians were committing more men and resources to the war, and that al-Nusra, the al-Qaeda front, was gaining strength and influence with rebel forces because their fighters were proving the most effective. I was tired of butting up against administration excuses that suppressing Assad's air defenses was too time-consuming and dangerous an undertaking. I spoke on the Senate floor to call for measures that could tip the balance without a full-out assault on Assad's SAMs and antiaircraft artillery. "More than seventy thousand Syrians have been killed indiscriminately," I noted,

> with snipers, artillery, helicopter gunships, fighter jets, and even ballistic missiles. Indeed . . . more than 4,300 civilians have been killed by Assad's airstrikes alone since July 2012.
>
> At the same time, Iran and its proxy Hezbollah are building a network of militias inside Syria, and the al Qaeda–aligned al Nusra Front has gained unprecedented strength on the ground. According to estimates that have been published in the media, some believe there were no more than a few hundred al Nusra fighters in Syria last year—but today, it is widely believed that there could be thousands of extremist fighters inside Syria.

I talked about the hundreds of thousands of Syrian refugees who were overwhelming Jordan and Lebanon. "Syria is becoming a failed state in the heart of the Middle East," I warned,

> overrun by thousands of al Qaeda–affiliated fighters, with possibly tons of chemical weapons, and poised to ignite a wider sectarian conflict that could profoundly destabilize the region.

We didn't have to take out the regime's air defenses, I argued, to arm and train vetted opposition forces, which was something the President's entire national security team had recommended he do, but that he continued to resist. And we could use precision strike capabilities to target Assad's aircraft and SCUD launchers without suppressing his defenses. We could use them against artillery, too, and use Patriot batteries to defend safe zones from aerial and missile attacks.

> Would any of these options immediately end the conflict? Probably not. But they could save innocent lives in Syria. They could give the moderate opposition a better chance to succeed in marginalizing radical actors.

I went to Turkey at the end of the month after convincing the State Department to let me enter northern Syria for a few hours. The Washington-based Syrian Emergency Task Force had arranged for me to meet with members of FSA units. I went with General Salim Idris, the head of the FSA's Supreme Military Council. I don't know what I had expected but crossing the border into a war turned out to be a pretty unremarkable experience. General Idris, Brose, two Syrian Emergency Task Force staffers, and I loaded into SUVs and drove less than a mile to a border crossing, where the guards were expecting us. They raised the gates and we crossed into Syria, and with that easy effort I became for the time being the highest-ranking U.S. official to visit Syria since the war began. Another short drive took us to the building where FSA commanders from around the country had gathered to meet us. They described recent fighting on various fronts where the regime was trying to retake territory, and how increasingly large a share of the fighting Hezbollah was conducting. They were doing all of the fighting in Homs, they said. There were more Russians in the country as well. They told me they were running low on ammunition and didn't have weapons they could use against aircraft. They also insisted Assad had already used chemical weapons several times. They asked me for the things I had been arguing for months they be provided with, antitank and antiaircraft weapons and air strikes. I told them I'd keep at it. We took a few photographs, and then we left for another uneventful border crossing.

When I got back to the hotel, I instructed my Washington office to tweet one of the pictures. I don't remember exactly how long it took, but some days if not weeks later, a Lebanese television station affiliated with Hezbollah accused two of the FSA commanders of being al-Nusra fighters who had been involved in kidnapping Shia pilgrims to Lebanon. The names mentioned didn't match any of the names of the people we had met with, and we soon determined the story was bullshit. But it lives forever on the Internet, in easy reach of McCain-hating conspiracy nuts everywhere. Some troll even went to the trouble of Photoshopping the head of ISIS leader Abu Bakr al-Baghdadi onto the body of one of the FSA leaders.

In the predawn hours of August 21, 2013, the regime fired as many as fifteen rockets at two densely populated rebel-held areas in the Damascus suburbs. They carried warheads filled with sarin gas. It wasn't long before video and photographs appeared of some of the victims, many of them children, gasping their last breaths. As many as fifteen hundred civilians were massacred. Assad denied his regime was culpable, and blamed the attacks on the rebels, as did Russia's foreign minister, Sergei Lavrov, whom I've gotten to know over the years at conferences in Munich and elsewhere, and who lies as easily as he breathes. But a U.N. inspection team confirmed that a sarin gas attack on sleeping civilians had occurred. On August 30, U.S. intelligence services revealed they had surveilled each step in the attack from preparing the rockets to after-action reports. President Obama's red line had been crossed. I believed he would retaliate as he had promised, and I hoped the force used to punish the regime would seriously degrade its military capabilities.

The President was reported to have decided on military action, and the strikes were thought to be imminent when he abruptly announced in the Rose Garden that he would ask Congress for authorization first. The day before, British prime minister David Cameron had lost a vote in Parliament authorizing military action against Syria. Americans were war-weary. Republicans were restive and not often disposed to vote for the President's policies whatever they were. Lindsey and I released a statement on the day of his announcement, August 31, urging a military response that would help change momentum on the battlefield, and saying we wouldn't support a few isolated cruise missile strikes, the damage from which could be quickly repaired and forgotten.

The President asked us to the White House on the following Monday, Labor Day. It was just Lindsey and me, the President, and National Security Advisor Susan Rice. The plan they laid out to us was surprisingly substantial. The strikes from carrier aircraft and cruise missiles would not be lasting but they would be big enough to degrade Assad's military capabilities. They were going to hit airfields, runways, SCUD batteries, and command and control, seriously degrading Assad's airpower, all the targets they had been insisting for years couldn't be touched without taking out the regime's air defenses. They were also going to upgrade assistance to the FSA, providing it weapons it had long needed, and train them far more seriously. They weren't prepared to create a no-fly zone, but I was satisfied that the plan would change the war's momentum, and I welcomed it. We held an impromptu press conference on the White House driveway, and I said the consequences of a vote against authorization would be "catastrophic." "A weak response," I added, "would also be catastrophic." Without disclosing details, I intimated that the strikes the President was contemplating would be serious rather than cosmetic.

We had been told the attacks were likely to launch in two days. We both got a call from General Dempsey a day later saying they had been delayed. The authorization never received a vote by the full Senate. It was approved by the Senate Foreign Relations Committee on September 4 by a vote of 10 to 7, both the ayes and nays were bipartisan. I had amended the resolution to include authorization for a use of force sufficient to change momentum on the battlefield. The President called it all off not long after. An aside by Secretary of State John Kerry that military action wouldn't be necessary if Assad surrendered his chemical weapons arsenal led to an offer from Sergei Lavrov to broker an agreement with Assad. Assad agreed to do it, and to join the Chemical Weapons Convention. He was lying, of course. The administration insisted the deal was a breakthrough, and commended it with every load of chemical weapons surrendered. But Assad retained some of his arsenal, and used chemical weapons again on his people. Neither Lindsey nor I received a heads-up that the President had changed his mind.

It was the worst decision of his presidency, I believe, and its consequences are felt to this day. His administration's credibility in the region was lost and with some of the region's worst actors. It was badly damaged everywhere, really. It shook the confidence of our allies and emboldened our adversaries, no one more so than Vladimir Putin. For the next couple years, the administration's policy for Syria was reduced to pleading with Russia to help convince Syria to negotiate a settlement to the war. Lavrov and Putin would string us along, and never deliver.

In September 2015, Putin jumped into the war with both feet. Russian air strikes on rebel targets in northwest Syria were the first act in Russia's decisive intervention in the conflict. Henceforth, Russian bombers would serve as Assad's air force. Moscow maintained it had intervened to fight ISIS and other terrorist groups fighting in Syria. But their attacks were usually focused on the FSA and other rebel militias that are part of the moderate opposition. Their intervention turned the tide of the war in the regime's favor. Russian airpower, used to devastating effect on rebel-held cities such as Palmyra and Aleppo, was indispensable to retaking the ruins of those ancient metropolises. Moreover, Putin has used his bombers as instruments of terror deliberately targeting hospitals and school rescue efforts, dropping cluster and barrel bombs, cheap, unguided munitions, indiscriminately in civilian areas. Last December, Russia's defense minister confirmed that Russia would maintain permanent air and naval bases in Syria, giving the Russians a military presence in the Middle East they haven't had since Anwar al-Sadat kicked them out of Egypt. In December 2016, rebel forces in Aleppo negotiated a cease-fire with the Russians to allow them to evacuate civilians and themselves from the destroyed city.

ISIS had begun seizing territory in northern and eastern Syria in early 2013, taking its declared capital, Raqqa, in March of that year. The administration refused to order air strikes against ISIS camps in Iraq in the fall of 2013, when the Iraqis were urging us to, and when ISIS fighters were more in the open. In January 2014, they took Fallujah and Ramadi and then Mosul in June, which seemed to shock the administration into action. Russia's and Assad's insistence to the contrary, the regime and its ally didn't concentrate their attacks on

ISIS, but on other rebel militias, which by the middle of 2014 were fighting ISIS in some areas more than they were the regime. President Obama announced in September 2014 his intention to bomb ISIS sites in Syria in concert with an international coalition, and to, at last, begin providing arms, including antitank weapons, to the FSA. U.S. Special Forces deployed to northern Syria in October 2015 to advise the Kurds' Syrian Democratic Forces and other forces fighting ISIS. By the end of last year, the coalition had launched nearly twelve thousand air strikes. As many as two thousand special operators and Marines were in Syria, and it appears that many of them will be there for a while. I went back to northern Syria in February of last year to meet with our Syrian Kurd allies who would bear the brunt of the fighting to take Raqqa, and with some of the brave Americans helping them. It would be the last time I shared the company of soldiers in the field risking their lives for a just cause, and as ever they were an antidote for despair.

ISIS was forced out of all its occupied territory in Syria and Iraq, though thousands of ISIS fighters are still present in both countries. Last April, Assad again used sarin gas, this time in Idlib Province, and Russia again used its veto to protect its client from condemnation and sanction by the U.N. Security Council. President Trump ordered cruise missile strikes on the Syrian airfield where the planes that delivered the sarin were based. It was a minimal attack, but better than nothing. A week before, I had condemned statements by Secretary of State Rex Tillerson and U.N. Ambassador Nikki Haley, who had explicitly declined to maintain what had been the official U.S. position that a settlement of the Syrian civil war had to include Assad's removal from power. "Once again, U.S. policy in Syria is being presented piecemeal in press statements," I complained, "without any definition of success, let alone a realistic plan to achieve it."

As this book goes to the publisher, there are reports of a clash between U.S. forces in eastern Syria and Russian "volunteers," in which hundreds of Russians were said to have been killed. If true, it's a dangerous turn of events, but one caused entirely by Putin's reckless conduct in the world, allowed if not encouraged by the repeated failures of the U.S. and the West to act with resolve to prevent his assaults against our interests and values.

In President Obama's last year in office, at his invitation, he and I spent a half hour or so alone, discussing very frankly what I considered his policy failures, and he believed had been sound and necessary decisions. Much of that conversation concerned Syria. No minds were changed in the encounter, but I appreciated his candor as I hoped he appreciated mine, and I respected the sincerity of his convictions. Yet I still believe his approach to world leadership, however thoughtful and well intentioned, was negligent, and encouraged our allies to find ways to live without us, and our adversaries to try to fill the vacuums our negligence created. And those trends continue in reaction to the thoughtless America First ideology of his successor. There are senior officials in government who are trying to mitigate those effects. But I worry that we are at a turning point, a hinge of history, and the decisions made in the last ten years and the decisions made tomorrow might be closing the door on the era of the American-led world order. I hope not, and it certainly isn't too late to reverse that direction. But my time in that fight has concluded. I have nothing but hope left to invest in the work of others to make the future better than the past.

As of today, as the Syrian war continues, more than 400,000 people have been killed, many of them civilians. More than five million have fled the country and more than six million have been displaced internally. A hundred years from now, Syria will likely be remembered as one of the worst humanitarian catastrophes of the twenty-first century, and an example of human savagery at its most extreme. But it will be remembered, too, for the invincibility of human decency and the longing for freedom and justice evident in the courage and selflessness of the White Helmets and the soldiers fighting for their country's freedom from tyranny and terrorists. In that noblest of human conditions is the eternal promise of the Arab Spring, which was engulfed in flames and drowned in blood, but will, like all springs, come again.

CHAPTER SIX

FIGHTING THE
GOOD FIGHT

(with and against Ted Kennedy)

IT WAS THE SUMMER OF 1993, AND A NEW ADMINISTRATION was still finding its footing. I had won my first reelection to the Senate, putting to rest doubts about my long-term prospects in the Senate that had arisen during the "Keating Five" scandal. A few Democrats had come to the Senate floor to speak in support of the new President, Bill Clinton's, budget. Several more were there to defend Clinton's surgeon general nominee, Joycelyn Elders, whose history of controversial remarks on abortion, the sexual activity of minors, and Republicans had, unsurprisingly, generated opposition in our caucus to her nomination. Barbara Boxer was there, speaking in her usual lacerating style, as were several others, including Carol Moseley Braun, the newly arrived senator from Illinois, who had beaten popular "Al the Pal" Dixon in the Democratic primary in 1992, and gone on to beat my friend and Reagan administration alumnus the late Rich Williamson in the general. The crux of the Democrats' complaint was that Republicans were filibustering the nomination even though the debate on her nomination was only a few hours old.

Republicans, feeling themselves unfairly abused, had started lining up to fight back. Don Nickles from Oklahoma was there, as was my closest Senate friend at the time, Phil Gramm. The Republican whip, Trent Lott, was there, too. I was just crossing the floor on my way out of the chamber. I hadn't paid any attention to the debate. I don't remember if I was even aware of the issue in contention. Nevertheless, I sensed the rising temperature in the room, and the irritation of my fellow Republicans, and I'm a sucker for a fight. One of the reasons I'd become close friends with Phil was because he was quick on his feet, and especially good in a really lively debate.

I stopped near the door to the Republican cloakroom where my administrative assistant was standing, and asked him what the fuss was about. He was starting to explain when Ted Kennedy interrupted Trent, which got my attention. I had been aware that Ted was sitting at his desk when I entered the chamber. You were always aware when Ted was on the floor. He had a booming voice and laugh that could be heard in private conversations with colleagues, often over the sound of whichever speaker was addressing the Senate at the time. He had a presence you noticed the moment he arrived, and a reputation for being a ferocious adversary in a floor fight, bombastic, to be sure, but his cutting sarcasm, his mockery is what you most feared. He was one of the most experienced members of the body, expert in its procedures and customs, and he always had one of the most talented staffs in Congress. Going up against him was never easy or lightly undertaken. As a rule, I tried to keep my distance from him. I hadn't wanted to make an enemy of him, but I also didn't want to fall under the spell of his camaraderie. He was good company, funny and hard to resist when he was in full-out charm mode. He could get you to agree to something you didn't want to do or at least something you sensed wasn't in your best political interests. But this, too, was part of his reputation: whatever he promised you in exchange for your help, he delivered. He kept his word, which is the Senate's principal virtue, or was for many of the years I served there.

I believe he had already spoken on the Elders nomination that day and was just reading papers at his desk. Until he interrupted Trent, he had seemed to be ignoring the debate as I had been. Senate procedure allows you to interrupt a senator who has the floor as long as the purpose of the interruption is to ask a question. In practice, the rule is used to interject criticism or an insult with a question mark punctuating the abuse, like the way contestants on the game show *Jeopardy!* have to frame their answers in the form of a question. *Mr. President, will my friend yield for a question? Can I ask my friend if he understands his position is the devil's own work and will surely destroy the Republic?*

As soon as Kennedy started interrupting to ask his question, I stomped down to my desk, picked up the mic, and started calling for "regular order," which demands that the presiding officer recognize the speaker who had the floor before the interruption. Ted kept asking questions, and I kept demanding regular order, both of us getting heated. Even after we sat down for a pause, we were both committed, and itching to get back into it.

Things had died down a bit when Moseley Braun sought recognition and began excoriating Republicans in personal terms. She compared Republicans to Torquemada, the Grand Inquisitor of the Spanish Inquisition. Don Nickles interrupted her and asked if she understood Rule 19, which states:

> *No Senator in debate shall, directly or indirectly, by any form of words, impute to another Senator or to other Senators any conduct or motive unworthy or unbecoming a Senator.*

This time it was Kennedy who demanded "regular order." Nickles responded that he wasn't making a motion to invoke the rule, only asking Moseley Braun if she was aware of it. Kennedy just ignored him and kept yelling "Regular order, regular order!" I shot to my feet, and demanded the same. "Regular order, Mr. President. Regular order!" Kennedy addressed me directly, "That's what we're asking, regular order." Nodding at Nickles, "He has to ask her a question." "I did," Nickles replied. "Regular order!" I insisted. "Regular order!" Ted shouted back. Anyone unfamiliar with Senate procedure and the behavior of senators, which is probably all but a tiny fraction of the American population, wouldn't have had any idea what the fight was about. The debate had become a free-for-all, ungoverned by Senate rules. The presiding officer looked confused and a little scared as he struggled to regain control. He was a recent addition to the Senate's ranks, appointed to finish Al Gore's unexpired term. An unfamiliar face to most of us, he would leave the Senate not long after with the same status. That day, he looked as if he would have liked to have gone back to Tennessee right then. Moseley Braun seemed bewildered, too; having somehow lost her right to the floor without relinquishing it, she had no idea how or if she should get it back.

I guess Ted and I felt our ability to address each other directly was too encumbered by the intercessions of our colleagues and the formalities of addressing the chair. Neither of us signaled the other. But in the very same instant, we both put down our mics, and charged to the well of the Senate. There, standing inches apart, we let each other have it in personal and profane terms. Reporters seated in the gallery above us leaned over the rail, straining to hear our unamplified exchange. A few of them caught the F word lending emphasis to the insults hurled back and forth. Our behavior was certainly unbecoming of senators and unworthy of the Senate, a place I have come to love.

After a minute or two we realized we were being observed from above, and retired to our respective corners. We stayed engaged in the debate for the time being, giving actual statements on the nomination rather than interrupting each other. But as things became a little less lively, our enthusiasm waned correspondingly. We left the floor at the same time through the same door. Ted threw an arm across my shoulder, and we both started laughing as we complimented each other's combativeness. It wasn't our first time sparring. We had exchanged a few shots before in Armed Services Committee hearings and members' meetings. But this one was memorable for how carried away we had gotten, and even more so for the fact that I think it might have been the first time we had made each other laugh.

We hadn't become fast friends or allies. We were just friendlier with each other after that, and respected each other more. It would be several more years before we started working closely together on a few issues, after I had lost the Republican nomination to George Bush in 2000. I had returned hoping my newly acquired national reputation would increase my influence in the Senate, as Ted had returned to the Senate in 1980 after losing the nomination to Jimmy Carter determined to make the most of his opportunities there. I wanted to get some things done in that Congress, particularly campaign finance reform, an issue that had been central to my campaign, and Ted was willing to help where he agreed. He was also, for a time, intent on convincing me to switch parties. The Senate was evenly divided, fifty-fifty, a fairly rare occurrence. Because Republicans had won the White House, and the vice president can break tie votes in the Senate, we were technically in the majority. A single defection would have given control to the Democrats. So, although we were friendly, Ted's interest in my political conversion wasn't exactly fraternal.

His relationship with Carter, never close to begin with, was reportedly permanently icy after their 1980 contest, each party nursing resentments. Maybe Ted thought I felt similarly about my victorious opponent, and saw an opening to take advantage of our disaffection. Various enticements were offered, including at some point the chairmanship of the Armed Services Committee. Tom Daschle, the Democratic leader, joined the discussions. I listened and was flattered, but insisted in every conversation that my differences with Democrats were more numerous than those I had with current Republican orthodoxy. After a while they relented.

In truth, there were some hard feelings after I lost. But I got over them a lot sooner than many people believed I had, and sooner than the lingering antagonism between our staffs had faded. I disagreed with President Bush on some issues, including a few big ones like his tax cuts. But I agreed with him on other things, most things, really, and I liked him. He's likable, and a good man. Last but not least, I was a Republican, a Reagan Republican. Still am. Not a Tea Party Republican. Not a Breitbart Republican. Not a talk radio or Fox News Republican. Not an isolationist, protectionist, immigrant-bashing, scapegoating, get-nothing-useful-done Republican. Not, as I am often dismissed by self-declared "real" conservatives, a RINO, Republican in Name Only. I'm a Reagan Republican, a proponent of lower taxes, less government, free markets, free trade, defense readiness, and democratic internationalism.

I also believe government should respond to our biggest problems and prepare for our biggest future challenges, be as transparent as possible and as efficient as possible. There are a lot of government responsibilities that have needed to be reformed for decades, especially one of my pet peeves, our broken government acquisition system. I believe the same can be said about the rules of contemporary politics, the way redistricting is done in most of the country, and the explosion of unlimited and dark money in campaigns, an invitation to corruption made possible by the Supreme Court's decision in the *Citizens United* case, a mistake made by five justices who never ran for any office and were more naive than a cloistered nun about the corrupting effect of unlimited money in politics. I believe in the separation of powers, a press free to report without fear or favor, and free to infuriate politicians—including me—as they do. Lastly, I believe in principled compromises that move the country forward, goodwill toward Man, and empirical facts.

Here's one fact fools ignore. Our Constitution and closely divided polity don't allow for winner-take-all governance. You need the opposition's cooperation to get most big things done. And so, I've worked with Democratic colleagues to do things I thought were important. Proudly. When I travel overseas, I like to travel in a bipartisan delegation. I've cultivated many relationships over the years with foreign politicians, journalists, and military leaders that made me a better proponent of my country's interests and values, and more knowledgeable about our allies and adversaries. I want more members of Congress from both parties to acquire that experience with the hope they will help thwart the spread of a form of nationalism that barely distinguishes enemy from friend, seeing every relationship as purely transactional with a winner and a loser. Congress can produce statesmen as well as the executive branch can, statesmen who will help retain our primacy in world affairs. I'm pleased to help that happen by introducing colleagues to foreign leaders, as John Tower and Scoop Jackson and others did for me.

I didn't accept Ted's invitation to become a Democrat. But we did start working together on some issues. Our first project was a patient's bill of rights, legislation that required HMOs to grant patients and doctors more decision-making authority. Specifically, the bill provided that doctors, not insurance company representatives, make medical decisions for their patients. It also guaranteed that patients could see medical specialists, and in a medical emergency go to the nearest emergency room. In exchange for these protections, I had hoped to include in the bill medical malpractice litigation reform. But one of our other co-sponsors, John Edwards, a trial lawyer who had, as the saying goes, "done well by doing good," raised the alarm with the powerful Democratic Party benefactor, the trial lawyers lobby, a main source of "soft" or unregulated money for Democrats. They got Democratic leaders to kill the idea.

The HMOs were opposed to the bill as was most of the medical insurance industry, and most Republicans. Nevertheless, with unanimous Democratic support and eight Republican votes, the bill passed the Senate comfortably, though not by a veto-proof margin. The times being what they were, with HMOs suffering adverse publicity from news stories in every state about patients being denied treatment prescribed by their doctors, Republicans knew they had to appear responsive to public concerns. The bill that House Republicans had passed included some of the assurances ours had, but unlike our bill, it did not include provisions to enforce them. The bills couldn't be reconciled in conference. We wanted a bill with teeth. House Republicans did not.

A patient's bill of rights wasn't my highest priority that year, but it was high on our agenda, and its failure was a disappointment. I'm sure it was for Ted, too, but one of the qualities I most admired about Ted was he didn't despair in defeat or get carried away in victory. He pressed on. Universal health care, as everyone knows, was his highest priority that year and every year he served in the Senate. And every year he was disappointed until Barack Obama was inaugurated President of the United States, and Senate Democrats began working on the Affordable Care Act, which would pass the Senate over united Republican opposition four months after Ted died. Three months later, Obamacare was the law of the land. I had strenuously opposed it, but I was very sorry that Ted had not lived to see his long crusade come to a successful end. He believed it was going to happen. He always had. And knowing him, he wouldn't have spent more than a day celebrating the achievement. He would have had other things to do, other crusades to wage. I would have opposed most of them, but cherished the few times here and there when I could work with him instead of against him.

He took the long view, Ted, and he hung in there. I had learned to do that as well, most notably during Russ Feingold's and my multiyear commitment to passing campaign finance reform. Ted knew when an issue was ready for a big push. I did, too. Campaign reform was the central issue of my 2000 campaign. I could see people react favorably to my thesis that campaign reform was a necessary prerequisite to other government reforms, that too much money from too few sources bred a dependency on narrow interests that frequently undermined the national interest. I saw it with my own eyes, in the size of my crowds and their enthusiasm. I knew it was time. We also had gotten an assist from the Enron scandal that blew up in the fall of 2001. I had come back to Washington determined to use the political capital I had accumulated to pass a reform bill in that Congress, the 107th, and we did, sending the Bipartisan Campaign Reform Act to President Bush in March 2002.

Ted had used his influence in his caucus to help overcome concerns about McCain-Feingold raised by important Democratic constituencies, including labor unions. The Democratic Party was more dependent on soft money than were Republicans. The Republican opposition was more up-front and vocal, led by my formidable friend, occasional opponent, and now majority leader, Mitch McConnell. Democratic opponents of the bill were more discreet, but they were very influential, and had the ear of senior Democratic leaders. In an exchange on the Senate floor overheard by one of my staffers, John Edwards, who had just finished speaking in support of the bill, asked Democratic leader Tom Daschle if anything could be done to stop it from passing. I'm sure most Senate Democrats genuinely supported reform, including senior senators such as Ted, whose public support meant that even Democrats who were cynical about the issue had to publicly endorse and vote for it, which was good enough for me. All but two Democrats voted for final passage, and ten Republicans joined me.

The harder task was in the House, which Republicans controlled. Although a substantial number of House Republicans supported the bill, enough to constitute with Democratic supporters a large majority in favor, Speaker Denny Hastert had declined to bring the bill up for a vote. House rules being what they are, leadership decisions aren't easily overridden as long as they represent "a majority of the majority." To get McCain-Feingold on the calendar over the speaker's refusal would require a discharge petition, which needed only a simple majority to pass. But a majority required fifteen or more Republican votes. For House Republicans or Democrats to oppose their leadership and the majority of their caucus to get a bill up for debate and vote is a brave thing to do. Leadership frowns on that kind of independence, and punishes it. Suddenly, you find yourself sitting on the postal service subcommittee and not in that seat you always coveted on Ways and Means. But the lead Republican sponsor of the bill, Chris Shays of Connecticut, did it. He got nineteen Republicans to vote for a discharge petition. His Democratic co-sponsor, Marty Meehan of Massachusetts, provided the necessary votes from his caucus with a major assist from the Democratic leader, Dick Gephardt, who was all in on campaign finance reform despite being a proficient soft money fundraiser. Dick was an impressive behind-the-scenes force. For only the second time in House history a discharge petition to force action on legislation passed. After that, the vote on the bill itself was anticlimactic. It passed easily with 41 Republicans voting with 198 Democrats in favor of it. The President signed it, unenthusiastically, a week later.

That's the formula for success for any major piece of legislation. Don't give up, be persistent. If you can't get it done in this Congress, try again in the next. Give the impression that you're going to make yourself as big a pain in the ass on the issue as you can until some accommodation to your view is made by negotiated compromise if possible or by a vote. Be alert to changes in the political environment.

Strike hardest when external events give you an advantage. Make necessary compromises to build a bipartisan coalition in favor of it. Use your friendships to recruit as many influential members to your side as you can. Friends on both sides of the aisle will warn you about problems you might not be aware of, they'll tell you who you can count on and who's quietly working against you. Box in the cynics with public and media attention, make sure the more transactional politicians know there's a cost to opposing the bill. Leave critical responsibilities to your hardest-nosed allies, and hope they'll stand up to threats and reprisals. Be the most hard-nosed advocate yourself to set an example. Gather all the pressure you can to move the process along as quickly as possible, even if it ruffles important feathers. A lot of momentum for an issue is illusory and based on excessive faith in the media's sustained attention to it and the potency of its public support. Get it done before your opponents figure out that's not the case. And get a little lucky. That's how the sausage gets made.

That's the formula we tried to follow, Ted and I and our fellow travelers, in our multiple attempts to pass comprehensive immigration reform. We failed twice, and then once more after Ted had passed away, despite big majorities in both houses of Congress in favor of it. I'd like to say I'll try again. But that is not up to me anymore. That's a harder disappointment than other defeats have been because first, it's something that most Americans want, and most members of Congress know is the right thing to do. But most of all, because it's something this country needs to do now, in this political moment, as old fears and animosities that have blighted our history appear to be on the rise again, exploited by opportunists who won't trouble their careers or their consciences with scruples about honesty or compassion for their fellow man.

Then there are the true believers in an exclusive America. It might be the cynics who are mainly responsible for inaction on immigration reform. They're Republicans mostly, in gerrymandered districts where the only challenge they're likely to face is from the Far Right. But people in both parties, people who know better, have used the lack of progress on immigration reform to their advantage. Their obstruction isn't durable. They'll change when the politics for them change. If and when being pro-immigration becomes a political advantage, they'll shelter immigrants in their own homes.

Although their numbers aren't large, it's the true believers who fear America is contaminated by the customs of non-European immigrants who make this moment so fraught. They believe the President shares their prejudice, and has promised to enact it into law. They're not only opposed to illegal immigration, they're opposed to immigration, at least immigration from south of the border, and the Caribbean, the Middle East, Africa, and Asia. They're still a small faction in the Republican Party. But they're the ones getting all the attention right now. They need to be confronted, not ignored or winked at or quietly dismissed as kooks. They need to be confronted before their noxious views spread further, and damage for generations the reputation of the Republican Party.

A backbench House Republican from Iowa, Steve King, has made a name for himself by regularly espousing ethnocentrism as the principal attribute of American exceptionalism and the foundation of Western civilization. Some days, King plays the social scientist with his openly expressed misapprehension that diversity and assimilation are incompatible. Other times, he seems to go out of his way to offend as many people as he can with his crude insults of folks who came to this country for freedom and opportunity.

In a tweet praising Dutch nationalist Geert Wilders, King wrote, "culture and demographics are our destiny. We can't restore our civilization with somebody else's babies." Leave aside the fact that our civilization isn't in need of restoration, and marvel at the breadth of King's ignorance of history. We built the civilization he wants to restore—the world's freest, most enlightened, and most prosperous civilization—with the help of babies whose parents came here from every corner of the world.

We've had periods of practically open immigration and periods where government severely restricted immigration. Through all our history, immigrants kept coming. They came with permission and without it. They came from south of the border, north of the border, across the Pacific and Atlantic Oceans. They came to escape violence, poverty, religious intolerance, and powerlessness. Most grasped the bottom rung of the ladder of opportunity and society, working jobs many American citizens wouldn't, living in ethnic ghettos, speaking their native language. They were objects of fear, resentment, disgust, and hate. They were accused of stealing jobs from the native-born. They were victims of prejudice and violence. They dressed oddly. They had strange habits and food and entertainment. Their music was different, their theater, too. They had different ideas about farming and business. And yet they assimilated. As they did, they changed our civilization with their additions to it, and they were changed by it. The amalgamation was a more varied, cosmopolitan, rich, accomplished, capable, visionary society held together by shared ideals. That's how assimilation works in this country, and what a country it has become as a result. Because all that's needed to assimilate in America is to embrace our founding convictions, the foundation of Western civilization, that all have an equal right to life, liberty, and the pursuit of happiness, to the protections of the law, to be governed by consent, to speak freely, practice their religion openly, go as far as their industry and talent can take them. That's it, and it's beautiful in its wise simplicity. People came to this country and brought their culture and languages and customs with them, infused them in the stew of American culture, and became Americans. You can speak Spanish or Mongolian. You can like Yiddish theater. You can hum music from the steppes of Central Asia. You can worship Jesus or Allah or your ancestors. You can celebrate Cinco de Mayo or St. Patrick's Day. You can be sentimental and proud of the heritage you brought with you. You can change American arts, food, and industry. Only our ideals must remain unaltered. You have to give your allegiance to those, and most immigrants do. They came here for the protection and opportunities our ideals provide. And often they do a good deal more than adhere to the country's values, they fight and die for them, too. The first American combat casualty of 2018 was an immigrant, Sergeant First Class Mihail Golin from Fort Lee, New Jersey, a thirty-four-year-old Green Beret, who emigrated from Latvia when he was twenty-one. He was the latest of many thousands of immigrants, authorized and unauthorized, who gave their lives for America.

As long as you respect the rights and property of your fellow Americans, you are entitled to their respect, whether they give it to you or not. You have the same rights. You are protected by the same laws. You're welcome to your opportunities. You're welcome to America, land of the immigrant's dream.

Steve King and his immigrant-bashing cohort—and let's be as clear about it as Mr. King has been, he's not just opposed to illegal immigration, but also to the current rules and levels of legal immigration—understand none of this for the very simple reason that they don't understand American exceptionalism. They believe exceptionalism is the quality of a culture dominated by the customs, beliefs, and experiences of a single race and religion, not just allegiance to ideals that, while they are part of that culture, are universal, endowed to humanity by our Creator.

Here is one of the best illustrations of American exceptionalism

I've ever heard, offered by an American President who believed this country was the most special place on earth, Ronald Wilson Reagan:

> America represents something universal in the human spirit. I received a letter not long ago from a man who said, "You can go to Japan to live, but you cannot become Japanese. You can go to France to live and not become a Frenchman. You can go to live in Germany or Turkey, and you won't become a German or a Turk." But then he added, "Anybody from any corner of the world can come to America to live and become an American."

What he meant was that in all those other countries you must be born there to be of there. Even if you're a legal resident of long standing, a citizen, even if you make a good living there, are protected by the same laws that protect the native-born, speak the language fluently, cheer for local sport teams, listen to the same music, cook the same food, fly the same flag, vote for the same candidates, even if you can run for public office there, you still can't assume the national identity if you were born elsewhere. You have to have been born a member of the tribe.

Anyone can become an American if they embrace our values. Anyone. You don't even have to speak the language. As a practical matter, you'll have an easier time of it here if you learn English. But even a common language isn't essential to assimilation. Not in this country. Spanish has been spoken in Arizona centuries longer than English has. Plenty of Italian, Polish, Serbian, Russian, German, and every other kind of non-English-speaking immigrants came to this country and struggled to learn the language. They relied mostly or exclusively on their native tongue to talk with family and friends, and yet managed to communicate with English-speaking Americans, while their children grew up bilingual.

There are valid arguments for and against high levels of immigration. You can argue that immigrants are depressing wages and taking jobs from native-born Americans, or taking more jobs than they're creating. You can argue they're a drain on public resources, straining school systems and human services, while not contributing enough to public treasuries or local economic growth to compensate. I think those arguments are mistaken, and the facts support my view. But they're not outlandish. Nor are they racist or expressions of the narrow-minded nationalism of Steve King and Steve Bannon, and those parts of the America First crowd that misunderstand American culture and exceptionalism. Demographics aren't destiny. Our culture isn't the work of one race or religion. To suggest otherwise is to contradict our ideals and to doubt their power.

What is behind that point of view? Often it's little more than a re-action to different behavior and tastes that are perceived as an attack on the culture, on the American way, especially in previously homogenous small towns and rural communities. Hearing a foreign language spoken where only English was ever heard. Seeing new restaurants and shops cater mostly to immigrants. Finding your kid's school pageant includes music from another country performed in another language. Driving by a familiar neighborhood and being taken aback by the colors the houses are painted or the way the yards are kept. In some communities, these sudden departures from the familiar can make folks worry America is being appropriated by a foreign culture. It's not. America is absorbing, as it always does, the latest contributions to our tastes and look and sound. It's new. It's foreign. But it isn't an assault on our culture. In Arizona, no one, Anglo or Hispanic, native-born or immigrant, would think twice about hearing Spanish spoken anywhere or the prevalence of Mexican restaurants or the prominence of Hispanic heritage in the local humanities.

To be sure, there is anger over illegal immigration in Arizona, too,

at times more than there is in parts of the country that have only recent experience with a wave of immigrants locating there. Arizona is a
border state and bears the brunt of the economic, environmental, and
criminal impact illegal immigration has on communities. Ranches and
towns along the border can be dangerous places for the unauthorized
immigrant and the native-born. But for centuries Hispanic influences
have played a prominent part in shaping the culture of the American Southwest. We identify with them. That's not to say there aren't
Arizonans who view immigration as a threat to civilization or share
resentments and fears harbored by people in other states. There are.
And there are also people here, as there are in every other place in this
country, whose views about immigrants, at least non-European immigrants, are just racist. They can be cruel. But their influence in the
immigration debate is marginal, limited usually to making themselves
and sometimes nonracist immigration restrictionists look bad.

Unlawful immigration is a serious legal, economic, commercial,
and security problem. It is not our biggest or most dangerous problem,
not by any stretch of the imagination. But it is a serious problem, especially for border states. A comprehensive policy to address the problem
should have been signed into law more than a decade ago. It's not that
complicated. Its provisions are obvious, practical, and humane. That a
compromise immigration reform policy is no closer to being enacted
today than it was when we first attempted it is mostly attributable to
the misinformation and downright lies that enflame opponents, which
have only gotten more pervasive and inflammatory over the last decade. Here's a little straight talk:

First, there are eleven to twelve million immigrants, give or take,
residing in this country without permission. Most of them are never
going to leave, and they're really isn't much we can do about it or that
we should want to do about it. About seven million are from Mexico
and Central America. The other four to five million came from all over,

from China to Ireland. Two-thirds of adult unauthorized immigrants have been here for at least a decade. They're integrated into the fabric of our communities. In a word, but for their illegal status, they are assimilated, and most of them aren't going anywhere. The physical and legal infrastructure and the nationwide hard-heartedness required to round up and deport eleven to twelve million mostly decent, hard-working, well-liked people will never exist. To attempt anything like it would produce an economic, social, and humanitarian catastrophe. It would hurt communities all over the country, shrink revenue bases, necessitate tax increases and cuts in services. Businesses large and small would be damaged or destroyed by sudden losses of employees and customers. Friendships would be lost, students hauled from schools, valued members of community organizations treated as criminals, families separated as teenaged children born here to immigrant parents are U.S. citizens, and many will stay to make their way on their own in their native land. It would destroy the spirit of communities and our reputation as a compassionate and practical people.

Second, the great majority of unauthorized immigrants came here to find work and raise their families, like most immigrants have throughout our history. They are not the rapists, killers, and drug dealers of fevered imaginations on the Right. They're not the cause of the opioid epidemic. They're decent people working hard to make better lives. Only a small fraction ever commit violent crimes, a much lower percentage than native-born violent criminals. Only 3 percent have committed a felony of any kind. About a third own their own homes. A third have children born here. They pay taxes, obey the laws, contribute positively to our economy and society, serve in our armed services, are killed and wounded in overseas conflicts, and live in fear they'll be discovered and expelled from the land of their dreams.

Third, since 2007 most immigrants who come here without permission simply outstay their visas. They don't cross the border illegally.

And since the Great Recession, net illegal immigration has been flat or negative as more immigrants voluntarily returned to their native countries as jobs were scarce. A wall along the southern border isn't going to solve the problem. It might make it worse. Spending tens of billions of dollars on a dubious barrier to illegal immigration takes resources away from more effective border security and enforcement. There are long stretches of the southern border where the topography makes a wall impractical. Where a physical barrier is feasible, fences are better than walls for an obvious reason, they're transparent. You can see what people on the other side are doing. Where barriers aren't feasible, drones, sensors, and cameras can provide better security. No matter what you build, a wall or a fence, no matter how high and forbidding it is, it can be scaled or tunneled under or breached in some way. Build a thirty-foot wall, and someone will get rich selling thirty-foot ladders. And walls and fences cannot apprehend anyone. You need people to do that, and there will never be enough Border Patrol agents to monitor twenty-four hours a day every stretch of a two-thousand-mile border, especially if you're spending $20 billion on a wall. We can make it harder to cross the border illegally. We can reduce the numbers of people walking over, wading across, digging under, climbing over the border. We can build a series of hugely expensive walls and fences that look impregnable. We can hire thousands of new Border Patrol agents. We can crack down on employers of unauthorized immigrants. We can do most of the things the opponents of comprehensive immigration reform demand, and they might significantly reduce the number of unauthorized immigrants entering the country. But people are still going to cross that border illegally every day. We can restrain illegal immigration. We cannot stop it altogether. There is one way to curtail illegal immigration that's more effective than all others. An economic downturn and lack of job opportunities here will do it as we saw during the last recession. Again, that's because virtually all adults entering our country illegally aren't doing it to commit crimes or live on welfare. They're seeking work they don't have in their home countries.

Fourth, unauthorized immigrants aren't depriving millions of native-born Americans of employment. Most jobs taken by immigrants are low-paying, and have the hardest conditions. Their employers have trouble filling payrolls. Many jobs are seasonal or otherwise irregular employment. Unauthorized immigrants are not sucking up all the blue-collar jobs in the country as their most hyperbolic antagonists insist. They make up approximately 5 percent of the workforce. Even in communities where immigrants have taken jobs that might otherwise have been taken by native residents, their economic activity, their spending on local goods and services creates new job opportunities for locals.

There are politicians today who would have Americans believe that illegal immigration is one of the worst scourges afflicting the country. Some who espouse that nonsense believe it to be true. Their opinions were formed in restricted information loops as they communicate mostly or exclusively with people who believe the same. Many more know it isn't so, and are cynically claiming otherwise for one of a couple reasons. I expect most are identifying a scapegoat people can blame for their dissatisfaction because it suggests there is an easy fix for difficult problems, an easy fix that's easy to campaign on. Others are doing it for more sinister reasons they're reluctant to acknowledge publicly, including racial prejudice. Whatever their reasons, the cynical and the ignorant promotion of false information and unnecessary fear have the same outcome. Decent, hardworking people who mean no harm are blamed for crime, unemployment, failing schools, and various other ills, and become in the eyes of many the objects of hate and fear.

The other consequence is that Americans who are having a hard time of it, people with fewer job opportunities than previous generations had, people with children in underperforming schools, families who have been victimized by crime or lost a loved one to drugs are deluded into believing there's a simple remedy for all of it—round up all the "illegals" and deport them. The cynic knows that isn't going to happen and even were such a "roundup" possible it wouldn't appreciably improve any of the problems they blamed on immigrants. Of course, they wouldn't ever admit their prescription was bullshit. They would just perpetuate the delusion, keep blaming "the Swamp" for not doing enough to rid the country of the scourge. Some politicians will always see an advantage in it, and some folks will always fall for it. But America's demographics are changing inexorably and with it public opinion as well. Soon scapegoating immigrants is going to help the Republican Party lose more elections than it helps win.

Nearly 57 million people living in the United States are Hispanic, about 18 percent of the population, a percentage that has been steadily growing for years. In one year, of the two and a half million people who were added to the population, almost half were Hispanic. In forty years, the number of Hispanic Americans is projected to reach 119 million, nearly 30 percent of the population. As a matter of survival, the Republican Party has to be competitive for the fastest-growing segment of the population. States such as Arizona and Texas, vote-rich, reliable red states, will become competitive for Democrats. Arizona will get there first. Trump only won it by 4 percent, less than half the margin Governor Romney won with in 2012. And when Texas goes, there is no conceivable way Republicans can win a presidential election given the Democrats' lock on New York and California (also related partly to Hispanic alienation from Republicans).

Let's use my state as an example. The Hispanic segment of Arizona's population is approaching one-third. More Hispanics are enrolled in Arizona schools than any other ethnic group. Forty-four percent of students are Hispanic. Two hundred ninety-one thousand Arizona

Hispanics voted in the 2008 presidential election. Eight years later, the number had almost doubled to 550,000. As a border state, Arizona confronts some of the worst problems associated with streams of unauthorized immigrants regularly entering the state, and that made for some distress and hard feelings, which resulted in legislation and referenda that seemed harsh and discriminatory, which in turn led to hard feelings and distrust among Arizona Hispanics. Exit polling in 2016 suggested that President Trump won more than 30 percent of Hispanics in Arizona. Analysis based on comprehensive and precise polling indicates his share of their vote could have been as low as 12 percent, which would partly explain why he won the state so narrowly. That isn't terribly surprising given his insulting references to unauthorized immigrants and the hard positions the state adopted in recent years to punish and apprehend them, exacerbated by the offensive statements and policies of Maricopa County's notorious former sheriff, convicted felon Joe Arpaio.

Yet for all that trouble, Arizona life is a blend of Hispanic and Anglo influences. We know each other. We're used to each other, having not merely coexisted for centuries, but having built together from a desert wilderness this thriving state. In other places in the country, disruptions caused by the sudden arrival of an immigrant community can include the shock of the new and different. Obviously, that's not the case here. And things have settled down in Arizona in recent years. Most Arizonans have a pretty practical take on the problem of illegal immigration. We know illegal immigration will never be stopped entirely. We know most people are coming because there's work here, because they're needed. We want the border made more secure. We want the rule of law respected. We want to save people from dying in the desert where they were left by unscrupulous "coyotes." We want to prevent the environmental and private property damage caused by illegal crossings. We want to interdict drugs flowing across the border and into the veins of kids. We want responsible officials to tackle these problems with sensible policies. And we want people treated with respect for their dignity.

Our own experiences inform our views of immigrants. A recent Arizona poll found that more than two-thirds of Arizonans don't want all unauthorized immigrants deported. Two-thirds don't think a border wall makes sense. Two-thirds don't believe immigrants increase crime rates. Three-quarters allowed that immigrants don't take jobs from citizens. Over 80 percent believe they're good for the economy and improve American society. It's not that Arizonans don't care about border security, of course we do. We deal every day with problems caused by unsecured borders. I campaigned on improving security, and every immigration bill I've sponsored has proposed measures to strengthen the border and provided the resources to do it. In a campaign ad, I called, notoriously my critics would say, for finishing "the dang fence." I probably wouldn't have emphasized the measure if it weren't very popular with my constituents. But I meant it. We need effective barriers on the border. Arizonans know from experience that fences are more practical in many places than a wall would be, but that doesn't mean they don't want improvements made. And familiarity has bred appreciation here for the character and culture of immigrants that I'm sure will be the case in time in other parts of the country, when people are no longer perceived as aliens but as neighbors.

Right now, Republicans are on the wrong side of that progress, and if we want to retain our competitiveness in the fastest-growing communities in the country we'll stop letting the zealots drive the debate, and fix the problem that gives them their soapbox. We can begin by permanently legalizing the status of unauthorized immigrants who were brought here as children, the so-called Dreamers. America is the only country they know. It would be a surpassingly cruel act to deport them, and it would earn Republicans the enmity of not only Hispanic

Americans, but the enmity of their neighbors and friends as well. Most Arizona high school seniors are Hispanic. Do you think most of them would consider voting for the party that pulled their friends out of school, took them away from their teams and clubs and neighborhoods, and put them on buses to Mexico?

We face much more difficult and complicated problems in this century than illegal immigration. If we have the political will, the solution isn't hard to envision, if for no other reason than because variations of the solution have been proposed three times in the last twelve years. But having the political will requires doing something Republican leadership isn't comfortable doing: acting over the objections of a minority of Americans, which on this issue is mostly comprised of Republicans.

Most of the provisions of an effective comprehensive immigration reform were included in the first immigration bill Ted Kennedy and I worked on in 2005 and 2006. The late Arlen Specter was the primary sponsor of the bill the Senate debated in 2006. He was chairman of the Senate Judiciary Committee at the time, which had jurisdiction over the issue and sent the bill to the full Senate. But it was an amended version of the bill Ted and I and our staffs had written and introduced in 2005, working with colleagues Chuck Hagel, Mel Martinez, Lindsey Graham, and prominent conservative Sam Brownback.

The House had passed a very different immigration bill near the end of 2005. Republicans had majorities in both the House and Senate. And while President George W. Bush wanted comprehensive immigration reform along the lines of our bill, many House Republicans' views on immigration reform were restricted to authorizing more money for border security and tougher enforcement of existing law, which is practically all the House bill included. The President's political standing at the time had been weakened by the Iraq War's unpopularity, and though there remained considerable affection for him among conservatives, bucking him wasn't politically risky. On this issue, with certain constituencies, it was advantageous. The issue was starting to heat up on the Far Right. Bashing illegal immigrants proved popular with conservative talk radio audiences, and if any industry enjoys beating dead horses, it's conservative talk radio. Honestly, having to dream up more hyperbole on the same damn subject day after day would bore the hell out of me. A few backbench Republicans were acquiring notoriety by taking a hard stance against any practical solution to the eleven or so million people living in the country without authorization. "No amnesty!" was their battle cry.

Things were different in the Senate. The rules of the place require bipartisan negotiation and agreement to pass most major bills. Ted and I thought we had hammered out a compromise that could attract twenty or more Republican votes and most of his caucus. And we had. Our bill added ample additional resources for border security, including hundreds of miles of new fencing, and new restrictions on employers who hired undocumented workers. It created a new guest worker program that would allow workers in the country for three years, with the possibility of one three-year extension, if they had standing employment offers for jobs that had not been filled after advertising their availability. Contrary to the complaints of immigration restrictionists and some labor leaders, there are a good many businesses all over this country that cannot get American citizens to take the jobs they offer, and not, as is often alleged, because the pay is so low. I once caught grief from talk radio blowhards for saying, "You can't get Americans to pick lettuce in Yuma in the summer if you paid them fifty dollars an hour." But it's the truth, whether the anti-immigration crowd wants to hear it or not.

Finally, the bill dealt practically with unauthorized immigrants already in the country, if somewhat convolutedly due to the political balancing required to get support from liberals and conservatives, by legalizing the status of all but the most recent arrivals. We proposed a three-tier system. If someone had been here for two years or less, they would be deported if found. Those here for two to five years would have to return to a border entry point and apply for a temporary guest worker visa. As long as they passed a criminal background check, they would be allowed to stay. Those who had been living in the country for more than five years would be offered a path to citizenship. After an eleven-year probationary period, in which they would have to come out of hiding, pay a penalty and any back taxes they might owe, submit to criminal background checks, and learn English, they could become citizens of the country they were already positively contributing to in numerous ways. We would make two more attempts at comprehensive reform after this one. But this remains the general outline of a prac-tical, workable, effective, fair, and decent solution to the problem of illegal immigration.

Debate on the bill began in May. Every day the bill was pending, the leading co-sponsors met with Ted and me in a room off the Sen-ate floor before we went into session. We shared intelligence and plot-ted strategies for the amendments that would be offered that day. We had an agreement that if either the Republicans or Democrats in the room considered an amendment a "poison pill," a deal breaker in other words, all would vote against it. A freshman senator who frequently joined our morning conference, an eloquent and ambitious addition to the Senate, declined to join our pact.

I had been eager to work with Barack Obama. There had been so much buzz about him the moment he arrived. The Democratic leader, Harry Reid, had already given him significant roles to play in some of the more politically charged debates his first year in the Senate. Like everybody else, I'd been impressed by his 2004 convention speech in Boston. Here's a guy, I thought, who talks about bridging partisan di-vides, who can really move people with a speech, and he's coming to an institution where we make a lot of them. Most of us, no matter how modest our talent for oratory, have tried more than once to convince our colleagues we are a Cicero. And most of us recognize the real thing when we see it. Barack Obama was the real deal when it came to public speaking, as the world would soon discover. I wanted to work with him, to enlist his voice in causes I cared about.

We did briefly work together early in his first Congress. I was trying to put together a bipartisan coalition for a series of ethics reform proposals, and approached him to join us, which he did. We got along perfectly well until Harry got his hooks into him, getting him to promote some ethics changes Harry wanted because they would put Republicans at a disadvantage. Harry was a character, and partisan to the core. We had our moments, he and I. We both liked the fights and we liked to fight. But even though there were times in our long association when I was seething over something Harry did, I could never quite sustain a permanent dislike for the guy. He was scrappy as hell. He had come up from nothing and had more than a little pride about it. Woe be to the opponent he felt didn't respect him. On this occasion, he had somehow convinced Obama to send me a letter criticizing some reform I had proposed that I thought Obama had agreed to support.

I was traveling overseas when the letter reached my office, about an hour after it had been sent to the press. My administrative assistant at the time, Mark Salter, got hold of it, and before he had finished reading it we started receiving press calls about it. When I called the office that day and Salter mentioned it to me, I told him to send a letter to Obama from me. "Brush him back," I instructed, the baseball term for when the pitcher tries to nearly, emphasis on nearly, hit a batter crowding the plate. Salter, the hothead, beaned him, penning a letter so loaded with sarcasm and insults that amused reporters welcomed it as a controversy suited for a couple days in the cable news blender. It blew over by the end of the week. Obama made a pretty funny, smartass rejoinder, and Salter and I might have made another smartass remark after that. But by the time I got back from my trip, I had let it go, and believed he had as well. I wanted Obama to join our immigration effort, and was pleased when he agreed.

I had been a man in a hurry when I arrived in the Senate in 1987. I recognized the type, and remembering how my ambitiousness had been so consuming, I had a sympathetic regard for those suffering the same ailment. I didn't know then that Barack Obama would run for President in 2008, the year I was contemplating another run. That took daring and confidence I'm not sure I possessed in those early days of my career. But I knew he would run for President someday. He had the bug and he had the chops. That was clear on first acquaintance.

It was clear, too, that he was focused on other objectives during that first effort at immigration reform. When he joined our morning conference, he usually had a note card in his shirt pocket with concerns about the bill he wanted addressed, and the interests who were most interested in those concerns were usually quite obvious. More often than not, they were concerns raised by the AFL-CIO or another important Democratic constituency. It was noticeably self-interested, but not an unfamiliar or unacceptable approach to legislation with the political impact immigration reform has. There were mornings when I wished he had spent more time helping us strategize how to beat back politically tricky amendments than he had advocating for amendments he wanted. That said, when he spoke on the floor on behalf of the bill he gave us good value.

Ted Kennedy gave value no other senator could. His influence on his caucus was greater than the influence any other senator in either caucus had. He could persuade, cajole, maneuver, humor, shame, and scare Democratic senators into doing what he wanted them to do. And with that booming voice he could be pretty intimidating. Barack got a taste of it during that first immigration fight. It happened one morning near the end of the Senate debate. Obama had made a couple of requests, and while I can't remember exactly what Ted said, it was something along the lines of "Why don't you pitch in and help, instead of making demands every morning," only louder. It stopped the conversation in the room for a minute. He had done it for the benefit of Republicans there, I'm sure, to remind us we could trust him. But I think he also intended to help Obama, whom he considered a unique talent. He told me he did. That day he was helping him learn how to "win friends and influence people" as the old marketing slogan goes, how to get stuff done. Obama took it in stride.

The bill passed on May 25, 2006, with a filibuster-proof majority, 62 votes, which included 23 Republicans and 38 Democrats (and one Independent). It was major legislation passed the only way most major legislation is ever passed: with a broad bipartisan majority built on compromises both sides could live with and good faith on the part of the senators most involved. The sponsors of the bill held a press conference after the win to thank supporters and urge the House to agree to a conference. When it was my turn at the mic, I paid tribute to Ted, "the last lion of the Senate."

We all expected the bill would have to become more conservative, for lack of a better word, in conference with the Republican House. Ted knew that, and was prepared to bring his caucus along. Regrettably, House Republicans weren't inclined to negotiate at all. When you serve in an institution where the majority almost always gets its way completely, giving in on anything is hard to accept, and disdain for the Senate with its compromising, split-the-difference ways runs high. House Republicans kept referring to the bill as the Reid-Kennedy bill instead of Kennedy-McCain as the rest of the world called it, as if that name change would fool anyone into believing that no Republican supported it. Many Republicans in Congress did, and polling made clear that a majority of Republicans in the country supported it. But it didn't have the support in the House of a "majority of the majority," Speaker Hastert's precondition for letting any legislation come to a vote. And so it died, despite the White House urging Senate and House Republicans to come to terms on a compromise.

In November of that year, Republicans were crushed in midterm elections, losing both houses of Congress. The loss was mostly attributable to dissatisfaction with the Iraq War, not Republican opposition to immigration reform. But I don't think the latter helped us any. In the silver lining category, with the Democrats now in charge of the House, proponents of comprehensive immigration reform would have an easier time passing a bill, or so we thought, anyway. But gridlock in Congress is not always strictly a partisan divide. In 1998, I had moved anti-tobacco legislation through the Commerce Committee, which I chaired at the time, with only one dissenting vote. We had gathered a wide coalition of most of the various interests affected by the bill, with the exception of the tobacco companies themselves, from tobacco-state senators to trial lawyers who had sued the tobacco companies. But when the bill got to the floor for debate by the full Senate, a tactical alliance formed between the most anti-tobacco progressives and conservative opponents of the bill when the latter offered amendments to entice the former, ostensibly to toughen sanctions against the tobacco companies, but in reality to weigh the bill down and bleed its support. The tobacco bill died in a blaze of anti–tobacco company indignation, equal parts cynical and earnest.

A similar fate awaited the new comprehensive immigration bill we introduced in 2007. Early that year, before the Senate had even convened, Ted and I had approached my friend and Arizona colleague Jon Kyl, a prominent conservative and thoughtful legislator, who had opposed our bill the year before but sincerely wanted to find a solution to the impasse. Working closely with the Bush White House and with Jon, we put together a bill that incorporated provisions from a bill Jon had sponsored with John Cornyn. While Lindsey and I and our staffs were involved in the discussions, the biggest changes to the bill were mostly a product of Ted's and Jon's negotiations with input from the White House. I was running for President at the time, and frequently out of town. I tried to be in the Senate for much of the debate, and my staff was involved in decisions on floor strategy. Two Democrats supporting the bill were running for President, too, Hillary Clinton and Barack Obama. Of the two, Barack was the more engaged in the effort. All of us were increasingly absent from the Senate. When I was on the campaign trail, I called Ted, Jon, and Lindsey several times a day for an update, and to offer suggestions. I missed the action when I wasn't in the Senate, and wished I could have temporarily suspended the campaign. This was in the period when we were in trouble and teetering on the brink of insolvency. I was also getting the hell kicked out of me for my immigration views by some of my Republican rivals, chiefly Mitt Romney, as well as a nuisance candidate and anti-immigration hard-liner from Colorado, Tom Tancredo. Once, when we were both in the same South Carolina restaurant, Tancredo sent my table an order of chips and salsa, meaning I'm not sure what. I guess he thought that since I didn't want to kick out of the country every Mexican-born immigrant, I must like chips and salsa.

The bill, thanks to Jon's contributions, should have been acceptable to the get-tougher-on-security-and-enforcement camp. It authorized over $4 billion more for border security, thousands of new Border Patrol agents, seven hundred miles of new fencing, infrared cameras, drones, and sensors that detected footsteps. It increased penalties on employers who knowingly hired undocumented workers, and created a central database of information on all immigrant workers provided by their employers, as well as a biometric identity card that immigrant workers would have to show employers to prove they were in the country legally. It terminated the existing family reunification policy for immigrants who became citizens, and substituted a more restrictive one that limited family visas to a naturalized citizen's spouse and children. And it established a merit-based point system for granting work visas, which would give preference to more skilled workers. These were all key demands of conservative critics, who had felt our previous effort hadn't been tough enough on illegal immigration.

We also established a guest worker program urged by the business community that would have given temporary visas to foreign workers who had job offers in the U.S. They would expire after two years, when the worker would have to return to his home country. The legislation incorporated the provisions of the Dream Act, which offered eventual citizenship to immigrants who were brought to the country as minors, and who were attending college or serving in the military. And the bill still offered a path to citizenship for the millions of unauthorized immigrants living and working here already. It was a longer and more conditional path than the one we had proposed the previous year. Anyone living in the country without a visa could, after passing a criminal background check, apply for a new "Z" visa in 2010, which would allow them to remain in the country. After eight years in the country, they could apply for permanent residence, or a "green card," if they paid a fine and back taxes. Existing law allows green card holders to apply for citizenship after five years. The entire process would have taken about sixteen years from the date of the bill's enactment. And the Z visa holder had to return to their home country to apply for a green card. It wasn't a generous or easy route to citizenship. But it was the product of practical politics based on the premise that we couldn't deport all or most or even a substantial minority of the undocumented immigrants in the country, and we shouldn't want to.

Democrats controlled both houses of Congress, and the White

House was fully behind the bill, having pushed with Kyl for many of the more restrictive changes to the bill. That opened up fissures with some of the other interests supporting comprehensive reform. Labor, not all unions, but certainly the AFL-CIO, hated the temporary worker provisions. Some immigrant groups were upset with changes to the family reunification policy, and with the point system. Those fissures were seen by conservative immigration restrictionists as opportunities to kill the bill. Despite the inclusion of many provisions they had long advocated, any bill that provided any kind of path to citizenship, no matter how attenuated and scrutinized and difficult a path, was "amnesty." The impracticality bordering on stupidity of such a position is equaled only by its inhumanity.

Many conservatives voted for amendments offered by Senate liberals at the behest of labor and by immigrant groups dissatisfied with the bill. In effect, conservative opponents helped make the bill less conservative and business-friendly, knowing that each successful amendment attracted new opposition to the bill or at least created confusion and chaos that extended the debate.

One of those amendments was offered by Barack Obama over the objections of the bill's other co-sponsors, who, as we had the year before, had pledged to act by consensus. It failed, but he co-sponsored another amendment objected to by the group, offered by Byron Dorgan of North Dakota, to sunset the temporary worker program after five years. It passed and it cost the bill some of its business community support. I wasn't there when it happened, but Lindsey called to describe it to me. When Obama informed the other co-sponsors that he was supporting and even offering amendments they agreed should be opposed, Ted tore into him in front of the others, at length, accusing him of bad faith. Obama objected that he had never agreed to act by consensus, and felt strongly that the changes he supported were needed. Ted, as he would have done with any other member of the body who needed the instruction, Democrat or Republican, explained that only senators who hold up their end of bargains get anything done there. However vociferous it was, the remonstration was again as much for Obama's benefit as it was for the Republicans in the room. Ted, the liberal lion of the Senate, was chastising a Democratic colleague for voting with other liberals. He was showing him the ropes, how to work the Senate, something Obama would need to know whether his presidential bid failed or succeeded. Lesson one: only give your word if you're sure you can keep it.

The opponents succeeded. Various tactical alliances formed, all intent on continuing the debate until they could get what they wanted in the bill or what they disliked out of it. We made three attempts to cut off debate, all three failed, and Harry Reid reluctantly pulled the bill from the floor. A golden opportunity to get immigration reform done was squandered. Republicans and Democrats had collaborated in its defeat. President Bush expressed his disappointment. So did its Senate proponents. I continued to get pummeled by my primary opponents for my immigration views as my campaign was on the brink of imploding. Ted called to tell me to keep my chin up, we'd get it done next time. I wasn't so sure.

There wasn't a next time for Ted. In January, at a big rally with his niece Caroline, he endorsed Barack Obama for President despite both Clintons beseeching him not to. It was a big deal. Ted's endorsement was one of the most influential in his party, and it came when Obama most needed it, not long after Hillary had won New Hampshire. Reportedly, Obama had assured Ted that were he elected, he would make an early and aggressive push for universal health care insurance. A couple days after the endorsement, Ted called me to check in. I was in our campaign bus rolling down some highway in a state I can't remember. Lindsey was with me. I had won the South Carolina primary a few days earlier. Ted congratulated me and said it looked like I'd be the nominee.

I told him I wasn't so sure, but that I expected him to start beating the hell out of me anyway. We traded gossip for a few minutes, and then Lindsey asked me to pass the phone to him. "Ted," he drawled, "can I have your hideaway office?" Senators have small offices in the Capitol building in addition to their official offices. Most are cubbyholes tucked away in the basement or a back hall. The most senior senators have grander ones, with views of the Mall. Ted's was the nicest.

"Why?" Ted asked.

"Because the Clintons are going to have you murdered," Lindsey explained.

I could hear Ted's laughter boom from the phone Lindsey held several feet away, over the din of the crowded bus.

Four months later, Ted had a seizure, and was diagnosed with brain cancer, glioblastoma. Surgeons removed as much of the tumor as they could in a long operation in June 2008, and he started chemotherapy and radiation to keep the cancer at bay as long as possible. He was back in the Senate the next month to help break a Republican filibuster of Medicare legislation, and he gave a speech at the Democratic convention in August from memory because he couldn't see well enough to read the teleprompter. After that, he withdrew from the public spotlight for longer periods as he fought his cancer. He attended Barack Obama's inauguration, but fell ill at the lunch in the Capitol that followed the ceremony. He came back to the Senate for a few important votes, and to help behind the scenes get a health care bill through the health committee he had chaired. I spoke with him a few times as he got weaker. He was as positive as he could be given the circumstances, but not self-deluding. He set a fine, brave example. He died the following August, at his beloved Hyannis Port home.

Early in President Obama's first term, a few immigration advocates we had worked closely with in the previous two attempts asked to meet with me in my Washington office. It was a short meeting. They started explaining what they wanted included in a new immigration bill, some of which they informed me they would work out with the new administration with a plan to introduce new legislation in the spring. I was, I expect, a little irritated and abrupt at being instructed. I was still chafing over attacks the Obama campaign had made on my immigration position, one ad likening me to Rush Limbaugh, who had regularly attacked me as "Amnesty John." I hadn't expected any of the immigration activists we had worked with to endorse my candidacy. They were Democrats. Their support for Obama was expected and fine with me. I was, however, disappointed that not one of them had come to my defense over the Limbaugh comparison. I told them to come see me when the White House had an immigration proposal they would like me to consider supporting. I would give it the attention it deserved. Then I nodded at the door.

There never was a White House immigration proposal. However, after Obama's reelection in 2012, I went to see Chuck Schumer to discuss putting together a bipartisan group to sponsor a new immigration bill. The Gang of Eight, we were styled by the press. Four Democrats and four Republicans. Lindsey joined us, and Jeff Flake, my new Arizona Senate colleague, Jon Kyl having retired. And another relative newcomer to the Senate, Marco Rubio, who had been elected in the Tea Party wave in the 2010 midterms, a Cuban American and gifted speaker, who was marked as an up-and-comer. Chuck; Dick Durbin, the Democrats' whip; Bob Menendez of New Jersey; and Michael Bennet of Colorado made up the Democratic quartet. I got along with all the Gang members. Each had skills for the fight I valued.

The White House helped us put together the bill, and the President shrewdly and with admirable discipline made sure to keep the attention focused on the Senate. The bill provided for more security and enforcement, more fencing, more customs and border control agents, a more elaborate employment verification system. It divided temporary

work visas into three categories, one for high-skilled workers, a guest
worker visa for low-skilled workers, and a separate category for agri-
cultural workers. To protect American workers, no temporary work
visas would be granted for jobs in areas of the country where unemployment was high. The path to citizenship, which began with a green
card application after five years for Dreamers, and ten years for people
who came here as adults, would be suspended if specific markers for
improved border security weren't met. One marker was a 90 percent
apprehension rate for people crossing the border. Stopping 90 percent
of illegal crossings was an awfully tall task that any rational, honest
observer would acknowledge was as close to a secure border as was
possible to achieve. The bill was a balanced, conservative, scrupulously
thorough and fair attempt to settle the immigration problem in a way
that would satisfy economic needs, the interests of American workers, justice, and human decency. I'm proud it passed the Senate with
a supermajority, 68 to 32, despite the furious protests of anti-reform
senators. For them, every realistic attempt to address the issue will always be an "amnesty bill," no matter how rigorous and fair the path to
legalized status for immigrants who have been here for years and will
stay here the rest of their lives no matter what we do.

Once again, another broadly popular, eminently fair, and workable
solution to the immigration problem was buried in the Republican
House. I've made calls to three Republican Speakers of the House to
plead the case for comprehensive reform. This time the Speaker who
declined to put a comprehensive immigration bill on the floor for a
vote was John Boehner, who I'm pretty sure agreed with my views on
the issue. But because the House Republican caucus, to John's frequent
frustration, is driven crazy by the incessant demands of the say-no-
to-everything crowd otherwise known as the Freedom Caucus, and
because more sensible Republicans are afraid of primary challenges,
this acceptable solution to a solvable problem that impacts the lives

of a great many souls never got a vote. If it ever did, it would pass the House easily with Democratic support. But we're at a place in our political history when passing legislation through the House with bipartisan support is considered by some folks a greater evil than the problem it's intended to solve.

I've come to the conclusion that to get an immigration bill through Congress and to the President's desk will require one of three things to happen. Either Democrats retake the House, or enough practical, problem-solving House Republicans vote for a discharge petition as happened with McCain-Feingold, or Republican leaders break with recent precedent and bring a bill to the floor for a vote that offends the Freedom Caucus. I'd vote for the latter, but it's not in my power to arrange, more's the pity. Like my friend Ted, I might have fought my last immigration battle. I've got another one in me. I feel sure of that as we write this, and I've co-sponsored a new immigration bill with Chris Coons of Delaware. I'm not as sure that I've sufficient time left to see it all the way through. That, alas, isn't my call to make.

I spoke at Ted's memorial service at the Kennedy Library. I recalled his generosity toward my youngest son, Jimmy, many years ago, when Russ Feingold and I had come to the library to receive an award for supporting campaign finance reform. It was Jimmy's birthday, and Cindy and I had worried we would be too busy with official activities to celebrate the occasion. Ted arranged for a Coast Guard cutter to carry us across Boston Harbor to the library. He had a cake on board, and he led a rousing rendition of "Happy Birthday." Later that night, he produced another cake, and sang "Happy Birthday" again with no loss of enthusiasm. Then I recalled our long-ago stormy and profane exchange over Carol Moseley Braun's speech, and how much we had enjoyed it. "I'll go back to the Senate," I said, "and I'll try to be as persistent as Ted was, and as passionate for the work. I know I'm privileged to serve there. But . . . the place won't be the same without him."

And it hasn't been. It's been a privilege, and I've enjoyed the last nine years. I've been reelected twice in that time, and I've fought hard for the causes that mattered most to me, as hard, I hope, as Ted would expect me to fight. But the fights would have been more fun were Ted one of the combatants. Whether he was fighting on my side or on the other, it wouldn't have mattered that much. I would've just been happy to hear his bombast resounding in the chamber, and give it back to him if I dared.

CHAPTER SEVEN

NYET

(Know Thine Enemy)

I REGULARLY ATTEND AN ANNUAL SECURITY CONFERENCE in Halifax, Nova Scotia. The only thing unusual about the November 2016 meeting was that it occurred just after the U.S. presidential election, and most of the formal and informal conversations among the conferees were about what to expect from the President-elect, Donald Trump. The subject was causing consternation among the governments, military, and intelligentsia of the West, including ours. I spent most of my time in Halifax reassuring friends that the United States government consists of more than the White House. Congress and, I hoped, the people the new President would appoint to senior national security positions would provide continuity in U.S. foreign policy, compensate for the lack of experience in the Oval Office, and restrain the occupant from impulsively reacting to world events.

Saturday evening, when the day's presentations were finished, a retired British diplomat, who had served as the United Kingdom's ambassador to Russia during Vladimir Putin's rapid ascent to the Russian presidency, Sir Andrew Wood, asked to have a word. I might have been introduced to him before at a previous conference, but I don't recall ever having had a conversation with him. Nevertheless, I agreed to sit down with him for a few minutes. We found a room off the main conference hall, with a few chairs scattered around a coffee table. Chris Brose of the Senate Armed Services Committee staff and David Kramer joined us. David is a former assistant secretary of state, who has extensive experience dealing with Russia. He was working at the time at the McCain Institute for International Leadership, a policy organization dedicated to preparing world leaders and advancing human rights founded by Arizona State University.

We briefly discussed Russia's interference in the election, the hacking of the Democratic National Committee's and John Podesta's emails, which U.S. intelligence services concurred had been part of a Kremlin attempt to sabotage Hillary Clinton's chances and improve Trump's. We speculated about what Putin hoped to gain by taking such a risk, and discussed how to dissuade him from similar mischief in the future. I'm of the opinion that unless Putin is made to regret his decision he will return to the scene of the crime again and again. Crime has most certainly paid for Vladimir Putin, while leaving his country underdeveloped and over-dependent on its oil and gas resources. I've heard it speculated that he might be the wealthiest person on earth, and every ruble of his wealth will have been stolen from the Russian people. Imposing sanctions on Putin and his closest confederates, freezing assets, travel bans, and financial and trade restrictions on Russian entities tied to the Kremlin are appropriate and helpful. But to make Putin deeply regret his assault on the foundation of our democracy—free and fair elections—we should seriously consider retaliating with the kinds of weapons he used. We are in an information war with Russia whether we want to recognize it or not, and in this war offense might be our best defense. We have cyber capabilities, too. They could be used to expose the epic scale of his regime's corruption or to embarrass him in other ways. Although discussions of how to utilize them should remain confidential, the West, led by the United States, must accept that Putin is and will remain our implacable foe, and act accordingly. He won't stop until he's made to stop. With his troll farms and hackers, he continues to this day to provoke and exacerbate political divisions within and between our countries, and undermine the operations of and confidence in our democracies. He will not stop until the political and personal price he's made to pay for his sabotage is greater than the advantages it has provided him. He never was, he is not now, and he never will be our partner. That delusional aspiration has led many Western governments to underestimate Putin's megalomania and the enmity he has for the United States.

After a few minutes, Sir Andrew came to the subject that was his reason for approaching us. He told me he knew a former MI6 officer by the name of Christopher Steele, who had been commissioned to investigate connections between the Trump campaign and Russian agents as well as potentially compromising information about the President-elect that Putin allegedly possessed. Steele had prepared a report that Wood had not read and conceded was mostly raw, unverified intelligence, but that the author strongly believed merited a thorough examination by counterintelligence experts. Steele was a respected professional, Wood assured us, who had good Russian contacts and long experience collecting and analyzing intelligence on the Kremlin. Both Steele and Wood were alarmed by what he had learned and worried that it would not be further investigated.

I was alarmed by Russian interference in the election. Any loyal American should be. I wanted to make Putin pay a steep price for it, and I worried the incoming administration would not be so inclined. I had strongly disagreed with candidate Trump's admiration for Vladimir Putin, which I put down to naïveté and a general lack of seriousness about Putin's antagonism to U.S. interests and values. But I was skeptical that Trump or his aides had actively cooperated with Russia's interference. And I certainly did not want to believe that the Kremlin could have acquired kompromat on an American President. There were some odd characters involved in Trump's campaign. But this was too strange a scenario to believe, something out of a le Carré novel, not the kind of thing anyone has ever actually had to worry about with a new President, no matter what other concerns you might have about him. But even a remote risk that the President of the United States might be vulnerable to Russian extortion had to be investigated. Our impromptu meeting felt charged with a strange intensity. No one wise-cracked to lighten the mood. We spoke in lowered voices. The room was dimly lit, and the atmosphere was eerie. Wood described Steele's research in general terms. He had not read it himself, but vouched for Steele's credibility. I was taken aback. They were shocking allegations. When Wood offered to arrange to provide me a copy of his research, I knew that were Steele as reputable as Wood claimed, I would have a duty to see that the report was placed in the hands of those who had the resources to investigate its contents. I thanked Wood warmly, told him he had done the right thing, and that I was grateful he had brought it to my attention.

David Kramer offered to go to London to meet Steele, confirm his credibility, and report back to me. I agreed to the idea. When David returned, and shared his impression that the former spy was, as Sir Andrew had vouched, a respected professional, and not to outward appearances given to hyperbole or hysteria, I agreed to receive a copy of what is now referred to as "the dossier." I reviewed its contents. The allegations were disturbing, but I had no idea which if any were true. I could not independently verify any of it, and so I did what any American who cares about our nation's security should have done. I put the dossier in my office safe, called the office of the director of the FBI, Jim Comey, and asked for a meeting. I went to see him at his earliest convenience, handed him the dossier, explained how it had come into my possession. I said I didn't know what to make of it, and I trusted the FBI would examine it carefully and investigate its claims. With that, I thanked the director and left. The entire meeting had probably not lasted longer than ten minutes. I did what duty demanded I do.

I don't know what is true, partially true, or not true in the dossier. I gave it to the people best equipped to answer those questions. Had I done any more, I would have exceeded my capability. Had I done any less I would be ashamed of myself. And if any of my colleagues in Congress had been in my situation and not done what I did, I would be ashamed of them.

I am very familiar with the persistence and the damage done by groundless conspiracy theories. Even before the Internet provided the medium for the proliferation of all manner of unhinged speculation, I had confronted more easily discredited conspiracy mongering. In the early 1990s, I was a member of a Senate committee investigating claims that American POWs were still held in Vietnam after the war. We refuted a variety of unfounded accusations that six presidential administrations had covered up the fact that we had left POWs behind in Vietnam. They were tales concocted by crazy people or con artists, and embraced by some families of the missing who were desperate for any hope their loved ones might still come home. It was cruel to raise false hopes like that, and I took strong exception to it with some of the people responsible. For my trouble, I became the subject of a conspiracy theory that claimed I was the Manchurian Candidate, brainwashed by Russians when I was a prisoner of war in Hanoi, and planted in the American political scene to do their bidding. The Russians were likely more amused by the idea than I was. As I recalled in an earlier chapter, my meeting with members of the Free Syrian Army a few miles inside the Syrian border was seized by Internet hysterics and converted into a secret meeting with ISIS. A photograph of the event was Photoshopped to place the head of ISIS emir Abu Bakr al-Baghdadi on the shoulders of one of the participants.

So, I've been to crazy town before, and I've seen how impervious to reason, facts, and common sense these delusions can be. Most are still the work of nuts and frauds, but they proliferate like never before and persist forever on the world wide web. I noted the traffic of absurd conspiracies in the 2016 campaign, and we know now that many of them were conceived and disseminated by Russia, which makes their embrace by politicians too gullible to dismiss them or too shameless to resist exploiting them all the more disconcerting. But those kinds of politicians were around before the advent of the Internet, too. From Joe McCarthy acolytes to moon landing deniers to 9/11 Truthers and Obama Birthers, there has always been a market for "the paranoid style in American politics," as historian Richard Hofstadter termed it. There were members of Congress who believed or took advantage of the improbable tales about our missing-in-action in Vietnam. Rand Paul believed the unsubstantiated charge that I had met with representatives of ISIS during my brief visit to Syria, and he said so publicly.

So, it shouldn't have surprised me that I've become a featured player in the fevered speculation about the dossier. Conspiracy theories have grown around what I did and why. I'm an agent of the "deep state." I'm a double agent for Russia. I acted out of jealousy that Donald Trump was elected President and I wasn't. I'm faking my illness to avoid investigators. I had to wear an orthopedic boot when I tore my Achilles tendon this fall, a side effect of my cancer treatment. It healed, but I tore my other Achilles as well, and had to transfer the boot to the other leg. That seemed to trigger a crowd of paranoids, who manned their smartphones and laptops to expose my perfidy on the Internet. It is more amusing than annoying, I suppose. Although the fact that ravings like these are communicated in the same social media used by the sane and the skeptical means that while their proponents might not have increased as a percentage of the population, their audience, involuntary though it may be, has widened.

I have the same answer to inquiries from the paranoid and from the skeptical. I did exactly what I've explained here, no more and no less. I did my duty, as I've sworn an oath to do. I had an obligation to bring to the attention of appropriate officials unproven accusations I could not assess myself, and which, were any of them true, would create a vulnerability to the designs of a hostile foreign power. I discharged that obligation, and I would do it again. Anyone who doesn't like it can go to hell. I trust the FBI and Special Counsel Robert Mueller, an experienced, skilled prosecutor, and a man of exceptional probity and character, to separate fact from fiction, and get to the bottom of the so-called dossier. If it is the product of slander or groundless fears, he'll say so. If any of it is true, he'll say so. It will be up to Congress and the judiciary to evaluate his conclusions and act on them if necessary, to do our duty, whatever it proves to be, as diligently, fairly, and nonpolitically as Mueller will have done his.

Why had I been given the dossier? That's the first accusatory question in every budding conspiracy theory about my minor role in the controversy. The answer is too obvious for the paranoid to credit. I am known internationally to be a persistent critic of Vladimir Putin's regime, and I have been for a long while. Wood and Steele likely assumed that my animosity toward Putin, which I unapologetically acknowledge, ensured that I would take their concerns seriously. They assumed correctly. Most Americans and Europeans believe that Putin changed around 2007, when he went from being a modernizing Russian leader the West could work with to a risk-taking autocrat and Russian nationalist who resented the West, especially the U.S. I think that's a fallacy. At the risk of sounding self-congratulatory, I've been a realist about Russia and its corrupt strongman for over two decades. Putin and I have history, you could say, each of us having regularly made known our low opinion of the other. Yet we have never actually met.

I was as excited as everyone else when the Soviet empire collapsed in the last decade of the twentieth century, and captive nations from Central Asia to the Baltic Sea claimed their independence, and Russia itself, haltingly and chaotically, tried to find a democratic future for a society that had never been governed by consent. But I soon had doubts that it would succeed.

I traveled to Russia in December 1993, as part of an international group monitoring elections to the Duma, Russia's legislature. The voting took place in the shadow of a confrontation in September between the previous legislature and President Boris Yeltsin that had turned violent and resulted in the military dissolving the Duma, and Yeltsin's call for new elections. The new election laws were confusing, and Russians had little experience casting votes that actually mattered. Nevertheless, for the first time Russia had held a mostly transparent, free, and legitimate national election. That was encouraging, but the results were judged to be victories for ultranationalist parties and the Communist Party, and defeats for those parties associated with Yeltsin. More political uncertainty and government dysfunction were sure to follow, which bred pessimism on the part of well-wishing observers like me.

One of the polling sites we visited was in an industrial area on the outskirts of Moscow. The people running the site were all women, and most of the Russians voting there were women. I asked through an interpreter, "Where are the men?" and one of the women in charge replied indifferently, "They're all drunk." Political analysis by anecdote is as unreliable as it is irresistible, but I didn't take that observation as a positive sign of Russians' civic-mindedness, at least on the part of the male portion of eligible Russian voters. Another anecdote from that trip made an even grimmer impression on me. Cindy and I had dinner late on election night with the American ambassador, the widely respected Tom Pickering, whom I'd known for years. It was lightly snowing and strangely quiet in Moscow after the polls had closed. We left the restaurant, which had been mostly empty, around eleven o'clock, and found the streets deserted as well. Pickering had left in an embassy car, and Cindy and I rode in a white van with a Russian driver. Moscow looks its best in the winter in a fresh snowfall, and we were looking out the windows admiring the wide avenues, empty and blanketed in white. All of a sudden what looked like a human tumbleweed rolled across the street in a flash right in front of us, forcing our driver to slam his brakes. It took a split second before my mind registered what we were actually seeing. Three men were beating another as he scrambled on his hands and knees trying to escape. They all carried automatic rifles, and they were clubbing the unfortunate soul with them. No one was trying to stop them. There were no cops on the scene, no Good Samaritans, no curious passersby, even. Just us. Our driver was pulling away, and I yelled at him to stop. "Nyet, nyet," he shouted back as he accelerated. Moscow is a city of nearly twelve million people. And that night, the night following the first successful free election in the city's modern history, it felt vacant and lawless, a dangerous place, the nighttime realm of criminals and drunks. That's unfair, obviously, and too censorious a judgment to draw from witnessing one violent encounter. But it gave me a sense of foreboding that has never entirely left me.

I felt that same apprehension on a trip in the mid-1990s to some former Soviet republics in what the Kremlin refers to as Russia's "near abroad." We went to the Crimean Peninsula and to the Russians' main Black Sea base at Sevastopol. I thought then, still the Yeltsin era, and a time of cooperative, mostly productive relations between former Cold War superpower foes, that in Moscow's view Ukrainian independence must always yield to the interests and power of its former imperial master. The Russians made it very clear their Sevastopol base would remain in their control without even the pretense of deference to the sovereign nation in whose territory it was located.

Later that same trip, we visited a Baltic Sea naval base in Estonia that the Soviets were in the process of vacating. More accurately, they were scuttling it. Sinking patrol boats at the pier. Razing buildings. Ripping cable from the ground. Taking with them everything of value they could, and destroying everything they couldn't take. I met with the admiral in command, in a dreary office on the top floor of a nondescript building overlooking the disassembled base. He sat at a metal desk beneath a large portrait of Lenin. We spoke through an interpreter, but his curt replies gave me the sense that he wasn't exactly pleased to see me. I think, more to the point, he wasn't pleased that I, an enemy, was seeing him and his command in such a reduced state. There was resentment evident in his demeanor, no hint of a smile, no insincere courtesy, no averting unpleasantness. He was unhappy they were surrendering the base. He made that clear, and gave the impression that were it up to him, these Estonians, with their independence and their Scandinavian dialect, could try to take it from him, and from the quarter of Estonia's population who were Russian and Russian-speaking. There was humiliation in his attitude, too, though he would never have acknowledged it.

Resentment and humiliation spread in Russia in the chaos, dislocation, and corruption of the erratic Yeltsin years, and eased the way for that striving, resentful KGB colonel, who seems to feel those emotions sharply and, to borrow an observation from *Game of Thrones*, used chaos as a ladder.

I have been an equal-opportunity skeptic of four administrations' policies toward Russia. While I might sometimes have been harsher in my judgments than I should have been, I was not wrong about the big picture. I've gotten plenty of things wrong in a long political career. Putin isn't one of them. I made a speech on the Senate floor in 1996, after I had returned from my trip alarmed by Russian attitudes, and warned of "Russia's nostalgia for empire." I urged an early and rapid expansion of NATO to include the former Baltic republics and Warsaw bloc countries who prudently feared an imperial restoration. I, too, feared what was coming, and my pessimism was out of step with the optimism that colored most expectations for the post–Cold War U.S.-Russian relationship. But that optimism was premised on a short view of Russian history, a view limited to Russia's seventy-three years of Communist Party rule. Resentment and insecurity had been powerful drivers of Russian history for centuries. An ideological component was added for three-quarters of the twentieth century, a mere blip. When the ideology failed, it was abandoned. The other pathologies are more deeply rooted.

When the Berlin Wall was destroyed, Putin left his KGB post in East Germany and went home to Saint Petersburg. He was given a position in the mayor's office, the head of the committee responsible for licensing new business ventures, and attracting foreign investment. He was investigated for corruption his first year in the job. But then as now, such suspicions weren't much of an obstacle to his upward mobility. Putin had a spy's instinct for knowing when to stay behind the scenes. He never stole the spotlight from his patrons, and appeared at all times loyal to them. Those traits, combined with his ruthless competence, helped make him a formidable overachiever. He was regularly assigned bigger responsibilities and ran the local branch of a political party founded by Russia's prime minister, Viktor Chernomyrdin. When his mentor lost his reelection as Saint Petersburg's mayor in 1996, Putin was recruited to Moscow. By the next year, he was deputy chief of Yeltsin's staff. The year after that, Yeltsin appointed him head of the Federal Security Service (FSB), the successor to the KGB. In August 1999, he was appointed prime minister by the Duma, and was Yeltsin's chosen successor. When Yeltsin resigned at the end of the year, Putin became acting president, and won election to the office in his own right in March 2000. Quite a rapid ascent up the greasy pole.

In Putin's first weeks as prime minister, bomb explosions destroyed apartment buildings in three Russian cities, including Moscow. Putin used the incident as grounds for starting a second Chechen war, and ordered the bombing of Grozny, Chechnya's capital. The inhumanity of the Russian assault was stunning. No caution, no discrimination, no trials, brutal and merciless, just kill people, fighters and civilians, and don't worry about the difference. As part of an international public relations campaign to obscure Russian brutality in Chechnya, Putin had an op-ed published in the *New York Times*, defending his actions as comparable to American responses to terrorist attacks. That disgusted me. FSB defector Alexander Litvinenko would later allege that the FSB had planted the bombs to improve Putin's prospects for succeeding to the presidency. The violent attack was an opportunity to show Putin in command, acting the strong leader, raining hell on Russia's enemies. Some Western journalists reiterated the allegation, while others disputed it. I've no idea if it's true. But I wouldn't be shocked if it were. Litvinenko would pay a terrible price for this and other accusations. He was poisoned in November 2006 in London with an extremely toxic chemical, polonium, by Russian agents acting on orders, a British investigation concluded, from the Russian government.

In the summer of 1999, after a seventy-eight-day NATO air campaign against Serbia, the government of Slobodan Milosevic agreed to withdraw its forces from Kosovo and accept a NATO peacekeeping force there. Russians were angered by NATO's bombing of their fellow Slavs, which complicated efforts to secure the Kremlin's agreement with a peacekeeping plan for Kosovo. Putin was head of the FSB at the time, and a central figure in negotiations over the question. When U.S. diplomats heard rumors that Russia would send its own peacekeeping force without coordinating its deployment with NATO, Putin assured them that nothing of the kind was planned. That same day an armored column carrying more than two hundred Russian paratroopers arrived at the airport in Pristina, Kosovo's capital. A British peacekeeping force arrived the next day, and the ensuing standoff resulted in public divisions between NATO allies when the British force commander refused an order from NATO's American commander, General Wes Clark, to block the runways to prevent Russian reinforcement. The matter was eventually resolved, but the small show of force by Russia had pleased the Russian public, and no doubt their soon-to-be President, who had learned something about NATO politics and the West's resolve, and how to weaken it by promoting divisions within it.

From these and other warning signs, I was starting to learn a thing or two about Putin. At a South Carolina primary debate during my 2000 run for president, I commented that Putin was "the kind of guy who makes the trains run on time." Russians ought to be warier of him, I implied, and so should the West.

As an advocate of NATO expansion, I traveled in 2001 to some of the Balkan aspirants and paid another visit to the three Baltic states. Hungary, Poland, and the Czech Republic had joined NATO in 1999. In 2000, ten other aspirants, Albania, Bulgaria, Croatia, Macedonia, Romania, Slovakia, Slovenia, Estonia, Latvia, and Lithuania formed the Vilnius Group to lobby for NATO membership. Seven of them would be invited in 2002 to begin negotiations to join, and were admitted in 2004—all of the Vilnius Group except Albania, Croatia, and Macedonia. Moscow was incensed by the inclusion of the Baltics. In meetings on that 2001 trip, Bulgarian and Romanian leaders had impressed me as very anxious to join NATO. Officials in Estonia, Latvia, and Lithuania appeared almost desperate. All feared Russian economic and diplomatic coercion, and meddling in their internal politics, no country more so than Estonia, with its large Russian population. But I was more surprised by how seriously they all took the threat of Russian military intervention, the Baltics especially.

I had dinner late one evening in Catherine the Great's palace on the Baltic Sea with Estonia's president, Lennart Meri, a writer, filmmaker, and a revered leader of Estonia's independence movement. I had just given a speech in Tallinn, calling for the Baltics' inclusion in NATO, and proclaiming, "No more Yaltas, no more spheres of influence." Meri spoke fluent English, as well as several other languages. We talked at length that night about what it had been like to have been a victim of great power politics, and of the bargains made for the sake of balance rather than justice. He assessed the Russian threat calmly, describing how Moscow intimidated its neighbors. He didn't fear an imminent invasion or any very risky action to restrict the independence of the Baltic states. Putin hadn't consolidated enough power yet. But he made it clear that without the protection afforded by NATO membership the day would come when the Kremlin would use all necessary means to restore to Russia the once-captive nations on the Baltic Sea.

I spent an entire afternoon on that same trip with Václav Havel, sitting alone with him in the tower of Prague Castle as the day ebbed to twilight. His health was very poor, and he was soon to leave office. He was in an expansive, philosophical mood. He talked about how to live with purpose. I told him he had a place in history and would never be forgotten. We talked about the Russians, too, but more of history than current events. We talked about what the West meant to oppressed peoples, and what it ought to continue to mean in this new and temporary period of American primacy. Humility was important and hard for us to sustain, he said, but he worried more that our faith in our ideals would erode when the world presented new trials for our leadership, and the temptation to cut deals, to divide into spheres, to balance one thing off another would reassert itself. And it soon would. This was the summer of 2001, and a fateful September lay ahead. It is as important to the souls of nations as it is to individuals to stand up for your ideals, Havel argued. We had both spent time in prison, he for his ideals, and me for my country's interests. The sentiment resonated with us both.

I traveled to Georgia on that trip as well, and met with President Eduard Shevardnadze, the former Soviet foreign minister, veteran of

Kremlin politics, and architect with U.S. secretary of state Jim Baker of an understanding between the disintegrating Soviet Union and the West that allowed the reunification of Germany, the liberation of the Warsaw Pact, and the dissolution of the Soviet Union to proceed peacefully.

Shevardnadze had returned to his homeland in 1992, following a coup that had triggered a civil war. He was elected president in 1995. Georgia was crawling out of the pit in 2001, still suffering widespread chaos and dislocation, its politics marred by corruption, regional chieftains asserting autonomy from Tbilisi, and violent Russian separatist movements in two semiautonomous regions, Abkhazia and South Ossetia. Shevardnadze governed as an authoritarian, but despite his deals with oligarchs, election rigging, and occasional ruthlessness, he was committed to Georgia's independence from Russia. And he was a fascinating man, who had seen a lot of history made and unmade. I enjoyed talking with him, but he struck me as a man who was starting to feel overtaken by events. He would be overthrown two years later in the Rose Revolution by reformers in his own party, led by Mikheil Saakashvili, whom I would come to know well. But in our discussions, Shevardnadze's principal worry was Putin. Russians were still occupying Soviet military bases in Georgia that they had committed to leaving years before. The Russian separatists in Abkhazia and South Ossetia had nearly severed the regions from Georgia. A quarter million Georgians had fled Abkhazia in 1993, and about a tenth that number had to leave South Ossetia in the same period. Territory in both regions was effectively ruled by Russia. The Putin cult of personality, that bare-chested, give-the-finger-to-the-West machismo he advertises to Russians living in Russia and abroad, that the West sneered at for years, was evident early on in those breakaway Georgian regions. On a congressional delegation trip to Georgia a few years after that first visit, when Saakashvili was president but before Russia invaded Georgia in 2008, we entered South

Ossetia without our Georgian hosts, who were forbidden to enter. Although it was sovereign Georgian territory, it had a border crossing and border guards and a gregarious Russian puppet running the place, who handed each of us huge floral arrangements. We were taken to a nearby farmhouse where we met with a bunch of Russian colonels. The first sight that greeted us after our bus "crossed the border" was an immense billboard with a smiling Vladimir Putin looking down on us, and written in Russian above him "Our President."

An early and profitable Putin move to consolidate power was the understanding he reached in 2000 with the oligarchs who had made their vast fortunes from the control of privatized state assets. They were allowed to continue operating without too much government interference as long as they publicly supported the regime, and privately shared their wealth with the ruling elite. Putin began making new oligarchs as well, whose loyalty to him was unquestioned. Most of the established oligarchs went along, except for three, Boris Berezovsky, Vladimir Gusinsky, and Mikhail Khodorkovsky, of whom Khodorkovsky was the most prominent and the richest. The head of Yukos, an oil conglomerate that owned valuable Siberian oil leases, he was reputed to be Russia's wealthiest man. He was also a generous supporter of NGOs working to build the institutions of civil society in Russia, and he established a foundation in London for that purpose, Open Russia. He was outspoken in his concerns about the growing authoritarianism and corruption of Putin's government. Khodorkovsky opened a Washington office of Open Russia in 2002, and became a familiar figure on Capitol Hill. He had business interests to represent here, of course, and lawyers and lobbyists to advocate for him. I met with him a few times, but our meetings were focused on his fears about Putin. He described how Putin was cracking down on those he perceived as a threat to his authority, opposition parties, independent media, disobedient billionaires. He warned that Putin would never be

a reliable partner to the West, that his long-term goal was to reestablish the Soviet empire. Khodorkovsky had an openness about him. He
seemed almost earnest and uncalculating, which didn't strike me as a
typical personality profile for a Russian oligarch. To be sure, he had
his own interests to protect. But I believed his support of democratic
values was sincere, as was his fear of Putin's ambitions.

Khodorkovsky was arrested on trumped-up fraud charges in July
2003. His real crime was criticizing the regime and supporting opposition parties. He was given a ten-month trial in 2004, at which few
defense witnesses were allowed to testify, convicted on all counts, and
sentenced to nine years' imprisonment. Two years were added to his
sentence in a subsequent trial. The state seized Yukos on bogus tax
evasion accusations, declared it bankrupt, and transferred most of its
assets to the state-owned oil company Rosneft. Khodorkovsky was sent
to a labor camp, where he was threatened, locked in solitary confinement, and physically assaulted. Putin finally let him go in 2013, and
Khodorkovsky left Russia for Switzerland, where he relaunched Open
Russia the next year.

Khodorkovsky's arrest and imprisonment was one of Putin's more
daring moves to date, and seemed to surprise many Western observers, who regarded Khodorkovsky as a modern, fairly transparent, and
honest international businessman. They had been less alarmed by
Moscow's war in Chechnya, the assaults on opposition parties and the
media, the Russian army occupation of breakaway regions in Georgia
and Moldova, and threats to the rest of the "near abroad" in its pursuit
of an empire of submissive neighbors. The body count for victims of
political assassinations was starting to mount, too. It was early days yet
for the latest Kremlin chapter of Murder Inc., but the lives of Russians
who dared investigate the darkest deeds of the regime were in grave
peril. Two Duma deputies who had begun investigating the Moscow
apartment bombing had died in mysterious circumstances. Journalists

were beaten for asking the wrong questions, and several were killed. All the murders were unsolved.

The West might have been appalled to see a well-regarded Russian businessman shackled and forced to endure an obvious show trial, recalling images of Soviet-style justice in the bad old days. But many Western governments continued to view Putin as a man they could do business with, literally and figuratively. Europeans relied on Russian natural gas supplies, and the U.S. and its allies continued to seek Russia's cooperation with various global and regional security challenges.

After their first summit meeting in Slovenia in 2001, President Bush said he had looked Putin in the eyes and was able to "get a sense of his soul." Two years later, I quipped that I saw the letters KGB in Putin's eyes, as I criticized Putin's escalating authoritarianism, which I described as a "creeping coup," and Russia's intimidation of its neighbors. In reaction to the regime's crackdown on the opposition, assaults on the press, endemic corruption, and attempts to subjugate its former republics, Joe Lieberman and I introduced a resolution calling for Russia's participation in G-8 summits to be suspended. The U.S. was scheduled to host the next summit of the world's leading industrial democracies in June 2004, and Russia, I argued, was anything but a democracy. In my statement introducing the resolution, I noted that:

The dramatic deterioration of democracy in Russia calls into question the fundamental premises of our Russia policy since 1991. American leaders must adapt U.S. policy to the realities of a Russian government that may be trending towards neo-imperialism abroad and authoritarian control at home. It is time to face unpleasant facts about Russia.

I understood the impulse for wishful thinking. The sudden end of the Cold War had left a lot of Americans, including me, giddy with optimism for what the future might hold for relations between the former superpower enemies. But at this point it was just wishful thinking to believe Putin would ever be our democratic partner. All that was in Putin's soul, I worried, "is the continuity of four hundred years of Russian oppression."

That message wasn't well received in Washington or the capitals of Europe. In truth, it was mostly ignored, as was our resolution, although Joe and I continued sounding the alarm about a revanchist Russia. Hardly a month passed when the Kremlin strongman didn't supply us with more evidence to substantiate the charge. The Duma regularly passed laws altering election rules, laws restricting NGOs, laws suborning the media, laws controlling political parties, trade unions, and the judiciary, laws against "extremism," all intended to serve one purpose above all others: to strengthen the authority and political security of the Kremlin and the man in charge.

In 2004, Putin ordered Russian security forces to storm a school in Beslan, North Ossetia, where Chechen terrorists were holding over a thousand hostages. Using tanks and rockets, the school was liberated at the cost of more than 330 innocent lives, 186 of them children. In a 2005 speech, Putin decried the dissolution of the Soviet Union as "the greatest political catastrophe of the 20th century." On October 7, 2006, Putin's birthday, courageous Russian journalist Anna Politkovskaya, who had made her international reputation reporting from Chechnya during the second Chechen war and had been poisoned as she traveled to Beslan to help negotiate the hostages' release, was shot several times at point-blank range in the elevator of her apartment building. The next month Alexander Litvinenko lay poisoned and wasting away in a London hospital.

In the same period, at a pace of one a year, color revolutions were overthrowing autocratic regimes in former Soviet republics, the Rose Revolution in Georgia in 2003, the Orange Revolution in Ukraine in

2004, and the Tulip Revolution in Kyrgyzstan in 2005. Putin reacted predictably with dark warnings about not letting the "post-Soviet space" succumb to "endless conflict," and with export bans, gas cutoffs, and other punitive measures meant to bring the former vassal states to heel.

Two thousand seven saw the advent of the "dissenters' protests," organized by the Other Russia, a broad coalition of opposition parties, right, left, and center. Former chess world champion Garry Kasparov, whom I've gotten to know well and admire a great deal, was one of the protest's most prominent leaders. He's a smart, honest, and brave advocate for democratic governance and the rule of law, and an unflinching Putin opponent, which can be a dangerous occupation. A welcome benefit of my reputation as an early Putin critic and human rights advocate is that my office is a frequent stop for visiting dissidents, opposition leaders, civil society builders, freedom fighters, humanitarian workers, and other defenders of human dignity from every part of the world. I'm proud of that, and I'm grateful. I've gotten to know and associate myself with some of the most inspiring people in the world. More than a few of them, like Garry Kasparov, were Russians.

Natan Sharansky, the stouthearted refusenik, gulag victim, legendary resister, and champion of the Rights of Man, has honored me with a couple visits. He is one of a few people on earth I'm content to let dominate our conversation. First, he is so fascinating and insightful and I'm smart enough to know I can learn a lot by listening to him. Second, it's really hard to get a word in edgewise with him. He has a bigger personality than most people I know, probably bigger than anyone I know. He speaks quickly, forcefully, and demonstratively. It's a riot of intelligent, passionately conveyed convictions and often brilliant analysis. We talk about Israel and the Middle East, of course. He's an Israeli politician. But he's come to see me because we are both democratic internationalists, and because we share the same view of

Putin, although his is informed by personal experiences more relevant than mine. George W. Bush's second term, which began with the introduction of his freedom agenda in his inaugural address, was an exciting time for democracy and human rights movements, and for guys like Sharansky and me, who were longtime democracy advocates and early skeptics of Putin. Regrettably, the Bush administration, for all its sincere commitment to helping support democratic movements, was much too slow to embrace that skepticism. When they finally did, it was too late. Sharansky was clear-eyed about what was happening in Russia, and about Putin's goals, and he encouraged my similar views. And he urged me to continue speaking out on the subject, reminding me how Reagan's speeches had sustained him when he was under duress. It was advice I was quite happy to follow.

The dissenters marched to protest rigged election rules in advance of the 2008 Russian presidential election. Thousands took to the streets in successive protests in Moscow and Saint Petersburg and three other cities, with marchers demanding new election laws and "Russia without Putin." The police turned out in force. They beat many protesters, and arrested hundreds, including Kasparov, who had marched in Moscow.

Two thousand seven also seemed to mark a turning point in the West's sense of Putin. The Litvinenko and Politkovskaya murders had an impact on Western opinion, as had Putin's reactions to the color revolutions and his crackdowns on the media and political opponents. Later that year, Russia launched a surprise expedition to the North Pole, to plant the Russian flag and claim disputed Arctic territory. And in November, Putin pulled Russia out of the treaty that limited conventional armed forces deployments in Europe. The Bush administration and most European governments now had a more realistic appreciation of the man in whom they had invested too much hope, and of the rapidly disappearing chances for a broadly cooperative relationship with him. But the evidence of his authoritarianism and corruption had been there all along. In an interview in 2006, I warned that "the glimmerings of democracy are very faint in Russia today," citing Putin's repression of dissent and the Russian press. We need "to be very harsh" in response, I urged.

I announced my presidential campaign in the spring of 2007, but I had been preparing to run for months, and, as I mentioned in an earlier chapter, I was widely viewed as the front-runner for the nomination. Among other effects, my higher profile widened the audience for my criticism of Russia. And Russia was starting to respond. I was an object of occasional but pointed criticism in various organs of the Kremlin's propaganda machine. Sometimes the complaints were from Russian government officials, lamenting my "old"—an adjective that my foreign and domestic critics overused in 2008—"Cold War mentality." Often the alarm about my hawkishness was given voice by random Russian citizens, chosen for their scrupulous honesty, no doubt, and the acuity of their political insights. A retired Red Army officer earned favorable press notice by claiming to have manned the surface-to-air missile in Hanoi that had destroyed my plane. He was a modest hero, a Russian newspaper tribute to him described, who had done his duty and earned the respect of his grateful nation.

In February 2007, Vladimir Putin attended the Munich Security Conference, a long-running annual gathering of government and military leaders. For most of its history, the conference was attended almost exclusively by officials and journalists from the West. It was a conference for committed Trans-Atlanticists. But in the post–Cold War era invitations were extended to officials of former and current adversaries of the West. Putin's defense minister and deputy prime minister, and at one time his expected successor, Sergei Ivanov, was a regular attendee whom I had gotten to know and had exchanged ideas with, so to speak, a few times. He and Putin had been friends since they had served together as young spies in the bad old days. We sat next to each other a few times at conference dinners over the years. I complimented his English once. He explained he had served in the KGB's London station. Putin had never attended the conference before, and his appearance in 2007 was eagerly anticipated.

I had been coming to the conference since the 1970s, when I was the Navy's liaison to the Senate, and had helped staff the Senate delegation led by the late John Tower. For the last twenty years, I had led the delegation myself. I was a familiar face there, and had made many friendships over the years that I value despite having a reputation for being argumentative, and too blunt sometimes—my critics might call it confrontational—about what I perceived as threats to the West's values and interests. Starting in the early years of the new century, my remarks at Munich usually identified Vladimir Putin's regime as one of those threats.

Like everyone there, I had expected Putin to be gracious and magnanimous, to sketch out a vision of cooperation with the West, and offer his hand in friendship to former adversaries and new friends, or some such hogwash. And I was prepared to denounce it as such. But he surprised us.

Putin delivered an angry diatribe, an extraordinary tirade about NATO, and especially the United States. "Today, we are witnessing an almost uncontained hyper use of force," he complained, meaning, of course, the United States. He warned that our efforts to dominate the world would destroy us. Our primacy was at an end. Our day was over. Russia and other great, proud nations of the world were asserting themselves again. He appeared angry that the U.S. hadn't accepted the role he assigned us. High on his list of complaints were the Baltics' admission into NATO, American support for democratic reform movements, the color revolutions in Russia's "near abroad," and U.S. plans to build a ballistic missile shield in Europe. He was, in essence, insisting that the world order again be based on spheres of influence, and there was nothing the U.S. should or could do to prevent it. I half expected him to start banging his shoe on the podium as Nikita Khrushchev is purported to have done at the U.N. For good measure, he threw in a threat to pull Russia out of the Intermediate-Range Nuclear Forces Agreement signed by Ronald Reagan and Mikhail Gorbachev in 1988. The audience was stunned. And Putin kept it up in the question-and-answer session that followed his speech. He professed to be enjoying himself, which he emphasized with his usual bravado, demanding the interrogator ask him more questions. "This is fun. I love it," he insisted.

The second most interesting aspect of the whole thing was that Putin glared at us almost the entire time he was delivering the speech, and I mean really glared. He would read a line or two from his prepared text, then look up, and fix a menacing stare at me, at Defense Secretary Bob Gates, at Joe Lieberman. I was sitting between Bob and Joe, at a table directly in front of Putin with Jon Kyl and California congresswoman Jane Harman. Lindsey, former national security advisor Brent Scowcroft, and other members of our delegation were seated just behind us. German chancellor Angela Merkel was seated at the table to our right. We all saw it, and felt the animosity behind it, and remarked about it afterward. It was weird. I don't know if it had been meant exclusively for me, as a U.S. presidential candidate with a record of being his detractor, or if it had been directed at all U.S. officials present in keeping with his speech's exaggerated attack, although in the Q&A he had managed to say a few nice words about President Bush. But I am certain he meant to convey hostility to someone in that room. "I'll be damned," I said. "That seemed kind of personal."

The reactions in the hall and in the capitals of the Atlantic Alliance were mostly restrained, expressing disappointment with the tone and substance, but repeating assurances that the West wanted a constructive relationship. Chancellor Merkel was diplomatic, calling

Putin "a reliable partner," but suggesting "we need to speak frankly to each other." Lindsey offered him a backhanded compliment. "He's done more to bring Europe and the U.S. together than any single event in the last several years," he told a reporter. Joe Lieberman criticized Putin's speech as "Cold War rhetoric." A White House spokesman expressed surprise, and disputed Putin's "accusations" before promising to continue "cooperation with Russia in areas important to the international community."

The American delegation huddled in a nearby control room to discuss how to respond. I was scheduled to speak to the conference the next day. My prepared remarks contained forceful criticism of Russia, a staple of my speeches in Munich for the last several years. The Europeans usually reacted by conceding my assessment was correct, but that we wouldn't get anywhere with the Russians by saying it to their face and pushing them away. I'm sure they expected me to fire back at Putin with all the indignation I could muster—and I can muster quite a bit when provoked. They might even have appreciated it a bit more than usual this time. Brent Scowcroft noted that Putin had an opportunity to come here and strengthen the arguments of the proponents of engagement, "but he whiffed. It was good he came. He froze himself out." Two of my foreign policy advisors, Richard Fontaine and Randy Scheunemann, were there, and assumed I would want to toughen up the already tough Russia criticism in my speech. But I decided a more effective approach would be a thoughtful, more-in-sorrow-than-anger response. I confess I liked the idea not just because it would confound expectations in the hall, although that had appeal. I liked it because it was the approach that would make Putin look the worse in comparison. "My God," you could imagine some Brussels snob remarking, "that Russian has managed to make McCain sound diplomatic."

I didn't plan to refrain from criticism. I wouldn't let Putin's accusations go unanswered, and I don't think anyone there wanted me to. But I would make my response almost an aside in a speech focused mainly on other subjects. And I would couch it in terms of "we," meaning the U.S. and Europe, the West, the Alliance, and not the U.S. versus Russia, as Putin would have it. Two short, temperate paragraphs in a twenty-five-hundred-word speech were all it would need. "I remain concerned about the long-term possibilities of Russian democracy and the direction of Moscow's foreign and energy policies," I noted, before pushing back on Putin's America-the-hyper-power-cowboy theme.

Today's world is not unipolar. The United States did not single-handedly win the Cold War in some unilateral victory. The *transatlantic alliance* won the Cold War, and there are power centers on every continent today. Russian leaders' apparent belief to the contrary raises a number of difficult questions. Will Russia's autocratic turn become more pronounced, its foreign policy more opposed to the principles of the western democracies and its energy policy used as a tool of intimidation? Or will it build, in partnership with the West, a democratic country that contributes to the international rules-based system? While our hopes are obviously for the latter choice, recent events suggest a turn toward the former. This is unfortunate, and the U.S. and Europe need to take today's Russian realities into account as we form our policies.

That was it. My brief, diplomatic reproach might have been only slightly less of a surprise in the hall than Putin's fiery one. But, contrary to my caricature, I can adjust my tone when circumstances call for it. I have spoken to many skeptical audiences in my career, skeptical of my views and skeptical of me. I might not have made converts of all of them, but I could communicate in terms and attitudes they appreciated. I value candor and directness in discourse. I think most people do. But having traveled as extensively as I have, and spoken to as many different audiences as I have, from the Oxford Union to Vietnam's Diplomatic Academy, I know how to manage subtlety and tactful persuasion when it's required. The bluntness typical of my Russian criticism was intended to disrupt the widespread attitude that letting Putin get away with some mischief here and there will placate him, and help get his cooperation on important things. It doesn't. It just convinces him he's on the right course, and encourages him to go further. The evidence for that could fill volumes.

Putin traded jobs in 2008 with his chosen successor, Prime Minister Dmitry Medvedev. Russian law at the time prevented him from serving a third consecutive term as president. The law has since been changed, as well as the law limiting a presidential term to four years. It's now six years. And Putin is running for a fourth term. His brief interval as prime minister didn't require him to relinquish any real power. Despite being "appointed" prime minister by the new president, he was subordinate to no one for those four years. Everyone knew who still called the shots in the Kremlin. It was Vladimir Putin. And it was Vladimir Putin who decided to invade the Republic of Georgia in the summer of 2008.

I had gotten to know Georgia's president, Mikheil "Misha" Saakashvili, quite well by then. I had been back in Georgia a couple times since the Rose Revolution, and I had seen Saakashvili when he came to Washington. I had actually first met him years before in 1994, when he was a law student at Columbia, and a young political activist. He was impressive. He won a seat in the Georgian parliament the next year as a member of Shevardnadze's party, and led an effort to reform the country's election laws. Five years later, he was minister for justice, the architect of sweeping reforms of Georgia's criminal justice system, and an anticorruption crusader who resigned to protest the government's systemic corruption. He started a new party, and when parliamentary elections in 2003 were judged by international observers to have been rigged, he and his party were in the vanguard of protests demanding Shevardnadze's resignation and new elections. Those peaceful protests attracted hundreds of thousands of Georgians to the streets and became the Rose Revolution. Shevardnadze resigned in November 2003. New elections were held the following January, and Saakashvili, just thirty-six years old then, won a massive majority and became Georgia's new democratically elected president. He was committed to a program of free market, government, and judicial reform. He released imprisoned dissidents, cut regulations and taxes, privatized industries, imposed transparency on business transactions, began massive infrastructure improvements, fired corrupt government officials and police, ensured public officials made a living wage, ended the bribery-based university admissions system, and began modernizing Georgia's military. In short, he was a force for open governance and liberal political values who believed his country's future depended on its association with the West, and not the angry giant to its north. I admired him.

My last trip to Georgia had been in 2006. It was during that visit that we had gone into South Ossetia. Georgia's problems with ethnic Russian separatists predated Saakashvili's presidency, but they worsened after his election, a development at least partly attributable to Saakashvili's pro-Western reputation and Moscow's displeasure with democratic uprisings in the neighborhood. Aslan Abashidze, a pro-Russian warlord, who ran another autonomous Georgian region, Adjaria, refused to recognize the authority of the national government, and cracked down on local supporters of the Rose Revolution. That precipitated a crisis that lasted five months and appeared on the verge of becoming a military confrontation, when Adjari paramilitary forces, armed and supplied by Russia, took up positions along the region's border while the Georgian army maneuvered nearby. Moscow backed Abashidze, of course, and Washington condemned him. The crisis was brought to an end by a combination of local protests, economic sanctions, military pressure, and negotiations. Abashidze resigned on May 6, 2004, and fled to Moscow. His success in Adjaria encouraged Saakashvili to confront separatists in South Ossetia and Abkhazia. In South Ossetia the confrontation was violent, as armed separatists fought Georgian armed forces to a draw, and negotiations in 2005 left the status quo in place. Georgia had better luck suppressing a rebellion in Abkhazia's Kodori Gorge in 2006.

From its first days in office, Saakashvili's government had pursued membership in NATO as the best guarantee of its territorial integrity. I think in those years Georgia's eventual admission was assumed to be likely, but not while its government was confronting breakaway regions within its borders. Moscow, of course, was fiercely opposed to the idea. Nevertheless, Saakashvili tried hard to prove Georgia's value as a military ally to the West, sending large contingents of troops to Iraq and Afghanistan. President Bush paid a state visit to Tbilisi in 2005. As he gave a speech in Freedom Square to a huge and receptive crowd of cheering Georgians, a onetime member of an Adjari separatist party threw a hand grenade at the podium, hoping to kill both presidents. It didn't detonate.

Russia had been openly hostile to the Georgian government from its inception, and intensely so since 2006. Putin seemed to have a special animus for Saakashvili, who wasn't the kind of person to show elaborate deference to the strongman of a hostile power. Misha was smart and committed and he had guts. He was a proven reformer and, I believe, genuinely committed to advancing liberal political values, and certainly to allying Georgia with the U.S. and Europe. He also had a not entirely undeserved international reputation, and not just in

Russia, as an impulsive, hardheaded risk-taker. I recognized that aspect of Misha's personality, but I admired his courage and vision, too, and appreciated the sincerity of his regard for the U.S. We had become friends, and I was seen in Washington as Georgia's leading supporter in the Senate. I was an advocate for Georgia's eventual entry into NATO, and a frequent critic of Putin's intimidation of the Saakashvili government, which he conveyed primarily by encouraging the militancy of separatists in Abkhazia and South Ossetia. I believe that by early 2008 Putin planned to provoke a war with Georgia.

His first move was to establish official ties with separatist authorities in April, for all practical purposes recognizing them as the legitimate governments of separatist territories. A Russian jet shot down a Georgian reconnaissance drone over Abkhazia that same month. Putin accused Georgian peacekeeping forces occupying the Kodori Gorge of preparing to invade Abkhazia, and threatened to retaliate. He deployed more "peacekeepers" to Abkhazia, permitted as part of the negotiated settlement of the separatist war there in 1993. Then he sent additional peacekeepers that exceeded the agreement's limits, claiming they were unarmed and didn't count against the total. In July, violent incidents in South Ossetia were bringing things to a boil, including an attack on the head of the Tbilisi-supported government, and the kidnapping of four Georgian soldiers. Georgia recalled its ambassador to Russia after Moscow ordered four military jets to overfly the territory. Russian troops conducted exercises in the northern Caucuses that same month, ostensibly to train peacekeepers, but in reality to prepare for an invasion. When the exercises concluded, the Russian soldiers didn't return to base. They stayed near the border.

August began with Ossetians blowing up a Georgian police truck and shelling some towns along the border. Georgians responded by shooting up some border checkpoints. Events spiraled from there, with exchanges of artillery and rifle fire intermittently continuing for several days. Saakashvili attempted to call Medvedev on August 6. The Russian president refused the call, and the worst shelling of the conflict to date continued through the night. The Georgians believed Russian forces had already entered South Ossetia. Saakashvili ordered a unilateral cease-fire the evening of the 7th. The Ossetians ignored the move and resumed artillery attacks. Around midnight the Georgians responded by shelling the South Ossetian capital, Tskhinvali. A few hours later, they marched three columns on the city and surrounding heights. Moscow denounced the Georgian "aggression." As they approached the city, Georgian soldiers exchanged fire with Russian peacekeepers at their base camp, and the fight rapidly escalated. The next morning, August 8, Russian forces poured into South Ossetia, and launched a missile attack on a Georgian resort town near the border. The Russian air force began bombing targets in the area. That afternoon, Russian air and artillery attacks had joined the fight for Tskhinvali, and Georgian air defenses succeeded in destroying a few Russian aircraft. Two Russian tank columns reached the city and started shelling Georgian infantry. Georgia gave up the offensive on Tskhinvali late on August 9, and began withdrawing. Saakashvili declared another unilateral cease-fire on the 10th and announced that he was pulling his forces out of South Ossetia. Russia ignored it. Russian planes indiscriminately bombed Gori, a Georgian town near South Ossetia, and the Russian army occupied the town on August 13. They attacked and occupied a key Georgian Black Sea port. Russian soldiers and Abkhazian separatists attacked Georgian soldiers in the Kodori Gorge and forced them to withdraw. Russian planes bombed Tbilisi and Russian troops threatened to march on the capital. Moscow waged a sophisticated cyber and disinformation campaign against the Georgians as well, giving the world its first good look at a form of warfare the Russians would prove adept at, which we would see again in Crimea and Eastern Ukraine, and, it pains me to say, in an American presidential election.

French president Nicolas Sarkozy helped negotiate a cease-fire agreement on August 12 that the Russians would eventually observe, but not with any haste. A subsequent agreement brokered by Sarkozy set the terms for the exchange of prisoners and the withdrawal of Russian forces from Georgia over the next month or so. They wouldn't leave Abkhazia and South Ossetia, of course. They were effectively lost to Georgia. Medvedev recognized their independence on August 26.

The West's reaction to Russia's aggression was, if not uniform, mostly based on the same opinions. In short, Russia was the aggressor and had provoked the war, but Misha was a fool for taking the bait and giving Moscow a pretext to invade. Moscow should, of course, be reprimanded, but nothing too punitive should be considered that would jeopardize long-term interests at stake. I think that view was shared by many in the U.S. as well. Misha learned how few friends he really had in the West. I was one. But there were not a great many others. The Bush administration denounced Russia's aggression, but decided against a military response or rushing arms and equipment to Georgia, although it did send a C-130 loaded with humanitarian supplies to Tbilisi, and left it parked on a runway the Russians had been preparing to crater. We also airlifted Georgian troops fighting with us in Afghanistan back to Georgia so they could defend their country. Administration officials claimed it signaled to Russia not to press the attack any further, and it worked. Maybe. The administration imposed some sanctions on Russia, including suspending meetings of the NATO-Russia Council, which was conceived to facilitate consultation and cooperation between the rival powers. I thought it was an inadequate response, and more likely to boost Putin's confidence than make him regret his aggressiveness. All the sanctions were dropped the following year, as part of the Obama administration's "reset" of relations with Russia.

Misha should have been shrewd enough to know what the Russians expected him to do and not have done it. But that didn't make him the aggressor or mitigate the ruthlessness and perilous implications of Putin's actions. He had shown the world that he would use force, in this instance a conventional military invasion, to command a sphere of influence in his "near abroad." And the West had mostly shrugged. That's on us, not Misha Saakashvili, whatever his flaws. We would see it again, Putin's use of force, and his exploitation of frozen conflicts to keep neighboring countries in his orbit. Russia's military hadn't fought particularly well in Georgia. Putin would see to it that its deficiencies were corrected. He would use it again to instruct a former republic in the limits of its independence or to improve Russia's standing in the world as a rival to American power. After Georgia, he had reason to believe he could get away with it.

I was the presumptive Republican nominee for President when Russia invaded Georgia, and most commentators credited my knowledge of the subject and of that part of the world, and acknowledged that my early skepticism about Putin appeared prescient. But that didn't mean that every comment I made in reaction to the crisis wouldn't be scrutinized skeptically by the press and liable to be exploited by the Democrats to limit whatever advantage I had for having more extensive national security experience than my opponent. This was before the global financial system collapsed. Foreign policy was still a relevant issue to voters, and Obama and I were running neck and neck in most polls.

I reacted to Russia's invasion by accusing Moscow of being the aggressor, and trying to rally support for the victim. "Today, we are all Georgians," I exclaimed at the outset of the invasion. I did scores of interviews explaining why the attacks on Georgia threatened our interests and the rules we established for the post–Cold War order, and why Putin should be made to answer for his transgressions. I repeated my call to bar Russia's participation in G-8 summits. I had urged that action regularly for the last five years, and it had been mostly ignored. Now I was assailed by foreign policy experts with Democratic proclivities and even a few who leaned Republican for making such a provoca-tive recommendation. Didn't I understand, they huffed, that pulling Russia into Western institutions was the only way to civilize it? Well, not if Russia rejects the institutions' norms, deriving benefits from the association without accepting the obligations that come with them. Fareed Zakaria, whom I like, called it "the most radical idea put for-ward by a major candidate for the presidency in twenty-five years." Goodness. As it happened, Putin would invade another neighbor in 2014, having had six more years' exposure to the civilizing effects of association with the West. After he seized the Crimean Peninsula from Ukraine, many of my more vociferous critics in 2008 joined the chorus to kick the Russians out of the G-8, which, happily, the Obama admin-istration finally did.

Democrats saw my statements as an opportunity to suggest that, like Saakashvili, I had an impulsive nature. After Iraq, they reasoned, we don't want another impulsive hawk in charge of things. But the charge didn't do much damage. We ticked up a little in the polls, which was largely credited to my high profile during the crisis. I was repeat-edly invited to express reservations about some of the Georgian presi-dent's decisions. But I wouldn't criticize a friendly government while it was under attack, an undeserved and premeditated attack, by a mutual adversary. On the contrary, throughout the duration of the Russo-Georgia war, I was regularly on the phone with Saakashvili, who called almost daily. He asked my advice, and I gave it to him. He couldn't win the war. I knew that. He couldn't count on the West to help him win it, just to help him get out of it, and I advised him to seek and cooperate with that help. He asked me to urge Washington to be more supportive, and I did, strenuously. He was surprised by the discovery that the nations of Europe, which he wanted his nation to emulate and associate with, valued their relations with Russia more than the ter-ritorial integrity of a friendly democracy. I told him that they would regret that misplaced allegiance someday, and they mostly have. Too late for Misha, he's long out of power in Georgia. But not, perhaps, for the country he tried hard to liberalize and hold together in the face of open and covert aggression from its former imperial master, and the audacious despot who ordered it.

With the inauguration of the Obama administration came its vaunted reset of relations with Russia, which sought Russian cooperation on arms control and other security issues at the cost of not troubling Moscow too much over its endemic corruption, repression, and intimidation of its neighbors. Sanctions imposed by the Bush administration the year before were lifted. Two missile defense sites under construction in Poland and the Czech Republic would be canceled to placate Russian objections despite the enormous domestic political challenge their location had been for the two host governments, who were upset by the reversal, to say the least. The following year we would sign a new strategic arms agreement with Russia, which required significant reductions in the U.S. arsenal but not Russia's. NATO enlargement was largely shelved. Albania and Croatia were admitted in April 2009, but they had been formally invited to join the year before. No other new members were added to the alliance for the duration of the Obama administration, although Montenegro was invited near the end of 2015, and would formally join in June 2017.

My old friend Joe Biden, the new vice president, introduced the new policy at the Munich Conference in February 2009. "The United States rejects the notion that NATO's gain is Russia's loss," he declared, "or that Russia's strength is NATO's weakness." Explain that to Putin, I thought to myself. There wasn't anything terribly offensive in the speech, and Joe noted areas where we would continue to have serious disagreements. It surely wasn't a profoundly idiotic statement as was

President Sarkozy's assertion at the same conference that Russia didn't constitute a military threat to the European Union and NATO. But the implication that much of the strain in our relations with Russia was simply caused by a misunderstanding was, as Poland's prime minister, Donald Tusk, put it, "naive."

Hillary Clinton, the new secretary of state, met with her Russian counterpart, Foreign Minister Sergei Lavrov, in Geneva the next month, and handed him a big red "reset" button, although she was rumored to have been somewhat skeptical of the initiative, as I know Defense Secretary Bob Gates, held over from the Bush administration, was. By the time Hillary left office in 2013 after the President's reelection, she was counseling the administration to snub Putin, and not "flatter [him] with high-level attention." By then, she had plenty of experience with how the Kremlin boss interpreted friendliness as weakness. She concluded, correctly, that "strength and resolve were the only language Putin would understand." But she was leaving office, and President Obama and her successor, John Kerry, didn't heed the advice.

It's fair to recognize welcome developments the reset might have encouraged. Russia agreed to let us fly military supplies to Afghanistan through their airspace. We had been flying over Kyrgyzstan, but Moscow had pressured the Kyrgyz to withdraw permission. Russia agreed to join the international sanctions regime against Iran. The administration would also credit the new START treaty to the reset. I didn't think that was a good deal, so I wouldn't include this among welcome developments. I didn't see many other benefits to our outreach to Russia. Nor did I expect any. Putin's personality wasn't the kind to be modified by positive reinforcement, which the advocates of the reset would eventually realize.

In September 2010, Bill Browder, whose hedge fund Hermitage Capital had been the largest private investment firm in Russia, came to see me with a tragic tale to tell. Putin had expelled Browder from

Russia in 2005 after Browder had publicly complained about rampant corruption in the state-owned Russian companies he had invested in. Interior Ministry police raided his Moscow offices, seized his corporate records, used them to forge change-in-ownership contracts, and transferred ownership of Hermitage's assets, which were used to create a billion dollars in phony tax liabilities, and, in one instance, fraudulently claim a refund for $230 million in taxes Hermitage had paid when Browder was in control. Browder hired a Russian tax lawyer and auditor, Sergei Magnitsky, to get to the bottom of it, which he did. Magnitsky's discoveries and subsequent testimony implicated Interior Ministry police, government officials, judges, and organized criminals in a massive fraud conspiracy. For his honesty and courage, he was arrested by some of the same police he had accused, imprisoned without trial, denied visits from his family, and beaten savagely to get him to withdraw his complaints. He never recanted or signed a false confession. On the contrary, throughout his imprisonment he continued to file complaints about his abusers and the perpetrators of the fraud he had uncovered. His conditions were awful, and his injuries and various illnesses were left untreated. In November 2009, after nearly a year in prison, he complained of severe abdominal pains, and was taken to the prison medical facility, and denied treatment. A quasi-official human rights committee reported to Medvedev two years later that rather than treating his stomach pains, Sergei Magnitsky was beaten with rubber truncheons by eight prison guards and orderlies, and then left to die alone in his cell. He was only thirty-seven years old, married, and the father of two children. The Russian government announced he had died of heart disease. Several of the people responsible for his death were promoted.

Browder went to war against the bastards who had murdered his lawyer. In that pursuit, he worked with Representative Jim McGovern and Senator Ben Cardin, both Democrats, to introduce legislation that would subject sixty Russians implicated in Sergei's arrest and death, and in the crimes he had uncovered, to a U.S. visa and banking ban. They needed a Republican co-sponsor. Browder told me Sergei's story in a very calm and matter-of-fact way, which gave it an even more powerful effect, and I was moved. I asked him what I could do to help, and he explained the sanctions legislation, the Sergei Magnitsky Rule of Law Accountability Act, and asked me to sponsor it. I said "I'm in," and told an aide to contact Ben Cardin's office and put me on the bill. Thus began a two-year fight to get the Obama administration to let us impress on Russia that there were misdeeds the U.S. would not ignore even in the interests of a reset relationship. To punish this misdeed, we intended to offend the mob-boss mentality of the Kremlin where it hurt the most, by cutting off access to the banks and real estate where they stashed their wealth, and the places where they enjoyed flaunting it. And we would encourage other Western governments to do the same. I don't think I had realized in the beginning how much that would matter to Putin Inc. I soon discovered it mattered a lot from the ferocity of Putin's opposition to the sanctions—when he spoke about them sometimes he was visibly angry—and from discussions with prominent Russian dissidents, Kasparov and Boris Nemtsov among them, who assured me nothing was more likely to upset them than telling them they couldn't travel, invest, and spend their money lavishly wherever they wanted, which for most of them was the whole purpose of stealing all that money.

We introduced the bill in May 2011, with a long list of co-sponsors. Impressed by the testimony of activists who identified numerous other transgressions against human rights in Russia, we widened the scope of the bill beyond those involved in the false arrest and murder of Sergei Magnitsky to include Russians guilty of abusing any of their fellow citizens. Despite overwhelming support in Congress, Moscow fought a determined diplomatic and public relations campaign to stop the bill.

A small army of lobbyists and public affairs specialists was engaged for that purpose. But the Kremlin's primary targets of persuasion weren't on Capitol Hill, they were in the administration, which, to preserve the mostly mythical reset, worked hard behind the scenes to impede the bill's progress. But it had too much support in both houses of Congress to be stopped.

The administration might not have realized it at the time, but the tens of thousands of Russians who poured into the streets of Moscow and other Russian cities to protest irregularities in Duma elections at the end of 2011 and Putin's election to a third presidential term in March 2012 would deal the final blow to the dream of partnership with Russia. Putin's party, United Russia, had won a plurality in the parliamentary elections, but its share of the vote was substantially reduced from the previous election, and witnesses had alleged thousands of election violations. In response to the protests, an incensed Putin launched his harshest crackdown yet on dissenters, the remaining independent media in Russia, and foreign NGOs working there. It was in this wave of repression that the members of the punk rock group Pussy Riot were arrested for "hooliganism."

Putin blamed the Obama administration for fomenting the protests, especially Secretary of State Clinton, who had appropriately stated the administration had "serious concerns about the conduct of the [December] election." "The Russian people," she continued, "deserve the right to have their voices heard and their votes counted." The new U.S. ambassador, Michael McFaul, who had been one of the architects of the Russian reset, welcomed a number of prominent opposition figures and leading protesters to the embassy, which didn't endear him to the objects of the protests. Putin had expected a more triumphant return to the Russian presidency. Instead, he heard masses of Russians chant "Putin is a thief." He was embarrassed and worried. The Arab Spring was under way and protests were rattling autocracies across the Middle East, and overthrowing some of them. I had by this time discovered the dubious pleasures of Twitter, and as I watched on cable TV the marchers in Moscow chant their anti-regime slogans, I tweeted the following, "Dear Vlad, The #ArabSpring is coming to a neighborhood near you."

I got more of a reaction from him than I expected. The embattled presidential candidate had already blamed the protests on Secretary Clinton's statements (and unbeknownst to her and every other American, he would seek revenge five years later by ordering his trolls and hackers and subcontractors at WikiLeaks to help defeat her). When he was asked about my mischievous insult on a televised call-in program a few days later, Putin unleashed quite a tirade. "Mr. McCain fought in Vietnam," he observed.

> I think that he has enough blood of peaceful citizens on his hands. It must be impossible for him to live without these disgusting scenes anymore. . . . He was captured and they kept him not just in prison, but in a pit for several years. Anyone would go crazy.

It wasn't the first time I had heard that insult, and I laughed it off. Putin normally affects insouciance when he's trying to offend a foreign critic who's annoyed him. The barely disguised fury in his response to my insolence told me two things: he doesn't like me, and he was genuinely worried about his political survival.

I think the campaign of repression Putin orchestrated to strengthen his hold on power effectively ensured the passage of the Magnitsky sanctions. But it took a while for the Obama administration to recognize that or that the Russian reset was another casualty of Putin's furious insecurity. The administration tried to bottle up the bill in the Senate Foreign Relations Committee, chaired by my friend John Kerry, who would succeed Hillary Clinton as secretary of state. We went around him. We still had a law on the books, Jackson-Vanik, that imposed restrictions on trade with the former Soviet Union to force it to let Russian Jews immigrate to Israel. The Soviet Union didn't exist anymore, the refuseniks had long immigrated, and Russia was preparing to enter the World Trade Organization. Jackson-Vanik had to be replaced by permanent normal trade status to allow WTO rules to apply to trade with the United States. Legislation to that effect was pending before the Senate Finance Committee, and I went to see the chairman, Max Baucus of Montana, to tell him that unless our Magnitsky sanctions were added to his trade legislation, I and several other sponsors of the sanctions would oppose it, ensuring its defeat. The threat was enough to convince the administration and John to relent. The Magnitsky sanctions passed the House overwhelmingly in November 2012. The Senate followed the next month. President Obama signed the bill on December 14, and Moscow retaliated by barring all American adoptions of Russian children, a cruel and ineffective response. U.S.-funded NGOs were barred from working in Russia as well. Moscow has continued to complain bitterly about the sanctions and litigate the issue ever since, even, as we recently discovered, seeking the assistance of President Trump's son during the 2016 campaign. Last year, the Kremlin accused Bill Browder of complicity in Sergei's murder, and registered a warrant with Interpol for his arrest, which resulted in his visa being denied by the State Department last year. An uproar ensued, and the decision was quickly reversed.

The dissidents who had advised that the sanctions proposed in the Magnitsky legislation would hurt the regime where it most mattered were proved right. In 2016, we passed the Global Magnitsky Act, subjecting human rights violators anywhere in the world to the same sanctions, a memorial that the honest and courageous lawyer for whom the law is named would have appreciated, may he rest in peace.

In 2013, Putin had an op-ed published in the *New York Times*, warning the U.S. not to intervene in the Syrian war on the side of the Syrians murdered with chemical weapons, or the millions of Syrians killed, injured, and dislocated by the Assad regime. Two years later, Putin would deploy Russian soldiers to Syria to fight on behalf of the murderers. I asked and was allowed to publish a response to Putin in *Pravda*. I began by addressing the falsehood that I was anti-Russian. "I am pro-Russian," I claimed. "I'm more pro-Russian than the regime that misrules you today.

> I make that claim because I respect your dignity and your right to self-determination. I believe you should live according to the dictates of your conscience, not your government. I believe that you deserve the opportunity to improve your lives in an economy that is built to last and benefits the many, not just the powerful few. You should be governed by a rule of law that is clear, consistently and impartially enforced and just. I make that claim because I believe the Russian people, no less than Americans, are endowed by our Creator with inalienable rights to life, liberty and the pursuit of happiness.

Much of the commentary in Washington about my op-ed was focused on the fact that it had been published on an online news site, Pravda.ru, and not in the old Communist Party organ, *Pravda*. Some analysts believed Russians would be offended by my criticism of the regime, despite the fact that the largest anti-regime protests of the last twenty years had just occurred. They seemed to think that the lies Putin published in the *Times* were more appealing than the truth I published in *Pravda*.

Nyet.

CHAPTER EIGHT

KNOW THYSELF

(Defending the West)

IN ALL MY YEARS OF TRAVEL, I HAD NEVER SEEN ANYTHING like it. I had wanted to come to Ukraine for months as events seemed to be leading toward a historic turning point for Ukraine and for Europe. Would Ukraine be a part of Europe or a client state of Russia? Would Europe move closer to the hopeful post–Cold War vision of a Europe whole, free, and at peace or would Putin drag it toward his regressive vision of a Europe divided into rival spheres of influence?

Ukrainian president Viktor Yanukovych had been deposed a decade earlier in the Orange Revolution after a fraudulent election and then returned to power in the 2010 presidential election. Though his election was judged by international observers to have been free and fair, Yanukovych had governed as a strongman. He threw his opponent, Prime Minister Yulia Tymoshenko, in jail on trumped-up charges and changed the Ukrainian constitution to strengthen the powers of the presidency. The endemic corruption Ukraine had suffered for decades was even more pervasive. However, Yanukovych by necessity appeared to embrace a European future for Ukraine. He had negotiated a formal association agreement with the European Union as the first step toward eventual EU membership. Ukraine was destitute. Corruption, reckless economic mismanagement, price gouging by Russia for its natural gas, had left it broke, deeply in debt, with its currency devalued, and facing a bleak future. Under the terms of the agreement, Ukraine would institute liberal political and economic reforms in exchange for loans, investment, and access to European markets. Association with the EU was popular with Ukrainians, especially with younger Ukrainians, or at least with much of the 80 percent of the population that is ethnic Ukrainian. Ethnic Russians, under 20 percent of Ukrainians, were less enthusiastic. Yanukovych was ethnic Russian and long seen as tied to the Kremlin, but he appeared determined to go through with the agreement. Moscow had waged an intense pressure campaign to persuade him to turn east and join the nascent customs union Russia was forming as a rival to the EU. Its only other members were Kazakhstan and Belarus, with a combined nominal GDP about the same as EU member Romania's. Putin viewed Ukraine's economic and political alliance as indispensable to a reconstituted Russian sphere of influence, and he was prepared to fight for it.

As I watched the contest intensify, I wanted to bring a Senate delegation to Ukraine to encourage the association with the EU. I had been a longtime supporter of Ukraine's pro-Western, democratic development, and had connections with a number of prominent Ukrainian reformers. But administration officials, primarily Assistant Secretary of State Toria Nuland and Vice President Biden, both good friends of mine, encouraged me to wait as U.S. and EU diplomats trooped regularly to Kiev and pushed Yanukovych to break with his Russian patrons. It didn't work. After all outstanding issues in the association agreement had been resolved, and most Ukrainians were excitedly waiting for the agreement to be signed, Yanukovych announced on November 21, 2013, that he was backing out. The announcement came just hours after the Ukrainian legislature had defeated a bill that would free former prime minister Tymoshenko from prison, which had been a condition of association with the EU.

Ukrainians took to the streets in protest. Three days later, the police used force to break up the demonstrations in Kiev. The demonstrators multiplied exponentially. The largest demonstration gathered in Kiev's Independence Square, from which the protest movement took its name, the Maidan, Ukrainian for "square," or the "Euromaidan," to recognize what it was the protesters were demonstrating for—a European identity. A large, specially trained police force attacked the square with flash bangs, truncheons, and tear gas on November 30, beating hundreds, including bystanders, and driving most of the protesters out of the square. But every use of force by the police seemed to strengthen the movement's resolve. That same night protesters rallied in another Kiev square, calling for "revolution." In early December, 800,000 people filled Independence Square in Kiev, many of them recently arrived from other cities. Most swore they wouldn't leave the Maidan until the government acquiesced to their demands, which now included Yanukovych's resignation. On December 11, the security police and civilian thugs in their employ made another run at clearing the Maidan, and an eight-hour battle ensued. Church bells rang, and reinforcements flooded into the square. Ukrainian veterans of the Soviet Union's war in Afghanistan formed their own Maidan security force and repelled police attempts to infiltrate it. I had waited longer than I cared to, and Toria and Joe had no further objections. They wouldn't have dissuaded me if they had. In mid-December, I left for Kiev, where I would join Connecticut senator Chris Murphy, a knowledgeable and like-minded member of the Senate Foreign Relations Committee.

I arrived on Saturday afternoon, December 14, and was briefed by embassy officials, who helped arrange meetings with individuals they hoped we could encourage to support, or at least not work to thwart, the Maidan's goals. We met with the Patriarchs of both the Ukraine and Russian Orthodox Churches. We met with several government officials, and put in a request to see Yanukovych. We saw half the oligarchs in the country, those who hadn't yet decided which side to support. Others were loyal to Yanukovych or more accurately, loyal to Moscow. Still others had embraced the Maidan, and one of them, Petro Poroshenko, was a prominent Maidan leader and financial backer. I was introduced to him that night, and met with other opposition leaders, including Vitali Klitschko, one of the famous Klitschko brothers, both heavyweight champion boxers. Vitali had never been knocked down in a fight. I was a fan, and had gotten to know him years before, when I had sponsored legislation to reform the sport. Now, both brothers were leaders in the fight for Ukrainian independence.

It was freezing, windy, and snowy that Saturday night as we drove to a trade union building, and took an elevator to a sixth-floor balcony that overlooked the Maidan. There might have been a half million people in the square that night, unafraid, confident, and joyous. Men, women, and children, young and old, and from all parts of the country. They held their cell phones aloft as they cheered the speakers, LED lights glowing in the swirling snow.

Martin Luther King, Jr., had called it "the fierce urgency of now," the transformational moment when aspirations for freedom must be realized, when the voice of a movement can't be stilled, when the heart's demands will not stand further delay. I saw it that night. I felt it. It was thrilling and affirming. If you told me I could choose to retain only a handful of memories from my long life, that night at the Maidan would be one of them. Ukraine's politics might be complicated by competing ethnic loyalties, but that's mostly because Russia stokes the anger and insecurities of ethnic Russians in Ukraine. There was nothing tribal about the Maidan that night. There were nationalist sentiments in evidence, of course, but in a common demand for independence from corruption, injustice, and imperial dominion. The fervent political movements of our age seem so often to be the workings of religious fanaticism or injured ethnic pride or dehumanizing ideologies of one kind or another, and the power seekers who profit from them. That night I witnessed a fervent mass movement for the universal ideals of freedom and justice. That's what a European identity meant to those people. It was humankind I saw in that square, in all its impossibly resilient dignity, known to God, and striving to be recognized and answered to by the powerful forces who had set themselves above them. Those ideals were my cause, the cause that gave meaning to my eventful life, a life that might otherwise have been squandered. All are created equal. All are endowed by their Creator with inalienable rights. The Maidan put the lie to rationalizations that those ideals can only thrive in some civilizations and not others. It was beautiful to see.

The next day was long and busy, but I was still inspired from the night before. We had breakfast with another oligarch the embassy was trying to enlist, Rinat Akhmetov from Donetsk, who denies having ties to organized crime though it's a familiar biographical detail among Russian and Ukrainian oligarchs, as is elective office. Akhmetov had been elected to parliament as a member of Yanukovych's party. The embassy knew he could bring a lot of powerful converts to the pro-Europe side and a lot of money. He engaged politely with us, but gave no indication whether he agreed with anything we said. Today, he's purported to provide financial support for Donetsk separatists.

The highlight of the day was our invitation to speak at the Maidan. I had planned brief remarks written as a series of one-sentence bullets, to make them easy to translate simultaneously, with a single message, that America supports Ukraine's sovereign right to seek its destiny in Europe. I stood onstage with Vitali and Chris, and a crowd of protest leaders, while an English-speaking Ukrainian diplomat translated. "Ukraine will make Europe better, and Europe will make Ukraine better," I promised. I wish our speeches had receptions at home as rousing as the one we got there. When I told them that "America is with you," chants of "thank you, thank you" in English came roaring back at me.

I had asked staff to find an appropriate line or two from a Ukrainian poet that I could use to end my remarks. "Love your Ukraine," I quoted the poet Taras Shevchenko, "love her in cruel times, love her in cruel moments, pray to God for her." Every politician likes to flatter themselves that they can move an audience. I don't succeed at that as often as I sometimes pretend to myself that I do. I didn't need to pretend that day. It wasn't my delivery that had the effect, just the message and the moment.

We spent a couple hours in the square talking and taking pictures, and soaking up the vibrancy of the experience. I made a point to commend some of the fifty-something Afghanistan vets who were protecting the demonstrators. They looked alike, big guys, with thick arms and long beards, wearing their old uniforms and their medals and patches. They were pretty imposing, and when the regime's goons attacked the square, they held the line.

We got word at seven o'clock that night that Yanukovych would meet us in his palatial residence. We arrived an hour later. Chris Murphy; the U.S. ambassador, Geoff Pyatt; my national security assistant, Chris Brose; and I were seated at a long conference table across from Yanukovych and two of his aides. We exchanged quick introductions, and then Yanukovych proceeded to speak uninterrupted for at least an hour. He dwelt in detail on a long litany of grievances. It had been an early start to the day, the room was overheated, and all of us had to struggle to stay awake. Finally, Chris interrupted him, explaining that we had hoped for more of a dialogue than a lecture. Bless him. If he hadn't spoken up, I swear we would have been there to ring in the New Year two weeks later. We spent another hour going back and forth with the beleaguered president. He had resumed discussions with EU officials in response to the protests, and the EU had called them off, he complained, because he still refused to release Yulia Tymoshenko. Yanukovych was stalling for time hoping the protests would lose momentum, and everyone knew it. What was there left to negotiate, we countered, you had an agreement all but signed. What is it you need to get you to sign it now? His response was to return to his grievances, citing all the ways Europe had mistreated him, one of which, I kid not, was a soccer game in which a European referee had called a goal wrong and cost Ukraine the game. He wanted to give us the sense that he understood our position, but that he was doing what he could in an impossible situation, caught between his country's interests and the ruthlessness of their colossus to the east. We had heard that before he had refused to sign the EU agreement, he had been summoned to Putin's dacha in Sochi, where the Russian had laid out all the ways the Kremlin would crush Ukraine's economy and his finances along with it. Yanukovych had used his presidency to join the ranks of the oligarchs, standard practice, sadly, in Ukraine and Russia. Sanctions targeted at certain wealthy men, Putin is purported to have warned him, trade cutoffs, export bans, the whole panoply of economic blackmail. Yanukovych returned to Kiev a changed man, it was said, self-preservation having become his sole occupation. Integration with Europe was now a fantasy from happier times. We tried to impress upon him that the Maidan movement had reached escape velocity. He wouldn't be able to stop it. If he tried, he would be swept from power. He could only complain that he had been ill-treated. Two days later, Putin would offer Yanukovych $15 billion in debt relief, and to slash the price for Russian gas deliveries to Ukraine. We left the next morning for home and the holidays, certain that Ukraine would overthrow its government, and certain, too, that we would be back in Ukraine soon.

By the time I returned in March with a large, bipartisan Senate delegation, the peaceful, festive protests of December had been eclipsed by a series of riots and general pandemonium caused by the government's attempts to suppress the demonstrations, and resulting assaults on the protesters, including killings, by the security police and thugs paid by the regime. Death squads had targeted some Maidan leaders. The prime minister resigned on January 28, and the legislature repealed anti-protest laws that had been enacted the week before. Putin again summoned Yanukovych to Sochi. Several days later a senior Putin advisor intimated that Russia might have to intervene to prevent a coup and continuing chaos. The same day a bomb exploded in the trade union building where I had watched the Maidan demonstrations. On February 18, protesters marched on parliament. Police fired on the marchers, who fought back. Dozens were killed, including ten policemen, and thousands injured. Within a few days, the government had essentially fallen, and Yanukovych had fled the capital, en route ultimately to Moscow.

Putin convened a meeting with his security services to plan the conquest of Crimea. Pro-Russian protests in Crimea began the next day in Sevastopol, and on February 27, Russian soldiers disguised as civilians seized the Crimean legislature and other government institutions. A puppet government led by Sergei Aksyonov, an ethnic Russian who had received 4 percent of the vote in the last election, was installed. He declared Crimea an autonomous republic, and invited Russian troops to serve as "peacekeepers." By March 2, Russian forces completely controlled the peninsula. A fraudulent referendum was staged on March 16, two days after our delegation arrived in Kiev, that overwhelmingly approved Crimea's federation with Russia. Two days later, Russia formally annexed it.

Eight of us had rushed to Kiev, five Republicans and three Democrats, in a show of American bipartisan solidarity with Ukraine as it confronted the Russian invasion. Just before we left the *Wall Street Journal* reported that the Obama administration had denied Ukraine's request for lethal assistance to defend its territory. Members of our delegation were divided on the subject, but not along party lines. I was in favor, and have argued continuously for the last three years that

Ukraine has the right to defend itself from Russian invasion, which would soon include the Donbass region in Eastern Ukraine, and the U.S. should help provide it weapons for that purpose. The administration remained opposed, however, until its last day in office, as did Chancellor Merkel, who feared a wider war, and spoke for most of the EU on the subject.

We met with the acting president and his cabinet, as well as the leaders of all the political parties who would be contesting a presidential election in May and parliamentary elections in October, including Vitali Klitschko and Petro Poroshenko, who was expected to be the next president. The next day we flew to Donetsk in the Donbass, where Kiev feared the Russians would next invade, which they did a few weeks later. Anti-Maidan, pro-Russian demonstrations had been building in Donetsk and other locations in Eastern Ukraine since the beginning of March and protesters had occupied the local government administration building. At every stop, and in every public statement, we pledged our support for the independence of Ukrainians, and condemned Russia's actions. Without the promise of defense assistance, however, Putin was unlikely to be concerned with our disapproval or be deterred.

The administration and the EU imposed sanctions on Russia, travel bans, and asset freezes that had been authorized by the Magnitsky Act, targeting individuals in Putin's inner circle. They went after Russian banks, too, and state-owned companies such as Rosneft. Russia was suspended from participation in G-8 summits. In retaliation, Moscow announced similar sanctions against eight American officials, including Speaker John Boehner, Majority Leader Harry Reid, a few White House staffers, and me. I was delighted. "I guess this means my spring break in Siberia is off," I joked.

The provisional national government promised to take back control of the Donbass. Russian separatists, mostly led by Russians from

Russia, seized other government buildings and demanded independence. By April it was a shooting war. Many of the militants, possibly the majority of them, were Russian paramilitaries. In July, they shot down a Malaysia Airlines passenger jet with Russian-supplied missiles. The war has ebbed and flowed over the last three years, and continues unresolved. Various cease-fires have been agreed to, announced, and promptly violated by the Russians. Minsk I and Minsk II and I'm sure whatever Minsk agreement comes next have wrung commitments from Moscow to cease its incursions, but Russians still fight in Ukraine. The insurrection would be finished without Putin's patronage. While we were in Ukraine, I had an op-ed published in the *New York Times* criticizing the administration's response. Whxile not blaming the Russian invasion on the administration or any policy of the U.S. and its allies, I did claim that the administration's lack of realism about Russia specifically and the state of the world generally had created a perception of weakness, and to Putin "weakness is provocative."

> For Mr. Putin, vacillation invites aggression. His world is a brutish, cynical place, where power is worshiped, weakness is despised, and all rivalries are zero-sum. . . . He does not accept that Russia's neighbors, least of all Ukraine, are independent countries. To him, they are Russia's "near abroad" and must be brought back under Moscow's dominion by any means necessary.

I attended Petro Poroshenko's presidential inauguration in June 2014, and have been back several times since then, reiterating my solidarity, and promising to keep pressing the administration for support. My last trip was just after Christmas in 2016, when I attended with President Poroshenko a meeting of the families of killed and missing Ukrainian soldiers. A mother of one of the casualties, who wasn't very old, but very stoic, stood quietly, with tears streaming down her face, as Poroshenko pinned a medal on her for her late son. Later that same trip I flew with Lindsey Graham and Amy Klobuchar, a Democrat from Minnesota, to Mariupol in Donetsk, and from there we traveled to an outpost on what constitutes the front in the war in Eastern Ukraine. We spent New Year's Eve with an impressive group of Ukrainian marines, all committed to the struggle with the powerful country that wants Ukraine subjugated. They made me a gift of a rifle, not an antique, but a modern assault rifle, an AK-47 or something similar. Jim Hickey, a retired career Army officer who serves on the Armed Services Committee staff, was there, and I handed the case containing the rifle to him. He carried it onto the airplane for me. Before the plane took off, he opened the case and found it had a full magazine and a round in the chamber. He cleared the chamber and ejected the magazine. For two years, I had argued the U.S. should provide the lethal arms Ukraine needed to defend itself from invaders. I had included authorization for that assistance in the defense bill every year. I had failed. Now, Ukrainians had given lethal arms to me. I wondered if they had meant it as a joke.

We had arrived in Mariupol soon after the Obama administration announced new sanctions against Russia for interference in the 2016 election. Russia had not announced retaliatory measures yet. We would later learn that was because President-elect Trump's incoming national security advisor, retired lieutenant general Mike Flynn, had urged the Russian ambassador in Washington not to impose new sanctions, presumably implying that once the new administration was in office they would reconsider the sanctions the White House had just announced. If that was indeed what happened, it was a terrible thing to do. A ruthless adversary had tried to sabotage our elections, aggravating our political divisions and worsening our government's dysfunction. Sparing Putin any serious penalty for his assault on our democracy doesn't just encourage further aggression, it tells the victims and potential victims of Russian aggression in Ukraine and Georgia, the Baltics, Poland, Moldova, and Montenegro, and in Russia itself, that the United States, the greatest power in the world, couldn't be relied on to defend its own democracy. It's a colossal strategic mistake, and a stain on our honor. In the last decade, I've traveled to all the countries named above, save Russia, and many others in the neighborhood. They are all scared of what Russia plans for them, and though they will never say it publicly, worried that the U.S. won't help defend them when it comes. Putin's kleptocracy has left the sluggish Russian economy overly dependent on its oil and gas reserves. Russia's population is declining at an alarming rate as birthrates plunge and life expectancy is static. Much of the wealth of the country has been plundered by the Russian ruling class and invested in the West. Putin's authoritarianism has bred more dissent in his country than the West credits. Russia's future is bleak, darkened by all the ills he and his collaborators have created for their country, and blamed on the United States. Putin is uniquely vulnerable and yet, from the Donbass to Syria to an American presidential election, he is on the attack. Because he has not encountered the resolve it will take to expose his precarious position, to shatter his ambitions. Until he does meet that resolve, there's no end to the trouble he'll cause, and the victims he'll claim.

The reader familiar with my public statements will have heard me make these arguments many times. What has any of it meant? All these trips, all these speeches, op-eds, press statements, interviews, professing support for Ukrainians and Georgians and Estonians and Montenegrins, condemning Putin, criticizing my own government? Did it change anything, improve anything? I hope so. But I know for certain it meant something to the people I meant to help because they've told me it has. It meant that there were Americans on their side, that we hear them, we acknowledge the justice of their cause, they aren't forgotten. Keep up the fight, hang on, have hope. Maybe we should do more to help you. We might argue among ourselves about that. But you're on the right side of history, and we're on your side. It matters. Scoop Jackson taught me that. Natan Sharansky taught me that. And the countless dissidents, political prisoners, freedom fighters, honest journalists, human rights activists, and defenders of the Western liberal order that I've had the privilege to meet have told me it matters.

I got involved in the case of Nadiya Savchenko, a Ukrainian army pilot who had volunteered to fight on the ground in the Donbass, and was captured in June 2014 and given to the Russians. They accused her of murdering two Russian journalists, who had been killed after her capture. She was tried and convicted and sentenced to twenty-two years in prison. She had been brave and defiant throughout her trial, speaking from a barred cage in the courtroom. When the judge pronounced her guilty, she sang a patriotic Ukrainian anthem. While in prison, she was elected to the Ukrainian parliament. Years before, she had served with a detachment of Ukrainians in Iraq to help America. We owed her. Her treatment was protested by the Obama administration, the Europeans, the Red Cross, almost every government and institution that observed the basic norms of conduct in war. I made a few statements on her behalf, and had sent a letter to Secretary Kerry, urging him to raise her case on an upcoming trip to Russia. It was nothing out of the ordinary, really. Just a standard expression of support for another victim of Russian aggression. Putin couldn't have cared less about any of it. She remained in prison for over two years, until she was included in a Russian prisoner swap with the Ukrainians. She came through Washington not long after and asked to see me. She thanked me profusely, more than I deserved. She was very emotional. All I could think to say was how brave and inspiring she had been in very difficult circumstances, and how proud her country was of her. "I do know a little of what you went through," I told her, referring to my own experiences as a prisoner of war. With that she began to weep. I had done something, but very little, to help a brave Ukrainian patriot, and it had mattered to her.

Boris Nemtsov was organizing another rally. The "spring march" was scheduled for Sunday, March 1, 2015, to protest the economic crisis Putin's policies and corruption had caused, and the casualties and criminality of his war in Eastern Ukraine. Boris had urged chronically quarreling opposition parties to put aside their differences for the day and present a united front of defiance to the regime that oppressed them all. He had mentioned to me that he was working on a report detailing the Russian involvement in the war when I had last seen him a month earlier. He had come to my Washington office in late January with his closest associate and friend, Vladimir Kara-Murza. We had a long conversation about Ukraine. There wasn't much Boris didn't know about the situation. He was as well informed about Ukraine as he was about Russia, and as well connected. He was often in Ukraine. He had seen the fighting in the east himself. He met with the families of Russian soldiers who had been killed there. He and the political party he chaired had endorsed the Maidan movement and Ukraine's integration in Europe. He had vociferously denounced the annexation of Crimea, and was blistering in his condemnation of Russian separatists in Eastern Ukraine, and their patron, Vladimir Putin. "This is not our war," he wrote in a Kiev newspaper, "this is not your war, this is not the war of twenty-year-old paratroopers sent out there. This is Vladimir Putin's war."

Boris was well known in the West as Putin's most outspoken and persistent scourge, to the point that many observers, even admirers, in and out of Russia thought him reckless. He appeared fearless, though I'm certain he had concerns that his antagonism for Putin was a more dangerous enterprise than he pretended. The stinging insults he hurled, the provocative but truthful charges he made, often seemed perfectly devised to expose Putin's personal corruption and, worse, prick the bubble of Putin's self-regard. He had been arrested, jailed, harassed, and threatened. He would rarely confess fears for his safety, and then only to his closest friends. But to Russia, to the rest of the world, and to me, he alternated between bravado and resignation. He was funny, irreverent, and full of himself, a big man with a big personality. He was entertaining as hell, self-assured, charming, impudent, and dismissive of the apprehensions and grudges of less sturdy souls. "My mother is worried," he acknowledged as he deflected another anxious inquiry, "but I'm not worried."

I think he rationalized he wouldn't be murdered because it would set a bad precedent for the Kremlin. He had served in senior government positions, a young crusading reformer representing Nizhny Novgorod in the early years of Russia's democratic transformation, a minister in Yeltsin's cabinet, and, like Putin, a deputy prime minister. He had been elected several times to both houses of the Russian parliament, the Federation Council and the Duma, and was one of the most prominent opposition leaders in the country, and had many friends in the West. To kill a man with that kind of résumé would be unprecedented even for the gangster regime Putin is running. He had been one of the first prominent critics of Putinism, and the sharpest. He and Vladimir Kara-Murza authored an editorial in 2004 denouncing Putin's encroachments on Russian democracy and growing despotism. He had been one of the organizers with Garry Kasparov and others of the Dissenters' March in 2007. He and Vladimir published numerous reports exposing official corruption, and Putin's personal accumulation of wealth and grandiose lifestyle. One of the most notable was their exposé of corruption plaguing the Sochi Olympics.

I first met Boris in 2011 on one of his periodic trips to Washington. He and other opposition leaders had recently been arrested at a

New Year's Eve protest and jailed for a couple weeks. Joe Lieberman and I had issued a statement condemning the arrests, which evidently received unfavorable attention in Moscow. A Duma committee chairman condemned our condemnation, and betraying a parochial view of the proper relationship between the legislative and executive branches of government, professed confusion that we would concern ourselves with Russian politics, since "Obama . . . [had] pledged not to . . . interfere in a foreign country's affairs and not to force democracy on anyone." Boris had asked to see me the next time he came through town. Vladimir came with him.

We hit it off instantly, and it became the first of many meetings with the two defiant democrats. Gregarious, charming, Boris made friends easily, and we became friends, genuine friends. He was especially good company. I usually met with them in Washington, but occasionally I'd see them both at an overseas conference where Russia was a subject of concern, and carve out some time to catch up. I admired both of them a great deal, and trusted them. I relied on their knowledge of Putin's regime, and their counsel on how the U.S. ought to confront it. Their insights about the impact the Magnitsky sanctions would have on Putin Inc. strengthened my own confidence in their utility. As mentioned, I found Boris's judgment about what Putin was up to in Ukraine, as well as in the other former republics and satellites of the Soviet Union, astute. Even with Syria, where Putin was setting himself up as an opponent of U.S. intervention, and where he was planning to intervene militarily himself later that same year, Boris understood that the West's episodic astonishment with Putin's unexpected adventurism revealed a lack of realism. Nothing Putin does abroad should be unexpected. He always signals his intentions and always follows through unless he encounters resistance that worries him.

Our last conversations were mostly focused on Ukraine, but increasingly on his own safety. By the time I saw him in January 2015, for the last time, I had heard reports from a variety of sources, many of whom had talked to Boris, that the threats against his life had proliferated in recent months, and that he was worried. He didn't show his concern to me. But I didn't get the full flourish of Boris's usual bravado, either, when I begged him—and that was exactly the verb I used—I begged him not to go back to Russia. He had a tired smile, but no fear in his voice, when he said something like, "I will never give up fighting for Russia's freedom, for the rule of law. What can I do. It's my country."

On an unusually warm winter night, February 27, two days before his "spring march," Boris Nemtsov and his girlfriend of three years walked through Red Square after dinner and across the nearby bridge to his apartment building. A white car pulled up behind them while they were on the bridge, and a gunman or gunmen shot him four times. He died instantly.

Russians who believed in the dream of freedom and equal justice were devastated, as were Boris's many friends abroad, as was I. The precedent that Boris had hoped wouldn't be set, had been. A prominent opposition leader and senior government official had been assassinated. Two years later, Vladimir Kara-Murza lay in a Moscow hospital, his organs failing, nearly dead from poison. But he survived, I'm relieved to say, and I've seen him quite a few times since that attempt. It was the second time he had been poisoned by, I have no doubt, someone who was directly or indirectly authorized by Vladimir Putin. I've begged him, too, to be careful. But what's he to do? It's his country.

The International Republican Institute posthumously awarded Boris our Freedom Award. I gave a brief tribute to the man who gave his life for a vision of Russia taking its place in the civilization of free people, governed by laws, not men, where human dignity was above the state. "Putin could never understand Boris," I explained.

He could never appreciate how someone could be impervious to threats and slander, to the lure of corruption and the oppression of fear. A man like Putin, who all his life has stood on the wrong side of history, of morality, of goodness, can't comprehend the power of righteousness. He is blind to the supremacy of love. He can't see that all lies are exposed eventually, hate is overcome by love, illicit power decays, while the truth endures.

The people who killed Boris and the regime that protects them are the enemies of the Russian people. They rob Russia of its wealth, its hopes, its future. They deny the God-given dignity of the people they misrule. They are thieves and murderers and cowards. They fear justice. They fear truth. They fear a society in which ideals and morality are the foundation of law and order.

Boris wasn't afraid. He knew his enemies. He knew what they were capable of, but he would not be oppressed. He would not be oppressed by unjust laws or by violence and fear. He was a free man, and bravely so. He was accustomed to danger. But he lived for love and justice and truth. He had been threatened repeatedly and demonized by the regime's propaganda apparatus. Yet when his enemies took his life in the shadow of the Kremlin, they found him walking in the open air, enjoying the evening, unafraid.

Not that long ago, Putin's English-language propaganda organ, Russia Today, compiled a list of the top ten Russia haters. I was number one. I don't hate Russia. I want for it the same freedom, justice, and prosperity that Americans have. I hate Putin, though. I make no bones about that. I've been accused more than once of taking Putin's crimes "personally." And I have. I have indeed. Vladimir Putin is an evil man. There is no better word for him. And he is intent on evil deeds, which include the destruction of the liberal world order, its values and its institutions. The world order that the United States of America led and defended all my lifetime. The world order that has brought more stability, prosperity, and freedom to humankind than has ever existed in history. He is assaulting those institutions from a position of weakness. Russia's future, its economy and stability, is bleak. And while he has an immense nuclear arsenal and modern armed forces, he's not using them to attack the West frontally. He employs his military in easier conquests. He is using our own weaknesses and virtues against us, the openness of our society and the increasingly acrimonious political divisions consuming us. He wants to widen those divides and paralyze us from responding to his aggression. He meddled in our election, and he will do it again because it worked, and because he has not been made to stop. He interfered in the last French presidential election. And he successfully helped reelect the president of the Czech Republic, a NATO ally, who opposes NATO and the EU and supports Putin's invasion and annexation of Crimea. He did it with the same means he used to interfere in our election. And yet, as of this writing, I don't see Washington prepared and focused to stop his continued assault on the integrity of our democratic processes.

Montenegro, a small, mountainous country on the Adriatic Sea, had been on track to join NATO since 2006, when it dissolved its union with Serbia, and entered the Partnership for Peace. The following year, the Montenegrin government signed an agreement with NATO allowing Alliance forces to transit the country. Montenegro's application for the Membership Action Plan was granted in 2009, and it began fulfilling the political and military requirements for accession. Disappointingly, Russia's annexation of Crimea is believed to have slowed Montenegro's progress as some NATO members worried about Russia's reaction to adding any new members. But by 2015, it appeared back on track, and a formal invitation was extended in December of that year. The member nations of the Alliance had to vote to ratify Montenegro's accession, as did the Montenegrin parliament, which would have to overcome the objections of pro-Russian opposition leaders, acting in concert with a furious Russian campaign to prevent ratification. Parliamentary elections were scheduled for October.

We started hearing reports in early 2016 of Russia working with the opposition to prevent ratification, including suspected efforts to subvert the parliamentary elections. I asked staff from the Armed Services Committee to go to Montenegro in July and get briefed by our embassy and by Montenegrin officials on the extent of the Russian interference. They reported back that the Montenegrins were alarmed about more than Russian meddling in their country's politics. They were worried about a violent attack on Montenegrin democracy.

Putin viewed Montenegro's pursuit of EU and NATO membership as a threat to Russia's geopolitical ambitions and an insult. Montenegro had been part of Serbia, Russia's traditional Slavic ally. And Montenegro had long been a favorite destination for Russian tourists, especially vacationing oligarchs and politicians. As much as 40 percent of the country's real estate is said to be in Russian hands. Montenegro's beaches are a popular haunt for heavyset Russians wearing Speedos and accompanied by their "nieces." More important to Moscow, though, is the country's strategic location. Russia had once sought to build a naval base there. Montenegro's membership in NATO would bring the Adriatic Sea within the Alliance's borders, and it would signal other countries in the Western Balkans, possibly even Serbia itself, that alignment with the West was a real possibility.

Putin had a lot at stake in the question, in terms of his imperial ambitions, nationalist pride, and protecting Putin Inc.'s financial investments in the country. As he is wont to do, he decided on a bold move. He doesn't need much incentive to choose to take a risk. As we now know, he was meddling in our election at the same time. And he would use some of the same means to disrupt Montenegro's election that he used here, chiefly cyberattacks and a disinformation war. In Montenegro, he also employed economic pressure, threats to cut off energy exports, bribery, financial support for opposition parties, co-opting the elements of the Serbian Orthodox Church to foment anti-Western sentiments, and protest rallies. As it turned out, Putin was prepared to use something else to bend Montenegro to his will. Violence.

Pro-Russian politicians had demanded a popular referendum on NATO membership, but Prime Minister Milo Djukanovic replied by stating the obvious: the October election would serve as a referendum. If he and other pro-NATO members won a majority, then ratification would happen. If the opposition won, it wouldn't.

On the morning of the election, October 16, Montenegrin authorities arrested twenty Serb nationals who had crossed into Montenegro the night before and charged them with planning a coup d'état. The Montenegrins were tipped off days before by one of the Serbian coup plotters who had gotten cold feet and defected. According to the subsequent indictment, the plotters planned to stage a protest rally in front of the parliament building on the day of the election, while fifty of them dressed as police stormed the building and killed Montenegrin security police posted there. The protesters would flood into the building and declare victory for the opposition. A new government would be formed, and Prime Minister Djukanovic would either be arrested or murdered. In the aftermath of the failed plot, two Russian military intelligence agents in Belgrade who had organized it made their way back to Moscow after hiring an assassin to kill the Montenegrin prime minister.

Initial reports beyond the announced arrests were murky. Government officials were cautious about speaking candidly, especially about Russia's involvement, fearing that they might still be at risk. They accused Russian nationalists of being responsible, and eventually arrested two opposition party leaders, but for more than a month they kept mostly quiet about Moscow's responsibility. By the end of November, the *New York Times* had reported that the failed coup had been conceived and supported by Russia, which the Montenegrin government soon confirmed, eventually issuing indictments for the two absconded Russian intelligence agents. Still, despite the allegations, the initial impression in the West about the bungled affair was that it had been a confused, inept, and probably not very serious threat to the Montenegrin government.

I took it seriously, and I thought the most effective way to prevent another attempt was to secure the thing that the coup had been meant to prevent, Montenegro's membership in NATO. I talked to the new Montenegrin prime minister on January 10, and pledged my full commitment to getting the Senate to ratify their accession. The vote had been stalled for months, blocked by two senators, Rand Paul and Mike Lee. Leadership hadn't felt it was urgently necessary to overcome their objections. I tried to convince the Senate it was. Only NATO membership was likely to prevent Russia from other attempts to overthrow the Montenegrin government. I tried to bring ratification up for a vote in early March, and Paul objected, which led to a sharp exchange between us that included my assertion that the Kentucky senator was "now working for Vladimir Putin." Senator Paul didn't appreciate that, and I'll grant that it was an intemperate thing to say. But it wasn't incorrect. He might not have worked wittingly for Putin, but he was doing exactly what the Russian wanted done. It took a couple more weeks, and a commitment to being a real pain in the ass, badgering leadership, and threatening to hold up other business, but we finally cleared the Paul and Lee holds on March 28, and the Senate voted 97 to 2 to ratify Montenegro's accession. I flew to Montenegro a few days later.

I met with the prime minister, and with senior officials prosecuting the coup plotters. They read the indictment to me, and it made clear how sophisticated and well prepared the attempt had been, and how Moscow had masterminded and directed it. It might very well have succeeded had it not been for the one defector who informed on his accomplices. I had the embassy translate the entire 135-page indictment into English, and brought it back to Washington, where I shared it with colleagues and reporters. Montenegro officially joined NATO on June 5, and is now protected by the Atlantic Charter's Article 5, that an attack on one member is an attack on us all.

I held a committee hearing on July 13, the anniversary of Montenegro's statehood, to examine the details of Russia's involvement, and I invited Montenegro's ambassador to testify. In my opening statement, I explained how nearly successful the coup had been, and I urged NATO to welcome other aspirants, and be prepared to resist Putin's covert and overt treachery to prevent it. I warned he would continue his attacks on our democracy, and offered suggestions for how to prevent them, and take the fight to Putin. "Most of all," I urged,

> we have to stop looking at Russia and its threat to our security and our democracy through the warped lens of politics. We cannot allow Putin to divide us . . . [and] undermine confidence in ourselves. . . . We must take our own side in this fight—not as Republicans, not as Democrats, but as Americans.

Despite the good efforts and good faith of many of my colleagues who have worked to understand the threat and defeat it, we have a way to go before all Americans realize that Putin's goal isn't to defeat a candidate or a party. He means to defeat the West. He will try to interfere, he already is, in our next election, and the election after that, and the election after that. He will keep doing it until we prevent him. And we're behind schedule in that responsibility.

I'm sure there are legions of committed national security officials working hard to figure out how to combat his cyberattacks, his disinformation campaigns, and his possible, even likely, effort to hack into our voting machines. But President Trump seems to vary from refusing to believe what Putin is doing to just not caring about it. Just last November he appeared to take Putin's denials at face value. "There's nothing 'America First,'" I pointed out, "about taking the word of a KGB colonel over that of the American intelligence community." And some House Republicans investigating Russian interference seem more preoccupied with their own conspiracy theories than with a real conspiracy by a foreign enemy to defraud the United States. Unless the elected leaders of our government provide persistent direction and leadership and resources to officials working to defend our democracy, we won't stop Putin's next assault. With a nominal investment of resources, and a bold disregard for our resistance, Putin's interference in our last election achieved all his objectives. He damaged Hillary Clinton's campaign, but that wasn't his most important priority. Encouraging our government's dysfunction, and disaffection and distrust in the polity were his main objectives. He sees evidence of his success every day in our polarization and gridlock.

Just a few weeks before I met with Boris for the last time, President Obama and Putin had spoken on the phone. The very next day Putin authorized fresh attacks on Ukrainian forces in the Donbass, breaking a cease-fire. He cannot be trusted. He has aided the slaughter of hundreds of thousands of Syrians, and made refugees of millions more. He has deliberately and repeatedly bombed hospitals there. He claims he is fighting terrorism. But he isn't. He's fighting freedom. He uses terrorism as an excuse and as a method of state power. To his credit, President Trump overturned the Obama policy and supplied lethal assistance to Ukraine, and I commend him for it. But he needs to comprehend the nature of the threat Putin poses. He needs to understand Putin's nature, and ours. Last year, he implied that our government was morally equivalent to Putin's regime: "We have a lot of killers, too. You think our country is so innocent," he told an interviewer. It was a shameful thing to say, and so unaware of reality. He said it as Vladimir Kara-Murza was near death, as Russian bombs fell on Aleppo hospitals, as Ukrainian soldiers defended their country from another Russian attack, as the most vile false accusations pitting Americans against Americans coursed through social media, disseminated by an army of trolls paid by Vladimir Putin to destroy the fraying bonds, established by law and norms, that hold our society together.

China is our greatest long-term challenge, and one we have yet to concentrate our resources and employ a strategy to counter. Regrettably, our shrewdest response to China's growing influence in the Pacific and challenge to our interests and values, the Trans-Pacific Partnership, was a casualty of the President's campaign demagoguery. The countries we would have partnered with are now negotiating a pact among themselves. The world is learning to live without our active leadership. That's not good for the world and it won't be good for us. That's the real damage our distractions are doing to our interests—the spurious nationalism animating our politics, our growing distrust of our institutions and of each other, facilitated by the activities of a committed enemy. When President Trump compares us neutrally to the regime of a murderer and thug, it causes our allies and adversaries to wonder, if Americans don't believe in themselves, why should we?

China is the challenge of the century, but Putin is the clear and present danger, the immediate threat to America, and to the world we have helped make and thrive in. We must fight him as cleverly and as determinedly as he fights us. We will stop him when we stop letting our partisan and personal interests expose our national security interests, even the integrity of our democracy and the rule of law, to his predation. We will stop him when we start believing in ourselves again, in our exceptionalism, and remember that our exceptionalism hasn't anything to do with what we are—prosperous, powerful, envied—but with who we are, people united by ideals, not ethnicity or geography, and how faithfully we stand by those values, not just within our shores but in the world.

We will stop him when we are confident of our strength in the world, not merely the strength of our arms, but the power of our ideals—government by consent, equal justice, free markets—to continue transforming the world into a broadening civilization that shares them. Americans who demand that we fight globalization are suffering from a kind of antihistorical hysteria. Whose values and interests do they think created the global economy? Ours. We don't have the confidence to compete in a global economy that operates by rules and economic principles that we practically invented? Globalization is a fact, not a policy. It won't disappear because we don't think we're succeeding in it. We can't withdraw from it any more than we can withdraw from the weather. It's where wealth is created, invested, dispersed, exchanged. It will continue making some industries obsolete in the West and propagating new ones. We have to adjust to those dislocations, help those hurt by them, and prepare their children for the opportunities to come. But we thrive in the global economy because we open our markets to other nations and help them thrive, and create new markets, new consumers for our goods and services, and, importantly, new converts to our way of doing things, to our principles. Open trading relations help make a safer, more stable world, a more prosperous world, a more just world, which is what we did throughout the Cold War and well into this century. We overcame grave threats and huge challenges to do it. And we can overcome Putin's less formidable challenge today. We just have to believe in ourselves and act as responsibly, as exceptionally, as four generations of Americans and twelve presidential administrations, six Democratic and six Republican, acted as we led the free world. We have to value the world we made, and not let someone who fought on the losing side of the struggle for the rules and values that govern it convince us it's not worth fighting for.

The Iraq War caused divisions in the West. Some of our closest allies were the most outspoken critics of our decision to invade, none of them more passionately so than Germany's foreign minister at that time, Joschka Fischer. We both attend the Munich Security Conference, where Fischer had famously directly replied to Rumsfeld's WMD justification for the war. "Excuse me, I am not convinced," he declared. I suspect some of Fischer's irritation had been caused by Rumsfeld's recent grumbling about criticism from Old Europe, presumably Germany and France, and other Western European countries, and support from New Europe, the nations of the former Warsaw Pact and new NATO members who were more supportive.

Fischer and I both spoke sharply about Iraq in Munich, he in heated opposition, and I in heated defense. We might have been confused as antagonists. But we were not. We were allies in disagreement. But allies nonetheless. He was a member of the Green Party in a coalition government with Chancellor Gerhard Schroeder's Social Democrats. Schroeder would prove in time to be a Putin admirer or at least a beneficiary of Putin's largesse. He's now on the board of Rosneft. But Fischer wasn't like that despite his party's pacifist philosophy. He is a good man, and a committed ally. He supported NATO's intervention in Kosovo, and advocated sending German troops to Afghanistan.

He asked to see me when he was next in Washington. I assumed he wanted to talk about Iraq. But he didn't, or at least not specifically. He acknowledged our differences on Iraq but deferred their resolution to the future. "History will prove one of us right," he noted with no rancor. What was worrying him most, he said, was the anti-Americanism spreading in Europe that our decision to go into Iraq exacerbated. He had grown up near a U.S. military base. The soldiers had been kind to him, and taught him English. Americans were part of Germany, part of Europe. Neither would be the same without the other. He went through this long, lovely recitation of the transatlantic values that united Europe with America, and how our relationship ended divisions and rivalries that had roiled the continent for centuries. Twice America had helped end wars Europeans had started, and after the last one we had promised never to leave. Our presence in Europe, our shared identity as the West, had had a profound effect on generations of Europeans, he said. Our alliance had made Europe better. It was an elegant, compelling appeal for American and European solidarity, and it moved me very much.

I had the same fear that we were losing the forest for the trees. The forest was our shared values, our history, the uniqueness of our continuing alliance. I have that same fear now, that we will let the distractions and follies of the moment debilitate our alliance, undermine our solidarity, and leave us vulnerable to the plots of a weak adversary. I addressed that fear last year at the Munich Security Conference. I hope to attend the conference again, to see old friends and talk about the future. But if I am unable to, then I am content for my speech from last year's conference to stand as my valedictory address as a proud ally in the world order the West has built.

> These are dangerous times, but you should not count America out, and we should not count each other out. We must be prudent, but we cannot wring our hands and wallow in self-doubt. We must appreciate the limits of our power, but we cannot allow ourselves to question the rightness and goodness of the West. We must understand and learn from our mistakes, but we cannot be paralyzed by fear. We cannot give up on ourselves and on each other. That is the definition of decadence. And that is how world orders really do decline and fall.
>
> This is exactly what our adversaries want. This is their goal.

They have no meaningful allies, so they seek to sow dissent among us and divide us from each other. They know that their power and influence are inferior to ours, so they seek to subvert us, and erode our resolve to resist, and terrorize us into passivity. They know they have little to offer the world beyond selfishness and fear, so they seek to undermine our confidence in ourselves and our belief in our own values.

We must take our own side in this fight. We must be vigilant. We must persevere. And through it all, we must never, never cease to believe in the moral superiority of our own values— that we stand for truth against falsehood, freedom against tyranny, right against injustice, hope against despair . . . and that even though we will inevitably take losses and suffer setbacks, through it all, so long as people of goodwill and courage refuse to lose faith in the West, it will endure.

That is why we come to Munich, year in and year out—to revitalize our common moral purpose, our belief that our values are worth the fighting for. Because in the final analysis, the survival of the West is not just a material struggle; it is now, and has always been, a moral struggle. Now more than ever, we must not forget this.

During one of the darkest years of the early Cold War, William Faulkner delivered a short speech in Stockholm upon receiving the Nobel Prize for Literature. "I decline to accept the end of man," Faulkner said. "I believe that man will not merely endure: he will prevail. He is immortal, not because he alone among creatures has an inexhaustible voice, but because he has a soul, a spirit capable of compassion and sacrifice and endurance."

Even now, when the temptation to despair is greatest, I refuse to accept the end of the West. I refuse to accept the demise of our world order. I refuse to accept that our greatest triumphs cannot once again spring from our moments of greatest peril, as they have so many times before. I refuse to accept that our values are morally equivalent to those of our adversaries. I am a proud, unapologetic believer in the West, and I believe we must always, always stand up for it—for if we do not, who will?

CHAPTER NINE

PART OF THE MAIN

(American Exceptionalism)

FRENCH WRITER AND AVIATOR ANTOINE DE SAINT-EXUPÉRY authored his best-known work, *The Little Prince*, while living in exile in New York after France's capitulation to Nazi Germany. He returned to the war in the spring of 1943, traveling in an American military convoy to Algiers, where he joined the Free French Air Force fighting with the Allies in North Africa. At forty-three, he was well past the age limit for pilots, and in pain from permanent injuries suffered in several crashes. At the end of July in 1944, he disappeared without a trace while flying a reconnaissance mission over southern France. His loss was widely mourned.

While crossing the Atlantic in the company of American soldiers, Saint-Exupéry was inspired by American idealism and gave testament to it in a letter to an American friend. "If the American soldiers had been sent to war merely in order to protect American interests," he reasoned,

> their propaganda would have insisted heavily on your oil wells, your rubber plantations, your threatened commercial markets. But such subjects were hardly mentioned. If war propaganda stressed other things, it was because your soldiers wanted to

hear about other things. And what were they told to justify the sacrifice of their lives in their own eyes? They were told of the hostages hanged in Poland, the hostages shot in France. They were told of a new form of slavery that threatened to stifle part of humanity. Propaganda spoke to them not about themselves, but about others. The fifty thousand soldiers of this convoy were going to war, not for the citizens of the United States, but for man, for human respect, for man's freedom and greatness.

Of course, the objects of wars aren't limited to humanitarian causes. Nations fight for their self-interest, their security interests, their economic interests, their cultural interests, all nations, including ours. But what has distinguished us in the great chapters of our history, the attitude that had so impressed Saint-Exupéry, whose observations are displayed today in the D-Day museum at Utah Beach, is that we have seen our interests in the world as inextricably linked to the global progress of our ideals.

I believe the United States has a special responsibility to champion human rights in all places, for all peoples, and at all times. I've believed that all my life. I was raised to believe it, to see it in the examples of gallantry put before me, in the histories and novels and poems I was encouraged to read, in the conduct of the heroes I admired, those to whom I was related or knew personally, and those who were commended to me. I am a democratic internationalist, a proud one, and have been all my public life. I could have been nothing else given my role models and influences. I took from Hemingway's For Whom the Bell Tolls that defending the dignity of others is never a lost cause whether you succeed or not. And I thrill to the exhortation in the poem that inspired the novel, to be "part of the main," to be "involved in mankind."

It's who we are. The right to life and liberty, to be governed by consent and ruled by laws, to have equal justice and protection of property, these values are the core of our national identity. And it is fidelity to them—not ethnicity or religion, culture or class—that makes one an American. To accept the abolition or abridgement of those rights in other societies should be no less false to Americans than their abridgment in our own society. Human rights are not our invention. They don't represent standards from which particular cultures or religions can be exempted. They are universal. They exist above the state and beyond history. They cannot be rescinded by one government any more than they can be granted by another. That's our creed. The authors put it right at the beginning of the manifesto they wrote to declare our independence. "We hold these truths to be self-evident, that all men are created equal, that they are endowed by their Creator with certain unalienable Rights."

That creed gave us a purpose in the world greater than self-interest, a cause that encompasses our interests but is not defined by us alone. As Harry Truman once said of America, "God has created us and brought us to our present position of power and strength for some great purpose." Where rulers abused their people, we spoke up, we protested, we drew attention, we identified with the abused, and demanded better from the abuser. We used diplomatic and economic pressure to protect dissidents, to free political prisoners, to restrain autocrats, to get them to stop resisting change or at least modify their behavior enough to let change eventually undo them.

Human rights advocacy isn't naive idealism. It's the truest kind of realism. Statesmen who think that all that really matters in international relations is how governments treat each other are wrong. The character of states can't be separated from their conduct in the world. Governments that protect the rights of their citizens are more likely to play a peaceful, constructive role in world affairs. Governments that are unjust, that cheat, lie, steal, and use violence against their own people are more likely to do the same to other nations.

Take Russia, for example. It's not a coincidence that as the Kremlin has reverted to autocracy at home under its crooked ex-KGB colonel, Vladimir Putin, it has become ever more aggressive abroad, occupying territories that belong to its neighbors; helping one of the cruelest regimes on earth, Bashar al-Assad's, slaughter hundreds of thousands of Syrians; interfering in an American presidential election with the intention of helping elect the candidate they believed would pose the least resistance to their ambitions. Not even that last offense is entirely surprising considering the character of revanchist Russia, and its vain and corrupt leader, who decried the collapse of the Soviet Union and its evil empire. Why? Because of all the good the Soviets did in the world? They were the eastern front against Nazi Germany. That is their only welcome political or military contribution to history. The rest is a saga of corruption, brute force, and atrocious inhumanity followed by decay and collapse.

If we don't accept that the nature of a regime shapes its conduct, we risk profoundly misreading international politics. We expect better behavior from despots than we have reason to. We miss what can be the most transformational force for good in the world: the anger of oppressed people, and their hope, their imperishable hope for change. That anger and hope filled the streets of East Berlin twenty-nine years ago, tore down a wall separating half a continent from liberty, and made the United States and our allies a whole lot safer. A world where the human rights of more people in more places are secure is not only a more just world, it's a safer world. For reasons of basic self-interest we must continue to lead the long, patient effort to make the world freer and more just.

I consider myself a realist. I have certainly seen my share of the world as it really is and not how I wish it would be. What I've learned is that it is foolish to view realism and idealism as incompatible or to consider our power and wealth as encumbered by the demands of justice, morality, and conscience. In the real world, as lived and experienced by real people, the demand for human rights and dignity, the longing for liberty and justice and opportunity, the hatred of oppression and corruption and cruelty is reality. By denying this experience, we deny the aspirations of billions of people, and invite their enduring resentment.

The benefits of promoting our values can be a long time coming. The rights of others will never be our only priority. But they must always be a high priority. Our interests will often necessitate dealing with some pretty bad actors. But we shouldn't pay for the privilege by declining to criticize how they mistreat their people. We should demonstrate to the oppressed that as we negotiate with their oppressors we haven't forsaken them, we are still on their side. Ronald Reagan negotiated with the Soviets when he believed it was in our security interests to do so. And while he did so, he routinely reminded them they were on the wrong side of history. He told Mikhail Gorbachev what he should do with his wall. He used engagement with our adversary as an opportunity to, among other things, demand better treatment for the captive peoples of the evil empire. And when he tempered his public criticisms of Soviet behavior it was in response to real progress on their part, not in exchange for engagement itself.

My youngest children have only read about the Berlin Wall. Their world was never divided by it. Their lives weren't affected by its shadow. But for those of us born before or during the Cold War that blessing was the achievement of "a long, twilight struggle." I remember the enormous sacrifice it entailed—the many brave souls, some of them my friends, who gave their lives to secure it. I remember a span of half a century when, for all our differences, Americans maintained a bipartisan commitment to the freedom and security of our allies. And together we kept faith with those on the other side of the walls that divided the free and the oppressed. We were confident they wanted the same things we did—freedom, equal justice, the rule of law, a fair chance to prosper by their own industry and talents. We kept the faith, and we prevailed.

No one of my acquaintance ever believed in that faith more sincerely, more ardently than Henry "Scoop" Jackson, U.S. senator from the state of Washington, and, in his time, the Senate's great apostle of freedom. I knew him when I was the Navy's liaison to the Senate, and escorted him on some of his many travels abroad. He was a champion for the world's oppressed, and an enemy to those who gained power for themselves by disregarding the humanity of others. He was a classic Cold War liberal, anticommunist to the bone. He complicated the Richard Nixon and Henry Kissinger policy of détente with the Soviets by insisting it not come at the expense of America's commitment to human rights. Over their objections, he passed legislation that conditioned trade with the Soviets and other autocratic regimes on the relaxation of emigration policies. He was a hero to Soviet Jews wishing to immigrate to Israel. I once escorted a large Senate delegation on a trip to Israel. The delegation included many strong supporters of the Jewish state, but only one man among them was greeted with the ecstatic approval more typical of a pop star's welcome. As the delegation's bus passed through the gates of Tel Aviv airport, a crowd of nearly a thousand, mostly former refuseniks and their families, had gathered to shout their gratitude and admiration for Scoop Jackson. They mobbed us, slowing the bus's progress to a crawl. Scoop and his beloved wife, Helen, were genuinely moved by the outpouring of affection. So was I, recognizing it, as Scoop surely did, as an outpouring of affection for America and our ideals.

We don't always appreciate as we should the value others place on the public statements of American officials. It matters what we say and what we don't say. The U.S. remains the world's leading power, and when our leaders speak, governments and people take notice. Natan

Sharansky told me how word of Reagan's statements on their behalf reached him and his fellow dissidents in prison, and sustained them, knowing they were not forgotten by the world's greatest power and most idealistic nation. Reagan's famous speech to the British Parliament in 1982 that envisioned the West's approaching victory in the Cold War, and committed America to vigorous support for democratic movements the world over, inspired the men and women who persevere through threats and setbacks to claim for their nations the universal values that bind ours. And the products of his Westminster speech, the National Endowment for Democracy, and its affiliated organizations, including the International Republican Institute, have given support and advice to many of those movements.

Our public support for the oppressed and criticism of their oppressors can effect change. I speak from personal experience. After America and the world learned that the POWs in North Vietnam were being mistreated, Hanoi was stunned by the criticism they received even from antiwar voices in the U.S. and in the capitals of other countries that opposed America's intervention, and our treatment improved.

Often the very act of supporting human rights overseas compels us to make our own "shining city upon a hill" worthier of such a boast. There's a story about Vice President Richard Nixon visiting the West African country of Ghana in 1957 to mark its official independence from the British Empire. Moved by the jubilant celebration, Nixon is reported to have asked one ecstatic Ghanaian after another, "How does it feel to be free?" until one young man replied, "I wouldn't know, sir. I'm from Alabama." Our support during the Cold War for the human rights of the peoples of the Soviet Union and its satellites helped force us to face up to our own failings more honestly. Russians, Cubans, Vietnamese, and just about every Marxist-Leninist regime in the world responded to our criticism of them with reminders that we continued to deny full citizenship to African Americans. Exposing our hypocrisy to the world played a part in forcing change in America, helping convince leaders to adopt laws that oblige us to live up to our values. The Voting Rights Act of 1965 and the Detainee Treatment Act forty years later were to an extent a response to accusations that our proselytizing on behalf of the God-given dignity of all people was cynical.

Most important of all, America's support, rhetorical and material, for the advance of freedom and justice to all peoples everywhere is sometimes the only expression of international solidarity that is known to the world's worst oppressed, the jailed and tortured and murdered, the only glimpse of hope in their despair, the only evidence they are not forsaken.

I traveled with a Senate delegation to Burma in January 2012. It was my second trip there in four months. The long-suffering Burmese people were on the cusp of real progress. The military junta that had misruled, mistreated, murdered, and imprisoned them had given way in 2011 to an elected government of mostly ex-military officers, not fairly elected, to be sure, but a government that appeared to recognize the need for political reform. Any sign of an opening in Burma, renamed Myanmar by the junta, was encouraging considering the many atrocities committed by the regime, from child conscripts to ethnic cleansing. Regime officials had opened talks with the last fairly elected leader of the country, Aung San Suu Kyi, whom I had met on my first trip to Burma in the 1990s, and who was a personal hero to me. Those talks led to genuine political reforms and a promise of parliamentary elections in April 2012 that Suu Kyi's party, the National League for Democracy, would win. I had gone to Burma in September 2011, to encourage the progress that had begun, to urge the release of all political prisoners, and to meet for the first time in fifteen years the woman I so admired. I came back the following January with friends Joe Lieberman, New

Hampshire Senator Kelly Ayotte, and Senator Sheldon Whitehouse of Rhode Island, after hundreds of prisoners had been released. Secretary of State Hillary Clinton had come the month before, the most senior U.S. official to visit the country in more than half a century. We were there to reinforce that a better relationship with the U.S. was within prospect, including the lifting of economic sanctions we had imposed on Burma, were the April elections, as promised, free and fair. We reminded our hosts that the Obama administration and Congress would be guided in those decisions by Suu Kyi's views.

It was a brief visit and a crowded schedule, but I'll remember one of our meetings for as long as I live. Full diplomatic relations between our two countries had yet to be reestablished, so we didn't have an ambassador in Burma. A chargé d'affaires led our country team there, and the meeting was held at his residence. The men we had come to meet, all in their fifties, were leaders of the 88 Generation, an organization of Burmese democratic activists that takes its name from the student protests in 1988 that culminated in a general strike and ultimately in Suu Kyi's election in 1990. The men had been active in the protests, which had been suppressed with terrible bloodshed, and were arrested in the ensuing crackdown. They formed the 88 Generation in 2005 and played a critical role in organizing massive protests against the regime in 2007, when hundreds of thousands of Burmese led by Buddhist monks took to the streets of Rangoon. The Saffron Revolution was the largest political demonstration since the 1988 uprising.

Min Ko Naing was sentenced to twenty years' imprisonment in 1988. Tortured, his health wrecked, and his case championed by Amnesty International and other human rights organizations, he was released after fifteen years in 2004. He was rearrested in September and imprisoned for several months. No charges were filed and no reason given for his release, shortly after which he helped found Generation 88. He was arrested again in August 2007 for his role in the Saffron

Revolution and sentenced with other 88 Generation leaders to sixty-five years in a remote prison where he was held in solitary confinement.

Ko Ko Gyi had been arrested and held briefly in 1989, then re-arrested in 1991. He was released in 2005, arrested in the same crackdown that claimed Min Ko Naing. Like Min, he was released without explanation in January 2007. With Min, he was arrested again during the Saffron Revolution, and sentenced to sixty-five years in the same remote prison.

Htay Kywe was arrested in 1991 and released in 2004, rounded up with Min and Ko in September 2005. Although he managed to evade capture a couple months longer than Min and Ko, he was again arrested in 2007, tried, and sentenced to sixty-five years' hard labor in another remote prison.

All three men had been released from prison in a general amnesty ten days before our meeting. Each had spent cumulatively more than twenty years in prison. All had been tortured, held in solitary confinement for long periods, and had suffered from poor conditions and malnourishment. Their cases had been publicized by Amnesty International, Human Rights Watch, and various other human rights organizations, as well as by the State Department and American politicians from both parties. I had been vocal about Burma since my first visit, had sponsored legislation sanctioning the regime, and had regularly made statements, signed letters, and given interviews on behalf of Suu Kyi and the 88 Generation prisoners, including the suffering souls I met that day. They had heard and seen all of it, all the advocacy in the West for their cause and for them personally. It had helped sustain them in dark hours. These simple, easily made gestures of solidarity had meant everything to them. They were emotional when we were introduced. One wept when I started to speak. My disembodied voice had become familiar to him from Voice of America and Radio Free Asia broadcasts. They embraced me over and over again and thanked me profusely as if I had saved their lives when all I had done was mention their names every now and again. It was one of the most touching encounters of my life. There is nothing so rewarding as contributing, even if only in the most modest way, to the defense of another human being's dignity, all the more so when the person is otherwise a stranger to you.

God bless the people who devote themselves to the liberation of the oppressed, to the spread of democracy and the rule of law in countries that are not their own, particularly those who do so at the risk of their own lives. Their example instructs us to speak up for our values and for people denied them wherever they are. Sometimes that's harder to do than on other occasions. Sometimes we have security interests at stake that loom larger on our list of priorities than the rights denied citizens in the country concerned, in Saudi Arabia, for example, with whom we have enemies in common. Sometimes the criticism falls on friends with whom we have more than just common enemies, but common values and shared causes.

I have admired few public figures more than I admire Aung San Suu Kyi. I have spoken and written of my admiration for her many times. And yet, if we are truly committed to the progress of democracy and justice in Burma, she must be held to higher standards than we expected from the regime that held her under house arrest for so many years. The atrocities perpetrated against Rohingya Muslims in the northern Burmese province of Rakhine by the Burmese military and, allegedly, by Buddhist monks in the world's latest episode of ethnic cleansing should be condemned by every decent person with knowledge of them. That surely includes the recognized leader of Burma's democrats. Many thousands have been killed, a half million have fled the country and are homeless, tales of their suffering are rife with accounts of rape and the most extreme physical abuse and cruelty. Yet Aung San Suu Kyi, who gave up her freedom, her family, her comfortable life in the West to help free her native country from tyranny, has been mostly silent about the inhumane treatment of the Rohingya. Political change in Burma is delicate and reversible. She has to be careful not to alienate the military, which allows her and her fellow democrats to govern and to move the country slowly toward a time when political reforms are firmly rooted. But that caution must not demand that a voice as important as hers be stilled when confronted with human rights abuses on a grand scale. Nor can ours be quiet out of respect for her. The rights of the Rohingya are as sacred as the rights of the 88 Generation. They, too, deserve to hear voices raised in their defense in the leading democracies of the world. They, too, deserve our respect for their dignity and our condemnation of those who oppress them. It's as wrong to refuse them our support as it would have been to refuse it to Suu Kyi, to the 88 Generation activists, to the Buddhist monks in the Saffron Revolution.

Yes, we often have important interests involved in relations with dictatorial regimes that those regimes will try to leverage to get us to turn a blind eye to corruption and human rights abuses. We can't let them. We have to trust that whatever interest the regime has in a relationship with us is more than a desire to buy our silence. Since 2001, we had relied on an air base in southeastern Uzbekistan, Karshi-Khanabad, or K2, to fly reconnaissance and air logistic missions, and to stage Special Forces operations. It was an important asset in our fight against the Taliban and al-Qaeda. Islam Karimov was elected the first president of Uzbekistan in 1991 after the dissolution of the Soviet Union. Once elected, he showed little interest in leaving to Uzbeks the decision of whether he continued in office. He was a former Party apparatchik and a thug. He arrested opponents and put down protests with force. In 2005, his security forces fired into a crowd of protesters in the city of Andijan, killing more than a thousand. Many of the victims were buried in secret mass graves, but word about the atrocity spread to the West.

As it happened I was planning a trip to the region around the same time with Joe Lieberman, Lindsey Graham, and New Hampshire senator John Sununu. We were going to visit Uzbekistan's neighbor, Kyrgyzstan, which had just had a color revolution of its own, the Tulip Revolution, and a new government had taken office. We were going to overfly Uzbekistan to get there. Having learned of the Andijan massacre, we decided to apply for visas and ask for a meeting with Uzbek officials to impress on them that Congress plays a role in making foreign policy, and we could use our influence to deny Uzbekistan some of the benefits of a relationship with the U.S. We were granted the visas but refused meetings with the government. Fine, we thought. We would still fly in, hold a press conference to protest the regime's abuses, demand an international investigation of the massacre, and fly right back out before the government could react.

I didn't know much more about Uzbekistan. I had a vague romantic notion of one of its cities, Samarkand, which I had always wanted to visit. It was on the Silk Road and featured in the title of a poem I had memorized as a child, "The Golden Road to Samarkand" by James Elroy Flecker.

> For lust of knowing what should not be known,
> We take the golden road to Samarkand.

But there would be no Samarkand visit on this trip. Nor ever, I regret to say. Just a ride from the airport in Tashkent, the capital, through its deserted, dreary streets in the shadow of Soviet-style cement apartment slabs to the U.S embassy, which, if memory serves, was a converted discotheque with office cubicles and a dim lighting system. There we met with a few representatives of the opposition, who seemed beleaguered but brave. Our ambassador at the time, Jon Purnell, was a talented professional, knowledgeable, self-assured, straightforward.

He knew we understood the importance of retaining access to K2, but he knew, too, that we have a moral obligation to condemn atrocities and hold the guilty parties accountable. Turning a blind eye encourages more Andijans.

We held our press conference, each of us condemning the regime in lacerating language, calling for an independent investigation and adjudication, and warning that our relationship, airfield or no airfield, couldn't continue if the regime were to commit crimes against humanity. The ambassador, who betrayed little visible discomfort at our stridency, although he wouldn't have been the intelligent diplomat he was had he not cringed a little, dutifully seconded our sentiments nevertheless. Then we loaded into embassy cars and returned to the airport, as relieved to get out of the place as I imagine Ambassador Purnell was to see us go. We hadn't been in the country much more than two hours.

Unfortunately, moments after our military aircraft had taken off, we'd had a bird strike, blood was all over one of the engines. We had to return to the airport. Nineteen fifties–era fire trucks raced out on the tarmac to meet us, a woman carrying an old black medical bag, a doctor I assumed, ascended the mobile staircase to treat the wounded. Fortunately, we didn't have any. The pilots wanted maintenance engineers to check that no serious damage had been done to the engine, and assuming there wasn't any, we would be shortly under way again. But an official from the Uzbek aviation authority informed us that we would have to file a new flight plan with her office, which was closed for the day. "What do you mean?" we asked. "You cannot leave today," came the answer. We assumed we were being subjected to an old Soviet form of bureaucratic abuse for foreign visitors who insulted the authorities. What other inconveniences might we suffer while spending an unscheduled night in Tashkent? The pilots pled our case to no avail. Purnell, who had left the airport, was summoned back. He was all business. He told us to remain on the plane while he negotiated our release. He started firing questions at the official. *Who do we have to file a flight plan with? Are they really closed? Who would we file with in an emergency?* For two hours, he negotiated on our behalf until his wearied interlocutor relented and let us go. We weren't the only people to condemn the Karimov regime. Most of the West did, including the United States government, and, as feared, Karimov reacted to the international denunciations by ordering the U.S. to vacate Karshi-Khanabad. But if the price for using the base was to ignore an atrocity of the magnitude of Andijan, which would signal to tyrants elsewhere that American values were transactional, then we were better off making other arrangements.

Scoop Jackson's opposition to Soviet tyranny and aggression, and his support for the world's oppressed, made him as much of an irritant to Jimmy Carter's administration as he had been to the governments of Richard Nixon and Gerald Ford. Scoop had his convictions, he believed in America's mission, and when it came to acting on his beliefs, he didn't particularly give a damn which party was in power. America's ideals came before party loyalty for him.

I've had disagreements with every presidential administration in office during the years I've served in Congress, even on occasion with the policies of President Reagan, a President I revered. I voted to override his veto of sanctions against South Africa's apartheid government, and I opposed his deployment of Marines to Beirut. I had had more numerous and stronger objections with the policies of other administrations, but it's fair to say that I've disagreed—sometimes too heatedly, and sometimes unfairly—with all of them. That's partly because of my nature. I can be as happy in opposition to government as I am in cooperating with it, sometimes happier. I like to fight, and I like people who like to fight, even if they're fighting with me, especially when the cause is worth fighting about.

There was much I admired about George W. Bush's focus on democratic internationalism and his defense of oppressed peoples. But I argued strenuously against his government's treatment of captured enemies because it violated the ideals he wanted to advance in the world. I didn't think the Obama administration paid sufficient attention to human rights concerns, and its support for democratic movements in closed societies was too subordinate to other priorities.

I've been accused of being too quick to propose that the U.S. intervene militarily in other countries' civil strife in support of embattled democratic movements. I have suggested on a few occasions limited U.S. military support for freedom fighters in civil wars that threaten vital U.S. security interests or where the regime has committed or is about to commit monstrous atrocities. I support using U.S. airpower to create safe zones in Syria, and I advocated using NATO airpower to prevent Muammar Qaddafi from slaughtering tens of thousands of Libyan rebels. More often, I've proposed providing material support, including, where appropriate, weapons to those fighting to liberate their country from violent oppression or foreign domination. Most often, all I've called for is that the government of the world's leading democracy in its relations with oppressive regimes speak loudly, persistently, and unambiguously in support of the brave souls who protest them.

Iran's Green Movement began in reaction to the fraudulent reelection of Mahmoud Ahmadinejad over the "reformer" Mir Hossein Mousavi in June 2009. Hundreds of thousands, if not millions, of Iranians, impatient for social change and international acceptance, poured into the streets of Tehran. The United States should have been on their side from the beginning, giving them public support, lending credence to their protest that the election had been stolen, and encouraging our allies to do the same. We might have offered the kinds of clandestine communications, financial, and other nonlethal support that we have provided other democratic movements. But barring riskier policies like that, we should have at least been full-throated in our support of the protests. Yet President Obama seemed reluctant from the outset to offer more than perfunctory rhetorical support for the protesters, never once to my recollection endorsing their principal demand, a fair election. He wanted to cultivate a better relationship with the Iranian regime than had existed since the Islamic Revolution of 1979, to, I assume, bring it into the world community with a goal of moderating its behavior and securing an agreement to suspend its nuclear weapons program. Perhaps the administration didn't believe the protests could succeed and didn't want to jeopardize other interests by vigorously defending them. But the idea that you could make any real progress toward integrating Iran into the international system and negotiating a nuclear deal while the virulent anti-American, Holocaust-denying Ahmadinejad was in office seems to me considerably more naive than to believe the Green Movement protesters could have forced real change in Iran. I didn't expect the President to abandon his other priorities in Iran or even to threaten the regime. I did want him to protest vociferously its antidemocratic nature and its inhumanity and call on the world community to do likewise. I wanted him to identify unmistakably with the protesters in the streets, the vast majority of them young people and the future of their country.

The Green Movement was violently suppressed. Ayatollah Khamenei endorsed the bogus election results. Security forces and Ahmadinejad thugs cracked down brutally. Scores were killed, hundreds injured, and thousands arrested, including many prominent reformers. On June 20, a sniper shot and killed Neda Agha-Soltan, a twenty-six-year-old musician, as she stood on the edge of a peaceful protest. A cell phone video captured her bleeding to death on the pavement. It went instantly viral, appalling many Americans and in some quarters shaming their conscience. It shamed mine. I want America to always identify with Neda and those like her, whom the world hasn't made cynical yet, who struggle against danger and daunting odds to claim the rights we fought a revolution to secure. I want to be in the streets with them, if only figuratively, raising our voices in support, and using our influence to encourage other governments to do the same. I want State Department and National Security Council officials to devise ways we can help them succeed, not just figure out how to take a stand without risking anything. They must be our priority, not our only priority, but a greater priority than placating the regime that persecutes them. In fairness, as the violence against the mostly peaceful protests mounted that summer, Obama's calls for restraint by the regime became somewhat more forceful. But it was late in coming, and never as forceful as it should have been from a President with his eloquence. Secret talks that led to negotiations for a nuclear deal were under way, and I'm sure he worried they would be jeopardized by greater pressure from us on behalf of the protesters. I worry that Iranians will remember our minimal engagement in their struggle, our tepid support, and when their day of liberation comes, our negligence will not be forgotten.

I had many disagreements with President Obama's policies that I argued publicly and sometimes vociferously. As I described in earlier chapters, I supported his decision to use NATO airpower in Libya, but was appalled when he quickly disengaged before Libya stabilized, rationalizing his irresolution as "leading from behind." I was angered by his refusal to provide Ukraine with the weapons it needs to defend itself from Russia's organized attacks on its sovereignty. And I thought his failure to make good on his threat of military action to punish the Assad regime's use of chemical weapons was a shockingly bad mistake, the biggest of his presidency, a strategic blunder that injured the security of our interests and the progress of our values throughout the Middle East and elsewhere. I never doubted the sincerity of President Obama's conviction that the ultimate goal of his administration's foreign policy was a safer, freer, and more just world. But he refused to make the hard calls that goal entails. I don't know if his irresolution stemmed from indecisiveness or a reluctance to do anything that risked failure. But whatever it was, it confounded allies, encouraged enemies, and left a lot of brave people struggling to live in freedom without meaningful support from the leader of the free world. That said, it's fair to also observe, that for all our disagreements I never doubted President Obama shared the seventy-five-year bipartisan consensus that American leadership of the free world was a moral obligation and a practical necessity. I think he tried to defer some of the responsibilities of that leadership, which weakened it. But I never believed he thought we should abandon it.

I'm not sure what to make of President Trump's convictions. At times as a candidate and as President, he has appeared to be more than merely a realpolitik adherent. He seemed to mock the idea that America has any business at all promoting its values abroad. I don't know if that is sincerely his view or if he believes that the global progress of democracy and the rule of law should be only a distant, notional goal of American statecraft. He threatened to deliberately kill the spouses and children of terrorists, implying that an atrocity of that magnitude would show the world America's toughness. His lack of empathy for refugees, innocent, persecuted, desperate men, women, and children, is disturbing. The way he speaks about them is appalling, as if welfare or terrorism were the only purposes they could have in coming to our country. His reaction to unflattering news stories, calling them "fake news," whether they're credible or not, is copied by autocrats who want to discredit and control a free press. He has declined to distinguish the actions of our government from the crimes of despotic ones. He seems uninterested in the moral character of world leaders and their regimes. The appearance of toughness or a reality show facsimile of toughness seems to matter more than any of our values. Flattery secures his friendship, criticism his enmity. He has showered with praise some of the world's worst tyrants. He said Putin was doing "a great job rebuilding Russia," failing to note that the "rebuilding" has come at the expense of liberty and justice in Russia, and, in many instances, at the cost of Russian lives. He has seemed just as smitten with Xi Jinping, despite the campaign of repression Xi waged as he consolidated his vast power.

He hardly ever talks about human rights as an object of his policies. He went on a two-week, five-country trip to Asia, and never raised the subject. Not in Vietnam, where political dissidence is a crime. Not in the Philippines, where the blustering Rodrigo Duterte holds murderous notions about criminal justice. President Trump's noticeably keen regard for Duterte feels more like an expression of genuine admiration than a realist's recognition that the Philippines is a valuable partner in the region. I'm a longtime advocate for better relations between the U.S. and Vietnam. I believe we share common interests, and I have visited the country many times, most recently last summer. I have never once gone to Hanoi and not raised human rights issues with my hosts. They would be surprised if I didn't or if any American on an official visit didn't appeal for greater freedom and justice in that country. That's what visiting American officials do. The world expects us to be concerned with the condition of humanity. We should be proud of that reputation. I'm not sure the President understands that.

Secretary of State Rex Tillerson compounded that perception when he warned State Department employees not to condition relations with nations "too heavily" on their adoption of values "we've come to after a long history of our own." That attitude feeds the notion that at best this administration believes human rights protests ought to be reserved for America's adversaries and not our friends or countries where we have other interests. Such an approach substantiates our adversaries' complaint that our support for human rights is cynical, that we use it only as a weapon against our enemies. We meddle in their domestic affairs and turn a blind eye to bad actors whose favor we need. That discredits our moral authority wherever we invoke it.

There have been glimmers of hope that the President recognizes our values have a place in the conduct of foreign policy or that his senior national security team has managed to prevent the idea from being banished altogether by the weirder members of this administration. I'm thankful that some of the latter were eventually shown the door, self-proclaimed nationalist radicals Steve Bannon and Sebastian Gorka among them. Bigger misfits haven't been seen inside a White House since William Taft got stuck in his bathtub.

Last December, the administration sanctioned five more Russians under the Magnitsky Act, and the President signed an executive order citing "serious human rights abuse and corruption around the world" that imposed on thirteen named individuals sanctions authorized by the provisions of the Global Magnitsky Act, which Ben Cardin and I also authored. The list of targeted people could have been longer, and some deserving individuals were spared. But the executive order actually expanded the reach of our bill and represents real progress toward the norm of American diplomacy, and I heartily welcome it.

The administration's recently released National Security Strategy document simultaneously offered hope and disappointment to human rights advocates. In one passage it avers, "We are not going to impose our values on others." In another, it promises, "We will continue to champion American values and offer encouragement to those struggling for human dignity in their societies."

As we write this, Iranians have taken to the streets again, and not just in Tehran, where the affluent and well-educated want to live in a more modern society. The protests began outside the capital and have spread to many cities, including the religious city of Qom. In 2009, the protests were focused on disputed election results. These protests are broader and, from the point of view of the regime, more subversive. Their criticism includes Iran's military adventurism in the region and the power of the mullahs. Some protesters are reported to have shouted "Death to Hezbollah," Iran's proxy in the Arab world. Others have demanded that Iran no longer continue as an "Islamic Republic." Another crackdown is sure to follow. As in 2009, the worst of it won't be public, but away from the cameras. To his credit, President Trump quickly identified with the protesters, and warned the regime that the world is watching. He has followed up with other statements. Will he persist? I don't know. He has been more outspoken thus far than our European allies, and that's something administration diplomacy should address. We're the leader of the free world, and we should work to rally our allies to the side of justice in Iran. Acting in unison with other nations will refute the regime's criticism that the Great Satan is behind the protests. The administration should negotiate an agreement on multilateral economic and diplomatic sanctions against the regime if the protests are violently suppressed and protesters killed or imprisoned. They should put on notice foreign companies that do business in Iran and the U.S. that they will be targeted if they are in any way, even indirectly, supplying materials or services to the security apparatus of the regime.

I also don't know if the President's engagement, much earlier and outspoken than his predecessor's, is mostly due to the fact that Iran is an adversary. I hope it's because he sees the connection there between America's interests and values, and that by promoting the latter he defends the former. Encouragingly, he unexpectedly criticized Saudi Arabia's blockade of Yemen around the same time, taking issue with an ally he was not previously willing to rebuke. I hope both actions indicate an evolution in his administration's view toward the understanding that our values are more than talking points with which to shame our enemies.

It is hard to know what to expect from President Trump, what's a pose, what's genuine. As in other areas, the character of the President will likely be reflected in the content and conduct of foreign policy. But the extent to which that is the case will depend on the restraining effect of his more experienced advisors' counsel, and, I genuinely hope, his growing recognition that "leader of the free world" is more than an honorific. It is a moral obligation more important than the person who possesses it.

There have been times in the past and there will be times in the future when America's conduct at home and in the world will fall short of our own high standards. That doesn't mean that our values are imperfect, only that we are. In those instances, our true friends will encourage us to change course. But we should never believe that our fallibility disqualifies us from supporting the rights of others. That isn't humility. It's an abdication of moral responsibility. What matters most is that we remain confident in our principles, mindful that they are not ours alone, and that we recognize that to be on the right side of history is to support people denied their basic rights.

Of course, we should recognize that some nations are more skeptical of American influence. And when dissidents there ask for our silence, we should respect their wishes. But when courageous people call on us by name, when they plea for our solidarity in peaceful demonstrations against their government, when they write their protest banners in English, that is a good indication that we can and should do more to support their cause.

When people peacefully appeal for their rights, we should encourage them. When they are thrown in prison, we should work for their release. When they face intimidation and violence, we should condemn it. This applies not only to our enemies, but to our friends whether they are long-standing partners like Saudi Arabia and Egypt or emerging partners like Vietnam. They won't enjoy these conversations. But if we really value these relationships, we will make the case to them that the only guarantee of their nations' long-term stability is the inclusion of all its peoples in the rights and protections their leaders possess and in the promise of a better future.

We will only get so far by urging abusive regimes, whether in private or public, to treat their people better. We also need to support those people directly wherever and however we can, to help them promote their aspirations and prepare for the day that they will govern themselves. What this help entails varies from country to country, but its aim is to strengthen civil society to balance the power of the state. It often includes providing access to factual information by broadcasting it ourselves or helping closed societies get it on their own. It can include support for political parties, the middle class, labor unions, student organizations, religious groups, and other associations. It can be strengthening the institutions of a free society—an independent media, legislatures, courts of justice, uncorrupt bureaucracies, election commissions and monitors. What form these institutions take is not up to us. America's institutions of governance are the result of 230 years of experimentation, trial and error, and our own unique experience. Other societies will develop in their own ways, consistent with their own cultures and traditions.

Critics, whether they call themselves realists or noninterventionists or just indifferent, maintain that active support for the political development of closed societies constitutes more than a strategy for changing the behavior of abusive regimes. It's a ploy to change the regimes themselves. Correct. And why shouldn't it be? I'm not suggesting armed revolution, but regime change achieved by giving people the tools and skills they need to work peacefully for it and build a better society. Why wouldn't we want autocracies replaced by democracies everywhere in the world? Our goal isn't to coexist eternally with regimes that are hostile to our most basic principles of justice. We deal with states like that because we have to, not because we wish them well.

And while we deal with them, we shouldn't forget that our ultimate goal is to see the victims of oppression supplant their oppressors.

It is one thing to recognize obstacles to change, and to understand the world as it is with all its corruption and cruelty. But it is a moral failure to believe tyranny and injustice are the inevitable tragedies of man's fallen nature, that there are some places in the world that will not change or aren't worth the effort to make better. They can be changed. They have been. And not only by force of arms as with Germany or Japan, but peacefully with international pressure and support. Every independent democratic country in the world once had a government less just and accountable, whether it was monarchical, dictatorial, or imperial. Progress toward a freer, more just world is the history of the world. Change doesn't always proceed as quickly as we want it to, but it comes. We were once the world's only democratic republic and now we're one of more than a hundred. The ranks of free nations have swelled thanks in large part to the example, leadership, and support of the United States. And thanks to all those people and organizations in every corner of the world, the philosophers, the politicians, the activists, and the ordinary decent men and women who throughout history have not let injustice stand without trying to right it. Thanks to idealistic realists in the National Endowment for Democracy, the International Republican Institute, the National Democratic Institute, Human Rights Watch, Amnesty International, Human Rights First, Freedom House, the International Rescue Committee, the McCain Institute, and countless other advocates. I have disagreed with their positions from time to time, but I'm proud to have worked with them for causes that are just and achievable. And thank you to those in the latest generation and in future generations who will be "involved in mankind," and make another, better world.

I'm grateful to have played a part in that progress. The gratification I've gotten from defending the rights of subjugated peoples has outlasted the satisfaction gained from personal successes and it has outlasted the sting of life's disappointments. The image I have of the Maidan in Kiev, of the massive crowd giving me their attention as I struggled to say a few words of encouragement, far surpasses in effect all the recognition given me because I managed to stay in the public spotlight as long as I have. I am grateful to the freedom fighters, the justice seekers, the change agents, and civil society builders the world over for the example they set for me, for their reminder that we are not inevitably the victims of our fallen nature. We are all sinners, far from perfection. But we can compensate a little for our flaws and the injuries we've caused when we fight for the dignity of our fellow man. We know our lives were not entirely squandered on ourselves. When you reach my age and condition that knowledge is a great relief, a little hope for God's mercy.

Even the smallest gestures in support of the hardest causes, the ones that seem futile, mean something to those struggling in them, and they are the ones that end up meaning the most to you. They're so appreciative of your support no matter how modest it is. But it's not their gratitude that moves you the most. It's their faith. They refuse to accept defeat, to face facts. They refuse to lose hope, no matter how long they're jailed, no matter how many of their friends are killed. They don't despair, they persist. It's an honor to stand with them, although most of the time all I can offer is my voice raised on their behalf or an open door to my office, an appeal to the administration, an introduction to other members of Congress.

I have done what little I can to stand in solidarity with forces of change in countries aligned with us and opposed to us, in Russia, in Ukraine, in Georgia and Moldova, in China, in Serbia, Kosovo, Montenegro, in Egypt, Libya, Tunisia, Syria, Saudi Arabia, and Turkey, in Iran, Uzbekistan, Kazakhstan, in Cuba, Nicaragua, in Zimbabwe and South Africa, and wherever else people fighting for their human rights wanted our help. I've protested killings, torture, and imprisonments. I worked to sanction oppressive regimes. I've encouraged international pressure on the worst offenders. I've helped secure support for people building the framework of an open society. I've monitored elections, consoled the families of political prisoners, worried about the risk-takers and mourned their deaths. I've gotten more from them than they've gotten from me. I've gotten their hope, their faith, and their friendship.

For the last twenty years, I've tried to help the opposition in Belarus overcome the ruthless regime of Alexander Lukashenko that has misruled that country since 1994. I've met with Belarusians from all backgrounds who are fighting to change their country, students, professors, lawyers, former government officials, retired military, businesspeople, technocrats, and actors. Joe Lieberman and I applied for visas to go to Belarus in 2004. The government refused to grant them, and we have been unwelcome there since. Opposition representatives have had to leave the country to meet with members of Congress enlisted in their cause. We have met in Vilnius, Lithuania, and in Riga, Latvia. We've met in Brussels and Washington. In solidarity with them, I denounced Lukashenko's fraudulent election in 2001 only to watch him steal another one in 2005, and another in 2010, and another in 2015. I called for the release from prison of Lukashenko's opponent in the 2001 election, Mikhail Marynich, only to see him remain behind bars for another five years after suffering a stroke. I've called for the release of other political prisoners with no greater success. I've watched Lukashenko work as closely with Putin's Russia as if Belarus were still a vassal state, then try to lead Belarus toward greater independence, and then always fall back into subservience to the Kremlin.

I've made countless statements, attended numerous conferences, helped pass legislation imposing sanctions on the regime, called on other nations to impose sanctions, and when they did, called for more. I made all manner of pleas and threats and promises, all focused on supporting the rights of the Belarus people to govern themselves. And to what effect? It doesn't appear to have had any. Lukashenko is still there. He's still jailing his opponents and worse. He's still obedient to Putin. In February and March 2017, tens of thousands of people took to the streets of Minsk and a dozen other cities. The regime responded with mass arrests. International calls for the release of protesters were ignored. In 2015, the *Guardian* published an analysis of the prospects for change in Belarus in the wake of the successful Maidan protests in Ukraine. It found Lukashenko's power secure and the opposition to be powerless, and declared "a revolution is impossible in Belarus." But, as Winston Churchill observed, "Success consists of going from failure to failure without loss of enthusiasm." Every time I meet with members of the Belarus opposition, they're as determined and sure of themselves, and as grateful for international support, as were the first dissidents I met all those years ago. Often, they are the same people I met with years ago. They believe, they fight, and they persist. They are a rebuke to the cynics, a tonic for the weary fatalism that can overcome even the happiest warrior.

Like them, I believe with all my heart that one day they or their children will prevail. And it won't be because they reached the end of history in Belarus, and it bent inevitably toward justice. It will happen as it's happened elsewhere, because brave men and women inside the country and loyal friends outside made painstaking and enduring efforts to make it happen. "In history," Nobel Laureate and freedom fighter Liu Xiaobo said, "nothing is fated."

Liu Xiaobo died in the summer of 2017 from multiple organ failure caused by liver cancer while under armed guard in a provincial capital in northeast China. His pleas and the appeals of his wife and his many supporters that he be allowed to receive treatment in the West were ignored, as were all previous appeals for his release from prison. He was a scholar and poet and one of the world's most eloquent proponents of Gandhian nonviolence in resistance to tyranny. He had been teaching at Columbia University when the student protests in Tiananmen Square began in 1989. He rushed home and joined them. He began a hunger strike on June 2. When the army moved in on the night of June 3 to massacre protesters and take the square, Liu urged the students to remain nonviolent, even wresting a rifle from the hands of one activist, and negotiated with the army to allow several thousand to leave the square peacefully. He was arrested two days later, fired from his university position, and his books banned. He was incarcerated for most of the next two years, and released after his conviction for counterrevolutionary incitement. Forbidden to write, he published his next book in Taiwan. He traveled back to the U.S. in 1993, and rejected advice from friends that he seek asylum here. He was arrested in 1995 and held under house arrest for nine months for starting a petition calling for political reforms. He was arrested again in October 1996 for calling for Taiwan's peaceful reunification with China, and sentenced to three years in a reeducation camp. For the next nine years, he was constantly surveilled by the police and harassed. His phone and Internet connection were cut after he wrote an essay in 2004 criticizing the regime.

Charter 08, which Liu helped write, was released on December 10, 2008. A political manifesto modeled on Charter 77 written by Václav Havel and other Czech dissidents, Charter 08 demanded democratic elections, an end to one-party rule, and the privatization of state-controlled industries. Liu was arrested two days before the Charter's release. The three hundred original signers of the document were interrogated to gather evidence against him. He was held in solitary confinement and denied access to a lawyer until he was formally charged with "inciting subversion" in June 2009. He was tried and convicted the following December and sentenced to eleven years in prison. His wife wasn't allowed to attend his trial. American embassy officials and officials from other Western embassies in Beijing requested permission to observe his trial and were denied. They stood outside the courthouse in solidarity. The court denied Liu's request to read testimony he had prepared for his trial, another appeal on behalf of human dignity that began "I have no enemies." The United States and the governments of many other nations condemned his conviction and petitioned Beijing for his release.

The next year, the Nobel Committee awarded Liu the 2010 Peace Prize. When he learned of the honor, he dedicated it to the "Tiananmen martyrs." He was, of course, forbidden to receive it in person. His wife, Liu Xia, was placed under house arrest and not allowed to travel to Oslo, either. An empty chair represented him at the ceremony, where the statement he had written for his trial was read.

He was among the most prominent political prisoners in the world. Hundreds of influential and powerful people spoke up for him and appealed for his release, presidents, prime ministers, monarchs, statesmen, celebrated writers and artists, representatives from the legislatures of many countries, including me. When I learned he had died, I said he would want it remembered that his imprisonment and lonely death were "only the latest example of China's assaults on human rights, democracy and freedom." He had been "relentless," I remembered, "in pursuit of a democratic China."

What had his relentlessness achieved? What had all the international attention focused on him done, all the public pressure applied to Beijing to win his release from prison, and when he was dying to get him out of the country? It hadn't succeeded. Nothing he did in his life can be said to have substantially moved China a step closer to the freedom he bravely and persistently urged for his compatriots. Nothing the world did can be said to have spared his suffering. Did any of it change anything? When Liu died, President Trump was in Paris offering what "great respect" he has for Xi Jinping. "A great leader . . . [who] loves China. Who wants to do what is right for China."

Maybe all we can say of his relentless struggle is that it was the right thing to do. He lived a righteous life. And a righteous life is its own reward. But I think we can say more. His struggle will inspire others to carry it forward. His suffering was for a purpose greater than himself, and that purpose won't be abandoned. Others will suffer for it. Others will die for it. But it will succeed in time. It might be many years, many decades, before the human rights of the Chinese people are secure in their own country. But it will happen. It will happen because the rationalization that Asia isn't the West, and Confucianism isn't compatible with individual liberty, is a lie. It is natural for human beings to want to live without fear of oppression. It is natural to want to make choices for yourself, all your choices. It's natural to the human mind to use our needs, wishes, desires, the ideas that interest us to direct our lives, to inform our choices about where to live, what to do for work, whom to love, how many children to have. If the state can control some of those decisions they can control all decisions, even who lives and dies. It's unnatural to the human heart, every human heart, to surrender its agency. Every generation of Chinese produces people who refuse to accept the state's authority over their conscience. They will read Liu Xiaobo, admire his courage, honor his sacrifice, learn from him, and press forward until some Chinese generation succeeds.

Those in the West who rallied to his defense were reminded by the regime's recalcitrance, by its refusal to be moved by expressions of outrage or appeals to human decency, that China is more than just a massive market and investment opportunity, more than the world's most populous nation of consumers, more than an economic, military, and political rival. China represents the alternative to Western civilization, an unjust and cruel alternative. But for all the vibrancy of its economy, all its commercial sophistication and enterprising people, China's rulers lack the vision to see around the corner of history because they lack faith in the human heart, and trust only power and fear to achieve their ends. We must persist, too. We have more than commercial interests at stake in our relationship with China, and even those are ultimately poorly served by letting China abuse its citizens without protest or sanction. We must appeal and insist and condition relations on China's progress toward a freer, more just society. The freer they are, the less of a threat they become.

Above all else, we must stand in solidarity with the imprisoned, the silenced, the tortured, and the murdered because we are a country with a conscience. It is a mistake to view foreign policy, as the Chinese would like us to view it, as simply transactional. It's a mistake and a dangerous idea. Depriving the oppressed of a beacon of hope could lose us the world we have built and thrived in. It could cost our reputation in history as the nation distinct from all others in our achievements, our identity, and our enduring influence on mankind. Our values are central to all three. Were they not, we would be one great power among the others of history. We would have acquired wealth and power for a time, before receding into the disputed past. But we are a more exceptional country than that. We saw the world as it was and we made it better.

CHAPTER TEN

REGULAR ORDER

SOMETHING WAS OFF. I DIDN'T KNOW EXACTLY WHAT. Fatigue mainly. I felt unusually tired. Of course, I'm in my eighties, and men my age are supposed to be tired. But my motor has always run at more rpms than the average geezer. I'm restless and curious and usually looking forward to something so that I don't tire easily. When I am a little beat, it's nothing I can't fix by taking a weekend off. I thank my 106-year-old mother. Her main attributes are enthusiasm, wanderlust, and good genes. Her vivaciousness is a force of nature. Even now, after a stroke has slowed her down, when her brisk pace is a memory and speaking can be a chore, and her twin sister's passing robbed her of her life's longest companion, there's still a spark in her, a brightness in her eyes that would light up the world if she could resume her peripatetic life. I've inherited modest measures of her qualities, sufficient to give me the energy for a busy life and the enthusiasm for it. I'm the son and grandson of admirals. That's the first line of my biography. But I am my mother's son. I always have been. Thank you, mother, thank you.

I attributed my weariness to the trip I had recently returned from, a five-day run to Afghanistan, Pakistan, and a brief stop in the UAE. I have made so many quick trips to the region like this one without jet lag bothering me very much. I didn't know why this one had made me so tired. It had been an interesting time. The highlight, as it is every year, was the promotion and reenlistment ceremony in Kabul on the Fourth of July, presided over by our delegation and the commanding officer of our forces in Afghanistan, General John Nicholson. I've spent the Fourth in Afghanistan or Iraq every year since 2003, and every visit I get choked up at a reenlistment ceremony. Hundreds of warriors, some having served multiple combat tours, celebrate our country's independence by voluntarily surrendering theirs and signing up for more hazard and stress. I look forward to the inspiration every year.

I also enjoyed the company. Whenever possible, I like to travel with a politically diverse delegation, ideally with a few new members of the Senate along, and I invite people with that idea in mind. This delegation included my old friend and road trip buddy Lindsey Graham. He's the second-funniest man I've met in this business, after the late Mo Udall, my Arizona congressional colleague and mentor. With an eye for the absurd, he can brighten up the dreariest day and make any journey, even the most exhausting slog, fun. He has a hard time not being amusing and amused. We had traveled to Kyrgyzstan in 2005, crossing paths in Bishkek, the capital, with a visiting delegation from the House of Representatives. Our ambassador to Kyrgyzstan had asked if we would mind combining delegations for a scheduled meeting with the new prime minister. Lindsey and I had both served in the House before we were elected to the Senate, and we both have friends there. But Senate snobbery being as pervasive as it is—ask any House member—we do have a not very republican attitude in the Senate that tends to look down at the so-called people's chamber. We serve six-year terms and the rules of the Senate allow each member considerable independence. Every man and woman a king, we like to think. Not so much in the House. Nevertheless, not wishing to impose on the prime minister's time any more than necessary, we consented to the request.

The House delegation was late. We started the meeting without them. The prime minister was an urbane fellow, and we were in the middle of a pleasant, interesting conversation when an aging elevator noisily stopped on the floor where we were meeting and disgorged its passengers, the tardy members of the House delegation. Introductions were made, and the previous discussion was suspended until our new cohort each had a few minutes to make brief introductory remarks. One of them, a nice guy from Tennessee, attempted to use his state's topography to establish a bond with our host. Like an Army scout trying to communicate with an Indian chief in a 1950s Western, he spoke slowly and loudly, using his hands to illustrate his message. "I come from a state with *biiiig* mountains," he offered. "Kyrgyzstan has *biiigger* mountains," he acknowledged, shaping the outline of a mountain peak with his hands. "Kyrgyzstan very beautiful. My state very beautiful." To which the prime minister responded nonchalantly and in very good English, "Yes, I know. I have a daughter at Vanderbilt." I almost didn't dare to look at Lindsey. When I did shoot him a glance, he was shaking from the pressure of not bursting out laughing. His eyes were leaking, and he was emitting little sounds that I guess were strangled cackles. Then I had to fight, with mixed results, to keep a straight face. We've had a regular laugh over that memory and scores of others from our travels ever since. He is the best company.

Sheldon Whitehouse, another frequent traveling companion and a smart, widely respected senator, had joined us on that July Fourth trip, too. And I had invited two other colleagues, both in their first terms, Dave Perdue of Georgia and Elizabeth Warren of Massachusetts. As I noted earlier, I always welcome a chance to introduce new senators to our national security challenges in person, so to speak. And I especially value those opportunities when the members hold opposing views. Dave and Elizabeth certainly fit that bill. Dave's very conservative and Elizabeth is very liberal, and there are very few issues where they would naturally find common ground.

That's one of the values of these trips. When you're traveling long distances in short amounts of time, much of it in the confined space of a military airplane, and keeping a crowded schedule on the ground, you put a premium on collegiality, courtesy, and good humor, not partisan affiliation. At dinner—and I always try to schedule at least one private, nonofficial dinner in a restaurant in each country visited—you enjoy a good joke or a story, and conversations that aren't strictly about politics and issues. You get to know people as more than the person across the Senate floor who disagrees with you or votes against your bill. Your staffs get to know each other, too. You become friendly, and sometimes you become friends. And while you will go on debating and voting against each other, you're less likely to resent it, and maybe, every once in a while, you'll find a way to work together on something beneficial to the country. That's the idea, anyway. It doesn't always work out that way, but it does often enough that it's worth continuing the effort. I'm not friends with all my Senate colleagues, and some, no doubt, will eagerly make the same disclaimer about me. But for all the times I haven't improved the comity of the Senate, the angry outburst, the heated exchange, the cutting sarcasm I'm guilty of from time to time, I also have a reputation for cross-party friendships and bipartisan collaboration. I led delegations overseas that have helped colleagues become better friends and better senators. If you ask me for a short list of accomplishments in my Senate career I'm proudest of, that would be one.

Usually I return from an interesting trip excited about the experience, and my mind occupied with things I had learned and want to follow up on. This time I felt run-down, and something else that I couldn't put my finger on. I didn't think it was serious, necessarily, just an unfamiliar sense that I wasn't myself. It worried me since it was the second time in a little more than a month that I had felt run-down and off-kilter. I had taken a more arduous trip in May with friends, John Barrasso from Wyoming and Chris Coons of Delaware, to Australia, Vietnam, and Singapore, seven days, each heavily scheduled with meetings and public events. I was bone-tired when I got back from that one, too, just a few days before former FBI director James Comey was scheduled to testify before the Senate Intelligence Committee.

I'm an ex officio member of the committee, which means I'm usually the last to ask the witness questions. When my turn finally came, I tried asking Mr. Comey a question that Lindsey had texted my staff. Something happened between reading the question and asking it. To this day, I'm really not sure what caused it. But as was widely noted at the time, I was incomprehensible. It was a high-profile hearing, carried live by the cable news networks. My strange performance was the focus of commentary on cable and fuel for Twitter. I felt embarrassed for myself and sorry for confusing Comey. It was one of the more mortifying experiences of my public career. Even now, I wince at the memory of it. I tried to move on, and put the whole thing down to a bad bout of jet lag. But a small concern nagged at me. And then I couldn't shake the fatigue from the July trip.

As luck had it, my regular physical at the Mayo Clinic in Scottsdale was scheduled for that Friday, July 14. I mentioned my general fatigue to my doctors as well as recent instances when I'd felt a little foggy mentally, and brief episodes of double vision. They added a brain scan to my exam. I left Mayo that afternoon and was happily driving north on I-17 to Hidden Valley for the weekend when my phone rang. It was my primary physician. She informed me that the scan had found something. She didn't say what. "Okay, I can be back there Monday morning," I agreed. "No," she replied emphatically, "you need to turn around and come back now."

A few hours later I was being prepped for surgery. A top neurosurgeon at Mayo, who I heard later had been called at the airport as he was about to depart on a long-planned trip, was enlisted to perform the operation, a minimally invasive craniotomy with eyebrow incision. In other words, they cut a hole in my skull along my left eyebrow to look at my brain's left frontal lobe and see what the trouble was. There they found a two-inch blood clot, and skillfully and thoroughly—according to every doctor who subsequently reviewed the surgeon's handiwork—removed it, and sent a tissue sample to the pathology lab. The operation took five and a half hours. When I came out of the anesthesia, one of my doctors asked if I knew the year. I answered correctly, which was, he informed me, the first time a patient of his could remember the year immediately following brain surgery. Brain scans after the surgery reaffirmed the clot had been entirely removed. I showed no signs of cognitive difficulty. I cracked a couple jokes to reassure myself as much as my doctors that I still had my wits. I was released the next day at my insistence, and went home feeling a little vain about how quickly I had gotten back on my feet, how tough I still was. I felt gratified when one of my doctors told me I showed an unusually high tolerance for pain, and I made sure to repeat the observation to friends. That might strike readers as a rather petty concern under the circumstances. But under the circumstances there's comfort to be found in one's lifelong idiosyncrasies.

I was back at Mayo the following Tuesday to meet with a medical team that included neuro-oncologists, and discuss the pathology report. It had revealed that the blood clot had been a primary brain tumor called a glioblastoma. I'd never heard the term before, and didn't immediately grasp the meaning of the diagnosis. I knew it was serious from the sober demeanor of the medical professionals in the room, and when someone, I don't remember who, mentioned it was the same cancer that Ted had, I got the picture. The Mayo team was confident the surgeon had gotten out all the tumor that was visible. But this kind of brain cancer has tentacles, they explained, that can lurk invisibly. It almost always comes back. I was otherwise in very good physical condition, they informed me, and recovering from the craniotomy with astonishing speed. Good to know. We discussed odds and averages, and courses of treatment, the standard approach being chemotherapy and radiation.

"How soon can I start?" I asked. Dates were suggested, and I said I'd rather start after I returned from Washington. I got some puzzled looks at that. "I want to go back to Washington," I explained. "We're in the middle of a big health care debate, and there will be votes I can't miss. How soon can I go back?"

Not soon, was the consensus. To which I replied, "Sooner." They didn't want me thirty thousand feet in the air and subjected to cabin pressure while I had a hole in my head, and maybe some swelling from the recent operation. They eventually relented and agreed I could leave a week from then following a quick exam to make sure I was fit to travel. We discussed what to do if there was a problem during the flight and what symptoms to watch for that might signal a stroke. We chartered a private plane and made plans to fly to Washington on Tuesday, July 25.

I had a lot to think about, obviously. A thing like that takes a little getting used to, for me and my family. My first reaction was to assign the news to the place in me where I store memories of adverse experiences, and not accord it greater significance than any other. "Here's another one," I thought, "just another one." In the blur of those first hours and days after the diagnosis, I knew I would have to concentrate on a purpose unrelated to my cancer or I would have been balled up with shock and anxiety. The news of my diagnosis was followed by an outpouring of sympathy and support. I heard from scores of people, presidents, colleagues, foreign leaders, people in business, sports, and entertainment. President Obama tweeted, "Cancer doesn't know what it's up against. Give it hell, John." I liked that quite a bit, especially since it came from someone to whom I had given a little hell from time to time. I heard from both Presidents Bush, too, and both Clintons, and from President Trump and the First Lady. I'm grateful to all of them. I had a long talk with an old friend, Joe Biden, whom I first got to know when I was the Navy's liaison to the Senate and he was a first-term senator, way back in the Jurassic era. His son Beau had succumbed to the same kind of brain cancer. Our conversation was equal parts practical and encouraging, an old friend helping another through a rough patch he had prior experience with. Joe and I have argued a lot over the years, but he is a first-class human being, and it's a lucky thing to be his friend.

Many well-wishers were friends and acquaintances, but most people who sent kind regards to me I had never met. They meant the most to me. Public figures sometimes complain about the abuse heaped on them by people who don't really know them. I've had my share, some of it deserved, no doubt, but it's nothing compared to the unearned kindnesses I received from strangers as I've walked through airports and ballparks and other public spaces. This won't last, I always told myself, and I tried to repay their generosity with a few moments of my time, asking their names, posing for pictures, making jokes. Now I was inundated with concern and prayers from kindhearted strangers. I felt unusually blessed. But as much as I appreciated it, the public attention to my condition was concentrating my attention on it as well. There is nothing to be gained by that, I told myself. What will be will be. So I focused on work. I wanted to go to work. I wanted to go back to the Senate.

Before the diagnosis, I had discussed with Mark Salter an idea for a speech I was thinking about giving that I wanted his help with. I hadn't liked the direction of Republican efforts to repeal and replace Obamacare, and had already made that clear in public remarks. Unable to find agreement among Senate Republicans for a replacement, the leadership was grasping for a minimalist proposal that could be acceptable at least temporarily to most Republicans. The House had already passed a bill, which I couldn't support. Senate leadership would eventually settle on an approach that could best be described as "repeal and good luck to you." No serious attempt had been made to see if Democrats would cooperate with us to address some of Obamacare's problems while we continued trying to find consensus among ourselves on a comprehensive alternative. Lamar Alexander and Patty Murray, the chair and ranking minority member of the Senate Health Committee, had been working on just such an approach. But the Republican leadership, primarily Mitch McConnell and his staff, were making most if not all of the decisions. They are experienced, skillful political tacticians. Health care is an issue that divides Republicans in both houses of Congress, not so much in our opposition to Obamacare, but over how to reduce the numbers of uninsured people. Not long ago, John Boehner, enjoying the freedom of expression that comes with retirement, observed that Republicans would never agree on a replacement for Obamacare. He was speaking a truth learned over many attempts at trying to reach such a consensus. It was never there, and it still isn't.

Republicans had just a two-vote margin in the Senate, three if you count the vice president's tie-breaker vote, so they could only afford to lose two Republicans. Susan Collins and Lisa Murkowski appeared to be likely no votes. Republican leaders looked for an alternative to Obamacare that would have the best chance of attracting the rest of us. They would come up with something they called "skinny repeal," which repealed key provisions of Obamacare and offered nothing as a replacement. Mitch and I have been on different sides of a few issues over the years, especially in campaign finance reform debates, where we were each other's principal antagonist. But contrary to Washington myth, we get along pretty well. We like and respect each other. We've known each other a long time. Both of us are in our fourth decade of Senate service. I admire his discipline, political IQ, and maturity. I also appreciate that he allows me an informal leadership role on national security issues. We're friends. Nevertheless, I felt Mitch had assumed too much control over health care legislation, with too little input from others, and no outreach to Democrats. I didn't think that approach would succeed.

I thought the best way to make some progress on the issue was to allow an organic, bottom-up effort to find a compromise or two or several that would be criticized by many, but acceptable to enough members on both sides in both houses of Congress. The way to do that was to allow legislation to proceed through regular order, the way most things used to be done here before we began trying to operate with minimal or no cooperation from the other side. Blocking amendments from being offered, limiting debate, putting everything we possibly can on the budget reconciliation measure, which requires only a simple majority to pass, and is how George W. Bush got his tax cuts and Barack Obama got Obamacare. Our dysfunction was years in the making, and it won't be quickly unmade. We're getting little done for the country, which exacerbates voters' alienation from Washington, which encourages them to elect more people to Washington determined to stop any compromise, and block genuine progress on anything. Both Democratic and Republican leaders have been instrumental in creating these conditions. Both have tried to control the place more than its customs and human nature tolerate. Gridlock is the result. We hadn't accomplished much more up to that point than confirming Neil Gorsuch's nomination. Returning to regular order would give the Senate a chance to work its will on an issue, to use our ideas, our friendships, our initiative to see if we could slowly, inefficiently, frustratingly stumble our way to a result.

In the health care debate, the issue would be referred to the committee or committees of jurisdiction—preferably Lamar and Patty's committee since they had already been working on related legislation—to consider a bill, vote on amendments offered by both sides, send the resulting legislation to the floor to be openly debated and amended by the full Senate, and then after a full debate, if it was clear some senators were filibustering the bill, file cloture to end the debate and bring it to a vote. That is exactly how the committee I chair, the Senate Armed Services Committee, succeeds every year in passing the defense authorization bill. It is always a bipartisan effort, always a series of compromises, always debated and amended openly in committee and on the floor, and always represents significant progress in meeting our security challenges.

I had started to make this argument before I learned I was sick, and I wanted to emphasize it after my diagnosis. I make fun of the Senate. I laugh at its pretensions, mock its byzantine customs, and bemoan its inefficiencies. But I love the place. I love it. I've known senators who were eminent statesmen, the equal of luminaries in the White House, Pentagon, and State Department. I've seen senators work diligently, collaboratively, and urgently in response to emergencies in war and peace, to meet a critical need or prevent a calamitous mistake, or to just make measurable, beneficial progress on the major problems of the day. I have made many friendships there that made my life richer and more purposeful. It's an honorable institution, with honorable people serving in it and working for it, and I am very proud, however much the maverick I have occasionally played, and grateful to be allowed to serve my country in their company. It is an extraordinary privilege to be one of the hundred Americans elected to the United States Senate, and I hope to be remembered for serving in it.

The health care debate was the right occasion for me to speak of the Senate as a place worthy of affection and respect. I planned to arrive in Washington right before the vote on a motion to allow the Senate to bring the health care bill up for debate and amendment. Leadership still hadn't announced what replacement for Obamacare they would offer as an amendment to the underlying legislation passed by the House. They wouldn't propose the aforementioned skinny repeal, which offered no replacement at all until after the vote on the motion.

Democrats had been blocking consideration of the House bill on the floor, and hoped to kill the entire effort by defeating the motion to proceed. They needed three votes. Mine would not be one of them. I wouldn't stop debate of the bill, but I wouldn't vote for final passage, either, if it weren't considerably improved in the process. I would ask for floor time after the vote to make the speech Salter and I had worked on during the flight from Arizona.

I wasn't prepared for the response to my sudden appearance on the Senate floor that day. I went directly from the airport to the Senate chamber, and arrived after every senator had voted on the motion. I walked through the door to the chamber, and all the senators gathered for the vote joined in sustained applause for a colleague who had often been a pain in the ass, but who had become, I guess, a part of the character of the place. It was, forgive the cliché, overwhelming. I was deeply moved, nearly to tears. Very few moments in my life have been as gratifying. I cast my vote for the motion, disappointing my friends on the other side of the aisle, no doubt. But when I asked for recognition after the vote on the motion had passed, I didn't see a single senator leave the chamber. That had never happened to me before, not once in my thirty-one years of service in the United States Senate. And while I might not be remembered as one of the Senate's legendary orators, I wanted to do my very best to deliver a speech that meant a great deal to me as it was intended as a tribute and encouragement to an institution I love. With the reader's indulgence, I submit it in full here.

Mr. President:

I've stood in this place many times and addressed as president many presiding officers. I have been so addressed when I have sat in that chair, as close as I will ever be to a presidency.

It is an honorific we're almost indifferent to, isn't it? In truth, presiding over the Senate can be a nuisance, a bit of a ceremonial bore, and it is usually relegated to the more junior members of the majority.

But as I stand here today—looking a little worse for wear, I'm sure—I have a refreshed appreciation for the protocols and customs of this body, and for the other ninety-nine privileged souls who have been elected to this Senate.

I have been a member of the United States Senate for thirty years. I had another long, if not as long, career before I arrived here, another profession that was profoundly rewarding, and in which I had experiences and friendships that I revere. But make no mistake, my service here is the most important job I have had in my life. And I am so grateful to the people of Arizona for the privilege—for the honor—of serving here and the opportunities it gives me to play a small role in the history of the country I love.

I've known and admired men and women in the Senate who played much more than a small role in our history, true statesmen, giants of American politics. They came from both parties, and from various backgrounds. Their ambitions were frequently in conflict. They held different views on the issues of the day. And they often had very serious disagreements about how best to serve the national interest.

But they knew that however sharp and heartfelt their disputes, however keen their ambitions, they had an obligation to work collaboratively to ensure the Senate discharged its constitutional responsibilities effectively. Our responsibilities are important, vitally important, to the continued success of our Republic. And our arcane rules and customs are deliberately intended to require broad cooperation to function well at all. The most revered members of this institution accepted the necessity of compromise in order to make incremental progress on solving America's problems and to defend her from her adversaries.

That principled mindset, and the service of our predecessors who possessed it, come to mind when I hear the Senate referred to as the world's greatest deliberative body. I'm not sure we can claim that distinction with a straight face today.

I'm sure it wasn't always deserved in previous eras, either. But I'm sure there have been times when it was, and I was privileged to witness some of those occasions.

Our deliberations today—not just our debates, but the exercise of all our responsibilities—authorizing government policies, appropriating the funds to implement them, exercising our advice and consent role—are often lively and interesting. They can be sincere and principled. But they are more partisan, more tribal more of the time than any other time I remember. Our deliberations can still be important and useful, but I think we'd all agree they haven't been overburdened by greatness lately. And right now, they aren't producing much for the American people.

Both sides have let this happen. Let's leave the history of who shot first to the historians. I suspect they'll find we all conspired in our decline—either by deliberate actions or neglect. We've all played some role in it. Certainly I have. Sometimes, I've let my passion rule my reason. Sometimes, I made it harder to find common ground because of something harsh I said to a colleague. Sometimes, I wanted to win more for the sake of winning than to achieve a contested policy.

Incremental progress, compromises that each side criticize but also accept, just plain muddling through to chip away at problems and keep our enemies from doing their worst isn't glamorous or exciting. It doesn't feel like a political triumph. But it's usually the most we can expect from our system of government, operating in a country as diverse and quarrelsome and free as ours.

Considering the injustice and cruelties inflicted by autocratic governments, and how corruptible human nature can be, the problem solving our system does make possible, the fitful progress it produces, and the liberty and justice it preserves, is a magnificent achievement.

Our system doesn't depend on our nobility. It accounts for our imperfections, and gives an order to our individual strivings that has helped make ours the most powerful and prosperous society on earth. It is our responsibility to preserve that, even when it requires us to do something less satisfying than "winning." Even when we must give a little to get a little. Even when our efforts manage just three yards and a cloud of dust, while critics on both sides denounce us for timidity, for our failure to "triumph."

I hope we can again rely on humility, on our need to cooperate, on our dependence on each other to learn how to trust each other again and by so doing better serve the people who elected us. Stop listening to the bombastic loudmouths on the radio and television and the Internet. To hell with them. They don't want anything done for the public good. Our incapacity is their livelihood.

Let's trust each other. Let's return to regular order. We've been spinning our wheels on too many important issues because we keep trying to find a way to win without help from across the aisle. That's an approach that's been employed by both sides, mandating legislation from the top down, without any support from the other side, with all the parliamentary maneuvers that requires.

We're getting nothing done. All we've really done this year is confirm Neil Gorsuch to the Supreme Court. Our health care insurance system is a mess. We all know it, those who support Obamacare and those who oppose it. Something has to be done. We Republicans have looked for a way to end it and replace it with something else without paying a terrible political price. We haven't found it yet, and I'm not sure we will. All we've managed to do is make more popular a policy that wasn't very popular when we started trying to get rid of it.

I voted for the motion to proceed to allow debate to continue and amendments to be offered. I will not vote for the bill as it is today. It's a shell of a bill right now. We all know that. I have changes urged by my state's governor that will have to be included to earn my support for final passage of any bill. I know many of you will have to see the bill changed substantially for you to support it.

We've tried to do this by coming up with a proposal behind closed doors in consultation with the administration, then springing it on skeptical members, trying to convince them it's better than nothing, asking us to swallow our doubts and force it past a unified opposition. I don't think that is going to work in the end. And it probably shouldn't.

The Obama administration and congressional Democrats shouldn't have forced through Congress without any opposition support a social and economic change as massive as Obamacare. And we shouldn't do the same with ours.

Why don't we try the old way of legislating in the Senate, the way our rules and customs encourage us to act. If this process ends in failure, which seems likely, then let's return to regular order.

Let the Health, Education, Labor, and Pensions Committee under Chairman Alexander and Ranking Member Murray hold hearings, try to report a bill out of committee with contributions from both sides. Then bring it to the floor for amendment and debate, and see if we can pass something that will be imperfect, full of compromises, and not very pleasing to implacable partisans on either side, but that might provide workable solutions to problems Americans are struggling with today.

What have we to lose by trying to work together to find those solutions? We're not getting much done apart. I don't think any of us feels very proud of our incapacity. Merely preventing your political opponents from doing what they want isn't the most inspiring work. There's greater satisfaction in respecting our differences, but not letting them prevent agreements that don't require abandonment of core principles, agreements made in good faith that help improve lives and protect the American people.

The Senate is capable of that. We know that. We've seen it before. I've seen it happen many times. And the times when I was involved even in a modest way with working out a bipartisan response to a national problem or threat are the proudest moments of my career, and by far the most satisfying.

This place is important. The work we do is important. Our strange rules and seemingly eccentric practices that slow our proceedings and insist on our cooperation are important. Our founders envisioned the Senate as the more deliberative, careful body that operates at a greater distance than the other body from the public passions of the hour.

We are an important check on the powers of the Executive. Our consent is necessary for the President to appoint jurists and powerful government officials and in many respects to conduct foreign policy. Whether or not we are of the same party, we are not the President's subordinates. We are his equal!

As his responsibilities are onerous, many, and powerful, so are ours. And we play a vital role in shaping and directing the judiciary, the military, and the cabinet, in planning and supporting foreign and domestic policies. Our success in meeting all these awesome constitutional obligations depends on cooperation among ourselves.

The success of the Senate is important to the continued success of America. This country—this big, boisterous, brawling, intemperate, restless, striving, daring, beautiful, bountiful, brave, good, and magnificent country—needs us to help it thrive. That responsibility is more important than any of our personal interests or political affiliations.

We are the servants of a great nation, "a nation conceived in liberty and dedicated to the proposition that all men are created equal." More people have lived free and prosperous lives here than in any other nation. We have acquired unprecedented wealth and power because of our governing principles, and because our government defended those principles.

America has made a greater contribution than any other nation to an international order that has liberated more people from tyranny and poverty than ever before in history. We have been the greatest example, the greatest supporter, and the greatest defender of that order. We aren't afraid. We don't covet other people's land and wealth. We don't hide behind walls. We breach them. We are a blessing to humanity.

What greater cause could we hope to serve than helping keep America the strong, aspiring, inspirational beacon of liberty and defender of the dignity of all human beings and their right to freedom and equal justice? That is the cause that binds us and is so much more powerful and worthy than the small differences that divide us.

What a great honor and extraordinary opportunity it is to serve in this body. It's a privilege to serve with all of you. I mean it. Many of you have reached out in the last few days with your concern and your prayers, and it means a lot to me. It really does. I've had so many people say such nice things about me recently that I think some of you must have me confused with someone else. I appreciate it, though, every word, even if much of it isn't deserved.

I'll be here for a few days, I hope managing the floor debate on the defense authorization bill, which, I'm proud to say, is again a product of bipartisan cooperation and trust among the members of the Senate Armed Services Committee.

After that, I'm going home for a while to treat my illness. I have every intention of returning here and giving many of you cause to regret all the nice things you said about me. And, I hope, to impress on you again that it is an honor to serve the American people in your company.

Thank you, fellow senators.

I remained on the Senate floor for a long while after my speech. Chuck Schumer spoke after me quite emotionally. Most of the senators present came up to me to say a few words, almost as if they were in a receiving line. They welcomed me back, offered their best wishes and prayers, complimented my remarks. Some were in tears, which was hard to see. At one time or another I had argued with every single one of them, and I'm certain I had offended more than a few of them. Their kindness to me in a difficult hour made my personal situation easier to accept. I mean that, and I hope they know that. Their concern and the generous regard they offered for the message I had delivered and for the messenger himself was more than just encouragement. It was an assurance that I meant something to the institution that means a great deal to me, that I have been of use there.

The next two days were busy with phone calls and meetings. Much of my time was spent thanking well-wishers. But a vote on a Republican Obamacare alternative was expected to occur late Thursday night, and I spent many hours trading intelligence about its likely contents, being lobbied by Republican and Democratic colleagues to support or oppose whatever proposal came to a vote, and seeking assurances from leadership that whatever happened with the health care bill, debate on the defense authorization bill, which I would manage, would be the next item on the calendar. As I mentioned, I take pride in the Armed Services Committee's track record in reporting out our bill every year and getting it passed with bipartisan majorities. I wanted very much to see it finished before I began cancer treatment. I tried to work out issues various colleagues had with the bill, and get an approximate number of the amendments likely to be offered to it, and a sense of which ones I could accept and which ones I would have to oppose. I didn't want to leave unfinished business behind when my return to the Senate was uncertain. Of course, the other members of the committee, who work closely together in a mostly nonpartisan way would have managed the bill on the floor in my absence quite competently. But I enjoy doing it and because I'm less abashed about pestering colleagues to move along, I can usually get the bill to final passage quicker than others can.

In my last Republican primary in 2016, my opponent accused me of being that lowest of characters in Washington, one of the wretches who lack the fortitude to disdain compromises and remain reliably useless at governing the country. "He's a champion of compromise," she warned. Yikes! What horrible transgressions might I yet be capable of committing were the voters of Arizona to send me back to Washington with another six-year mandate to help govern the country?

Well, they did send me back. And you're damn right, I'm a champion of compromise in the governance of a country of 325 million opinionated, quarrelsome, vociferous souls. There is no other way to govern an open society, or more precisely, to govern it effectively. Principled compromises aren't unicorns. They can be found when we put political advantage slightly second to the problem we're trying to solve. The health care sector represents a sixth of our economy. I think it appropriate we try to find, if not a consensus on major changes to it, at least bipartisan agreement on how to incrementally improve it. Muddling through, hashing out policy agreements that thrill no one, but are acceptable to most is a useful achievement in a republic. Maybe "champion" is too grand a designation for the believers in these more mundane pursuits. Perhaps practical problem solving is a more appropriate description of the only governing approach that works in our system whatever your political philosophy. There are still plenty of people in both houses of Congress who recognize that to govern is to compromise, but they need reinforcements.

Paradoxically, voters who detest Washington because all we do is argue and never get anything done for them frequently vote for candidates who are the most adamant in their assurances that they will never ever compromise with those bastards in the other party. Instead they complain about Senate rules that don't let them command obedience from the opposition; or the court that ruled some foolish executive order unconstitutional; or the fake news that's in the other side's back pocket; or unelected bureaucrats who won't follow orders; or foreign governments that won't be governed by us; or any handy entity they can blame for their failure to get anything done despite the moral superiority of their my-way-or-the-highway approach. When they eventually quit or lose an election and return from whence they came, they leave little behind but the memory of an impediment to the country's progress. Yes, I'd rather have a few more problem solvers than purists in Washington. Their zeal may be commendable, but not, as it usually happens, terribly productive.

There are a lot of contributing factors to the gridlock that frustrates so many. Chief among them is how much more polarized we are as a society. We are secluding ourselves in ideological ghettos. We don't have to debate rationally or even be exposed to ideas that contradict ours. We have our own news sources. We exchange ideas mostly or exclusively with people who agree with us, and troll those who don't. Increasingly, we have our own facts to reinforce our convictions and any empirical evidence that disputes them is branded as "fake." That's a social trend that is going to be very hard to turn around given the prevalence in our daily lives of media and communications technologies that enable it. It will require a persistent effort to identify and insist on what is objectively true and what isn't by the press, by media companies, by honest people in public life, and by broadly popular figures in all kinds of professions, business, sports, entertainment, who know that there is more to moving the country forward than winning an argument or an election. We have to recover our sense that we're part of a community that's larger than our political cohort, that we all, despite our disagreements, have shared interests and values.

That requires, paradoxically, taking politics more and less seriously. If you're alarmed by our descent into all-consuming partisanship, by the fact that much of the grassroots energy in both parties is with the closed-minded absolutists on the fringes, what are you doing about it? Are you voting in primary elections? Are you helping choose party leaders for your county, your state? Are you running for leadership positions yourself? Are you showing up for precinct committee meetings, district elections, town halls with your elected officials? Because I guarantee you, voters on the Far Right and Far Left are. They show up. And if those are the voices party leaders and elected officials hear from most then those voices will exercise influence over the local and state parties, over the national party, and over our national affairs that exceeds the strength of their actual numbers. If you want politics to be more civil, if you want Congress to argue less and get more done, then show up. Represent. Play as big a role in the mundane activities of politics as the zealots do. It's important.

At the same time, we need to recover some perspective about how much someone's politics is a testament to their character. When did politics become the principal or only attribute we use to judge people? Republicans and Democrats can be good neighbors, loving parents, loyal Americans, decent human beings. I don't remember another time in my life when so many Americans considered someone's partisan affiliation a test of whether that person was entitled to their respect. Ted Kennedy and I never voted for the same candidate for President. Nor did Joe Biden and I. Nor Russ Feingold and I. Nor any number of Democrats whose friendship made my life richer, and made me a better senator and a better person.

There are things other than personal commitment and reflection we can do to improve our politics and our government. We can change some of the rules and practices of politics that favor dysfunction. We can take on gerrymandering, and stop surrendering total control over the drawing of state legislative and congressional district lines to politicians motivated solely by the desire to opposition-proof as many seats as they can. Too many members of Congress can't lose a general election because their districts are preposterously drawn and overwhelmingly populated by fellow partisans. The only challenge they ever have to fear is from their right or left flanks in a primary, which, again, amplifies the voices on the fringes, and gives them greater influence over state legislatures and Congress.

I joined an amicus brief against gerrymandering last year, with anti-gerrymandering Republicans John Kasich, Arnold Schwarzenegger, and others, in a case pending before the Supreme Court. Democrats in Wisconsin sued the state, claiming that new legislative and congressional districts were intended to put Democrats at such an electoral disadvantage that they were practically disenfranchised. A lower court ruled in their favor. I don't know how the Supreme Court will rule. I'm not terribly optimistic, given my previous exposure to the Court majority's uninformed views of modern campaign practices in the *Citizens United* case. Who knows, maybe they'll surprise me. But

Americans don't have to wait for the courts to mandate basic fairness in elections. We can demand it from our elected representatives. We can vote on it. In states that have ballot initiatives, we can support referenda that would establish a nonpartisan redistricting system. We can vote in state legislative races for candidates who commit to drawing lines that fairly represent the entire population. Organize and vote. That is and always will be our greatest power over our government.

We can demand a less secretive and corrupting campaign finance system. The Court, in its current configuration, will continue to argue that money is speech, and as with mansions and yachts, rich Americans simply get to buy more of it than Americans of more modest means can afford. But you can still change the law to require that 501(c)(4)s, so-called nonprofit social welfare organizations, are required to disclose their donors. They're often financed by one or two or several billionaires, who can spend unlimited amounts of money effectively in support of a candidate or candidates, and consequently yield enormous influence over the positions and votes of those candidates while their identities remain a secret. Opponents of campaign finance reform have always argued that the most effective corrective to corruption is full disclosure, identifying donors and subjecting them to public scrutiny and pressure. Time to make them put up or shut up.

As always, more important than any political reforms is the discernment of voters. Here's my unsolicited advice to the American voter. If a candidate for Congress pledges to ride his white horse to Washington and lay waste to all the scoundrels living off your taxes, to never work or socialize or compromise with any of them, to make an example of them, and then somehow get them to bow to your will and the superiority of your ideas, don't vote for that guy. It sounds exciting, but it's an empty boast and a commitment to more gridlock, and gridlock is boring. If a candidate modestly promises to build relationships on both sides of the aisle, to form alliances to promote their ideas, to respect other points of view, and split differences where possible to make measurable progress on national problems, ask that candidate to run for President. Their humility and honesty commend them for the job.

There is a scarcity of humility in politics these days. I suspect it's never been in abundant supply in most human enterprises. And I don't mean modesty. Any politician worth a damn can fake modesty. Humility is the self-knowledge that you possess as much inherent dignity as anyone else, and not one bit more. Among its other virtues, humility makes for more productive politics. If it vanishes entirely, we will tear our society apart. No one will feel we owe each other the truth, much less our respect.

In the course of a long career, I've seen a decline in civility and cooperation, and increased obstructionism. But there are still enough statesmen in Congress and the executive branch committed to meeting the challenges of the hour, and putting the country they're honored to serve before narrower interests. They might not be the most colorful politicians in town, but they're usually the ones who get the most done. And it's not like there was ever a golden age of politics when everybody acted strictly in the public interest, and set aside personal ambitions to promote peace and brotherhood with the opposition. There is still corruption here, as there is in any human institution. But far, far less of it than in past times, when bribery of one sort or another was practically standard practice. We've drifted into stasis. Because the permanent campaign is a reality in this century, we too often blur the distinction between the requirements of campaigning and the responsibilities of the elective office.

This is my last term. If I hadn't admitted that to myself before this summer, a stage 4 cancer diagnosis acts as ungentle persuasion. I'm freer than colleagues who will face the voters again. I can speak my mind without fearing the consequences much. And I can vote my conscience without worry. I don't think I'm free to disregard my constituents' wishes, far from it. I don't feel excused from keeping pledges I made. Nor do I wish to harm my party's prospects. But I do feel a pressing responsibility to give Americans my best judgment and to take good care to keep my personal interests and my party's subordinate to the national interest. That is what I tried to do in last summer's debate on legislation to repeal Obamacare.

I received calls in my office, in the Republican cloakroom, on my cell phone, and at home. I was buttonholed on the floor, in the halls, and in visits to my office, urging me to support whatever Mitch and the White House proposed. Democratic friends entreated me to force the bipartisan cooperation I had advocated in my speech by helping defeat the Republican proposal, whatever it turned out to be. I had already been called a hypocrite by liberal detractors for allegedly betraying the sentiments expressed in my speech when I voted for the motion to proceed. As noted, I was skeptical that the final product of last-minute Republican scrambling and lobbying would be something I could support. And I had stated quite explicitly in my speech that I wouldn't support the underlying bill or any bill that offered as few or fewer protections to people who could lose their health insurance. But I wouldn't close a door on a Republican bill before I knew for certain what was in it. I had filed three amendments to address problems that my governor, Doug Ducey, had called to my attention. I thought it a reasonable position to wait to see if the bill would be improved before deciding whether or not to support it. But it did make me a target for persuasion, and I was the beneficiary of quite a lot of it, some subtle, some impassioned, some well-reasoned, some pleading.

On the nay side of the Obamacare repeal effort, the Democratic leader, Chuck Schumer, spoke with me most often, pledging his caucus's good faith in efforts to work out a bipartisan bill in Lamar and Patty's committee. I heard from Democratic friends in and out of the Senate. My old pal Joe Lieberman, who had left the Senate in 2012, called. He had called me earlier to sympathize about my recent bad luck, and promised to pray for me, which if you know Joe, is a sincere and thorough undertaking. When he called again, we commiserated some more and he reminded me he was praying for me. Then he gently lobbied me to vote no. I promised him I would give it my full consideration. I talked to Susan and Lisa, who were almost certain no votes. Joe Biden, in our long talk about my cancer diagnosis and treatment, managed to tell me he was sure I would do the right thing. I wasn't entirely sure what at that moment was the right thing to do. I kept an open mind to arguments on both sides.

I realized when leadership formally confirmed that their minimalist compromise, the aforementioned skinny repeal, would be their substitute to the underlying House bill, that I would likely vote against it. I had campaigned on repealing and replacing Obamacare. Skinny repeal would have killed off essential provisions of Obamacare, likely causing the whole thing to collapse, and offered literally nothing with which to replace it. Leadership assured us that a replacement could be found in conference with the House. But given the wide differences on the issue between House and Senate Republicans, I thought that unlikely. I feared that all the conferees would be able to do was accept the Senate bill, repealing but not replacing Obamacare and robbing millions of Americans of their health insurance. If that were the case, only the House would have to vote on the bill again because only the House bill would have been changed. If it were entirely unchanged from the bill passed by the Senate, we wouldn't get another opportunity to reject the final product. On Thursday, the last day of the debate, Lindsey convinced me to join him in a press conference to criticize the Republican bill and demand assurances that there would be a conference. Speaker Paul Ryan publicly and privately gave us those assurances. But what he couldn't guarantee is that the conference would produce a better bill or at least a bill that we would be able to vote against. He couldn't promise that skinny repeal wouldn't be the final measure sent to the President's desk.

We would be in session until the early morning hours of Friday. There were votes on various amendments to the bill, most of them decided by party line. Over the course of that long day and night, I heard from a good many people, some on their own initiative, but most pressed into service by the White House and the leadership, urging me to support the Republican measure. I spoke with Tom Price, the secretary of health and human services, and with my old friend Phil Gramm. Governor Ducey, who had previously expressed serious reservations about the bill, called to say on balance he thought it was worth voting for. My closest advisors were divided on what I should do. Some believed I should vote no, others thought I should give the bill a chance to be improved in conference. A few were agnostic on the question.

When I walked to the Senate floor around eleven o'clock that evening, I had mostly made up my mind that I would vote against the Republican substitute. Reporters pressed me for my decision, and I offered a smartass remark, "Wait for the show," which sounded like I was trying to heighten suspense. That wasn't my intention. I was just being a smartass with reporters, which, as most congressional reporters will tell you, is a daily routine for me. It would have been easier and certainly less dramatic had I announced my intention before the final vote. I knew the moment I stepped onto the floor that I would be lobbied by colleagues on both sides of the debate. I would listen respectfully and give a final consideration to the pros and cons, but I intended to let colleagues on each side know before the press knew which way I was leaning.

I had a brief word with Chuck Schumer right after I entered the chamber to confirm I was likely to vote no. His smile probably alerted Republicans and reporters in the gallery to my intention, and I immediately apprised Republican friends of the same, including Lindsey,

Mitch, and the Republican whip, John Cornyn. Others were delegated to try to change my mind. I was called into the cloakroom to take calls from Phil Gramm and Doug Ducey. I sat at my desk next to Lindsey for the first of two votes that started around midnight, and went over my reasons for voting no. I let Susan and Lisa know I was with them. Vice President Mike Pence was present that night in the event he had to break a tie vote. He talked to me at length, making the case for the bill and asking if there were any assurances he or the President could offer that would change my mind. He didn't give me a hard time. Our exchanges were relaxed and respectful. No one did, really. There was an urgency to their task understandably, but no one lost their temper, including me. No one threatened me or did anything other than implore me to give it more thought. Word spread on both sides. And a little after one o'clock in the morning, shortly before the vote on skinny repeal would start, I stood with a group of Democrats, making small talk and a few wisecracks. We didn't discuss the vote, although some observers assumed that's what we were talking about. They already knew how I would vote, as did most of the Senate. Orrin Hatch came over and gave me a hug. Just before one-thirty, Mike Pence asked to talk to me again off the Senate floor. I left the chamber with him, and he handed me his phone. President Trump was on the other end. I listened quietly as he asked me to reconsider. I don't remember exactly how I responded, but it was a polite rebuff. Then I walked back into the chamber to vote.

Nearly every senator had already voted, and most of them knew what I was about to do. Mitch was standing in the well with his arms crossed. I was genuinely sorry to disappoint him. He had worked hard to find a way to keep a commitment Republicans had made to our voters. I disagreed with his top-down approach and the bare-bones measure it had produced, but I took no pleasure in rejecting it. I got the attention of the clerk, extended my right arm, and gave a thumbs-down. People made a big deal about the drama of the moment, but it didn't feel that dramatic to me at the time. I didn't feel everyone watching me. Many members signal their vote with a hand gesture, typically a thumbs-up or -down. That's how I always vote. The clerk can't always hear "yeas" and "nays," so we accompany them with hand gestures to make sure our votes are recorded accurately. I heard a gasp when I voted from someone who must not have gotten the word, and a smattering of applause from the other side, which Chuck discouraged. I felt bad about that. I felt bad about disappointing my caucus. I didn't want Democrats to celebrate in the moment. It was a natural reaction, but would be seen by some on my side as rubbing salt in the wound.

I got a kick out of stories the next day that diagrammed my colleagues' reactions to my vote, pointing out the look on that senator's face and how this senator craned her neck to see better. I suspect you could take a photograph of the chamber during any routine vote and invest the tableau with conjectured excitement. There is always tension in the chamber when legislation of that magnitude is defeated or passed by a single-vote margin. And unlike more routine votes, senators won't typically remain on the floor until the last of their colleagues has voted. Still, it was hardly as intense and shocking as it was made out to be. It was a hard vote that I didn't make easily, but not one I would hesitate to make again. I went home that night hopeful that Senators Alexander and Murray would have renewed impetus to reach agreement on Obamacare reforms. And I looked forward to starting debate on the defense bill the next day.

But Rand Paul decided we wouldn't start debate on the defense bill that morning or any other morning before I went back to Arizona for treatment and the Senate recessed for the summer. We needed unanimous consent to bring up the bill, and he objected. I'm not sure why. Maybe he resented my vote the night before. Maybe he had another reason. It's hard to tell. I would have liked to have gotten a vote on the bill and sent it to conference before I started chemotherapy and radiation. But it didn't matter that much. I fooled them again. I came back in September and got the bill done then. After all these years, I've learned to have a little patience.

I was thanked for my vote by Democratic friends more profusely than I should have been for helping save Obamacare. That had not been my goal. I had campaigned on repeal and replace. The bill we voted on would only have repealed it. I'm not sure we'll ever agree on a replacement, and so perhaps all we can do is try to fix parts of Obamacare. I would prefer something more comprehensive, but that might not be attainable in the near future. As I've noted already, sweeping changes aren't easily achieved in our system of government. Incremental reform is often all that is possible, and there's value and honor in that.

Among the people who called to thank me was President Obama. I appreciated his call, but, as I said, my purpose hadn't been to preserve his signature accomplishment but to insist on a better alternative, and to give the Senate an opportunity to work together to find one. He hadn't called to lobby me before the vote, which I had appreciated. He had last called me not long after the November election, during the transition to the Trump administration, to congratulate me on my reelection. He added that he was counting on me to be an outspoken and independent voice for the causes I believed in as I had been during his presidency. I thanked him, and said I would try to be.

HIDDEN VALLEY

I WAS ROOTLESS FOR MORE THAN HALF OF MY EIGHTY-ONE years, beginning with my itinerant childhood. My father's Navy career required us to move constantly, just as my grandfather's service had disrupted his childhood. My father was born in Council Bluffs, Iowa, not because his family resided there or had some connection to the town, but because his parents were moving to the West Coast at the time, and he arrived on the way. I lost track of how many places we lived, how many schools I attended. The actual moving, of course, was undertaken by my capable, adventurous mother, hauling three kids across the country, detouring here and there to visit some natural wonder or cultural attraction. Eventually, my parents sent me to a boarding school, Episcopal High School in Alexandria, Virginia, so that I could receive my secondary education and have the same circle of friends in one location for longer than a year. We didn't see my father for long stretches during his deployments. He was gone almost all of World War II, and at sea for much of the Korean War, serving as an executive officer on a cruiser. We spent time together when he had shore duty. Even then he was at work most of the time, including weekends and holidays.

In the summers, when he was stateside, he would take us to the McCain family estate in the Mississippi Delta, a cotton plantation purchased in 1851 by my great-great-grandfather William Alexander McCain, and named for the local area, "Teoc." My great-uncle Joe, my grandfather's younger brother, ran Teoc back then. It was a big place, a couple thousand acres, with a comfortable but modest home that had replaced a more impressive manor house lost to a fire generations before, a company store with a gasoline pump, a cotton gin, and tenant farmers descended from the slaves, who had been held in bondage by my ancestors and taken the name McCain. I hunted, fished, and rode horses there, and enjoyed time with my father and my teasing, funny Uncle Joe. Those are cherished memories, but my connection to the place was fleeting, and many summers and years of my childhood were spent entirely without my father. We learned to live with and respect his absences.

My own Navy career meant more of the same, frequent moves and extended absences from my family and country. I didn't mind the life, really, at least not when I was single and could find fun and adventure in any temporary residence. But I knew how difficult my professional transience would be on my first wife, Carol, and our children. Until I remarried, left the Navy, and moved to Cindy's home, Arizona, the only time I lived in the same place longer than a year was an unexpectedly lengthy stay in a foreign country that wouldn't let me leave (and preferred I'd never come). Among the few advantages of my five and a half years in Hanoi was that Carol and the kids could live in one place, Orange Park, Florida, the entire time I was gone.

I think the experience of my wandering youth is one of the reasons I've always been restless. As I noted in the previous chapter, my curiosity and eagerness for new sights and experiences I likely got from my indefatigable mother. I didn't regret not having a hometown. Before I moved to Arizona, whenever I was asked where I was from, I just answered "all around" or "the States," and I felt not the least bit sorry that I couldn't be more specific. But something changed in the years after I left the Navy. I began to appreciate the comfort and solace that could be found in belonging to a place smaller and more intimate than an entire country.

Cindy and I decided we would raise our family in Arizona, and

I would commute to Washington. Given Congress's short workweek, that usually meant I could leave Washington on Thursday night or Friday morning and return Monday afternoon, and regular recesses would allow me to spend weeks at home. Of course, there were weekends and recess periods when I couldn't be in Arizona, when Congress had to work into the weekend or when I campaigned for Republican candidates in other states. My travel abroad as a member of the Armed Services Committee consumed many recess periods as well. But still, I've been able to spend more time with my family in the same home than I had ever thought would be possible.

In my first year in Congress, I had a meeting with members of the Arizona Farm Bureau. After an hour spent discussing issues theretofore unfamiliar to me, I mentioned a matter Cindy and I had recently started discussing. We were living in a small house in Tempe we had just acquired so I would meet my district's residency requirements. We didn't have any children yet, but we were planning to, and contemplating finding a place in the northern part of the state where our family could spend time together on weekends and holidays. "Say, if any of you know of a place that's for sale up north that's on water," I added as we were exchanging goodbyes, "let me know. My wife and I might be interested in it."

As everyone knows, water is scarce in Arizona, and finding property for a reasonable price that's near any isn't an easy assignment. But some months later, I received a call from the head of the Farm Bureau. He had heard of a place for sale near Cottonwood. "It's on Oak Creek," he informed me. "You might want to take a look at it." I called Cindy and she drove the 120 miles from Mesa to the spot in Yavapai County, near Cornville, Arizona, where a winding, bumpy dirt road takes you down a steep hill to an oasis.

Mormon pioneers were settled in the Salt Lake Valley in 1847, not long after the U.S. claimed the Utah Territory after the war with Mexico. Brigham Young was declared president of the Mormon Church, and in that capacity he dispatched missionaries to other parts of the Southwest newly acquired from our defeated foe. Mormons founded communities in all parts of Arizona, including quite a few small towns in the high, beautiful, desolate country in the northern part of the state, towns like Eagar, St. Johns, and Snowflake. Many hardy souls staked claims in even more isolated locations if there were reliable water sources nearby, including land along a horseshoe bend of Oak Creek.

Oak Creek is a Verde River tributary that carves a spectacularly beautiful gorge, Oak Creek Canyon, from Flagstaff down to Sedona, and continues on past Cornville to its confluence with the Verde south of Cottonwood. It is one of the few streams in the high desert of Northern Arizona that run all year. The creek bend that makes our valley verdant and fertile, and the stagecoach from Flagstaff to Prescott that passed nearby, attracted the first settlers to Hidden Valley in the 1870s. The previous residents, Yavapai and Apache peoples, had been forcibly relocated after a cruel march to the San Carlos Reservation in eastern Arizona.

It was a hard life for those early settlers, and a lonely one, I imagine. The valley is surrounded by steep hills, canyon walls, really. Getting in and out of here wouldn't have been easy. It still isn't. It was a life of ceaseless toil and hardship. The place is pretty far north and at a high elevation so it frequently suffers late freezes, a regularly recurring catastrophe for crops and the families and livestock that depended on them. Families worked this valley until the 1950s, when they began breaking up property and selling off parcels. One last ranching couple remained, a World War II veteran from Kansas and his wife, until they died, he in the late 1960s and she in the early 1970s.

When Cindy first saw our property with its single, small, three-bedroom cabin, it was lovely and green. But much of the rest of the valley had been neglected, leaving it uncultivated, dusty, and rocky. The settlers had dug an irrigation system across the entire valley that remained in operation, having been grandfathered into recently passed laws that forbade the diversion of water resources. There were trees here then, and we would plant many more. Many cottonwoods grace the property, they're fast growers, and we have fruit orchards, apple, peach, plum, and cherry trees. The cottonwoods whisper in the wind. And the fruit trees in blossom are a mesmerizing sight. But it's the slow-growing sycamores, so resilient in harsh climates, that give the place its majesty. They are just magnificent.

The courtyard of the old palace in Istanbul, the sultan's residence from the fifteenth century to the nineteenth, is lined by immense sycamores, some of which are believed to be five hundred years old. They are as splendid as the palace they guard. We have a sycamore standing near the north bend of the creek that's close to two hundred years old. With its massive trunk, great height, and sprawling limbs, it commands your attention. And the birds love it.

Cindy said she knew instantly we would love the place. She made an offer for it that day. That was in 1983. The property was about a quarter of the size that it is today. We only had the one little cabin then. We soon built a guest cottage across an irrigation ditch from our house. In the 1990s we bought the adjacent property to house our kids as they got older, and we added a deck to it, where I used to grill our meals. Our friends, the Harpers, have a home next to us. Not long after, we bought two small places near the south bend of the creek as guesthouses. We built a new main house in 2010 to replace the original cabin, and we just finished building a new place for our kids, who are starting families of their own now.

But the improvements we made that matter most to me are not architectural but natural. We planted more cottonwoods and fruit trees, mimosas and mulberry bushes for the birds, flowers of all kinds, with rose vines clinging to the fences. We established rolling lawns of rich green grass, shaded by tree canopies, and shimmering in the light filtered through the foliage. We dug ponds and stocked them with fish. It was called Hidden Valley Ranch before we owned it. Now it's practically invisible. From the tops of the surrounding hills you can barely make out the structures and roads below. It's just a mass of green, wooded and lush, with a symphony of birdsong in the air, and the buzz of cicadas in summer.

So many birds make their home here, sixty-eight different species the Audubon Society estimates, from hummingbirds darting around the mimosas to a pair of black hawks, a protected species, that return each spring to a nest in a sycamore. They teach their fledglings to fly and hunt, taking advantage of the fish in the creek and the trust that has come to exist between them and us, before flying back to Mexico for the winter. Several years ago, we bought land on the other side of the creek, the ghost ranch we call it, from the heirs of the self-sufficient old couple who had been the last to ranch here. We're turning it into a wildlife sanctuary to attract even more birds, planting only what is native to the area, cactus and desert willow. When we're finished the Audubon Society will designate it a special birding area, and the thought of that pleases me very much. There are Indian caves in the hills and waterfalls past the creek bends, and all kinds of wildlife: deer, javelina, coyote, fox, skunk, and rattlesnakes. We had a cougar one summer, but they're transient animals, and he moved on after he had culled the deer population.

We've spent all the time we could here. We celebrated holidays and birthdays. We swam in the creek, fished the ponds, hiked the hills, and barbequed. The place always teemed with kids, our own and the Harpers', and their friends'. Until the mid-2000s, when I started spending the Fourth of July with the troops in Afghanistan and Iraq, we always celebrated the holiday here with dozens of friends we invited for all manner of recreation, Wiffle ball games, forced marches up the hills to an Indian cave, swimming at the falls, lively dinners along the bank of the creek. We came here after elections to celebrate victories and for consolation after losses; the prescription for both included grilled ribs and a slowly sipped vodka on ice.

The McCain Institute convenes a weekend forum every spring at a resort in Sedona, attended by prominent figures in government, business, education, and the military. Foreign and defense ministers and even a few heads of government have come. We host a dinner on Saturday night for the attendees. It's especially beautiful here in the spring, and the property has made such an impression on our guests that word of Hidden Valley's charms has spread worldwide. Carlos Slim, the billionaire from Mexico City, one of the world's wealthiest men, told me he thought it was one of the nicest places he had ever been. I receive regular solicitations from senior officials of foreign governments. "I hear you have a beautiful place near Sedona. I'd love to see it someday."

Yes, I loved it when I first saw it, and had a vision of what it might become. And now we're nearly there, and I love it all the more.

I lived so much of my life on the move, compensated in other ways for the hometown I was denied. I had no connection to one place; no safe harbor where I could rest carelessly. Landscapes and communities passed too quickly to form lasting attachments of shared history that calm you when old age finally confounds your restlessness. I was almost forty-five when I moved to Arizona. In the nearly four decades that have passed since, Arizona has enchanted and claimed me.

Near the end of his life, Barry Goldwater, a great outdoorsman, tried to describe his affection for the state. "Arizona is 113,400 square miles of heaven that God cut out." Then he paused to choke back tears before managing to add, "I love it so much."

I have experienced every scene of spectacular natural beauty this magnificent state possesses. I've hiked Canyon de Chelly, and the Grand Canyon rim to rim. I've rafted down the Colorado and houseboated on Lake Powell. I've walked the trails in Saguaro National Park, been struck mute by the landscape of Monument Valley, and spent countless hours happily following hidden paths in wilderness areas. I've driven through the desert in the spring after a wet winter and gasped at the profusion of color, the mesmerizing beauty of desert wildflowers in sudden bloom. I love it so much. And I am so grateful for the privilege of representing the state and its people in the United States Senate.

I've been to just about every community that Arizonans carved from the wilderness and made thrive; places that never stopped growing and places that were abandoned to history when opportunities were exhausted; places that rose and declined were reimagined and made to prosper again by the hardworking, self-starting dreamers Arizona attracts in such great numbers. I've been astonished by the resourcefulness of generations of Arizonans in Yuma and Page, Jerome and Kingman, Bisbee and Flagstaff, who struggled, achieved, lost, and struggled again to build from their freedom and opportunities strong, prospering, decent communities in the challenging and beautiful place that had won their hearts.

We will change as all places do. More people will come, as I once came, to make a new home or find the only home they ever really have in towns and cities and rural communities that will be better for their presence. Some will come from other states, and some will come from other countries. They will face the challenges of their time and place. They'll suffer setbacks. And they will stick with it and prevail. And years from now their stories, character, and accomplishments will inspire other lucky newcomers, as I was once inspired, who came to live in beauty, and make the most of their lives.

I won't see it, but I wish I could. I don't know how much longer I'll be here. Maybe I'll have another five years. Maybe, with the advances in oncology, they'll find new treatments for my cancer that will extend my life. Maybe I'll be gone before you read this. My predicament is, well, rather unpredictable. But I'm prepared for either contingency, or at least I'm getting prepared. I have some things I'd like to take care of first, some work that needs finishing, and some people I need to see. And I want to talk to my fellow Americans a little more if I may.

My fellow Americans. No association ever mattered more to me. We're not always right. We're impetuous and impatient, and rush into things without knowing what we're really doing. We argue over little differences endlessly, and exaggerate them into lasting breaches. We can be selfish, and quick sometimes to shift the blame for our mistakes to others. But our country "'tis of Thee." What great good we've done in the world, so much more good than harm. We served ourselves, of course, but we helped make others free, safe, and prosperous because we weren't threatened by other people's liberty and success. We need each other. We need friends in the world, and they need us. The bell tolls for us, my friends. Humanity counts on us, and we ought to take measured pride in that. We have not been an island. We were "involved in mankind."

Before I leave I'd like to see our politics begin to return to the purposes and practices that distinguish our history from the history of other nations. I would like to see us recover our sense that we are more alike than different. We are citizens of a republic made of shared ideals forged in a new world to replace the tribal enmities that tormented the old one. Even in times of political turmoil such as these, we share that awesome heritage and the responsibility to embrace it. Whether we think each other right or wrong in our views on the issues of the day, we owe each other our respect, as long as our character merits respect, and as long as we share, for all our differences, for all the rancorous debates that enliven and sometimes demean our politics, a mutual devotion to the ideals our nation was conceived to uphold, that all are created equal, and liberty and equal justice are the natural rights of all. Those rights inhabit the human heart, and from there, though they may be assailed, they can never be wrenched. I want to urge Americans, for as long as I can, to remember that this shared devotion to human rights is our truest heritage and our most important loyalty.

Then I would like to go back to our valley, and see the creek run after the rain, and hear the cottonwoods whisper in the wind. I want to smell the rose-scented breeze and feel the sun on my shoulders. I want to watch the hawks hunt from the sycamore. And then take my leave, bound for a place near my old friend Chuck Larson in the cemetery on the Severn, back where it began.

"The world is a fine place and worth the fighting for and I hate very much to leave it," spoke my hero, Robert Jordan, in *For Whom the Bell Tolls*. And I do, too. I hate to leave it. But I don't have a complaint. Not one. It's been quite a ride. I've known great passions, seen amazing wonders, fought in a war, and helped make a peace. I've lived very well and I've been deprived of all comforts. I've been as lonely as a person can be and I've enjoyed the company of heroes. I've suffered the deepest despair and experienced the highest exultation. I made a small place for myself in the story of America and the history of my times.

I leave behind a loving wife, who is devoted to protecting the world's most vulnerable, and seven great kids, who grew up to be fine men and women. I wish I had spent more time in their company. But I know they will go on to make their time count, and be of useful service to their beliefs, and to their fellow human beings. Their love for me and mine for them is the last strength I have.

What an ingrate I would be to curse the fate that concludes the blessed life I've led. I prefer to give thanks for those blessings, and my love to the people who blessed me with theirs. The bell tolls for me. I knew it would. So I tried, as best I could, to stay a "part of the main." I hope those who mourn my passing, and even those who don't, will celebrate as I celebrate a happy life lived in imperfect service to a country made of ideals, whose continued success is the hope of the world. And I wish all of you great adventures, good company, and lives as lucky as mine.

Requiem

Under the wide and starry sky
Dig the grave and let me lie.
Glad did I live and gladly die,
And I laid me down with a will.

This be the verse you grave for me:
"Here he lies where he longed to be;
Home is the sailor, home from sea,
And the hunter home from the hill."

—*Robert Louis Stevenson*

ACKNOWLEDGMENTS

The authors would like to thank the following individuals for their invaluable assistance in our latest collaboration. Two people have played critical roles in our literary sideline over a span of two decades. We would have never produced a word without the trust and guidance of our publisher and editor, Jonathan Karp, or the dedication of our agent, Philippa Brophy. Thank you for everything, especially your friendship. Several people gave generously of their time to help summon and fact-check the memories recalled in these pages: dos amigos, Lindsey Graham and Joe Lieberman; traveling companions and trusted advisors Daniel Twining, Richard Fontaine, Christian Brose; and consigliere, Randy Scheunemann. Many thanks also to Ellen Cahill, Virginia Pounds, and Arjun Nijhawan for helping us produce a narrative that doesn't rely entirely on our rather unreliable memories of dates and places. To the team at Simon & Schuster—Fred Chase, Lisa Erwin, Jonathan Evans, Larry Hughes, Kristen Lemire, Elisa Shokoff, Emily Simonson, Dana Trocker—who made this book so much better than it otherwise would have been, thank you for your hard work and kindness to two writers who are amateurs saved from embarrassment by your professionalism. We wish to express our deep gratitude to three friends of long standing, whose support we have relied on in this and many other endeavors—Richard Davis, Carla Eudy, and Joseph Donoghue. And last but never least, our love to Diane and Cindy, for putting up with this project and everything else.

INDEX

INDEX

Bouazizi, Mohamed, 151, 152
Boumediene v. Bush (2008), 96
Boxer, Barbara, 195
Bradbury, Steven, 93, 95–96
brain cancer
    of Biden (Beau), 346; of Kennedy (Ted), 5, 229, 344; of McCain, 339–40, 342–46, 363, 364, 378–79
breaches: and torture debate, 94–97
Breitbart, 45
Bremer, Paul, 109, 113, 116
Brennan, John, 100–101, 102
Brose, Chris, 173, 176, 177, 178–79, 186, 236, 282
Browder, Bill, 270–72, 275
Brownback, Sam, 218
Bulgaria, 247
Burma, 314–18
Burns, Bill, 167
Bush, Barbara, 6, 7
Bush, George H.W., 1, 2, 6, 7–8
Bush, George W.
    and campaign finance reform, 203, 204; elections of 2000 and, 31, 199; elections of 2008 and, 37–38, 48; endorsement of McCain by, 37–38; and financial crisis, 48, 62, 63; freedom agenda of, 255; and Georgia, 263, 266; and Hurricane Katrina, 37; immigration reform and, 218–19, 225, 228; and Iraq, 15, 16, 37, 108, 122, 123, 127, 218; and McCain brain cancer, 345; McCain relationship with, 200; McCain views about, 200, 321–22; and 9/11, 69; Putin and, 252, 258; and Rumsfeld resignation, 121; and Russian-U.S. relations, 252, 255–56, 258, 266, 269; taxes and, 200, 348; and torture debate, 74, 76, 80, 84, 92, 96–97, 98, 99, 322
Bybee, Jay, 77, 87

California
    elections of 2008 in, 36; and immigration, 215
Callahan, Billy, 12
Cameron, David, 188
Camp David Accords, 166
campaign finance reform, 199, 200, 203–4, 232, 347, 362
Campaign Reform Act (2002), 203
Canal Hotel (Iraq): bombing at, 109
Cardin, Ben, 271–72, 327

Carter, Jimmy, 199, 321
Casey, George, 115, 116, 117, 120, 121, 122, 123, 124
Central Intelligence Agency. *See* CIA
change
    and American exceptionalism, 330–34; in Arizona, 378; elections of 2008 and, 28, 37–38, 43, 49, 56, 61; and incremental reform, 369; McCain views about, 369; of rules and practices of politics, 361
character
    and human rights, 309; of immigrants, 217; McCain views about, 379; of nations, 309; and politics, 360–61; of Russia, 310; of Trump, 329; Trump views about, 325
Charter 08 (political manifesto), 335
Charter 77 (political manifesto), 335
Chechnya, 246, 251, 253
Chemical Weapons Convention, 189
Cheney, Richard "Dick," 7, 83, 91–92, 98, 102, 114–15
Chernomyrdin, Viktor, 245
Chiarelli, Peter, 122, 123, 124
China, 181, 301, 332, 334–38
Christian, Mike, 148–49
Churchill, Winston, 19, 334
CIA (Central Intelligence Agency)
    and Belhaj-McCain meeting, 76; and Benghazi attack, 178; computer hacking by, 101; Feinstein Committee report about, 99–104; Inspector General report about, 82–83; interrogations and EITs by, 73, 74, 76, 79–80, 81–83, 87, 91, 92, 93, 95, 96–98, 99–104, 176; McCain views about, 97; as misleading government officials, 98–104; and 9/11, 69; and taping of interrogations, 73, 74, 80, 82, 97, 99
Citizens United decision, 200, 361
Clark, Wesley, 247
Clinton, Bill, 195, 228, 229, 345
Clinton, Hillary
    Afghanistan trip of, 118–19; and Benghazi attack, 178–79; Burma visit by, 315; elections of 2008 and, 13, 28, 29, 37, 38, 42, 53, 225, 228, 229; elections of 2016 and, 236, 274, 300; and immigration, 225; and Iraq, 129, 134, 136; and Kennedy (Ted) endorsement of Obama, 228, 229; and Libya, 172, 174, 178–79; McCain views about, 117–18; and McCain's brain cancer, 345;

INDEX

Edwards, John, 201, 203

Egypt

and American exceptionalism, 329; anti-Semitism in, 165, 166; Arab Spring in, 138, 152, 153, 158–69; assault on American humanitarians in, 162–65; change in, 332; and Congress, 161; constitution for, 165, 166; elections in, 159, 160, 161, 165; Feingold resolution about, 159; government in, 158; McCain trips to, 154, 158, 160–61, 165–66; and media, 168; and Muslim Brotherhood, 160, 161, 163, 164, 165, 166–67, 168; and Palestinians, 159–60; role of religion in, 164; and Russia, 190; and Sisi-Graham-McCain Four Seasons Hotel meeting, 168–69

82nd Airborne Division, U.S., 87–88, 90

88 Generation, 315–16, 318

800th Military Police Brigade, 84

EITs. See enhanced interrogation techniques

Elders, Joycelyn, 195–96, 197

elections of 1964, 43

elections of 1980, 199

elections of 1996, 54

elections of 2000

and campaign finance reform, 203; Lieberman and, 51; McCain candidacy in, 14, 17, 18, 26, 27, 29, 31–32, 33, 35, 45, 199, 203, 247; Straight Talk Express motto for, 31–32

elections of 2006, 15, 17, 121, 224

elections of 2008

ads for, 46–48; biography tour during, 38; "Black Belt" tour during, 38–40; change message and, 28, 37–38, 43, 49, 56, 61; debates for, 43, 44, 57–58, 60, 62, 63–64; endorsements of McCain in, 36, 37–38; funding for, 13–14, 18, 20, 22, 24, 31, 35, 43, 44, 57, 61, 65; general campaign during, 37–42, 60–66, 230; Kennedy (Ted) endorse-ment of Obama in, 228; McCain acceptance speech for, 58–60; McCain announce-ment of candidacy for, 13, 256; McCain as primary candidate in, 228–29; McCain as Republican nominee in, 267; McCain campaign strategy for, 43–44; McCain concerns about, 17–18, 20, 21–22; McCain concession speech and, 11, 66–67; McCain favorite memories of, 29, 40; McCain imperatives for, 42–43; McCain reactions to

losing, 11–13, 66–67, 200; McCain reasons for candidacy in, 52, 59–60; and McCain trip to Iraq, 18–20; McCain views about, 58, 66–67; media and, 18, 21, 22–23, 24, 25–26, 27, 33, 37, 39, 41, 42, 44–45, 46, 47, 48, 56, 57, 64, 65; "No Surrender Tour" in, 25–26; Obama acceptance of nomination for, 56; Obama-McCain comparison during, 28, 42–43, 47; Obama-McCain relationship and, 222; Republican convention for, 52, 58–59; Republican divisiveness during, 51–52; Republican primaries for, 13–30, 31–37, 228–29; and Russia-U.S. relations, 256, 268; and Russian criticisms of McCain, 256; staff for, 18, 20, 21; vice presidential selection for, 49–58; White House meeting during, 62–63

elections of 2012, 37, 215, 230

elections of 2016

conspiracy theories and, 240; immigration and, 215, 216; Republican primaries in, 358; Russian interference in, 236, 237–38, 240, 265, 274, 275, 287, 295, 296, 299, 300; and Russian-U.S. relations, 267; Western nations concerns about, 235

enhanced interrogation techniques (EIT)

and accuracy/reliability of information, 80, 81, 82, 91, 92, 98–100, 103; CIA and, 73, 76, 79–80, 81–83, 87, 91, 92, 93, 95, 96–98, 99–104; congressional briefings about, 101; and human rights organizations, 73; and McCain apology to Belhaj, 75–76; as pros-ecutable war crimes, 95–96; public support for, 104; secret authorization for, 83; and torture debate, 70, 73, 76, 79–80, 81–83, 87, 91, 92, 93–104

Ennahda Party (Tunisia), 154, 155–56

Enron scandal, 203

Episcopal High School (Alexandria, Virginia)

McCain as student at, 371; McCain biographical speech (2008) at, 38

Estonia, 243–44, 247–48

ethics reform: Obama-McCain letters about, 221–22

Europe: anti-Americanism in, 303–4

European Union, 157, 270, 277–78, 282–83, 285, 290, 295, 296

Facebook, 151, 154, 155

Fallujah (Iraq): battle of, 116

INDEX

air strikes in, 113, 114, 115, 117, 122, 123, 130–31, 135–38, 139, 140, 143; U.S. withdrawal from, 17, 127, 130, 134–35, 136–38; and weapons of mass destruction, 107, 108, 303; winning in, 124; *See also* Abu Ghraib; Anbar Province; Ramadi; *specific person*
Iraq Study Group, U.S. Congress, 127
ISIS
conspiracy theories about, 239, 240; in Iraq, 139, 140, 141, 190, 191; and Libya, 179; and Syria, 139, 181, 183, 187, 190–91
Islamic Revolution (1979), 323
Islamic Revolutionary Guard Corps (IRGC), Iranian, 139
Islamic State of Iraq, 135
Israel
Jewish immigration to, 275, 312; McCain trips to, 154, 312; Morsi comments about, 166; and Muslim Brotherhood, 166; Obama trip to, 45; Sharansky-McCain discussion about, 254
Issawi, Rafi al-, 138
Ivanov, Sergei, 256–57

Jackson, Helen, 312
Jackson, Henry "Scoop," 201, 289, 312, 321
Jackson-Vanik law, 275
Jamadi, Manadel al-, 83
Jebali, Hamadi, 156
Jeffrey, Jim, 132–33, 134, 135
Jibril, Mahmoud, 173–74, 175, 177
jobs
and immigration, 206, 207, 208, 210–15, 216–18, 219–20, 225–26, 230, 231; *See also* economy
Johnson, Lyndon B., 40, 44
Jones, Dan, 100, 101–2
Jordan, 45, 154, 156, 186
Judiciary Committee, Senate, 218
Justice Department, U.S.: and torture debate, 76, 77–80, 82, 100

Kagan, Fred, 122
Kagan, Kim, 122
Kara-Murza, Vladimir, 290, 291, 292, 293, 301
Karimov, Islam, 318, 321
Karzai, Hamid, 106
Kasich, John, 361
Kasparov, Garry, 254, 255, 272, 291
Kazakhstan, 278, 332

Keane, Jack, 122
Keating, Charles IV, 140
"Keating Five" scandal, 195
Kennedy, Caroline, 228
Kennedy, Edward "Ted"
brain cancer of, 5, 229, 344; and campaign finance reform, 199, 203–4; combativeness of, 199; death of, 202, 229; and Elders nomination, 196, 197–99; elections of 1980 and, 199; Graham "hideaway office" comment to, 229; and health care, 202, 229; and immigration reform, 14, 205, 218–20, 222–23, 224, 225, 227–28, 232; influence of, 222–23; last days in Senate of, 229; and McCain as Republican 2008 candidate, 228–29; and McCain as switching parties, 199–200, 201; McCain heated exchange with, 197–99, 232; and McCain (Jimmy) birthday, 232; McCain legislative activities with, 14, 201–2, 203–4, 218–20, 222–23, 224, 225, 227–28; McCain relationship with, 5, 196, 199, 202, 232–33; McCain tribute to, 223; memorial service for, 232; and Obama, 222–23, 227–28; and partisanship-respect, 361; and patient's bill of rights, 201–2; personality of, 196–97, 202, 222–23; reputation of, 196
Kennedy, John F. "Jack," 43
Kentucky: elections of 2008 and, 40–41
Kerry, John, 160–61, 172, 189, 270, 274–75, 289
Khalilzad, Zal, 121
Khamenei, Ayatollah, 323
Khodorkovsky, Mikhail, 250–51
Khrushchev, Nikita, 258
King, Martin Luther, 280
King, Steve, 206, 207, 208, 210
Kissinger, Henry, 312
Klitschko, Vitali, 280, 281, 285
Klobuchar, Amy, 287
Ko Ko Gyi, 316
Kolbe, Jim, 108
Korean War, 371
Kosovo, 246–47, 303, 332
Kramer, David, 236, 238
Krepinevich, Andy, 122
Kurds, 110, 133–34, 138–39, 140, 191
Kuwaiti, Abu Ahmed al-, 98–99
Kyl, Jon, 94, 224–25, 227, 230, 258
Kyrgyzstan, 254, 270, 319, 340–41
Kywe, Htay, 316

393

INDEX

National Security Strategy (Trump administration), 327
National Transitional Council (NTC), Libya,
71, 72, 169, 171–72, 173, 174, 175
nationalism, 9, 201, 210, 301
NATO (North Atlantic Treaty Organization)
and Baltic republics, 244, 247, 248, 257; and
Czech Republic, 295; and Georgia, 263, 264;
and Iraq, 303; and Libya, 71–72, 152, 156,
171–73, 175, 176, 180, 322, 324; membership in, 247; and Montenegro, 295–96,
297–99; Putin comments about, 257; and
Russia, 266, 269, 270; and Serbia, 246–47
Naval Academy, U.S., 1, 2, 5, 38, 145
Nemtsov, Boris, 272, 290–94
New Hampshire
elections of 2000 in, 14, 17, 29; elections of
2006 in, 17; elections of 2008 in, 17, 21–23,
24–26, 27–28, 29, 30, 31, 34, 60, 228; and
Savage request, 23–24
New Jersey: elections of 2008 in, 36
New Orleans, Louisiana: McCain 2008
campaign in, 41
New York State
elections of 2008 in, 36; and immigration,
215
New York Times
McCain's Ukraine op-ed in, 286; and
Montenegro, 298; MoveOn.Org Iraq ad
in, 129; and Obama as an Arab, 65; Putin's
op-ed in, 246, 276; and torture debate, 70,
80, 97
New Yorker magazine, 41, 83
Newsweek magazine, 48
Nicaragua, 332
Nicholson, John, 340
Nickles, Don, 196, 197, 198
Nixon, Richard M., 1, 35, 312, 313, 321
Nobel Peace Prize: for Liu Xiaobo, 336
North Ossetia: Russian storming of school in,
253
North Pole: Russian expedition to, 255
Novgorod, Nizhny, 291
Nuland, Toria, 278, 279

Obama, Barack
and Afghanistan, 130, 141–42, 143, 144,
145; American exceptionalism and,
324–25; approach to world leadership of,
192; and Arab Spring in Middle East, 153;

bipartisanship and, 325; and Burma, 315;
conspiracy theories about, 240; Democratic
convention speech (2004) of, 220; elections
of 2008 and, 11, 13, 28, 37, 38, 41–49,
55, 56, 58, 59, 60, 62–65, 66, 67, 222, 225,
228, 229, 267; elections of 2012 and, 230;
ethics reform and, 221–22; and financial
crisis, 62–64; goal of, 324–25; Graham-
Rice-McCain meeting about Syria and,
188–89; health care and, 202, 228, 348, 369;
human rights and, 322; immigration and,
220, 222–23, 225, 227–28, 230; and Iran,
323, 324; and Iraq, 129, 130–31, 132, 133,
134, 136–37, 139, 141; and Kennedy (Ted),
222–23, 227–28; "leading from behind"
phrase of, 173, 324; and Libya, 169, 172–73,
174, 176, 324; McCain compared with, 28,
42–43, 47; McCain conversations/meetings
with, 192, 369; McCain defense of, 64–65;
McCain letter exchange with, 221–22;
McCain relationship with, 59, 221–22, 369;
McCain views about, 130, 192, 220–21, 222,
322, 324–25; and McCain's brain cancer,
345; media and, 37, 42, 45; overseas trip
(2008) of, 45–46; and Russian-U.S. relations, 266, 267, 268, 269, 270, 272, 273, 274,
275, 287, 292, 300; and Savchenko case, 289;
State of the Union address (2013) of, 146;
and Syria, 180, 182, 183–84, 186, 188–90,
191, 324; torture debate and, 97–98, 99,
102; and Ukraine, 284–85, 300, 324; and
U.S. role in world, 325
Obamacare
McCain views about, 353–54, 369; passage
of, 202, 348; Republican efforts to repeal
and replace, 346–50, 353–54, 357–58,
364–69; "skinny repeal" of, 347, 349, 365,
366, 367
Odierno, Ray, 123, 124, 125, 127, 130, 131, 135
Office of Legal Counsel. *See* Justice
Department, U.S.
official statements, 312–13
oligarchs
in Russia, 250, 296; in Ukraine, 280, 281,
283; *See also specific person*
101st Airborne Division, U.S. Army, 119
Open Russia, 250, 251
Operation Enduring Freedom, 105
Orange Revolution, 253, 277
Other Russia, 254

396

Putin, Vladimir (*Continued*)
 professional background of, 245; and
 Russian interference in 2016 elections, 236,
 237; and sanctions on Russia, 272; and
 Savchenko case, 289; and Schroeder, 303;
 and Serbia-NATO peacekeeping plans,
 246–47; Sharansky-McCain discussion
 about, 254–55; Shevardnadze concern
 about, 249; and social media, 301; and
 Syria, 190, 192, 292, 300; Trump and,
 237–38, 300–301, 326; and Ukraine, 277,
 278, 283, 284, 285, 286, 290, 292; and
 U.S.-Russian relations, 257–58, 273; use of
 force by, 266–67; views about U.S. of, 241,
 257–58; wealth of, 236, 288, 291; Western
 relations with, 252–53, 255–56, 257–61;
 Yanukovych and, 283, 284
Pyatt, Geoff, 282

Qaddafi, Muammar al-, 70, 71, 72, 73, 74, 152,
 156–57, 158, 170–71, 172, 173, 174, 175,
 176, 322
Qatar, 71, 72, 138, 169

race issues
 elections of 2008 and, 39–40, 44, 46–49,
 64–65; and human rights, 313–14; and
 immigration, 211, 214; McCain views
 about, 67
Radio Free Asia, 316
Rahman, Gul, 81–82
Raines, Franklin, 48
Ramadi (Iraq)
 battle for, 116, 121, 126–27; ISIS capture/
 control of, 139, 140, 190; MacFarland-
 McCain meeting in, 125–26; violence in,
 138
Reagan, Nancy, 36, 44
Reagan, Ronald, 200, 209, 255, 258, 311, 313,
 321
realism: and idealism, 310–11
Red Cross, 289
redistricting: McCain views about, 200
reenlistment ceremonies, 147–49, 340. *See also*
 Fourth of July
refugees
 from Syria, 183, 186, 192, 300; and Trump,
 325
regular order
 and health care debate, 348, 354; McCain

views about, 348–49, 353, 354; need for
 return to, 348, 353, 354; and Senate rules,
 197–98
Reid, Harry, 62, 129, 220, 221, 228, 285
religion: role in public life of, 164
Republican Party
 divisions within, 51–52, 347; importance of
 immigration reform to, 206, 215, 217; and
 McCain as Reagan Republican, 200; and
 McCain as switching parties, 199–200, 201;
 See also specific person, election, or topic
Rice, Susan, 172, 188–89
Risha, Abdul Sattar Abu, 126
Rodriguez, Jose, 80, 97, 99
Rolling Stone: McCrystal comments to, 144–45
Romania, 247, 278
Romney, George, 32
Romney, Mitt
 elections of 2008 and, 13, 14, 21, 26–27, 29,
 31, 32–33, 34, 35, 36, 37, 225; elections of
 2012 and, 37, 215; and immigration, 225;
 McCain relationship with, 36–37; McCain
 views about, 26–27, 49; as vice presidential
 candidate (2008), 49
Roosevelt, Theodore, 67
Rose Revolution, 249, 253, 261, 262
Rosneft (Russian oil company), 251, 285, 303
Ross, Donald, 7
Rubio, Marco, 230
Rumsfeld, Donald
 and Fontaine letter, 88; and Iraq, 15, 108,
 112, 114–15, 117, 122, 303; resignation of,
 121; and torture debate, 84–85, 86–87, 88
Russia
 and adoption of Russian children, 275; and
 American exceptionalism, 310–12, 313, 332;
 bomb explosions in, 245–46; and change,
 332; characteristics of, 310; and collapse of
 Soviet Union, 241–42, 249, 253, 310; and
 color revolutions, 253–54, 257; compromising of Trump by, 237–38; corruption
 in, 250, 252, 269, 271, 310; criticisms of
 McCain by, 256; détente policy with, 312;
 dissent/protests in, 254, 255, 273–74, 276,
 290–93; economy of, 288, 295; elections in,
 242, 243, 245, 253, 255, 273; and European
 Union, 270, 285; future of, 288, 295; and
 G-8 summits, 252, 267–68, 285; haters of,
 294; Havel-McCain discussion about, 248;
 and human rights, 272–73, 313; interfer-

ABOUT THE AUTHORS

Senator John McCain entered the Naval Academy in June of 1954, and served in the United States Navy until 1981. He was elected to the U.S. House of Representatives from Arizona in 1982 and to the Senate in 1986. He was the Republican Party's nominee for President in the 2008 election.

Mark Salter has collaborated with John McCain on all seven of their books, including *Faith of My Fathers*, *Worth the Fighting For*, *Why Courage Matters*, *Character Is Destiny*, *Hard Call*, and *Thirteen Soldiers*. He served on Senator McCain's staff for eighteen years.